SELECTED ESSAYS

DAVID HUME was born in Edinburgh in 1711. He was raised as a Scottish Calvinist and attended the University of Edinburgh between the ages of 13 and 14. *A Treatise of Human Nature*, his first major work and the basis upon which his modern reputation rests, was completed when he was 26 years of age. It was largely ignored by his contemporaries. He then turned to writing essays on a wide range of subjects. The first edition of his *Essays Moral and Political*, published in 1741–2, was better received, and the essays were republished and expanded throughout his life. In 1745 Hume was unsuccessful in his attempt to gain an academic appointment, standing for the Chair of 'Ethics and Pneumatic Philosophy' at the University of Edinburgh. The *Treatise* was recast as the *Enquiries concerning Human Understanding and concerning the Principles of Morals* (1748 and 1752), but again Hume was disappointed with their reception. His contemporary fame grew with the publication of his *History of Great Britain* (1754–62), until he was regarded as a man of letters equal in stature to Voltaire and Rousseau. In 1762 Boswell described him as 'the greatest Writer in Brittain'. Hume returned to Edinburgh in 1769 and died seven years later.

STEPHEN COPLEY is a lecturer in English in the School of English Studies, Journalism and Philosophy, University of Wales, Cardiff.

ANDREW EDGAR is a lecturer in Philosophy in the School of English Studies, Journalism and Philosophy, University of Wales, Cardiff.

OXFORD WORLD'S CLASSICS

*For almost 100 years Oxford World's Classics have brought
readers closer to the world's great literature. Now with over 700
titles—from the 4,000-year-old myths of Mesopotamia to the
twentieth century's greatest novels—the series makes available
lesser-known as well as celebrated writing.*

*The pocket-sized hardbacks of the early years contained
introductions by Virginia Woolf, T. S. Eliot, Graham Greene,
and other literary figures which enriched the experience of reading.*

*Today the series is recognized for its fine scholarship and
reliability in texts that span world literature, drama and poetry,
religion, philosophy and politics. Each edition includes perceptive
commentary and essential background information to meet the
changing needs of readers.*

OXFORD WORLD'S CLASSICS

DAVID HUME

Selected Essays

Edited with an Introduction and Notes by
STEPHEN COPLEY
and
ANDREW EDGAR

Oxford New York
OXFORD UNIVERSITY PRESS

Oxford University Press, Great Clarendon Street, Oxford OX2 6DP

Oxford New York

Athens Auckland Bangkok Bogotá Buenos Aires Calcutta
Cape Town Chennai Dar es Salaam Delhi Florence Hong Kong Istanbul
Karachi Kuala Lumpur Madrid Melbourne Mexico City Mumbai
Nairobi Paris São Paulo Singapore Taipei Tokyo Toronto Warsaw

and associated companies in Berlin Ibadan

Oxford is a registered trade mark of Oxford University Press

Introduction, Note on the Text, Select Bibliography, Chronology, and
Explanatory Notes © Stephen Copley and Andrew Edgar 1993

First published as a World's Classics paperback 1996
Reissued as an Oxford World's Classics paperback 1998

British Library Cataloguing in Publication Data

Data available

Library of Congress Cataloging in Publication Data
Hume, David, 1711–1776.
[Essays. Selections]
Selected essays / David Hume; edited with an introduction by
Stephen Copley and Andrew Edgar.
p.   cm.—(World's classics)
Includes bibliographical references.
1. Philosophy.   2. Political science.
I. Copley, Stephen, 1954–
II. Edgar, Andrew.   III. Title.   IV. Series.
B1455.C65   1993   192—dc20   92–44092
ISBN 0–19–283621–8

1 3 5 7 9 10 8 6 4 2

Printed in Great Britain by
Caledonian International Book Manufacturing Ltd.
Glasgow

CONTENTS

INTRODUCTION

THE outline of Hume's career is well known from his own short published autobiography. Born in 1711 in Edinburgh, he inherited a small patrimony which provided him with modest financial independence. After half-hearted attempts to begin careers in the law and in trade, he settled for three years in France, where he wrote the *Treatise of Human Nature*, published in 1739 and 1740. As he writes in his autobiography, the work 'fell dead-born from the press', provoking little reaction, favourable or unfavourable. In 1741 and 1742 he published the first collection of his essays, under the title *Essays Moral and Political*. This was better received, as were the subsequent editions published in his lifetime. From 1745 to 1747, he held posts as a tutor and as a secretary on diplomatic missions. Concluding that the failure of the *Treatise* 'had proceeded more from the manner than the matter', Hume recast the first part as the *Enquiry concerning Human Understanding* (1748), and later parts as the *Enquiry concerning the Principles of Morals* (1752), but was once again disappointed by their reception, although he considered the latter 'of all my writings, historical, philosophical, or literary, incomparably the best'. In 1752 he published the collection of essays known as the *Political Discourses*, which was well received. He also became librarian to the Faculty of Advocates in Edinburgh, and began work on the *History of England under the Tudors and Stuarts*, which appeared between 1754 and 1761. *The Natural History of Religion* appeared in 1757. In the late 1760s he again held diplomatic posts, and saw his reputation increase and financial position strengthen. He completed the *Dialogues concerning Natural Religion* shortly before he died in 1776.

Essays Moral, Political, and Literary

In the Advertisement to the posthumous 1777 edition of the *Essays*, which included most of Hume's general essays and

the *Enquiries*, Hume presents the work as a reworking of
'the principles and reasonings' of the 'juvenile' *Treatise of
Human Nature*. He disowns the earlier work, and insists
that 'Henceforth, the Author desires that the following
Pieces may alone be regarded as containing his philosophical
sentiments and principles.' To modern philosophers this
claim has seemed strange, and they have accordingly disregarded it, first by continuing to regard the *Treatise* as
Hume's major philosophical work, at most only comple-
mented by the *Enquiries*; and second, by largely ignoring
the general essays. This latter decision is symptomatic of the
way in which Hume has fallen victim to the specialization of
modern academic disciplines. Many of the essays in this
selection have become individually well known in other disciplines. It is only relatively recently, however, that serious
attempts have been made to read the full range of Hume's
writings, including the *Essays*, in relation to each other, and
in the historical context of the Scottish Enlightenment and
of eighteenth-century ideas of 'polite' culture and learning.
Seen in this context the *Essays* are central to Hume's work,
and to the exposition of his 'philosophical sentiments and
principles'.

The writings of the Scottish Enlightenment have rightly
been seen as primary influences on the development of
modern disciplines of thought as diverse as political economy
and economics, sociology, aesthetics, and linguistics. It
is important to remember, however, that many of the
Enlightenment figures now regarded as early exponents of
those disciplines wrote voluminously in a number of areas,
without seeing their various interests as distinct or incompatible. Instead they worked from the basis of the older,
more generally defined and interrelated disciplines of moral
philosophy, rhetoric, jurisprudence, and civics; and some,
such as Adam Ferguson or Adam Smith, held academic
posts in a number of these disciplines in the course of their
careers. David Hume's work exerted a formative influence
on the course of Scottish inquiries in a wide range of fields,
and it illustrates the characteristics of Enlightenment
thought very clearly. His writing was particularly influenced

by the political and cultural context in which it was produced, in eighteenth-century Scotland. The extraordinary
flowering of intellectual and cultural life in Scotland in
the century after the Act of Union centred on the historic
Scottish universities, and on the new middle-class reading
public that emerged in the lowlands and urban centres.
Hume's writings were shaped to a peculiar degree by his
attempts to bridge the gap between the learned world of
the academy, and the world of 'polite' civil society and the
literary market. Faced with the publishing failure of the
Treatise, much of his later career was geared to finding
the means of popularizing his ideas. This endeavour helped
dictate the form of the *Essays*, and explains the attention he
paid to their repeated revision, as well as throwing considerable light on his preoccupations in them.

The Polite Essay and the Scottish Enlightenment

The prose essay has a history dating back to Bacon and
Montaigne. For Hume, however, the immediate models for
the *Essays* were the English periodical essays of the early
eighteenth century. This debt is acknowledged in the
Advertisement to the first edition of his *Essays* (1741),
where he writes that 'Most of these ESSAYS were wrote with
a View of being published as WEEKLY-PAPERS, and were
intended to comprehend the Designs both of the SPECTATORS
& CRAFTSMEN . . .'. The claim is slightly puzzling in that the
Spectator and the *Craftsman* are somewhat different types of
publication. Together, however, the two models do suggest
something of Hume's initial purpose in the *Essays*. Addison
and Steele's *Spectator* was one of the most culturally influential English publications of the eighteenth century, and
played a formative role in shaping Scottish polite culture
after the Union. Appearing in daily instalments from March
1711 to December 1714, it offered a new, extended, middle-
class reading public not only entertainment, but more
importantly educative guidance in the areas of manners,
morals, aesthetics, and general knowledge necessary for
them to take their place as 'polite' citizens in society. In

doing so, it was instrumental in defining the boundaries of polite knowledge and accomplishment. For the *Spectator* writers, such polite knowledge is general, non-specialized, non-vocational, and accessible. It is also avowedly apolitical: the periodical claims to address a cross-section of society across political and social divides, and to preach the lessons of moderation and non-partisanship. Of course these lessons are not as apolitical as they seem to be: in effect they involve acceptance of the contemporary social and political establishment and celebration of the values of middle-class morality as central to social life. Ideologically, the *Spectator* and the periodicals that followed it represented, reflected, and shaped the values of an increasingly culturally assertive middle-class reading public. The *Craftsman* differs from the *Spectator* in being more narrowly political in its concerns, and avowedly partisan in its allegiances. Produced as the mouthpiece of the opposition to Robert Walpole's ministry in the 1720s, it is perhaps most interesting as an acknowledged influence on Hume's essays in assessing the implications of his historical writings and commentaries on contemporary politics, and is discussed below.

The influence of the periodical essayists is perhaps at its clearest in the two short essays with which we have begun this selection. Both make explicit arguments and assumptions which can be traced in various implicit guises in many of the later essays. In particular, 'Of the Middle Station of Life' draws on the argument of many periodical essays that virtue does not necessarily reside with birth, to claim that the middle station 'is more favourable to happiness, as well as to virtue and wisdom' than either higher or lower social ranks, but it pointedly does not develop this claim to socially challenging ends. Meanwhile 'Of Essay Writing' defines the limits of Hume's projected audience—'the elegant part of mankind, who are not immersed in mere animal life'—and announces his project of acting as 'a kind of resident or ambassador from the dominions of learning to those of conversation', as well as rather coyly considering the appropriate terms of address for his male and female readers. Both discussions throw interesting light on the more elaborate arguments put forward in the other essays.

Those other essays cover several broad and overlapping areas. Although most are self-contained, Hume does also develop cumulative arguments in several areas, sometimes to the extent of picking up claims from previous essays and developing or qualifying them in later ones. His major concerns can be identified under several broad headings—with the important proviso, already mentioned, that the categories below are often merged or overridden in the course of his discussions.

Civil Society and Manners

It is no exaggeration to say that the central area of inquiry in the Scottish Enlightenment is the development and functioning of civil society. This concern underlies and informs Enlightenment historical accounts of the 'progress' of different societies, and emerges in surveys of the 'manners' of their members. The term 'manners' itself has an extended meaning in the period, akin to 'mores': in this sense it is used to describe the broad patterns of cultural behaviour of the members of a society, so that general discussion of 'manners' often provides the framework for particular discussions of questions in taste, politics, or economics. At the same time, however, the word is used by Scottish writers in endorsement of particular patterns of polite good conduct, when, for example, they chart 'the development of manners', and the progress of refinement. These concerns are clear in Hume's essays. In many respects his arguments in each of the areas outlined below can be related directly back to his concern with civil society, or read as complementary aspects of that concern, while the generalized discussions to which the essays often lead can be seen to grow from his overarching interest in 'manners'. To some extent this is true even of the most obviously 'philosophical' essays, in their particular emphasis on social conduct; and it is clear in Hume's discussions in every other area.

Philosophy

The philosophical content of four of the essays is signalled by their titles. 'The Epicurean', 'The Stoic', 'The Platonist', and 'The Sceptic' are all concerned with the problem of the highest end to which human life can be devoted, and thus to the nature of pleasure and virtue. They are not intended to be commentaries on philosophical systems. Rather, as Hume admits, the title of each essay is determined by an affinity that the essay shows with the ancient philosophy.

The affinity is perhaps closest in the 'The Epicurean'. As a moral hedonist, Epicurus argued that the achievement of pleasure and the elimination of pain alone are good. Pleasure may be bodily, and as such is perfected in physical health. However, the superior forms of pleasure are mental, perfected in freedom from anxiety. Because some pleasures also bring pain, and wisdom allows the avoidance of such pleasures, the greatest virtue is wisdom and the sober reasoning that searches out the motives for all choice. The wise, who have nothing to fear from those around them, can ultimately find their pleasure in friendship. Epicurus further employed the mechanistic theory of atomism as a response to the superstitious fear of gods and demons, thereby countering both the unhappiness that superstitions cause, and the fear of death. As the atoms of which the soul is composed disperse upon death, humans need not fear death, because they cannot survive it. In exploring the source and nature of pleasure, Hume, like Epicurus, rejects mere sensuality, but he revises Epicurus' stress on friendship, presenting it in terms of the 'cheerful discourse' of polite society and the companionship of a lover.

'The Stoic' continues, paradoxically, with certain themes and ideas typical of the Epicureans (e.g. 'Happiness cannot possibly exist where there is no security'), albeit now interwoven with clearly Stoic propositions. The essay's initial thesis (that nature forces human beings to exercise their art and industry), while taking up something of the Stoic concern with the relationship between nature and humanity, is not itself a Stoic doctrine.

The treatment of the figure of the sage demonstrates something of the subtlety of Hume's relationship to Stoicism. In early Stoicism, the sage exemplified virtue not merely by living in harmony with the rationality of nature, but also by understanding that rationality, and so consciously assenting to it. Hume presents the Stoic concern with the harmony of the universe in an analogy of the sage to the master workman, who puts several parts together and 'moves them according to just harmony and proportion'. For the Stoics the passions pose a threat to this virtuous existence. The sage thus uses reason to dominate their passions, engendering an apathy or indifference towards them. Hume's assertion that the 'true philosopher . . . subdues his passions, and has learned, from reason, to set a just value on every pursuit' is coherent with Stoicism, but lies in an ironic tension to the *Treatise*'s assertion that 'reason is, and ought only to be the slave of passion'.[1]

The later Stoics provide the model for much of the detail of Hume's argument. Hume's image of the sage who looks with compassion upon unhappy humanity may echo Marcus Aurelius' dictate to consider the viewpoint of the wrongdoer, and so come to be sorry for humanity. Similarly, Hume's appeal to the sentiments of humanity (defined as 'a feeling for the happiness of mankind, and a resentment of their misery'),[2] and the social virtues (or those characteristics, such as justice, obedience to law, and charity, that tend 'to promote the interests of our species, and bestow happiness on human society'),[3] reflects a general Stoic concern with the individual's duties towards all humanity. The Stoic concept of 'duty' derives from conduct that is in accord with the rationality of nature. For Epictetus, training for a virtuous life would include capacity to perform one's duty, and so act as a true citizen, brother,

[1] D. Hume, *A Treatise of Human Nature*, ed. L. A. Selby-Bigge and P. H. Nidditch (Oxford, Oxford University Press, 1978), 415.

[2] D. Hume, *Enquiries concerning Human Understanding and concerning the Principles of Morals*, ed. L. A. Selby-Bigge and P. H. Nidditch (Oxford, Oxford University Press, 1975), 286.

[3] Ibid. 181.

etc. For many Stoics, and most famously for Seneca, the extreme act of duty was that of suicide. Hence Hume comments that: 'Toils, dangers, death itself, carry their charms, when we brave them for the public good.' However, his concluding comments on glory, as the reward for virtue, while coherent with the other essays in this group, are alien to Stoicism.

'The Platonist' has only a tenuous relationship to the work of Plato or his followers. The essay centres upon the proposition that the human soul is 'made for the contemplation of the Supreme Being, and of his works', and that the most perfect happiness comes from the contemplation of the beauty of the universe and the virtue of the Deity. The perfecting of this contemplation is an endless task. A partially analogous doctrine may be found in the Platonic theory of forms. For example, in the *Meno*, Socrates argues that, 'All nature is akin, and the soul has learned everything, so that when a man has recalled a single piece of knowledge . . . there is no reason why he should not find out all the rest, if he keeps a stout heart and does not grow weary of the search.'[4]

Yet it might also be suggested, following Hume's subtitle, that the Platonist is merely a person of 'philosophical devotion', and so is the figure attacked in the essay for valuing artefacts over nature. The work of Plato's Academy, precisely because the education it offered embraced the gamut of the sciences and grounded political and practical abilities in more abstract and theoretical study, attracted accusations of obscurity from Plato's contemporaries.[5]

The very title of 'The Sceptic' suggests the essay's closeness to Hume's work in the *Treatise* and *Enquiries*, where he develops his own philosophy through a critical engagement with scepticism. As a doctrine, scepticism entails that the possibilities of human knowledge are limited. It is thereby opposed to all forms of dogmatism. Pyrrho of Elis (*c*.300 BC) proposed scepticism as a solution to the un-

---

[4] Plato, *Meno*, 81d, trans. W. K. Guthrie (Penguin Classics).
[5] See Plato, *Epistle* vii. 341b–e.

happiness caused by the intellectual chaos brought about by conflicting philosophies. While sceptical arguments were principally directed at metaphysical and epistemological assumptions (and especially those of the Epicureans and the Stoics), the goal of scepticism was practical. Through the abandonment of the futile search for ultimate truth, it sought peace of mind.

It has been argued that Hume's final position in the *Treatise* and *Enquiries* is closer to ancient scepticism (specifically as it was summarized by Sextus Empiricus) than Hume himself realized. Hume is highly critical of the nihilistic extremes of scepticism, that attempted 'to destroy reason by arguments and ratiocination'.[6] However, there is 'a more mitigated scepticism or academical philosophy' that while derived from Pyrrhonism is 'corrected by common sense and reflection'.[7] While the extremes of philosophical reasoning may be technically irrefutable, the sceptic's position is reduced to absurdity precisely because a human being cannot live in society without opinion and conviction. The four philosophical essays all echo the critical boundary that the *Treatise* places about philosophy. Specifically, philosophy gives way to, and finds its ground in, the company of polite society.[8]

Most fortunately it happens, that . . . nature herself . . . cures me of this philosophical melancholy and delirium. . . . I dine, I play a game of backgammon, I converse, and am merry with my friends; and when after three or four hour's amusement, I would return to these speculations, they appear so cold, and strained, and ridiculous, that I cannot find in my heart to enter into them any farther.

Despite Hume's disclaimer, this appeal to 'nature', which is further supported by the role that habit and custom pay throughout the *Treatise* and *Enquiries*, is merely a refinement of Pyrrhonism. Pyrrho himself argued that custom, tradition, and State law may all afford a norm by which practical life may be conducted.

'On the Immortality of the Soul' and 'Of Suicide' are both

---

[6] *Enquiries*, 155.   [7] Ibid. 161.   [8] *Treatise*, 269.

dependent upon Hume's mitigated scepticism. These essays
are part of a corpus of works, including the *Dialogues
concerning Natural Religion* and *Natural History of Religion*,
in which Hume attacked organized religion. In both essays
philosophical reason is pitted against religious dogmatism.
This follows Hume's exhortation in the *Treatise* to take
philosophy rather than superstition as a guide, because
philosophy contents itself with an examination of the visible
world rather than opening up worlds of its own, and so
is less disruptive of our lives. 'Generally speaking, the
errors in religion are dangerous; those in philosophy only
ridiculous.'[9] The *Treatise* however remains more guarded
than the *Essays* in establishing its relationship to religion.
After a critical discussion of the substance of the soul,
Hume provides an ironic apology should his reasoning have
offended religious belief. It is 'an evident principle, that
whatever we can imagine, is possible', and hence while
metaphysical arguments for the immortality of the soul
remain inconclusive, Hume mildly concludes that his cri-
ticisms can have taken nothing from religion.[10]

Criticism and Taste

'Of the Delicacy of Taste and Passion', 'Of Tragedy', and
'Of the Standard of Taste' are concerned with the modern
discipline of aesthetics. 'Of the Standard of Taste' is the
most important of these essays, and in many respects is the
most important philosophical document in the *Essays*. It
provides the fundamental theory that may have informed
the projected fifth part of the *Treatise*, on Criticism.[11]
Perhaps in consequence, there is little irony in its tone.

In 'The Sceptic' Hume distinguishes judgements of fact
from moral or aesthetic value judgements. While the former
are true or false according to the nature of the external
world, the latter depend upon the felt sentiments of the
person who judges. Reason, dealing with knowledge of
truth and falsehood, is thereby put in opposition to taste,

[9] *Treatise*, 272.   [10] Ibid. 250–1.   [11] Ibid. p. xii.

that 'gives the sentiment of beauty and deformity, vice and virtue'.[12] In the *Treatise* Hume notes, with respect to vice, that '[y]ou never can find it, till you turn your reflection into your own breast and find a sentiment of disapprobation, which arises in you, towards this action. . . . It lies in yourself, not in the object.'[13] Of beauty, he argues that it 'is such an order and construction of parts, as either by primary constitution of our nature, by custom, or by caprice, is fitted to give a pleasure and satisfaction to the soul'.[14] This is developed from a general theory, to the effect that value judgements respond to passions (or 'impressions of reflection') that are the pleasant or painful feelings accompanying sensations and perceptions.[15]

Differences in the constitution of individual humans, or of the spatial and temporal proximity of the individual to the object judged, will lead to the experiencing of different passions, and so make for different value-judgements of the same action or object. Hume's position may then be taken to entail an extreme subjectivism. While all will approve of what they call the 'virtuous' or 'elegant', they may apply the terms to different people, actions, and objects. In the *Treatise*, Hume avoids moral subjectivism by examining such examples as the greater approval we give to a close aquaintance than to a great figure in history. A servant may then be praised more highly than Marcus Brutus. This misjudgement is corrected in our use of language, such that the communication of our sentiments is only possible if we 'correct the momentary appearance of things, and overlook our present situation'. Correct moral judgement requires that 'we fix on some steady and general points of view'.[16] In the *Enquiries*, this general viewpoint is achieved by greater social intercourse and conversation, so that language comes to be grounded in general views.[17] 'Of the Standard of Taste' develops a variety of similar and complementary approaches to the problem of aesthetic subjectivity. Underpinning the methods by which a delicacy of taste may be

[12] *Enquiries*, 294.   [13] *Treatise*, 468–9.   [14] Ibid. 299.
[15] Ibid. 8.   [16] Ibid. 581–2.   [17] *Enquiries*, 228.

cultivated and recognized are the propositions that judgements are distorted by the momentary distractions of authority and prejudice, and that a suitably general viewpoint, overcoming the restricted viewpoint of a particular age or country, will reveal the universal principles of taste.

Political Economy

Hume's essays on economic matters, published in a group in Part II of the original edition, and here represented by some of the most important pieces, had a considerable influence on the development of Scottish political economy. They are typical of Scottish inquiries in the field (most notably pursued by Adam Smith) in embracing a range of social, cultural, and historical concerns beyond the purely economic in their discussions. They thus include consideration of various aspects of the development of civil society, the state of manners and morals, and questions of taste such as those discussed above, alongside and in relation to more technical questions of economic behaviour and policy.

Economic matters had been widely treated in print in England in the late seventeenth and early eighteenth centuries, when the technical inquiries of political arithmeticians such as Temple and Petty, and translations of French works, were counterparted by a considerable body of general commentary in books and periodicals. Defoe's *Compleat English Tradesman*, for instance, shares its concerns with his *Review*, which is largely devoted to explaining the elements of commerce to a lay audience. Similarly the *Spectator*, *Guardian*, and *Freeholder* include many essays on the area, including famous ones on credit and the stock exchange. Hume draws on these sources, and on the economic arguments of earlier commentators from the classical period on. Indeed his arguments can be seen as attempts to renegotiate the terms of a tradition of civic humanist political discourse in the light of contemporary economic circumstances and theories. The civic tradition is concerned above all with the moral well-being of society conceived as a republic. In this context, commerce is usually presented as a suspicious and potentially dangerous area, laying society open to the risk of succumbing to luxury and so falling into corruption. Some eighteenth-century apologists attempt to find terms in which to make the new commercial economy of the period morally acceptable, while others, such as Bernard Mandeville, launch shocking justifications of the economic workings of contemporary society, which set out to undermine the moral claims of civic humanism by insisting on the lack of relation between economics and morality, and suggesting that, in economic terms, the 'private vices' of consumption are 'public benefits'.

In his economic essays, Hume sets out to develop the work of earlier apologists for commerce, and in particular to negotiate a positive place for luxury as the foundation of prosperity, economic progress, and refinement in society, without falling back on Mandeville's shockingly amoral claims. His arguments are strikingly innovative in some areas, particularly in their treatment of luxury. The category is introduced immediately at the start of 'Of Refinement in the Arts' (an essay which is itself entitled 'Of Luxury' in some editions). Hume attempts to distinguish the 'good' and 'bad' 'signification' of the word, and argues that in the positive sense 'luxury' fosters 'refinement' in all its senses. His argument involves the inversion of traditional humanist claims about the corrupting effects of luxury, and in particular the claim that the Roman empire collapsed under the influence of Eastern luxury. Typically, it issues in a larger claim for the all-round cultural benefits of economic progress and refinement, as 'the spirit of the age' affects all the arts and stimulates sociability, politeness, and moderation. Notably, that 'spirit' is said to inform the 'mechanical' as well as the 'liberal' and 'polite' arts, although it is the latter that are of particular concern to Hume.

The essays depart from earlier commentaries in other significant ways. In particular, earlier commentators almost universally work from a model of the economy in which the economic functioning of society depends upon the existence of a class of subsistence labourers, whose efforts support the leisure and the luxury expenditure of their superiors, but who are themselves necessarily denied access to those things. In 'Of Commerce' Hume apparently departs from this model and argues for a high wage economy, in which all can be, to some extent, producers and consumers of luxury goods. In this respect he sets the agenda for later Scottish writers, including Adam Smith, although it is worth noting that he provides his own rationales for economic hierarchy and privilege in society which to some extent supply the place of those he attacks. In more strictly technical areas, the essays are at the forefront of contemporary economic theory on matters such as the nature of money and interest, value, credit, labour, public finance, and the benefits of free trade. Although we have not been able to include all Hume's particular essays on these matters in this selection, his general economic arguments are echoed from one essay to another, and their direction will, we hope, be apparent.

The other large area dealt with by Hume, which eventually comes to be regarded as a key concern of classical political economy, is demography. The longest essay in the collection is an exhaustive (or at least exhausting) survey of classical records of population, entitled 'Of the Populousness of Ancient Nations'. The essay makes an important contribution to a wide-ranging eighteenth-century debate. Hume was aware of Robert Wallace's work on the populousness of the ancient world. This was referred to in a footnote to the earliest editions of the essay, and was later published as *A Dissertation on the Numbers of Mankind in Antient and Modern Times* (1753). The argument that a large population signifies a happy and virtuous nation—and consequently that a decline in population is a sign of the moral corruption of the society involved—has its roots in civic humanist discussions of the moral health of society, and of the historical cycles of progress and decline. The terms and direction of the eighteenth-century argument were eventually and decisively reversed by T. R. Malthus (1766–1834), whose *Essay on the Principle of Population* (1798–1830) became a key document in classical political economy, alongside the works of Smith and Ricardo. In the first version of the *Essay* Malthus argues that the permanent pressure of expanding population on means of subsistence is an inevitable natural impediment to social amelioration, and so severs the connection made earlier between expanding population and the health of society.

Politics and History

Hume is still listed in the British Library catalogue as 'David Hume, historian'—an index of the importance and popularity of his historical writings. Several of the most important concerns of the *History of Great Britain* are prefigured in the *Essays*. The political histories and histories of civil society produced by, amongst others, Hume, Robertson, Lyttleton, Ferguson, Smollett, and Gibbon are marked by their negotiations between traditional patterns of exemplary history and newer models of 'scientific' historical inquiry. In his historical essays, and in his commentaries on contemporary political affairs, Hume is concerned to provide 'objective' accounts and assessments of public events. His endeavour has an avowed political purpose in teaching the lessons of detachment and moderation of judgement. At times his attempts at disinterested commentary themselves have the potential to be read as politically provocative. Claims for detachment, such as those made in 'Of the Parties of Great Britain', inevitably laid him open to the sort of partisan charges of covert political favouritism that later assailed the first volumes of the *History*; and he clearly recognized the dangers of provoking controversy when he withheld 'Of the Protestant Succession' from the 1748 edition of the *Essays*, in case its exposition of the cases for and against the Stuart succession could be read as an incitement to Jacobitism. Ultimately in this last essay, and consistently elsewhere, Hume's lessons in political moderation emerge as lessons in conservatism and acceptance of the *status quo*. In 'Of the Original Contract', for instance, his scepticism about the generally accepted contemporary Whig political orthodoxies derived from Locke's contract theory of government, and insistence that 'almost all' governments 'have been founded originally, either on usurpation or conquest, or both', does not lead him to advocate democracy (which might create such a contract, but is described only as 'the dissolution of government'). Instead it issues in an alternative rationale of subordination. Thus 'the general obligation, which binds us to government, is the interest and necessities of society', and this obligation is strong no matter what form the government takes, or how 'legitimate' its original claims to power. Even in the 'Idea of a Perfect Commonwealth', Hume prefaces his discussion with covering remarks about his merely speculative thoughts, and about how, despite them, 'the magistrate' will discern 'infinite advantage' in 'an established government . . . by that very circumstance, of its being established'.

Finally, Hume's political and historical inquiries repeatedly return to the patterns of cultural behaviour which result from (or give rise to) different political and social systems; and to endorsements of the systems most likely to encourage 'progress', 'liberty', and 'refinement' in civil society, in the terms he elsewhere endorses. Essays such as 'Of Some Remarkable Customs' illustrate his argumentative claims in compact form, but the full range of his concerns, and of the connections made between them in his arguments, is best illustrated in an essay such as 'Of the Rise and Progress of the Arts and Sciences', in which his broadly historical 'philosophical' inquiries dwell on the influence of particular political systems and other economic and geographical influences on the development of manners and aesthetic taste, and provide an excellent index of the concerns and characteristic modes of argument of the Scottish Enlightenment.

NOTE ON THE TEXT

THE textual history of Hume's *Essays Moral, Political, and Literary* is very complex. Sixteen editions of some or all of the essays appeared under various titles during Hume's lifetime, with a further authorized edition shortly after his death, in 1777. Different collections added or excluded essays, and individual essays were extensively, and sometimes repeatedly, revised. Modern standard editions by T. H. Green and T. H. Grose (Longman's, Green, and Co., London, 1889) and Eugene Miller (Liberty Classics, Indianapolis, 1985) take the 1777 edition as their copy text wherever possible. We have followed suit, but have included some textual variants in our endnotes where these are of particular interest. We have tried to offer an approachable reading edition of the selected essays: we have preserved much eighteenth-century spelling and capitalization, but have tactfully regularized both and modernized punctuation where this will aid comprehension. We have also silently standardized Hume's footnote references to classical texts to the appropriate modern Loeb editions. Hume's original footnotes and significant textual variations in earlier editions are signalled in the text by a dagger, our own explanatory notes by an asterisk.

BIBLIOGRAPHY

Ayer, A. J., *Hume* (Oxford, 1980).

Box, M. A., *The Suasive Art of David Hume* (Princeton, NJ, 1990).

Bryson, G., *Man and Society: The Scottish Inquiry of the Eighteenth Century* (Princeton, NJ, 1945).

Chappell, V. C. (ed.), *Hume* (New York, 1966).

Christensen, Jerome, *Practicing Enlightenment: Hume and the Formation of a Literary Career* (Madison, Wis., 1987).

Flage, Daniel E., *David Hume's Theory of Mind* (London and New York, 1990).

Flew, Antony, *David Hume: Philosopher of Moral Science* (Oxford, 1986).

Forbes, Duncan, *Hume's Philosophical Politics* (Cambridge, 1975).

Ginsberg, Robert (ed.), *The Philosopher as Writer: The Eighteenth Century* (Selinsgrove, Pa., 1987).

Haakonssen, Knud, *The Science of a Legislator: The Natural Jurisprudence of David Hume and Adam Smith* (Cambridge, 1981).

Hilson, J. C., 'Hume: The Historian as Man of Feeling', in *Augustan Worlds*, ed. J. C. Hilson, M. M. B. Jones, and J. R. Watson (New York, 1978).

Hirschman, Albert O., *The Passions and the Interests: Political Arguments for Capitalism before its Triumph* (Princeton, NJ, 1977).

Hont, Istvan, and Ignatieff, Michael (eds.), *Wealth and Virtue: The Shaping of Political Economy in the Scottish Enlightenment* (Cambridge, 1983).

Jones, Peter, *Hume's Sentiments: Their Ciceronian and French Context* (Edinburgh, 1982).

Livingston, D. W., *Hume's Philosophy of Common Life* (Chicago and London, 1984).

Livingston, D. W., and King, J. T. (eds.), *Hume: a Re-Evaluation* (New York, 1976).

Miller, David, *Philosophy and Ideology in Hume's Political Thought* (Oxford, 1981).

Merrill, Kenneth R., and Shahan, Robert W. (eds.), *David Hume: Many-Sided Genius* (Norman, Okla., 1976).

Morice, C. P. (ed.), *David Hume: Bicentenary Papers* (Edinburgh, 1977).

Mossner, E. C., *The Life of David Hume* (Oxford, 1980).

Norton, D. Fate, *David Hume: Common-Sense Moralist, Sceptical Metaphysician* (Princeton, NJ, 1982).

Noxon, James, *Hume's Philosophical Development* (Oxford, 1973).

Passmore, J. A., *Hume's Intentions* (London, 1968).

Phillipson, Nicholas, *Hume* (London, 1989).

Price, J. V., *The Ironic Hume* (Austin, Tex., 1965).

—— *David Hume* (New York, 1968).

Smith, N. Kemp, *The Philosophy of David Hume: A Critical Study of its Origins and Central Doctrines* (London, 1941).

Stewart, John B., *The Moral and Political Philosophy of David Hume* (New York, 1963).

Stewart, M. A. (ed.), *Studies in the Philosophy of the Scottish Enlightenment* (Oxford, 1990).

Todd, W. B. (ed.), *Hume and the Enlightenment: Essays Presented to Ernest Campbell Mossner* (Austin, Tex., 1974).

Wexler, V., *David Hume and the History of England* (Philadelphia, Pa., 1979).

CHRONOLOGY

1711   Birth of David Hume in Edinburgh.

1714   Accession of George I.

1715   Jacobite Rebellion.

1721   Beginning of Walpole's administration.

1723   Hume attends Edinburgh University.

1734–7   Hume lives in France, first at Rheims and then at La Flèche, writing the *Treatise*.

1739–40   *A Treatise of Human Nature* published.

1741–2   First edition of *Essays Moral and Political* published.

1742   End of Walpole's administration.

1744–5   Hume fails to obtain the Chair of Moral Philosophy at Edinburgh.

1745   Hume becomes tutor to the Marquess of Annandale.

1745   Jacobite Rebellion.

1748   Hume appointed secretary to General St Clair on diplomatic missions to Vienna and Turin.

1748   *Philosophical Essays concerning Human Understanding* (later entitled *Enquiry concerning Human Understanding*) published.

1751   *Enquiry concerning the Principles of Morals*.

1752   Hume fails to obtain the Chair of Moral Philosophy at Glasgow.

1752   *Political Discourses* published.

1752–7   Hume appointed Keeper of the Advocates' Library, Edinburgh.

1754   *The History of Great Britain, Containing the Reigns of James I and Charles I* published.

1756   *The History of Great Britain, Containing the History of the Interregnum to the Revolution of 1688* published.

1757   *The Natural History of Religion* published.

1759   *The History of England, Under the House of Tudor* published.

1762   *The History of England from the Invasion of Julius Caesar to the Accession of Henry VII* published.

1763–5   Hume appointed secretary to Lord Hertford in Paris.

1767–8   Hume appointed Under-Secretary of State, Northern Department.

1769   Hume settles in Edinburgh.

1776   Death of Hume.

CHRONOLOGY

1711	Birth of David Hume in Edinburgh.
1714	Accession of George I
1715	Jacobite Rebellion.
1721	Beginning of Walpole's administration.
1723	Hume attends Edinburgh University.
1734–7	Hume lives in France, first at Rheims and then at La Flèche, writing the *Treatise*.
1739–40	*A Treatise of Human Nature* published.
1741–2	First edition of *Essays Moral and Political* published
1742	End of Walpole's administration.
1744–5	Hume fails to obtain the Chair of Moral Philosophy at Edinburgh.
1745	Hume becomes tutor to the Marquess of Annandale.
1745	Jacobite Rebellion.
1746	Hume appointed secretary to General St Clair on diplomatic missions to Vienna and Turin.
1748	*Philosophical Essays concerning Human Understanding* (later entitled *Enquiry concerning Human Understanding*) published.
1751	*Enquiry concerning the Principles of Morals*.
1752	Hume fails to obtain the Chair of Moral Philosophy at Glasgow.
1752	*Political Discourses* published.
1752–7	Hume appointed Keeper of the Advocates' Library, Edinburgh.
1754	*The History of Great Britain, Containing the Reigns of James I and Charles I* published
1756	*The History of Great Britain, Containing the History of the interregnum to the Revolution of 1688* published.
1757	*The Natural History of Religion* published.
1759	*The History of England, Under the House of Tudor* published.
1762	*The History of England from the Invasion of Julius Caesar to the Accession of Henry VII* published.
1763–5	Hume appointed secretary to Lord Hertford in Paris.
1767–8	Hume appointed Under-Secretary of State, Northern Department.
1769	Hume settles in Edinburgh
1776	Death of Hume.

SELECTED ESSAYS

OF ESSAY WRITING

THE elegant part of mankind, who are not immersed in mere animal life, but employ themselves in the operations of the mind, may be divided into the *learned* and *conversable*. The learned are such as have chosen for their portion the higher and more difficult operations of the mind, which require leisure and solitude, and cannot be brought to perfection, without long preparation and severe labour. The conversable world join to a sociable disposition, and a taste for pleasure, an inclination for the easier and more gentle exercises of the understanding, for obvious reflections on human affairs, and the duties of common life, and for the observation of the blemishes or perfections of the particular objects that surround them. Such subjects of thought furnish not sufficient employment in solitude, but require the company and conversation of our fellow-creatures, to render them a proper exercise for the mind; and this brings mankind together in society, where every one displays his thoughts in observations in the best manner he is able, and mutually gives and receives information, as well as pleasure.

The separation of the learned from the conversable world seems to have been the great defect of the last age, and must have had a very bad influence both on books and company: for what possibility is there of finding topics of conversation fit for the entertainment of rational creatures, without having recourse sometimes to history, poetry, politics, and the more obvious principles, at least, of philosophy? Must our whole discourse be a continued series of gossiping stories and idle remarks? Must the mind never rise higher, but be perpetually

> Stunn'd and worn out with endless chat,
> Of Will did this, and Nan did that?*

This would be to render the time spent in company the most unentertaining, as well as the most unprofitable, part of our lives.

On the other hand, learning has been as great a loser by being shut up in colleges and cells, and secluded from the world and good company. By that means every part of what we call *belles lettres** became totally barbarous, being cultivated by men without any taste for life or manners, and without that liberty and facility of thought and expression which can only be acquired by conversation. Even philosophy went to wreck by this moping recluse method of study, and became as chimerical* in her conclusions, as she was unintelligible in her style and manner of delivery; and, indeed, what could be expected from men who never consulted experience in any of their reasonings, or who never searched for that experience, where alone it is to be found, in common life and conversation?

It is with great pleasure I observe, that men of letters in this age have lost in a great measure that shyness and bashfulness of temper, which kept them at a distance from mankind; and, at the same time, that men of the world are proud of borrowing from books their most agreeable topics of conversation. It is to be hoped that this league betwixt the learned and conversable worlds, which is so happily begun, will be still further improved to their mutual advantage; and to that end, I know nothing more advantageous than such *Essays* as these with which I endeavour to entertain the public. In this view, I cannot but consider myself as a kind of resident or ambassador from the dominions of learning to those of conversation, and shall think it my constant duty to promote a good correspondence betwixt these two states, which have so great a dependence on each other. I shall give intelligence to the learned of whatever passes in company, and shall endeavour to import into company whatever commodities I find in my native country proper for their use and entertainment. The balance of trade we need not be jealous of, nor will there be any difficulty to preserve it on both sides. The materials of this commerce must chiefly be furnished by conversation and common life: the manufacturing of them alone belongs to learning.

As it would be an unpardonable negligence in an ambassador not to pay his respects to the sovereign of the state where he is commissioned to reside; so it would be altogether inexcusable in me not to address myself with a particular respect to the fair sex, who are the sovereigns of the empire of conversation. I approach them with reverence; and were not my countrymen, the learned, a stubborn independent race of mortals, extremely jealous of their liberty, and unaccustomed to subjection, I should resign into their fair hands the sovereign authority over the republic of letters. As the case stands, my commission extends no further than to desire a league, offensive and defensive, against our common enemies, against the enemies of reason and beauty, people of dull heads and cold hearts. From this moment let us pursue them with the severest vengeance: let no quarter be given, but to those of sound understandings and delicate affections; and these characters, it is to be presumed, we shall always find inseparable.

To be serious, and to quit the allusion before it be worn threadbare, I am of opinion that women, that is, women of sense and education (for to such alone I address myself) are much better judges of all polite writing than men of the same degree of understanding; and that it is a vain panic, if they be so far terrified with the common ridicule that is levelled against learned ladies, as utterly to abandon every kind of books and study to our sex. Let the dread of that ridicule have no other effect than to make them conceal their knowledge before fools, who are not worthy of it, nor of them. Such will still presume upon the vain title of the male sex to affect a superiority above them: but my fair readers may be assured, that all men of sense, who know the world, have a great deference for their judgment of such books as lie within the compass of their knowledge, and repose more confidence in the delicacy of their taste, though unguided by rules, than in all the dull labours of pedants and commentators. In a neighbouring nation, equally famous for good taste, and for gallantry, the ladies are, in a manner, the sovereigns of the *learned* world, as well as of the *conversable*; and no polite writer pretends* to venture before the public, without the approbation of some celebrated judges of that sex. Their verdict is, indeed, sometimes complained of; and, in particular, I find, that the admirers of *Corneille*, to save that great poet's honour upon the ascendant that *Racine* began to take over him, always said, that it was not to be expected, that so old a man could dispute the prize, before such judges, with so young a man as his rival. But this observation has been found unjust, since posterity seems to have ratified the verdict of that tribunal: and *Racine*, though dead, is still the favourite of the fair sex, as well as of the best judges among the men.

There is only one subject of which I am apt to distrust the judgment of females, and that is concerning books of gallantry and devotion, which they commonly affect as high flown as possible; and most of them seem more delighted with the warmth, than with the justness of the passion. I mention gallantry and devotion as the same subject, because, in reality, they become the same when treated in this manner; and we may observe, that they both depend upon the very same complexion.* As the fair sex have a great share of the tender and amorous disposition, it perverts their judgment on this occasion, and makes them be easily affected, even by what has no propriety in the expression or nature in the sentiment. Mr *Addison's* elegant discourses on religion have no relish with them, in comparison of books of mystic devotion: and *Otway's* tragedies are rejected for the rakes of Mr *Dryden*.

Would the ladies correct their false taste in this particular, let them accustom themselves a little more to books of all kinds; let them give encouragement to men of sense and knowledge to frequent their company; and finally, let them concur heartily in that union I have projected betwixt the learned and conversable worlds. They may, perhaps, meet with more complaisance from their usual followers than from men of learning; but they cannot reasonably expect so sincere an affection: and, I hope, they will never be guilty of so wrong a choice, as to sacrifice the substance for the shadow.

OF THE MIDDLE STATION OF LIFE

THE moral of the following fable will easily discover itself, without my explaining it. One rivulet meeting another, with whom he had been long united in strictest amity, with noisy haughtiness and disdain thus bespoke him—'What, brother! still in the same state! Still low and creeping! Are you not ashamed, when you behold me, who though lately in a like condition with you, am now become a great river, and shall shortly be able to rival the *Danube* or the *Rhine*, provided those friendly rains continue which have favoured my banks, but neglected yours?' 'Very true,' replies the humble rivulet, 'You are now, indeed, swollen to a great size; but methinks you are become withal somewhat turbulent and muddy. I am contented with my low condition and my purity.'

Instead of commenting upon this fable, I shall take occasion from it to compare the different stations of life, and to persuade such of my readers as are placed in the middle station to be satisfied with it, as the most eligible of all others. These form the most numerous rank of men that can be supposed susceptible of philosophy; and therefore all discourses of morality ought principally to be addressed to them. The great are too much immersed in pleasure, and the poor too much occupied in providing for the necessities of life, to hearken to the calm voice of reason. The middle station, as it is most happy in many respects, so particularly in this, that a man placed in it can, with the greatest leisure, consider his own happiness, and reap a new enjoyment, from comparing his situation with that of persons above or below him.

Agur's prayer* is sufficiently noted. *Two things have I required of thee; deny me them not before I die: remove far* *from me vanity and lies; give me neither poverty nor riches; feed me with food convenient for me, lest I be full and deny thee, and say, who is the Lord? Or lest I be poor, and steal, and take the name of my GOD in vain.* The middle station is here justly recommended, as affording the fullest *security* for virtue; and I may also add, that it gives opportunity for the most ample *exercise* of it, and furnishes employment for every good quality which we can possibly be possessed of. Those who are placed among the lower ranks of men, have little opportunity of exerting any other virtue besides those of patience, resignation, industry, and integrity. Those who are advanced into the higher stations, have full employment for their generosity, humanity, affability, and charity. When a man lies betwixt these two extremes, he can exert the former virtues towards his *superiors*, and the latter towards his *inferiors*. Every moral quality which the human soul is susceptible of, may have its turn, and be called up to action; and a man may, after this manner, be much more certain of his progress in virtue, than where his good qualities lie dormant, and without employment.

But there is another virtue that seems principally to lie among *equals*, and is, for that reason, chiefly calculated for the middle station of life. This virtue is FRIENDSHIP. I believe most men of generous tempers are apt to envy the great, when they consider the large opportunities such persons have of doing good to their fellow-creatures, and of acquiring the friendship and esteem of men of merit. They make no advances in vain, and are not obliged to associate with those whom they have little kindness for, like people of inferior stations, who are subject to have their proffers of friendship rejected, even where they would be most fond of placing their affections. But though the great have more facility in acquiring friendships, they cannot be so certain of the sincerity of them, as men of a lower rank, since the favours they bestow may acquire them flattery, instead of good-will and kindness. It has been very judiciously remarked, that we attach ourselves more by the services we perform than by those we receive, and that a man is in danger of losing his friends by obliging them too far. I should, therefore, choose to lie in the middle way, and to have my commerce with my friend varied both by obligations given and received. I have too much pride to be willing that all the obligations should lie on my side, and should be afraid, that, if they all lay on his, he would also have too much pride to be entirely easy under them, or have a perfect complacency in my company.

We may also remark of the middle station of life, that it is more favourable to the acquiring of *wisdom* and *ability*, as well as of *virtue*, and that a man so situate has a better chance for attaining a knowledge both of men and things, than those of a more elevated station. He enters with more familiarity into human life: every thing appears in its natural colours before him; he has more leisure to form observations; and has, besides, the motive of ambition to push him on in his attainments, being certain that he can never rise to any distinction or eminence in the world, without his own industry. And here I cannot forbear communicating a remark, which may appear somewhat extraordinary, *viz.* that it is wisely ordained by Providence, that the middle station should be the most favourable to the improving our natural abilities, since there is really more capacity requisite to perform the duties of that station, than is requisite to act in the higher spheres of life. There are more natural parts, and a stronger genius requisite to make a good lawyer or physician, than to make a great monarch. For let us take any race or succession of kings, where birth alone gives a title to the crown; the *English* kings, for instance, who have not been esteemed the most shining in history. From the Conquest to the succession of his present majesty, we may reckon twenty-eight sovereigns, omitting those who died minors. Of these, eight are esteemed princes of great capacity, *viz.* the *Conqueror*, *Harry* II, *Edward* I, *Edward* III, *Harry* V and VII, *Elizabeth*, and the late King *William*. Now, I believe every one will allow, that, in the common run of mankind, there are not eight, out of twenty-eight, who are fitted by nature to make a figure either on the bench or at the bar. Since *Charles* VII, ten monarchs have reigned in *France*, omitting *Francis* II. Five of those have been esteemed princes of capacity, *viz. Louis* XI, XII, and XIV, *Francis* I, and *Harry* IV. In short, the governing of mankind well requires a great deal of virtue, justice, and humanity, but not a surprising capacity. A certain Pope, whose name I have forgot, used to say, *let us divert ourselves, my friends; the world governs itself.* There are, indeed, some critical times, such as those in which *Harry* IV lived, that call for the utmost vigour; and a less courage and capacity, than what appeared in that great monarch, must have sunk under the weight. But such circumstances are rare; and even then fortune does at least one half of the business.

Since the common professions, such as law or physic, require equal, if not superior capacity, to what are exerted in the higher spheres of life, it is evident, that the soul must be made of still a finer mould, to shine in philosophy or poetry, or in any of the higher parts of learning. Courage and resolution are chiefly requisite in a commander; justice and humanity in a statesman; but genius and capacity in a scholar. Great generals and great politicians are found in all ages and countries of the world, and frequently start up at once, even amongst the greatest barbarians. *Sweden* was sunk in ignorance, when it produced *Gustavus Ericson*, and *Gustavus Adolphus*: *Muscovy*, when the *Czar** appeared: and perhaps *Carthage*, when it gave birth to *Hannibal*. But *England* must pass through a long gradation of its *Spencers*, *Jonsons*, *Wallers*, *Drydens*, before it arise at an *Addison* or a *Pope*. A happy talent for the liberal arts and sciences is a kind of prodigy among men. Nature must afford the richest genius that comes from her hands; education and example must cultivate it from the earliest infancy; and industry must concur to carry it to any degree of perfection. No man needs be surprised to see *Kouli-Kan** among the *Persians*; but *Homer*, in so early an age among the *Greeks*, is certainly matter of the highest wonder.

A man cannot show a genius for war, who is not so fortunate as to be trusted with command; and it seldom happens in any state or kingdom, that several at once are placed in that situation. How many *Marlboroughs* were there in the confederate army, who never rose so much as to the command of a regiment? But I am persuaded there has been but one *Milton* in *England* within these hundred years, because every one may exert the talents of poetry who is possessed of them; and no one could exert them under greater disadvantages than that divine poet. If no man were allowed to write verses, but the person who was beforehand named to be *laureate*, could we expect a poet in ten thousand years?

Were we to distinguish the ranks of men by their genius and capacity, more than by their virtue and usefulness to the public, great philosophers would certainly challenge the first rank, and must be placed at the top of human kind. So rare is this character, that perhaps there has not as yet been above two in the world who can lay a just claim to it. At least, *Galileo* and *Newton* seem to me so far to excel all the rest, that I cannot admit any other into the same class with them.

Great poets may challenge the second place; and this species of genius, though rare, is yet much more frequent than the former. Of the *Greek* poets that remain, *Homer* alone seems to merit this character: of the *Romans, Virgil, Horace*, and *Lucretius*: of the *English, Milton* and *Pope*: *Corneille, Racine, Boileau*, and *Voltaire*, of the *French*: and *Tasso* and *Ariosto* of the *Italians.**

Great orators and historians are perhaps more rare than great poets; but as the opportunities for exerting the talents requisite for eloquence, or acquiring the knowledge requisite for writing history, depend in some measure upon fortune, we cannot pronounce these productions of genius to be more extraordinary than the former.

I should now return from this digression, and show that the middle station of life is more favourable to *happiness*, as well as to *virtue* and *wisdom*: but as the arguments that prove this seem pretty obvious, I shall here forbear insisting on them.

OF THE DELICACY OF TASTE AND PASSION

SOME People are subject to a certain *delicacy* of *passion*, which makes them extremely sensible to all the accidents of life, and gives them a lively joy upon every prosperous event, as well as a piercing grief when they meet with misfortune and adversity. Favours and good offices easily engage their friendship, while the smallest injury provokes their resentment. Any honour or mark of distinction elevates them above measure, but they are sensibly touched with contempt. People of this character have, no doubt, more lively enjoyments, as well as more pungent sorrows, than men of cool and sedate tempers. But, I believe, when every thing is balanced, there is no one who would not rather be of the latter character, were he entirely master of his own disposition. Good or ill fortune is very little at our disposal; and when a person that has this sensibility of temper meets with any misfortune, his sorrow or resentment takes entire possession of him, and deprives him of all relish in the common occurrences of life, the right enjoyment of which forms the chief part of our happiness. Great pleasures are much less frequent than great pains, so that a sensible temper must meet with fewer trials in the former way than in the latter. Not to mention, that men of such lively passions are apt to be transported beyond all bounds of prudence and discretion, and to take false steps in the conduct of life, which are often irretrievable.

There is a *delicacy* of *taste* observable in some men, which very much resembles this *delicacy* of *passion*, and produces the same sensibility to beauty and deformity of every kind, as that does to prosperity and adversity, obligations and injuries. When you present a poem or a picture to a man possessed of this talent, the delicacy of his feeling makes him be sensibly touched with every part of it; nor are the masterly strokes perceived with more exquisite relish and satisfaction, than the negligences or absurdities with disgust and uneasiness. A polite and judicious conversation affords him the highest entertainment; rudeness or impertinence is as great punishment to him. In short, delicacy of taste has the same effect as delicacy of passion. It enlarges the sphere both of our happiness and misery, and makes us sensible to pains as well as pleasures which escape the rest of mankind.

I believe, however, every one will agree with me, that notwithstanding this resemblance, delicacy of taste is as much to be desired and cultivated, as delicacy of passion is to be lamented, and to be remedied, if possible. The good or ill accidents of life are very little at our disposal; but we are pretty much masters what books we shall read, what diversions we shall partake of, and what company we shall keep. Philosophers have endeavoured to render happiness entirely independent of every thing external. This degree of perfection is impossible to be *attained*; but every wise man will endeavour to place his happiness on such objects chiefly as depend upon himself; and *that* is not to be *attained* so much by any other means as by this delicacy of sentiment. When a man is possessed of that talent, he is more happy by what pleases his taste, than by what gratifies his appetites, and receives more enjoyment from a poem, or a piece of reasoning, than the most expensive luxury can afford.[†]

Whatever connection there may be originally between these two species of delicacy, I am persuaded that nothing is so proper to cure us of this delicacy of passion, as the cultivating of that higher and more refined taste, which enables us to judge of the characters of men, of the compositions of genius, and of the productions of the nobler arts. A greater or less relish for those obvious beauties which strike the senses, depends entirely upon the greater or less sensibility of the temper; but with regard to the sciences and liberal arts, a fine taste is, in some measure, the same with strong sense, or at least depends so much upon it that they are inseparable. In order to judge aright of a composition of genius, there are so many views to be taken in, so many circumstances to be compared, and such a knowledge of human nature requisite, that no man, who is not possessed of the soundest judgment, will ever make a tolerable critic in such performances. And this is a new reason for cultivating a relish in the liberal arts. Our judgment will strengthen by this exercise. We shall form juster notions of life. Many things which please or afflict others, will appear to us too frivolous to engage our attention; and we shall lose by degrees that sensibility and delicacy of passion which is so incommodious.

But perhaps I have gone too far, in saying that a cultivated taste for the polite arts extinguishes the passions, and renders us indifferent to those objects which are so fondly* pursued by the rest of mankind. On further reflection, I find, that it rather improves our sensibility for all the tender and agreeable passions; at the same time that it renders the mind incapable of the rougher and more boisterous emotions.

> *Ingenuas didicisse fideliter artes,*
> *Emollit mores, nec sinit esse feros.* *

For this, I think, there may be assigned two very natural reasons. In the *first* place, nothing is so improving to the temper as the study of the beauties either of poetry, eloquence, music, or painting. They give a certain elegance of sentiment to which the rest of mankind are strangers. The emotions which they excite are soft and tender. They draw off the mind from the hurry of business and interest; cherish reflection; dispose to tranquillity; and produce an agreeable melancholy, which, of all dispositions of the mind, is the best suited to love and friendship.

In the *second* place, a delicacy of taste is favourable to love and friendship, by confining our choice to few people, and making us indifferent to the company and conversation of the greater part of men. You will seldom find that mere men of the world, whatever strong sense they may be endowed with, are very nice* in distinguishing characters, or in marking those insensible differences and gradations, which make one man preferable to another. Any one that has competent sense is sufficient for their entertainment. They talk to him of their pleasures and affairs, with the same frankness that they would to another; and finding many who are fit to supply his place, they never feel any vacancy or want in his absence. But to make use of the allusion of a celebrated French† author, the judgment may be compared to a clock or watch, where the most ordinary machine is sufficient to tell the hours; but the most elaborate alone can point out the minutes and seconds, and distinguish the smallest differences of time. One that has well digested his knowledge both of books and men, has little enjoyment but in the company of a few select companions. He feels too sensibly, how much all the rest of mankind fall short of the notions which he has entertained. And, his affections being thus confined within a narrow circle, no wonder he carries them further than if they were more general and undistinguished. The gaiety and frolic of a bottle companion improves with him into a solid friendship; and the ardours of a youthful appetite become an elegant passion.

THAT POLITICS MAY BE REDUCED TO A SCIENCE

IT is a question with several, whether there be any essential difference between one form of government and another and, whether every form may not become good or bad, according as it is well or ill administered?† Were it once admitted, that all governments are alike, and that the only difference consists in the character and conduct of the governors, most political disputes would be at an end, and all *Zeal* for one constitution above another must be esteemed mere bigotry and folly. But, though a friend to moderation, I cannot forbear condemning this sentiment, and should be sorry to think, that human affairs admit of no greater stability, than what they receive from the casual humours and characters of particular men.

It is true, those who maintain that the goodness of all government consists in the goodness of the administration, may cite many particular instances in history, where the very same government, in different hands, has varied suddenly into the two opposite extremes of good and bad.

Compare the FRENCH government under HENRY III and under HENRY IV.* Oppression, levity, artifice on the part of the rulers; faction, sedition, treachery, rebellion, disloyalty on the part of the subjects: these compose the character of the former miserable era. But when the patriot and heroic prince, who succeeded, was once firmly seated on the throne, the government, the people, every thing, seemed to be totally changed; and all from the difference of the temper and conduct of these two sovereigns. Instances of this kind may be multiplied, almost without number, from ancient as well as modern history, foreign as well as domestic.

But here it may be proper to make a distinction. All absolute governments must very much depend on the administration; and this is one of the great inconveniences attending that form of government. But a republican and free government would be an obvious absurdity, if the particular checks and controls, provided by the constitution, had really no influence, and made it not the interest, even of bad men, to act for the public good. Such is the intention of these forms of government, and such is their real effect, where they are wisely constituted: as, on the other hand, they are the source of all disorder, and of the blackest crimes, where either skill or honesty has been wanting in their original frame and institution.

So great is the force of laws, and of particular forms of government, and so little dependence have they on the humours and tempers of men, that consequences almost as general and certain may sometimes be deduced from them, as any which the mathematical sciences afford us.

The constitution of the ROMAN republic gave the whole legislative power to the people, without allowing a negative voice either to the nobility or consuls. This unbounded power they possessed in a collective, not in a representative body. The consequences were: when the people, by success and conquest, had become very numerous, and had spread themselves to a great distance from the capital, the city tribes, though the most contemptible, carried almost every vote: they were, therefore, most cajoled by every one that affected popularity: they were supported in idleness by the general distribution of corn, and by particular bribes, which they received from almost every candidate: by this means, they became every day more licentious, and the CAMPUS MARTIUS* was a perpetual scene of tumult and sedition: armed slaves were introduced among these rascally citizens, so that the whole government fell into anarchy; and the greatest happiness which the ROMANS could look for, was the despotic power of the CAESARS. Such are the effects of democracy without a representative.

A Nobility may possess the whole, or any part of the legislative power of a state, in two different ways. Either every nobleman shares the power as a part of the whole body, or the whole body enjoys the power as composed of parts, which have each a distinct power and authority. The VENETIAN aristocracy is an instance of the first kind of government; the POLISH,* of the second. In the VENETIAN government the whole body of nobility possesses the whole power, and no nobleman has any authority which he receives not from the whole. In the POLISH government every nobleman, by means of his fiefs, has a distinct heredi- tary authority over his vassals, and the whole body has no authority but what it receives from the concurrence of its parts. The different operations and tendencies of these two species of government might be made apparent even *a priori*.* A VENETIAN nobility is preferable to a POLISH, let the humours and education of men be ever so much varied. A nobility, who possess their power in common, will preserve peace and order, both among themselves, and their subjects; and no member can have authority enough to control the laws for a moment. The nobles will preserve their authority over the people, but without any grievous tyranny, or any breach of private property; because such a tyrannical government promotes not the interests of the whole body, however it may that of some individuals. There will be a distinction of rank between the nobility and people, but this will be the only distinction in the state. The whole nobility will form one body, and the whole people another, without any of those private feuds and animosities, which spread ruin and desolation everywhere. It is easy to see the disadvantages of a POLISH nobility in every one of these particulars.

It is possible so to constitute a free government, as that a single person, call him a doge, prince, or king, shall possess a large share of power, and shall form a proper balance or counterpoise to the other parts of the legislature. This chief magistrate may be either *elective* or *hereditary*; and though the former institution may, to a superficial view, appear the most advantageous; yet a more accurate inspection will discover in it greater inconveniences than in the latter, and such as are founded on causes and principles eternal and immutable. The filling of the throne, in such a government, is a point of too great and too general interest, not to divide the whole people into factions: whence a civil war, the greatest of ills, may be apprehended, almost with certainty, upon every vacancy. The prince elected must be either a *Foreigner* or a *Native*: the former will be ignorant of the people whom he is to govern; suspicious of his new subjects, and suspected by them; giving his confidence entirely to strangers, who will have no other care but of enriching themselves in the quickest manner, while their master's favour and authority are able to support them. A native will carry into the throne all his private animosities and friendships, and will never be viewed in his elevation without exciting the sentiment of envy in those who formerly considered him as their equal. Not to mention that a crown is too high a reward ever to be given to merit alone, and will always induce the candidates to employ force, or money, or intrigue, to procure the votes of the electors: so that such an election will give no better chance for superior merit in the prince, than if the state had trusted to birth alone for determining the sovereign.

It may, therefore, be pronounced as an universal axiom in politics, *That an hereditary prince, a nobility without vassals, and a people voting by their representatives, form the best* MONARCHY, ARISTOCRACY, *and* DEMOCRACY. But in order to prove more fully, that politics admit of general truths, which are invariable by the humour or education either of subject or sovereign, it may not be amiss to observe some other principles of this science, which may seem to deserve that character.

It may easily be observed, that though free governments have been commonly the most happy for those who partake of their freedom; yet are they the most ruinous and oppressive to their provinces: and this observation may, I believe, be fixed as a maxim of the kind we are here speaking of. When a monarch extends his dominions by conquest, he soon learns to consider his old and his new subjects as on the same footing; because, in reality, all his subjects are to him the same, except the few friends and favourites with whom he is personally acquainted. He does not, therefore, make any distinction between them in his *general* laws; and, at the same time, is careful to prevent all *particular* acts of oppression on the one as well as the other. But a free state necessarily makes a great distinction, and must always do so, till men learn to love their neighbours as well as themselves. The conquerors, in such a government, are all legislators, and will be sure to contrive matters, by restrictions on trade, and by taxes, so as to draw some private, as well as public advantage from their conquests. Provincial governors have also a better chance, in a republic, to escape with their plunder, by means of bribery or intrigue; and their fellow-citizens, who find their own state to be enriched by the spoils of the subject provinces, will be the more inclined to tolerate such abuses. Not to mention, that it is a necessary precaution in a free state to change the governors frequently; which obliges these temporary tyrants to be more expeditious and rapacious, that they may accumulate sufficient wealth before they give place to their successors. What cruel tyrants were the ROMANS over the world during the time of their commonwealth! It is true, they had laws to prevent oppression in their provincial magistrates; but CICERO informs us, that the ROMANS could not better consult the interests of the provinces than by repealing these very laws. For, in that case, says he, our magistrates, having entire impunity, would plunder no more than would satisfy their own rapaciousness; whereas, at present, they must also satisfy that of their judges, and of all the great men in

ROME, of whose protection they stand in need. Who can read of the cruelties and oppressions of VERRES* without horror and astonishment? And who is not touched with indignation to hear, that, after CICERO had exhausted on that abandoned criminal all the thunders of his eloquence, and had prevailed so far as to get him condemned to the utmost extent of the laws, yet that cruel tyrant lived peaceably to old age, in opulence and ease, and, thirty years afterwards, was put into the proscription by MARK ANTONY, on account of his exorbitant wealth, where he fell with CICERO himself, and all the most virtuous men of ROME? After the dissolution of the commonwealth, the ROMAN yoke became easier upon the provinces, as TACITUS informs us;† and it may be observed, that many of the worst emperors, DOMITIAN,† for instance, were careful to prevent all oppression on the provinces. In TIBERIUS's time,† GAUL was esteemed richer than ITALY itself: nor do I find, during the whole time of the ROMAN monarchy, that the empire became less rich or populous in any of its provinces; though indeed its valour and military discipline were always upon the decline. The oppression and tyranny of the CARTHAGINIANS over their subject states in AFRICA went so far, as we learn from POLYBIUS,† that, not content with exacting the half of all the produce of the land, which of itself was a very high rent, they also loaded them with many other taxes. If we pass from ancient to modern times, we shall still find the observation to hold. The provinces of absolute monarchies are always better treated than those of free states. Compare the *Pais conquis** of FRANCE with IRELAND, and you will be convinced of this truth; though this latter kingdom, being in a good measure peopled from ENGLAND, possesses so many rights and privileges as should naturally make it challenge better treatment than that of a conquered province. CORSICA is also an obvious instance to the same purpose.

There is an observation of MACHIAVEL,* with regard to the conquests of ALEXANDER the Great, which, I think, may be regarded as one of those eternal political truths, which no time nor accidents can vary. It may seem strange, says

that politician, that such sudden conquests, as those of
ALEXANDER, should be possessed so peaceably by his
successors, and that the PERSIANS, during all the confusions
and civil wars among the GREEKS, never made the smallest
effort towards the recovery of their former independent
government. To satisfy us concerning the cause of this
remarkable event, we may consider, that a monarch may
govern his subjects in two different ways. He may either
follow the maxims of the Eastern princes, and stretch his
authority so far as to leave no distinction of rank among his
subjects, but what proceeds immediately from himself; no
advantages of birth; no hereditary honours and possessions;
and, in a word, no credit among the people, except from his
commission alone. Or a monarch may exert his power after
a milder manner, like other European princes; and leave
other sources of honour, beside his smile and favour: birth,
titles, possessions, valour, integrity, knowledge, or great
and fortunate achievements. In the former species of
government, after a conquest, it is impossible ever to shake
off the yoke; since no one possesses, among the people, so
much personal credit and authority as to begin such an
enterprise: whereas, in the latter, the least misfortune, or
discord among the victors, will encourage the vanquished to
take arms, who have leaders ready to prompt and conduct
them in every undertaking.†

Such is the reasoning of MACHIAVEL, which seems solid
and conclusive; though I wish he had not mixed falsehood
with truth, in asserting that monarchies, governed according
to Eastern policy, though more easily kept when once
subdued, yet are the most difficult to subdue; since they
cannot contain any powerful subject, whose discontent and
faction may facilitate the enterprises of an enemy. For,
besides, that such a tyrannical government enervates the
courage of men, and renders them indifferent towards the
fortunes of their sovereigns; besides this, I say, we find
by experience, that even the temporary and delegated
authority of the generals and magistrates, being always, in
such governments, as absolute within its sphere as that of
the prince himself, is able, with barbarians accustomed to a

blind submission, to produce the most dangerous and fatal revolutions. So that in every respect, a gentle government is preferable, and gives the greatest security to the sovereign as well as to the subject.

Legislators, therefore, ought not to trust the future government of a state entirely to chance, but ought to provide a system of laws to regulate the administration of public affairs to the latest posterity. Effects will always correspond to causes; and wise regulations, in any commonwealth, are the most valuable legacy that can be left to future ages. In the smallest court or office, the stated forms and methods by which business must be conducted, are found to be a considerable check on the natural depravity of mankind. Why should not the case be the same in public affairs? Can we ascribe the stability and wisdom of the VENETIAN government, through so many ages, to any thing but the form of government? And is it not easy to point out those defects in the original constitution, which produced the tumultuous governments of ATHENS and ROME, and ended at last in the ruin of these two famous republics? And so little dependence has this affair on the humours and education of particular men, that one part of the same republic may be wisely conducted, and another weakly, by the very same men, merely on account of the differences of the forms and institutions by which these parts are regulated. Historians inform us that this was actually the case with GENOA. For while the state was always full of sedition, and tumult, and disorder, the bank of St GEORGE,* which had become a considerable part of the people, was conducted, for several ages, with the utmost integrity and wisdom.†

The ages of greatest public spirit are not always most eminent for private virtue. Good laws may beget order and moderation in the government, where the manners and customs have instilled little humanity or justice into the tempers of men. The most illustrious period of the ROMAN history, considered in a political view, is that between the beginning of the first and end of the last PUNIC war; the due balance between the nobility and people being then fixed by the contests of the tribunes, and not being yet lost by the extent of conquests. Yet at this very time, the horrid practice of poisoning was so common, that, during part of the season, a *Praetor* punished capitally for this crime above three thousand[†] persons in a part of ITALY; and found informations of this nature still multiplying upon him. There is a similar, or rather a worse instance,[†] in the more early times of the commonwealth; so depraved in private life were that people, whom in their histories we so much admire. I doubt not but they were really more virtuous during the time of the two *Triumvirates*; when they were tearing their common country to pieces, and spreading slaughter and desolation over the face of the earth, merely for the choice of tyrants.[†]

Here, then, is a sufficient inducement to maintain, with the utmost zeal, in every free state, those forms and institutions by which liberty is secured, the public good consulted, and the avarice or ambition of particular men restrained and punished. Nothing does more honour to human nature, than to see it susceptible of so noble a passion; as nothing can be a greater indication of meanness of heart in any man than to see him destitute of it. A man who loves only himself, without regard to friendship and desert, merits the severest blame; and a man, who is only susceptible of friendship, without public spirit, or a regard to the community, is deficient in the most material part of virtue.

But this is a subject which needs not be longer insisted on at present. There are enough of zealots on both sides, who kindle up the passions of their partisans, and, under pretence of public good, pursue the interests and ends of their particular faction. For my part, I shall always be more fond of promoting moderation than zeal; though perhaps the surest way of producing moderation in every party is to increase our zeal for the public. Let us therefore try, if it be possible, from the foregoing doctrine, to draw a lesson of moderation with regard to the parties into which our country is at present divided; at the same time, that we allow not this moderation to abate the industry and passion, with which every individual is bound to pursue the good of his country.

Those who either attack or defend a minister in such a government as ours, where the utmost liberty is allowed, always carry matters to an extreme, and exaggerate his merit or demerit with regard to the public. His enemies are sure to charge him with the greatest enormities, both in domestic and foreign management; and there is no meanness or crime, of which, in their account, he is not capable. Unnecessary wars, scandalous treaties, profusion of public treasure, oppressive taxes, every kind of maladministration is ascribed to him. To aggravate the charge, his pernicious conduct, it is said, will extend its baneful influence even to posterity, by undermining the best constitution in the world, and disordering that wise system of laws, institutions, and customs, by which our ancestors, during so many centuries, have been so happily governed. He is not only a wicked minister in himself, but has removed every security provided against wicked ministers for the future.

On the other hand, the partisans of the minister make his panegyric run as high as the accusation against him, and celebrate his wise, steady, and moderate conduct in every part of his administration. The honour and interest of the nation supported abroad, public credit maintained at home, persecution restrained, faction subdued; the merit of all these blessings is ascribed solely to the minister. At the same time, he crowns all his other merits by a religious care of the best constitution in the world, which he has preserved in all its parts, and has transmitted entire, to be the happiness and security of the latest posterity.

When this accusation and panegyric are received by the partisans of each party, no wonder they beget an extraordinary ferment on both sides, and fill the nation with violent animosities. But I would fain persuade these party zealots, that there is a flat contradiction both in the accusation and panegyric, and that it were impossible for either of them to run so high, were it not for this contradiction. If our constitution be really *that noble fabric, the pride of* BRITAIN, *the envy of our neighbours, raised by the labour of so many* centuries, repaired at the expense of so many millions, and cemented by such a profusion of blood;† I say, if our constitution does in any degree deserve these eulogies, it would never have suffered a wicked and weak minister to govern triumphantly for a course of twenty years, when opposed by the greatest geniuses in the nation, who exercised the utmost liberty of tongue and pen, in parliament, and in their frequent appeals to the people. But, if the minister be wicked and weak, to the degree so strenuously insisted on, the constitution must be faulty in its original principles, and he cannot consistently be charged with undermining the best form of government in the world. A constitution is only so far good, as it provides a remedy against maladministration; and if the BRITISH, when in its greatest vigour, and repaired by two such remarkable events as the *Revolution* and *Accession*,* by which our ancient royal family was sacrificed to it; if our constitution, I say, with so great advantages, does not, in fact, provide any such remedy, we are rather beholden to any minister who undermines it, and affords us an opportunity of erecting a better in its place.

I would employ the same topics to moderate the zeal of those who defend the minister. *Is our constitution so excellent?* Then a change of ministry can be no such dreadful event; since it is essential to such a constitution, in every ministry, both to preserve itself from violation, and to prevent all enormities in the administration. *Is our constitution very bad?* Then so extraordinary a jealousy and apprehension, on account of changes, is ill placed; and a man should no more be anxious in this case, than a husband, who had married a woman from the stews, should be watchful to prevent her infidelity. Public affairs, in such a government, must necessarily go to confusion, by whatever hands they are conducted; and the zeal of *patriots* is in that case much less requisite than the patience and submission of *philosophers*. The virtue and good intention of CATO and BRUTUS* are highly laudable; but to what purpose did their zeal serve? Only to hasten the fatal period of the ROMAN government, and render its convulsions and dying agonies more violent and painful.

I would not be understood to mean, that public affairs deserve no care and attention at all. Would men be moderate and consistent, their claims might be admitted; at least might be examined. The *country party* might still assert, that our constitution, though excellent, will admit of maladministration to a certain degree; and therefore, if the minister be bad, it is proper to oppose him with a *suitable* degree of zeal. And, on the other hand, the *court party* may be allowed, upon the supposition that the minister were good, to defend, and with *some* zeal too, his administration. I would only persuade men not to contend, as if they were fighting *pro aris et focis*,* and change a good constitution into a bad one, by the violence of their factions.

I have not here considered any thing that is personal in the present controversy. In the best civil constitutions, where every man is restrained by the most rigid laws, it is easy to discover either the good or bad intentions of a minister, and to judge whether his personal character deserve love or hatred. But such questions are of little importance to the public, and lay those who employ their pens upon them, under a just suspicion either of malevolence or of flattery.†

OF THE FIRST PRINCIPLES OF GOVERNMENT

NOTHING appears more surprising to those who consider human affairs with a philosophical eye, than the easiness with which the many are governed by the few; and the implicit submission, with which men resign their own sentiments and passions to those of their rulers. When we inquire by what means this wonder is effected, we shall find, that, as Force is always on the side of the governed, the governors have nothing to support them but opinion. It is, therefore, on opinion only that government is founded; and this maxim extends to the most despotic and most military governments, as well as to the most free and most popular. The soldan* of EGYPT, or the emperor of ROME, might drive his harmless subjects, like brute beasts, against their sentiments and inclination. But he must, at least, have led his *mamalukes* or *praetorian bands*,* like men, by their opinion.

Opinion is of two kinds, to wit, opinion of INTEREST, and opinion of RIGHT. By opinion of interest, I chiefly understand the sense of the general advantage which is reaped from government; together with the persuasion, that the particular government which is established is equally advantageous with any other that could easily be settled. When this opinion prevails among the generality of a state, or among those who have the force in their hands, it gives great security to any government.

Right is of two kinds; right to POWER, and right to PROPERTY. What prevalence opinion of the first kind has over mankind, may easily be understood, by observing the attachment which all nations have to their ancient government, and even to those names which have had the sanction of antiquity. Antiquity always begets the opinion of right; and whatever disadvantageous sentiments we may entertain of mankind, they are always found to be prodigal both of blood and treasure in the maintenance of public justice. There is, indeed, no particular in which, at first sight, there may appear a greater contradiction in the frame of the human mind than the present. When men act in a faction, they are apt, without shame or remorse, to neglect all the ties of honour and morality, in order to serve their party; and yet, when a faction is formed upon a point of right or principle, there is no occasion where men discover a greater obstinacy, and a more determined sense of justice and equity. The same social disposition of mankind is the cause of these contradictory appearances.

It is sufficiently understood, that the opinion of right to property is of moment in all matters of government. A noted author* has made property the foundation of all government; and most of our political writers seem inclined to follow him in that particular. This is carrying the matter too far; but still it must be owned, that the opinion of right to property has a great influence in this subject.

Upon these three opinions, therefore, of public *interest*,

of *right to power*, and of *right to property*, are all governments founded, and all authority of the few over the many.
There are indeed other principles which add force to these,
and determine, limit, or alter their operation; such as *self-
interest*, *fear*, and *affection*. But still we may assert, that
these other principles can have no influence alone, but
suppose the antecedent influence of those opinions above
mentioned. They are, therefore, to be esteemed the sec-
ondary, not the original, principles of government.

For, *first*, as to *self-interest*, by which I mean the expectation of particular rewards, distinct from the general
protection which we receive from government, it is evident
that the magistrate's authority must be antecedently established, at least be hoped for, in order to produce this
expectation. The prospect of reward may augment his
authority with regard to some particular persons, but
can never give birth to it, with regard to the public. Men
naturally look for the greatest favours from their friends
and acquaintance; and therefore, the hopes of any considerable number of the state would never centre in any
particular set of men, if these men had no other title to
magistracy, and had no separate influence over the opinions
of mankind. The same observation may be extended to the
other two principles of *fear* and *affection*. No man would
have any reason to *fear* the fury of a tyrant, if he had no
authority over any but from fear; since, as a single man, his
bodily force can reach but a small way, and all the further
power he possesses must be founded either on our own
opinion, or on the presumed opinion of others. And though
affection to wisdom and virtue in a *sovereign* extends very
far, and has great influence, yet he must antecedently be
supposed invested with a public character, otherwise the
public esteem will serve him in no stead, nor will his virtue
have any influence beyond a narrow sphere.

A Government may endure for several ages, though the
balance of power and the balance of property do not coincide. This chiefly happens where any rank or order of the
state has acquired a large share in the property; but, from
the original constitution of the government, has no share in

the power. Under what pretence would any individual of that order assume authority in public affairs? As men are commonly much attached to their ancient government, it is not to be expected, that the public would ever favour such usurpations. But where the original constitution allows any share of power, though small, to an order of men who possess a large share of property, it is easy for them gradually to stretch their authority, and bring the balance of power to coincide with that of property. This has been the case with the House of Commons in ENGLAND.

Most writers that have treated of the BRITISH government, have supposed, that, as the lower house represents all the commons of GREAT BRITAIN, its weight in the scale is proportioned to the property and power of all whom it represents. But this principle must not be received as absolutely true. For though the people are apt to attach themselves more to the House of Commons than to any other member of the constitution, that House being chosen by them as their representatives, and as the public guardians of their liberty: yet are there instances where the House, even when in opposition to the crown, has not been followed by the people, as we may particularly observe of the *tory* house of commons in the reign of king WILLIAM.* Were the members obliged to receive instructions from their constituents, like the DUTCH deputies, this would entirely alter the case; and if such immense power and riches, as those of all the commons of GREAT BRITAIN, were brought into the scale, it is not easy to conceive, that the crown could either influence that multitude of people, or withstand that balance of property. It is true, the crown has great influence over the collective body in the elections of members; but were this influence, which at present is only exerted once in seven years, to be employed in bringing over the people to every vote, it would soon be wasted, and no skill, popularity, or revenue, could support it. I must, therefore, be of opinion, that an alteration in this particular would introduce a total alteration in our government, and would soon reduce it to a pure republic; and, perhaps, to a republic of no inconvenient form. For though the people, collected in a body like the ROMAN tribes, be quite unfit for government, yet, when dispersed in small bodies, they are more susceptible both of reason and order; the force of popular currents and tides is in a great measure broken; and the public interests may be pursued with some method and constancy. But it is needless to reason any further concerning a form of government which is never likely to have place in GREAT BRITAIN, and which seems not to be the aim of any party amongst us. Let us cherish and improve our ancient government as much as possible, without encouraging a passion for such dangerous novelties.[†]

OF THE ORIGIN OF GOVERNMENT

MAN, born in a family, is compelled to maintain society from necessity, from natural inclination, and from habit. The same creature, in his further progress, is engaged to establish political society, in order to administer justice, without which there can be no peace among them, nor safety, nor mutual intercourse. We are, therefore, to look upon all the vast apparatus of our government, as having ultimately no other object or purpose but the distribution of justice, or, in other words, the support of the twelve judges. Kings and parliaments, fleets and armies, officers of the court and revenue, ambassadors, ministers, and privy counsellors, are all subordinate in their end to this part of administration. Even the clergy, as their duty leads them to inculcate morality, may justly be thought, so far as regards this world, to have no other useful object of their institution.

All men are sensible of the necessity of justice to maintain peace and order; and all men are sensible of the necessity of peace and order for the maintenance of society. Yet, notwithstanding this strong and obvious necessity, such is the frailty or perverseness of our nature! it is impossible to keep men faithfully and unerringly in the paths of justice. Some extraordinary circumstances may happen, in which a man finds his interests to be more promoted by fraud or rapine, than hurt by the breach which his injustice makes in the social union. But much more frequently he is seduced from his great and important, but distant interests, by the allurement of present, though often very frivolous temptations. This great weakness is incurable in human nature.

Men must, therefore, endeavour to palliate what they cannot cure. They must institute some persons under the appellation of magistrates, whose peculiar office it is to point out the decrees of equity, to punish transgressors, to correct fraud and violence, and to oblige men, however reluctant, to consult their own real and permanent interests. In a word, OBEDIENCE is a new duty which must be invented to support that of JUSTICE, and the ties of equity must be corroborated by those of allegiance.

But still, viewing matters in an abstract light, it may be thought that nothing is gained by this alliance, and that the factitious duty of obedience, from its very nature, lays as feeble a hold of the human mind, as the primitive and natural duty of justice. Peculiar interests and present temptations may overcome the one as well as the other. They are equally exposed to the same inconvenience; and the man who is inclined to be a bad neighbour, must be led by the same motives, well or ill understood, to be a bad citizen or subject. Not to mention, that the magistrate himself may often be negligent, or partial, or unjust in his administration.

Experience, however, proves that there is a great difference between the cases. Order in society, we find, is much better maintained by means of government; and our duty to the magistrate is more strictly guarded by the principles of human nature, than our duty to our fellow-citizens. The love of dominion is so strong in the breast of man, that many not only submit to, but court all the dangers, and fatigues, and cares of government; and men, once raised to that station, though often led astray by private passions, find, in ordinary cases, a visible interest in the impartial administration of justice. The persons who first attain this distinction, by the consent, tacit or express, of the people, must be endowed with superior personal qualities of valour, force, integrity, or prudence, which command respect and confidence; and, after government is established, a regard to birth, rank, and station, has a mighty influence over men, and enforces the decrees of the magistrate. The prince or leader exclaims against every disorder which disturbs his society. He summons all his partisans and all men of probity to aid him in correcting and redressing it; and he is readily followed by all indifferent persons in the execution of his office. He soon acquires the power of rewarding these services; and in the progress of society, he establishes subordinate ministers, and often a military force, who find an immediate and a visible interest in supporting his authority. Habit soon consolidates what other principles of human nature had imperfectly founded; and men, once accustomed to obedience, never think of departing from that path, in which they and their ancestors have constantly trod, and to which they are confined by so many urgent and visible motives.

But though this progress of human affairs may appear certain and inevitable, and though the support which allegiance brings to justice be founded on obvious principles of human nature, it cannot be expected that men should beforehand be able to discover them, or foresee their operation. Government commences more casually and more imperfectly. It is probable, that the first ascendent of one man over multitudes begun during a state of war; where the superiority of courage and of genius discovers itself most visibly, where unanimity and concert are most requisite, and where the pernicious effects of disorder are most sensibly felt. The long continuance of that state, an incident common among savage tribes, inured the people to submission; and if the chieftain possessed as much equity as prudence and valour, he became, even during peace, the arbiter of all differences, and could gradually, by a mixture of force and consent, establish his authority. The benefit sensibly felt from his influence, made it be cherished by the people, at least by the peaceable and well disposed among them; and if his son enjoyed the same good qualities, government advanced the sooner to maturity and perfection; but was still in a feeble state, till the further progress of improvement procured the magistrate a revenue, and enabled him to bestow rewards on the several instruments of his administration, and to inflict punishments on the refractory and disobedient. Before that period, each exertion of his influence must have been particular, and founded on the peculiar circumstances of the case. After it, submission was no longer a matter of choice in the bulk of the community, but was rigorously exacted by the authority of the supreme magistrate.

In all governments, there is a perpetual intestine struggle, open or secret, between AUTHORITY and LIBERTY; and neither of them can ever absolutely prevail in the contest. A great sacrifice of liberty must necessarily be made in every government; yet even the authority, which confines liberty, can never, and perhaps ought never, in any constitution, to become quite entire and uncontrollable. The sultan is master of the life and fortune of any individual; but will not be permitted to impose new taxes on his subjects: a French monarch can impose taxes at pleasure; but would find it dangerous to attempt the lives and fortunes of individuals. Religion also, in most countries, is commonly found to be a very intractable principle; and other principles or prejudices frequently resist all the authority of the civil magistrate; whose power, being founded on opinion, can never subvert other opinions equally rooted with that of his title to dominion. The government, which, in common appellation, receives the appellation of free, is that which admits of a partition of power among several members, whose united authority is no less, or is commonly greater, than that of any monarch; but who, in the usual course of administration, must act by general and equal laws, that are previously known to all the members, and to all their subjects. In this sense, it must be owned, that liberty is the perfection of civil society; but still authority must be acknowledged essential to its very existence: and in those contests which so often take place between the one and the other, the latter may, on that account, challenge the preference. Unless perhaps one may say (and it may be said with some reason) that a circumstance, which is essential to the existence of civil society, must always support itself, and needs be guarded with less jealousy, than one that contributes only to its perfection, which the indolence of men is so apt to neglect, or their ignorance to overlook.

OF THE PARTIES OF GREAT BRITAIN

WERE the BRITISH government proposed as a subject of speculation, one would immediately perceive in it a source of division and party, which it would be almost impossible for it, under any administration, to avoid. The just balance between the republican and monarchical part of our constitution is really in itself so extremely delicate and uncertain, that, when joined to men's passions and prejudices, it is impossible but different opinions must arise concerning it, even among persons of the best understanding. Those of mild tempers, who love peace and order, and detest sedition and civil wars, will always entertain more favourable sentiments of monarchy than men of bold and generous spirits, who are passionate lovers of liberty, and think no evil comparable to subjection and slavery. And though all reasonable men agree in general to preserve our mixed government, yet, when they come to particulars, some will incline to trust greater powers to the crown, to bestow on it more influence, and to guard against its encroachments with less caution, than others who are terrified at the most distant approaches of tyranny and despotic power. Thus are there parties of PRINCIPLE involved in the very nature of our constitution, which may properly enough be denominated those of COURT and COUNTRY.† The strength and violence of each of these parties will much depend upon the particular administration. An administration may be so bad, as to throw a great majority into the opposition; as a good administration will reconcile to the court many of the most passionate lovers of liberty. But however the nation may fluctuate between them, the parties themselves will always subsist, so long as we are governed by a limited monarchy.

But, besides this difference of *Principle*, those parties are very much fomented by a difference of INTEREST, without which they could scarcely ever be dangerous or violent. The crown will naturally bestow all trust and power upon those whose principles, real or pretended, are most favourable to monarchical government; and this temptation will naturally engage them to go greater lengths than their principles would otherwise carry them. Their antagonists, who are disappointed in their ambitious aims, throw themselves into the party whose sentiments incline them to be most jealous of royal power, and naturally carry those sentiments to a greater height than sound politics will justify. Thus *Court* and *Country*, which are the genuine offspring of the BRITISH government, are a kind of mixed parties, and are influenced both by principle and by interest. The heads of the factions are commonly most governed by the latter motive; the inferior members of them by the former.[†]

As to ecclesiastical parties, we may observe, that, in all ages of the world, priests have been enemies to liberty;[†] and, it is certain, that this steady conduct of theirs must have been founded on fixed reasons of interest and ambition. Liberty of thinking, and of expressing our thoughts, is always fatal to priestly power, and to those pious frauds on which it is commonly founded; and, by an infallible connection, which prevails among all kinds of liberty, this privilege can never be enjoyed, at least has never yet been enjoyed, but in a free government. Hence it must happen, in such a constitution as that of GREAT BRITAIN, that the established clergy, while things are in their natural situation, will always be of the *Court* party; as, on the contrary, dissenters of all kinds will be of the *Country* party; since they can never hope for that toleration which they stand in need of, but by means of our free government. All princes that have aimed at despotic power have known of what importance it was to gain the established clergy; as the clergy, on their part, have shown a great facility in entering into the views of such princes.[†] Gustavus Vasa* was, perhaps, the only ambitious monarch that ever depressed the church, at the same time that he discouraged liberty. But the exorbitant power of the bishops in SWEDEN, who at that time overtopped the crown itself, together with their attachment to a foreign family, was the reason of his embracing such an unusual system of politics.

This observation, concerning the propensity of priests to the government of a single person, is not true with regard to one sect only. The *Presbyterian* and *Calvinistic* clergy in HOLLAND, were professed friends to the family of ORANGE; as the *Arminians*, who were esteemed heretics, were of the LOUVESTEIN faction,* and zealous for liberty. But if a prince have the choice of both, it is easy to see that he will prefer the episcopal to the presbyterian form of government, both because of the greater affinity between monarchy and episcopacy, and because of the facility which he will find, in such a government, of ruling the clergy by means of their ecclesiastical superiors.[†]

If we consider the first rise of parties in ENGLAND, during the great rebellion,* we shall observe that it was conformable to this general theory, and that the species of government gave birth to them by a regular and infallible operation. The ENGLISH constitution, before that period, had lain in a kind of confusion, yet so as that the subjects possessed many noble privileges, which, though not exactly bounded and secured by law, were universally deemed, from long possession, to belong to them as their birthright. An ambitious, or rather a misguided, prince arose, who deemed all these privileges to be concessions of his predecessors, revocable at pleasure; and, in prosecution of this principle, he openly acted in violation of liberty during the course of several years. Necessity, at last, constrained him to call a parliament: the spirit of liberty arose and spread itself: the prince, being without any support, was obliged to grant every thing required of him: and his enemies, jealous and implacable, set no bounds to their pretensions. Here, then, began those contests, in which it was no wonder that men of that age were divided into different parties; since, even at this day, the impartial are at a loss to decide concerning the justice of the quarrel. The pretensions of the parliament, if yielded to, broke the balance of the constitution, by rendering the government almost entirely republican. If not yielded to, the nation was, perhaps, still in danger of absolute power, from the settled principles and inveterate habits of the king, which had plainly appeared in every concession that he had been constrained to make to his people. In this question, so delicate and uncertain, men naturally fell to the side which was most conformable to their usual principles; and the more passionate favourers of monarchy declared for the king, as the zealous friends of liberty sided with the parliament. The hopes of success being nearly equal on both sides, *interest* had no general influence in this contest: so that ROUNDHEAD and CAVALIER were merely parties of principle, neither of which disowned either monarchy or liberty; but the former party inclined most to the republican part of our government, the latter to the monarchical. In this respect, they may be considered as court and country party, inflamed into a civil war, by an unhappy concurrence of circumstances, and by the turbulent spirit of the age. The commonwealth's men, and the partisans of absolute power, lay concealed in both parties, and formed but an inconsiderable part of them.

The clergy had concurred with the king's arbitrary designs; and, in return, were allowed to persecute their adversaries, whom they called heretics and schismatics. The established clergy were episcopal, the nonconformists presbyterian; so that all things concurred to throw the former, without reserve, into the king's party, and the latter into that of the parliament.

Every one knows the event of this quarrel; fatal to the king first, to the parliament afterwards. After many confusions and revolutions, the royal family was at last restored, and the ancient government reëstablished. CHARLES II was not made wiser by the example of his father, but prosecuted the same measures, though, at first, with more secrecy and caution. New parties arose, under the appellation of *Whig* and *Tory*, which have continued ever since to confound and distract our government. To determine the nature of these parties is perhaps one of the most difficult problems that can be met with, and is a proof that history may contain questions as uncertain as any to be found in the most abstract sciences. We have seen the conduct of the two parties, during the course of seventy years, in a vast variety of circumstances, possessed of power, and deprived of it, during peace, and during war: persons, who profess themselves of one side or other, we meet with every hour, in company, in our pleasures, in our serious occupations: we ourselves are constrained, in a manner, to take party; and, living in a country of the highest liberty, every one may openly declare all his sentiments and opinions: yet are we at a loss to tell the nature, pretensions, and principles, of the different factions.

When we compare the parties of WHIG and TORY with those of ROUNDHEAD and CAVALIER, the most obvious difference that appears between them consists in the principles of *passive obedience*, and *indefeasible right*, which were but little heard of among the CAVALIERS, but became the universal doctrine, and were esteemed the true characteristic of a TORY. Were these principles pushed into their most obvious consequences, they imply a formal renunciation of all our liberties, and an avowal of absolute monarchy; since nothing can be greater absurdity than a limited power, which must not be resisted, even when it exceeds its limitations. But, as the most rational principles are often but a weak counterpoise to passion, it is no wonder that these absurd principles were found too weak for that effect. The TORIES, as men, were enemies to oppression; and also as ENGLISHMEN, they were enemies to arbitrary power. Their zeal for liberty was, perhaps, less fervent than that of their antagonists, but was sufficient to make them forget all their general principles, when they saw themselves openly threatened with a subversion of the ancient government. From these sentiments arose the *revolution*;* an event of mighty consequence, and the firmest foundation of BRITISH liberty. The conduct of the TORIES during that event, and after it, will afford us a true insight into the nature of that party.

In the *first* place, they appear to have had the genuine sentiments of BRITONS in their affection for liberty, and in their determined resolution not to sacrifice it to any abstract principle whatsoever, or to any imaginary rights of princes. This part of their character might justly have been doubted of before the *revolution*, from the obvious tendency of their avowed principles, and from their compliances with a court, which seemed to make little secret of its arbitrary designs. The *revolution* showed them to have been, in this respect, nothing but a genuine *court party*, such as might be expected in a BRITISH government; that is, *Lovers of liberty, but greater lovers of monarchy*. It must, however, be confessed, that they carried their monarchical principles further even in practice, but more so in theory, than was in any degree consistent with a limited government.

Secondly, Neither their principles nor affections concurred, entirely or heartily, with the settlement made at the *revolution*, or with that which has since taken place. This part of their character may seem opposite to the former, since any other settlement, in those circumstances of the nation, must probably have been dangerous, if not fatal, to liberty. But the heart of man is made to reconcile contradictions; and this contradiction is not greater than that between *passive obedience*, and the *resistance* employed at the *revolution*. A TORY, therefore, since the *revolution*, may be defined, in a few words, to be *a lover of monarchy, though without abandoning liberty, and a partisan of the family of* STUART: as a WHIG may be defined to be *a lover of liberty, though without renouncing monarchy, and a friend to the settlement in the* PROTESTANT *line.*[†]

These different views, with regard to the settlement of the crown, were accidental, but natural additions, to the principles of the *court* and *country* parties, which are the genuine divisions in the BRITISH government. A passionate lover of monarchy is apt to be displeased at any change of the succession, as savouring too much of a commonwealth: a passionate lover of liberty is apt to think that every part of the government ought to be subordinate to the interests of liberty.

Some, who will not venture to assert that the *real* difference between WHIG and TORY was lost at the *revolution*, seem inclined to think, that the difference is now abolished, and that affairs are so far returned to their natural state, that there are at present no other parties among us but *court* and *country*; that is, men who, by interest or principle, are attached either to monarchy or liberty. The TORIES have been so long obliged to talk in the republican style, that they seem to have made converts of themselves by their hypocrisy, and to have embraced the sentiments, as well as language of their adversaries. There are, however, very considerable remains of that party in ENGLAND, with all their old prejudices; and a proof that *court* and *country* are not our only parties, is, that almost all the dissenters side with the court, and the lower clergy, at least of the church of ENGLAND, with the opposition. This may convince us, that some bias still hangs upon our constitution, some extrinsic weight, which turns it from its natural course, and causes a confusion in our parties.[†]

OF SUPERSTITION AND ENTHUSIASM

THAT *the corruption of the best of things produces the worst*, is grown into a maxim, and is commonly proved, among other instances, by the pernicious effects of *superstition* and *enthusiasm*, the corruptions of true religion.

  These two species of false religion, though both pernicious, are yet of a very different, and even of a contrary nature. The mind of man is subject to certain unaccountable terrors and apprehensions, proceeding either from the unhappy situation of private or public affairs, from ill health, from a gloomy and melancholy disposition, or from the concurrence of all these circumstances. In such a state of mind, infinite unknown evils are dreaded from unknown agents; and where real objects of terror are wanting, the soul, active to its own prejudice, and fostering its predominant inclination, finds imaginary ones, to whose power and malevolence it sets no limits. As these enemies are entirely invisible and unknown, the methods taken to appease them are equally unaccountable, and consist in ceremonies, observances, mortifications, sacrifices, presents, or in any practice, however absurd or frivolous, which either folly or knavery recommends to a blind and terrified credulity. Weakness, fear, melancholy, together with ignorance, are, therefore, the true sources of SUPERSTITION.

But the mind of man is also subject to an unaccountable elevation and presumption, arising from prosperous success, from luxuriant health, from strong spirits, or from a bold and confident disposition. In such a state of mind, the imagination swells with great, but confused conceptions, to which no sublunary beauties or enjoyments can correspond. Every thing mortal and perishable vanishes as unworthy of attention; and a full range is given to the fancy in the invisible regions, or world of Spirits, where the soul is at liberty to indulge itself in every imagination, which may best suit its present taste and disposition. Hence arise raptures, transports, and surprising flights of fancy; and, confidence and presumption still increasing, these raptures, being altogether unaccountable, and seeming quite beyond the reach of our ordinary faculties, are attributed to the immediate inspiration of that Divine Being who is the object of devotion. In a little time, the inspired person comes to regard himself as a distinguished favourite of the Divinity; and when this phrensy once takes place, which is the summit of enthusiasm, every whimsey is consecrated: human reason, and even morality, are rejected as fallacious guides; and the fanatic madman delivers himself over, blindly and without reserve, to the supposed illapses of the Spirit, and to inspiration from above. Hope, pride, presumption, a warm imagination, together with ignorance, are therefore the true sources of ENTHUSIASM.

These two species of false religion might afford occasion to many speculations; but I shall confine myself, at present, to a few reflections concerning their different influence on government and society.

My first reflection is, *that superstition is favourable to priestly power, and enthusiasm not less, or rather more contrary to it, than sound reason and philosophy.* As superstition is founded on fear, sorrow, and a depression of spirits, it represents the man to himself in such despicable colours, that he appears unworthy, in his own eyes, of approaching the divine presence, and naturally has recourse to any other person, whose sanctity of life, or perhaps impudence and cunning, have made him be supposed more favoured by the Divinity. To him the superstitious intrust their devotions: to his care they recommend their prayers, petitions, and sacrifices: and by his means, they hope to render their addresses acceptable to their incensed Deity. Hence the origin of PRIESTS,[†] who may justly be regarded as an invention of a timorous and abject superstition, which, ever diffident of itself, dares not offer up its own devotions, but ignorantly thinks to recommend itself to the Divinity, by the mediation of his supposed friends and servants. As superstition is a considerable ingredient in almost all religions, even the most fanatical; there being nothing but philosophy able entirely to conquer these unaccountable terrors; hence it proceeds, that in almost every sect of religion there are priests to be found: but the stronger mixture there is of superstition, the higher is the authority of the priesthood.[†]

On the other hand, it may be observed, that all enthusiasts have been free from the yoke of ecclesiastics, and have expressed great independence in their devotion, with a contempt of forms, ceremonies, and traditions. The *quakers* are the most egregious, though, at the same time, the most innocent enthusiasts that have yet been known; and are perhaps the only sect that have never admitted priests among them. The *independents*, of all the ENGLISH sectaries, approach nearest to the *quakers* in fanaticism, and in their freedom from priestly bondage. The *presbyterians* follow after, at an equal distance, in both particulars. In short, this observation is founded in experience; and will also appear to be founded in reason, if we consider, that, as enthusiasm arises from a presumptuous pride and confidence, it thinks itself sufficiently qualified to *approach* the Divinity, without any human mediator. Its rapturous devotions are so fervent, that it even imagines itself *actually* to *approach* him by the way of contemplation and inward converse; which makes it neglect all those outward ceremonies and observances, to which the assistance of the priests appears so requisite in the eyes of their superstitious votaries. The fanatic consecrates himself, and bestows on his own person a sacred character, much superior to what forms and ceremonious institutions can confer on any other.

My *second* reflection with regard to these species of false religion is, *that religions which partake of enthusiasm, are, on their first rise, more furious and violent than those which partake of superstition; but in a little time become more gentle and moderate.* The violence of this species of religion, when excited by novelty, and animated by opposition, appears from numberless instances; of the *anabaptists* in GERMANY, the *camisars* in FRANCE, the *levellers*, and other fanatics in ENGLAND, and the *covenanters* in SCOTLAND.* Enthusiasm being founded on strong spirits, and a presumptuous boldness of character, it naturally begets the most extreme resolutions; especially after it rises to that height as to inspire the deluded fanatic with the opinion of Divine illuminations, and with a contempt for the common rules of reason, morality, and prudence.

It is thus enthusiasm produces the most cruel disorders in human society; but its fury is like that of thunder and tempest, which exhaust themselves in a little time, and leave the air more calm and serene than before. When the first fire of enthusiasm is spent, men naturally, in all fanatical sects, sink into the greatest remissness and coolness in sacred matters; there being no body of men among them endowed with sufficient authority, whose interest is concerned to support the religious spirit; no rites, no ceremonies, no holy observances, which may enter into the common train of life, and preserve the sacred principles from oblivion. Superstition, on the contrary, steals in gradually and insensibly; renders men tame and submissive; is acceptable to the magistrate, and seems inoffensive to the people; till at last the priest, having firmly established his authority, becomes the tyrant and disturber of human society, by his endless contentions, persecutions, and religious wars. How smoothly did the ROMISH church advance in her acquisition of power? But into what dismal convulsions did she throw all EUROPE, in order to maintain it? On the other hand, our sectaries,* who were formerly such dangerous bigots, are now become very free reasoners; and the *quakers* seem to approach nearly the only regular body of *deists** in the universe, the *literati*, or the disciples of CONFUCIUS in CHINA.†

My *third* observation on this head is, *that superstition is an enemy to civil liberty, and enthusiasm a friend to it*. As superstition groans under the dominion of priests, and enthusiasm is destructive of all ecclesiastical power, this sufficiently accounts for the present observation. Not to mention that enthusiasm, being the infirmity of bold and ambitious tempers, is naturally accompanied with a spirit of liberty; as superstition, on the contrary, renders men tame and abject, and fits them for slavery. We learn from ENGLISH history, that, during the civil wars, the *independents* and *deists*, though the most opposite in their religious principles, yet were united in their political ones, and were alike passionate for a commonwealth. And since the origin of *whig* and *tory*, the leaders of the *whigs* have either been *deists* or professed *latitudinarians* in their principles; that is, friends to toleration, and indifferent to any particular sect of *christians*: while the sectaries, who have all a strong tincture of enthusiasm, have always, without exception, concurred with that party in defence of civil liberty. The resemblance in their superstitions long united the high-church *tories* and the *Roman catholics*, in support of pre-rogative and kingly power; though experience of the tolerating spirit of the *Whigs* seems of late to have recon-ciled the *Catholics* to that party.

The *molinists* and *jansenists* in FRANCE have a thousand unintelligible disputes,* which are not worthy the reflection of a man of sense: but what principally distinguishes these two sects, and alone merits attention, is the different spirit of their religion. The *molinists*, conducted by the *jesuits*, are great friends to superstition, rigid observers of external forms and ceremonies, and devoted to the authority of the priests, and to tradition. The *jansenists* are enthusiasts, and zealous promoters of the passionate devotion, and of the inward life; little influenced by authority; and, in a word, but half catholics. The consequences are exactly conformable to the foregoing reasoning. The *jesuits* are the tyrants of the people, and the slaves of the court: and the *jansenists* preserve alive the small sparks of the love of liberty which are to be found in the FRENCH nation.

OF THE DIGNITY OR MEANNESS OF HUMAN NATURE

THERE are certain sects which secretly form themselves in the learned world, as well as factions in the political; and though sometimes they come not to an open rupture, they give a different turn to the ways of thinking of those who have taken part on either side. The most remarkable of this kind are the sects founded on the different sentiments with regard to the *dignity of human nature*; which is a point that seems to have divided philosophers and poets, as well as divines, from the beginning of the world to this day. Some exalt our species to the skies, and represent man as a kind of human demigod, who derives his origin from heaven, and retains evident marks of his lineage and descent. Others insist upon the blind sides of human nature, and can discover nothing, except vanity, in which man surpasses the other animals, whom he affects so much to despise. If an author possess the talent of rhetoric and declamation, he commonly takes part with the former: if his turn lie towards irony and ridicule, he naturally throws himself into the other extreme.

I am far from thinking that all those who have depreciated our species have been enemies to virtue, and have exposed the frailties of their fellow-creatures with any bad intention. On the contrary, I am sensible that a delicate sense of morals, especially when attended with a splenetic temper, is apt to give a man a disgust of the world, and to make him consider the common course of human affairs with too much indignation. I must, however, be of opinion, that the sentiments of those who are inclined to think favourably of mankind, are more advantageous to virtue than the contrary principles, which give us a mean opinion of our nature. When a man is prepossessed with a high notion of his rank and character in the creation, he will naturally endeavour to act up to it, and will scorn to do a base or vicious action which might sink him below that figure which he makes in his own imagination. Accordingly we find, that all our polite and fashionable moralists insist upon this topic, and endeavour to represent vice unworthy of man, as well as odious in itself.[†]

We find few disputes that are not founded on some ambiguity in the expression; and I am persuaded that the present dispute, concerning the dignity or meanness of human nature, is not more exempt from it than any other. It may therefore be worth while to consider what is real, and what is only verbal, in this controversy.

That there is a natural difference between merit and demerit, virtue and vice, wisdom and folly, no reasonable man will deny: yet it is evident that, in affixing the term, which denotes either our approbation or blame, we are commonly more influenced by comparison than by any fixed unalterable standard in the nature of things. In like manner, quantity, and extension, and bulk, are by every one acknowledged to be real things: but when we call any animal *great* or *little*, we always form a secret comparison between that animal and others of the same species; and it is that comparison which regulates our judgment concerning its greatness. A dog and a horse may be of the very same size, while the one is admired for the greatness of its bulk, and the other for the smallness. When I am present, therefore, at any dispute, I always consider with myself whether it be a question of comparison or not that is the subject of controversy; and if it be, whether the disputants compare the same objects together, or talk of things that are widely different.

In forming our notions of human nature, we are apt to make a comparison between men and animals, the only creatures endowed with thought that fall under our senses. Certainly this comparison is favourable to mankind. On the one hand, we see a creature whose thoughts are not limited by any narrow bounds, either of place or time; who carries his researches into the most distant regions of this globe, and beyond this globe, to the planets and heavenly bodies; looks backward to consider the first origin, at least the history of the human race; casts his eye forward to see the influence of his actions upon posterity, and the judgments which will be formed of his character a thousand years hence; a creature, who traces causes and effects to a great length and intricacy; extracts general principles from particular appearances; improves upon his discoveries; corrects his mistakes; and makes his very errors profitable. On the other hand, we are presented with a creature the very reverse of this; limited in its observations and reasonings to a few sensible objects which surround it; without curiosity, without foresight; blindly conducted by instinct, and attaining, in a short time, its utmost perfection, beyond which it is never able to advance a single step. What a wide difference is there between these creatures! And how exalted a notion must we entertain of the former, in comparison of the latter!

There are two means commonly employed to destroy this conclusion: *First*, by making an unfair representation of the case, and insisting only upon the weakness of human nature. And, *secondly*, by forming a new and secret comparison between man and beings of the most perfect wisdom. Among the other excellences of man, this is one, that he can form an idea of perfections much beyond what he has experience of in himself; and is not limited in his conception of wisdom and virtue. He can easily exalt his notions, and conceive a degree of knowledge, which, when compared to his own, will make the latter appear very contemptible, and will cause the difference between that and the sagacity of animals, in a manner, to disappear and vanish. Now this being a point in which all the world is agreed, that human understanding falls infinitely short of perfect wisdom, it is proper we should know when this comparison takes place, that we may not dispute where there is no real difference in our sentiments. Man falls much more short of perfect wisdom, and even of his own ideas of perfect wisdom, than animals do of man; yet the latter difference is so considerable, that nothing but a comparison with the former can make it appear of little moment.

It is also usual to *compare* one man with another; and finding very few whom we can call *wise* or *virtuous*, we are apt to entertain a contemptible notion of our species in general. That we may be sensible of the fallacy of this way of reasoning, we may observe, that the honourable appellations of wise and virtuous are not annexed to any particular degree of those qualities of *wisdom* and *virtue*, but arise altogether from the comparison we make between one man and another. When we find a man who arrives at such a pitch of wisdom as is very uncommon, we pronounce him a wise man: so that to say there are few wise men in the world, is really to say nothing; since it is only by their scarcity that they merit that appellation. Were the lowest of our species as wise as TULLY or lord BACON, we should still have reason to say that there are few wise men. For in that case we should exalt our notions of wisdom, and should not pay a singular homage to any one who was not singularly distinguished by his talents. In like manner, I have heard it observed by thoughtless people, that there are few women possessed of beauty in comparison of those who want it; not considering that we bestow the epithet of *beautiful* only on such as possess a degree of beauty that is common to them with a few. The same degree of beauty in a woman is called deformity, which is treated as real beauty in one of our sex.

As it is usual, in forming a notion of our species, to *compare* it with the other species above or below it, or to compare the individuals of the species among themselves; so we often compare together the different motives or actuating principles of human nature, in order to regulate our judgment concerning it. And, indeed, this is the only kind of comparison which is worth our attention, or decides any thing in the present question. Were our selfish and vicious principles so much predominant above our social and virtuous, as is asserted by some philosophers, we ought undoubtedly to entertain a contemptible notion of human nature.

There is much of a dispute of words in all this controversy. When a man denies the sincerity of all public spirit or affection to a country and community, I am at a loss what to think of him. Perhaps he never felt this passion in so clear and distinct a manner as to remove all his doubts concerning its force and reality. But when he proceeds afterwards to reject all private friendship, if no interest or self-love intermix itself; I am then confident that he abuses terms, and confounds the ideas of things; since it is impossible for any one to be so selfish, or rather so stupid, as to make no difference between one man and another, and give no preference to qualities which engage his approbation and esteem. Is he also, say I, as insensible to anger as he pretends to be to friendship? And does injury and wrong no more affect him than kindness or benefits? Impossible: he does not know himself: he has forgotten the movements of his heart; or rather, he makes use of a different language from the rest of his countrymen, and calls not things by their proper names. What say you of natural affection? (I subjoin), Is that also a species of self-love? Yes; all is self-love. *Your* children are loved only because they are yours: *your* friend for a like reason: and *your* country engages you only so far as it has a connection with *yourself*. Were the idea of self removed, nothing would affect you: you would be altogether unactive and insensible: or, if you ever give yourself any movement, it would only be from vanity, and a desire of fame and reputation to this same self. I am willing, reply I, to receive your interpretation of human actions, provided you admit the facts. That species of self-love which displays itself in kindness to others, you must allow to have great influence over human actions, and even greater, on many occasions, than that which remains in its original shape and form. For how few are there, having a family, children, and relations, who do not spend more on the maintenance and education of these than on their own pleasures? This, indeed, you justly observe, may proceed from their self-love, since the prosperity of their family and friends is one, or the chief, of their pleasures, as well as their chief honour. Be you also one of these selfish men, and you are sure of every one's good opinion and good-will; or, not to shock your ears with these expressions, the self-love of every one, and mine among the rest, will then incline us to serve you, and speak well of you.

In my opinion, there are two things which have led astray those philosophers that have insisted so much on the selfishness of man. In the *first* place, they found that every act of virtue or friendship was attended with a secret pleasure; whence they concluded, that friendship and virtue could not be disinterested. But the fallacy of this is obvious. The virtuous sentiment or passion produces the pleasure, and does not arise from it. I feel a pleasure in doing good to my friend, because I love him; but do not love him for the sake of that pleasure.

In the *second* place, it has always been found, that the virtuous are far from being indifferent to praise; and therefore they have been represented as a set of vainglorious men, who had nothing in view but the applauses of others. But this also is a fallacy. It is very unjust in the world, when they find any tincture of vanity in a laudable action, to depreciate it upon that account, or ascribe it entirely to that motive. The case is not the same with vanity, as with other passions. Where avarice or revenge enters into any seemingly virtuous action, it is difficult for us to determine how far it enters, and it is natural to suppose it the sole actuating principle. But vanity is so closely allied to virtue, and to love the fame of laudable actions approaches so near the love of laudable actions for their own sake, that these passions are more capable of mixture, than any other kinds of affection; and it is almost impossible to have the latter without some degree of the former. Accordingly we find, that this passion for glory is always warped and varied according to the particular taste or disposition of the mind on which it falls. NERO had the same vanity in driving a chariot, that TRAJAN had in governing the empire with justice and ability. To love the glory of virtuous deeds is a sure proof of the love of virtue.

OF CIVIL LIBERTY

THOSE who employ their pens on political subjects, free from party rage, and party prejudices, cultivate a science, which, of all others, contributes most to public utility, and even to the private satisfaction of those who addict themselves to the study of it. I am apt, however, to entertain a suspicion, that the world is still too young to fix many general truths in politics, which will remain true to the latest posterity. We have not as yet had experience of three thousand years; so that not only the art of reasoning is still imperfect in this science, as in all others, but we even want sufficient materials upon which we can reason. It is not fully known what degree of refinement, either in virtue or vice, human nature is susceptible of, nor what may be expected of mankind from any great revolution in their education, customs, or principles. MACHIAVEL was certainly a great genius; but, having confined his study to the furious and tyrannical governments of ancient times, or to the little disorderly principalities of ITALY, his reasonings, especially upon monarchical government, have been found extremely defective; and there scarcely is any maxim in his *Prince**
which subsequent experience has not entirely refuted. *A weak prince*, says he, *is incapable of receiving good counsel; for, if he consult with several, he will not be able to choose among their different counsels. If he abandon himself to one, that minister may perhaps have capacity, but he will not long be a minister. He will be sure to dispossess his master, and place himself and his family upon the throne*. I mention this, among many instances of the errors of that politician, proceeding, in a great measure, from his having lived in too early an age of the world, to be a good judge of political truth. Almost all the princes of EUROPE are at present

governed by their ministers, and have been so for near two centuries; and yet no such event has ever happened, or can possibly happen. SEJANUS might project dethroning the CAESARS, but FLEURY, though ever so vicious, could not, while in his senses, entertain the least hopes of dispossessing the BOURBONS.

Trade was never esteemed an affair of state till the last century; and there scarcely is any ancient writer on politics who has made mention of it.[†] Even the ITALIANS have kept a profound silence with regard to it, though it has now engaged the chief attention, as well of ministers of state, as of speculative reasoners. The great opulence, grandeur, and military achievements of the two maritime powers,[*] seem first to have instructed mankind in the importance of an extensive commerce.

Having therefore intended, in this Essay, to make a full comparison of civil liberty and absolute government, and to show the great advantages of the former above the latter; I began to entertain a suspicion that no man in this age was sufficiently qualified for such an undertaking, and that, whatever any one should advance on that head, would in all probability be refuted by further experience, and be rejected by posterity. Such mighty revolutions have happened in human affairs, and so many events have arisen contrary to the expectation of the ancients, that they are sufficient to beget the suspicion of still further changes.

It had been observed by the ancients, that all the arts and sciences arose among free nations; and that the PERSIANS and EGYPTIANS, notwithstanding their ease, opulence, and luxury, made but faint efforts towards a relish in those finer pleasures, which were carried to such perfection by the GREEKS, amidst continual wars, attended with poverty, and the greatest simplicity of life and manners. It had also been observed, that, when the GREEKS lost their liberty, though they increased mightily in riches by means of the conquests of ALEXANDER, yet the arts, from that moment, declined among them, and have never since been able to raise their head in that climate. Learning was transplanted to ROME, the only free nation at that time in the universe; and having

met with so favourable a soil, it made prodigious shoots for
above a century; till the decay of liberty produced also the
decay of letters, and spread a total barbarism over the
world. From these two experiments, of which each was
double in its kind, and showed the fall of learning in absolute
governments, as well as its rise in popular ones, Longinus*
thought himself sufficiently justified in asserting, that the
arts and sciences could never flourish but in a free government. And in this opinion he has been followed by several
eminent writers† in our own country, who either confined
their view merely to ancient facts, or entertained too great a
partiality in favour of that form of government established
among us.

But what would these writers have said to the instances of
modern Rome and Florence? Of which the former carried
to perfection all the finer arts of sculpture, painting, and
music, as well as poetry, though it groaned under tyranny,
and under the tyranny of priests: while the latter made
its chief progress in the arts and sciences after it began to
lose its liberty by the usurpation of the family of Medici.
Ariosto, Tasso, Galileo, no more than Raphael or
Michael Angelo, were not born in republics. And though
the Lombard school was famous as well as the Roman, yet
the Venetians have had the smallest share in its honours,
and seem rather inferior to the other Italians in their genius
for the arts and sciences. Rubens established his school at
Antwerp, not at Amsterdam. Dresden, not Hamburgh,* is
the centre of politeness in Germany.

But the most eminent instance of the flourishing of
learning in absolute governments is that of France, which
scarcely ever enjoyed any established liberty, and yet has
carried the arts and sciences as near perfection as any other
nation. The English are, perhaps, greater philosophers; the
Italians better painters and musicians; the Romans were
greater orators: but the French are the only people, except
the Greeks, who have been at once philosophers, poets,
orators, historians, painters, architects, sculptors, and
musicians. With regard to the stage, they have excelled even
the Greeks, who far excelled the English. And, in common

life, they have, in a great measure, perfected that art, the most useful and agreeable of any, *l'Art de Vivre*, the art of society and conversation.

If we consider the state of the sciences and polite arts in our own country, HORACE's observation, with regard to the ROMANS, may in a great measure be applied to the BRITISH.

> Sed in longum tamen aevum
> Manserunt, hodieque manent *vestigia ruris.**

The elegance and propriety of style have been very much neglected among us. We have no dictionary of our language, and scarcely a tolerable grammar. The first polite prose we have was writ by a man who is still alive.[†] As to SPRAT, LOCKE, and even TEMPLE, they knew too little of the rules of art to be esteemed elegant writers. The prose of BACON, HARRINGTON, and MILTON, is altogether stiff and pedantic, though their sense be excellent. Men, in this country, have been so much occupied in the great disputes of *Religion*, *Politics*, and *Philosophy*, that they had no relish for the seemingly minute observations of grammar and criticism. And, though this turn of thinking must have considerably improved our sense and our talent of reasoning, it must be confessed, that even in those sciences above mentioned, we have not any standard book which we can transmit to posterity: and the utmost we have to boast of, are a few essays towards a more just philosophy, which indeed promise well, but have not as yet reached any degree of perfection.

It has become an established opinion, that commerce can never flourish but in a free government; and this opinion seems to be founded on a longer and larger experience than the foregoing, with regard to the arts and sciences. If we trace commerce in its progress through TYRE, ATHENS, SYRACUSE, CARTHAGE, VENICE, FLORENCE, GENOA, ANTWERP, HOLLAND, ENGLAND, &c., we shall always find it to have fixed its seat in free governments. The three greatest trading towns now in EUROPE, are LONDON, AMSTERDAM, and HAMBURGH; all free cities, and protestant cities; that is, enjoying a double liberty. It must, however, be observed, that the great jealousy entertained of late with regard to the commerce of FRANCE, seems to prove that this maxim is no more certain and infallible than the foregoing, and that the subjects of an absolute prince may become our rivals in commerce as well as in learning.

Durst I deliver my opinion in an affair of so much uncertainty, I would assert, that notwithstanding the efforts of the FRENCH, there is something hurtful to commerce inherent in the very nature of absolute government, and inseparable from it; though the reason I should assign for this opinion is somewhat different from that which is commonly insisted on. Private property seems to me almost as secure in a civilized EUROPEAN monarchy as in a republic; nor is danger much apprehended, in such a government, from the violence of the sovereign, more than we commonly dread harm from thunder, or earthquakes, or any accident the most unusual and extraordinary. Avarice, the spur of industry, is so obstinate a passion, and works its way through so many real dangers and difficulties, that it is not likely to be scared by an imaginary danger, which is so small, that it scarcely admits of calculation. Commerce, therefore, in my opinion, is apt to decay in absolute governments, not because it is there less *secure*, but because it is less *honourable*. A subordination of rank is absolutely necessary to the support of monarchy. Birth, titles, and place, must be honoured above industry and riches; and while these notions prevail, all the considerable traders will be tempted to throw up their commerce, in order to purchase some of those employments, to which privileges and honours are annexed.

Since I am upon this head, of the alterations which time has produced, or may produce in politics, I must observe, that all kinds of government, free and absolute, seem to have undergone, in modern times, a great change for the better, with regard both to foreign and domestic management. The *balance* of power is a secret in politics, fully known only to the present age; and I must add, that the internal POLICE of states has also received great improvements within the last century. We are informed by SALLUST, that CATILINE'S army was much augmented by the accession of the highwaymen about ROME; though I believe, that all of that profession who are at present dispersed over EUROPE would not amount to a regiment. In CICERO's pleadings for MILO, I find this argument, among others, made use of to prove that his client had not assassinated CLODIUS. Had MILO, said he, intended to have killed CLODIUS, he had not attacked him in the daytime, and at such a distance from the city; he had waylaid him at night, near the suburbs, where it might have been pretended that he was killed by robbers; and the frequency of the accident would have favoured the deceit. This is a surprising proof of the loose policy of ROME, and of the number and force of these robbers, since CLODIUS[†] was at that time attended by thirty slaves, who were completely armed, and sufficiently accustomed to blood and danger in the frequent tumults excited by that seditious tribune.

But though all kinds of government be improved in modern times, yet monarchical government seems to have made the greatest advances towards perfection. It may now be affirmed of civilized monarchies, what was formerly said in praise of republics alone, *that they are a government of Laws, not of Men*. They are found susceptible of order, method, and constancy, to a surprising degree. Property is there secure, industry encouraged, the arts flourish, and the prince lives secure among his subjects, like a father among his children. There are, perhaps, and have been for two centuries, near two hundred absolute princes, great and small, in EUROPE; and allowing twenty years to each reign, we may suppose, that there have been in the whole two thousand monarchs, or tyrants, as the GREEKS would have called them; yet of these there has not been one, not even PHILIP II of SPAIN, so bad as TIBERIUS, CALIGULA, NERO, or DOMITIAN, who were four in twelve among the ROMAN emperors. It must, however, be confessed, that though monarchical governments have approached nearer to popular ones in gentleness and stability, they are still inferior. Our modern education and customs instil more humanity and moderation than the ancient; but have not as yet been able to overcome entirely the disadvantages of that form of government.

But here I must beg leave to advance a conjecture, which seems probable, but which posterity alone can fully judge of. I am apt to think, that in monarchical governments there is a source of improvement, and in popular governments a source of degeneracy, which in time will bring these species of civil polity still nearer an equality. The greatest abuses which arise in FRANCE, the most perfect model of pure monarchy, proceed not from the number or weight of the taxes, beyond what are to be met with in free countries; but from the expensive, unequal, arbitrary, and intricate method of levying them, by which the industry of the poor, especially of the peasants and farmers, is in a great measure discouraged, and agriculture rendered a beggarly and slavish employment. But to whose advantage do these abuses tend? If to that of the nobility, they might be esteemed inherent in that form of government, since the nobility are the true supports of monarchy; and it is natural their interest should be more consulted in such a constitution, than that of the people. But the nobility are, in reality, the chief losers by this oppression, since it ruins their estates, and beggars their tenants. The only gainers by it are the *Financiers*; a race of men rather odious to the nobility and the whole kingdom. If a prince or minister, therefore, should arise, endowed with sufficient discernment to know his own and the public interest, and with sufficient force of mind to break through ancient customs, we might expect to see these abuses remedied; in which case, the difference between that absolute government and our free one would not appear so considerable as at present.

The source of degeneracy which may be remarked in free governments, consists in the practice of contracting debt, and mortgaging the public revenues, by which taxes may, in time, become altogether intolerable, and all the property of the state be brought into the hands of the public. The practice is of modern date. The ATHENIANS, though governed by a republic, paid near two hundred per cent. for those sums of money which any emergence made it necessary for them to borrow; as we learn from XENOPHON.[†] Among the moderns, the DUTCH first introduced the practice of bor-

rowing great sums at low interest, and have wellnigh ruined
themselves by it. Absolute princes have also contracted
debt; but as an absolute prince may make a bankruptcy
when he pleases, his people can never be oppressed by his
debts. In popular governments, the people, and chiefly
those who have the highest offices, being commonly the
public creditors, it is difficult for the state to make use of
this remedy, which, however it may sometimes be necessary,
is always cruel and barbarous. This, therefore, seems to be
an inconvenience which nearly threatens all free governments, especially our own, at the present juncture of affairs.
And what a strong motive is this to increase our frugality of
public money, lest, for want of it, we be reduced, by the
multiplicity of taxes, or, what is worse, by our public impotence and inability for defence, to curse our very liberty,
and wish ourselves in the same state of servitude with all the
nations who surround us?

OF THE RISE AND PROGRESS OF THE
ARTS AND SCIENCES

NOTHING requires greater nicety, in our inquiries concerning human affairs, than to distinguish exactly what is
owing to *chance*, and what proceeds from *causes*; nor is
there any subject in which an author is more liable to
deceive himself by false subtilties and refinements. To say
that any event is derived from chance, cuts short all further
inquiry concerning it, and leaves the writer in the same state
of ignorance with the rest of mankind. But when the event
is supposed to proceed from certain and stable causes, he
may then display his ingenuity in assigning these causes;
and as a man of any subtilty can never be at a loss in
this particular, he has thereby an opportunity of swelling
his volumes, and discovering his profound knowledge in
observing what escapes the vulgar and ignorant.

The distinguishing between chance and causes must
depend upon every particular man's sagacity in considering

every particular incident. But if I were to assign any general rule to help us in applying this distinction, it would be the following: *What depends upon a few persons is, in a great measure, to be ascribed to chance, or secret and unknown causes: what arises from a great number, may often be accounted for by determinate and known causes.*

Two natural reasons may be assigned for this rule. *First*, If you suppose a die to have any bias, however small, to a particular side, this bias, though perhaps it may not appear in a few throws, will certainly prevail in a great number, and will cast the balance entirely to that side. In like manner, when any *causes* beget a particular inclination or passion, at a certain time, and among a certain people, though many individuals may escape the contagion, and be ruled by passions peculiar to themselves, yet the multitude will certainly be seized by the common affection, and be governed by it in all their actions.

Secondly, Those principles or causes which are fitted to operate on a multitude, are always of a grosser and more stubborn nature, less subject to accidents, and less influenced by whim and private fancy, than those which operate on a few only. The latter are commonly so delicate and refined, that the smallest incident in the health, education, or fortune of a particular person, is sufficient to divert their course and retard their operation; nor is it possible to reduce them to any general maxims or observations. Their influence at one time will never assure us concerning their influence at another, even though all the general circumstances should be the same in both cases.

To judge by this rule, the domestic and the gradual revolutions of a state must be a more proper subject of reasoning and observation than the foreign and the violent, which are commonly produced by single persons, and are more influenced by whim, folly, or caprice, than by general passions and interests. The depression of the lords, and rise of the commons in ENGLAND, after the statutes of alienation, and the increase of trade and industry, are more easily accounted for by general principles, than the depression of the SPANISH, and rise of the FRENCH monarchy, after

the death of CHARLES QUINT.* Had HARRY IV, Cardinal
RICHELIEU, and LOUIS XIV been SPANIARDS, and PHILIP II,
III, and IV, and CHARLES II been FRENCHMEN, the history of
these two nations had been entirely reversed.

For the same reason, it is more easy to account for the
rise and progress of commerce in any kingdom than for that
of learning; and a state, which should apply itself to the
encouragement of one, would be more assured of success
than one which should cultivate the other. Avarice, or the
desire of gain, is an universal passion, which operates at all
times, in all places, and upon all persons: but curiosity, or
the love of knowledge, has a very limited influence, and
requires youth, leisure, education, genius, and example, to
make it govern any person. You will never want booksellers
while there are buyers of books: but there may frequently
be readers where there are no authors. Multitudes of people,
necessity and liberty, have begotten commerce in HOLLAND:
but study and application have scarcely produced any
eminent writers.

We may therefore conclude, that there is no subject in
which we must proceed with more caution than in tracing
the history of the arts and sciences, lest we assign causes
which never existed, and reduce what is merely contingent
to stable and universal principles. Those who cultivate the
sciences in any state are always few in number; the passion
which governs them limited; their taste and judgment
delicate and easily perverted; and their application disturbed with the smallest accident. Chance, therefore, or
secret and unknown causes, must have a great influence on
the rise and progress of all the refined arts.

But there is a reason which induces me not to ascribe
the matter altogether to chance. Though the persons who
cultivate the sciences with such astonishing success as to
attract the admiration of posterity, be always few in all
nations and all ages, it is impossible but a share of the same
spirit and genius must be antecedently diffused throughout
the people among whom they arise, in order to produce,
form, and cultivate, from their earliest infancy, the taste
and judgment of those eminent writers. The mass cannot

be altogether insipid from which such refined spirits are extracted. *There is a God within us*, says OVID, *who breathes that divine fire by which we are animated.*† Poets in all ages have advanced this claim to inspiration. There is not, however, any thing supernatural in the case. Their fire is not kindled from heaven. It only runs along the earth, is caught from one breast to another, and burns brightest where the materials are best prepared and most happily disposed. The question, therefore, concerning the rise and progress of the arts and sciences is not altogether a question concerning the taste, genius, and spirit of a few, but concerning those of a whole people, and may therefore be accounted for, in some measure, by general causes and principles. I grant that a man, who should inquire why such a particular poet, as HOMER, for instance, existed at such a place, in such a time, would throw himself headlong into chimera, and could never treat of such a subject without a multitude of false subtilties and refinements. He might as well pretend to give a reason why such particular generals as FABIUS and SCIPIO lived in ROME at such a time, and why FABIUS came into the world before SCIPIO. For such incidents as these no other reason can be given than that of HORACE:

> Scit genius, natale comes, qui temperat astrum,
> Naturae Deus humanae, mortalis in unum—
> Quodque caput, vultu mutabilis, albus et ater.*

But I am persuaded that in many cases good reasons might be given why such a nation is more polite and learned, at a particular time, than any of its neighbours. At least this is so curious a subject, that it were a pity to abandon it entirely before we have found whether it be susceptible of reasoning, and can be reduced to any general principles.

My first observation on this head is, *That it is impossible for the arts and sciences to arise, at first, among any people, unless that people enjoy the blessing of a free government.*

In the first ages of the world, when men are as yet barbarous and ignorant, they seek no further security against mutual violence and injustice than the choice of some rulers, few or many, in whom they place an implicit confidence, without providing any security, by laws or political institutions, against the violence and injustice of these rulers. If the authority be centred in a single person, and if the people, either by conquest or by the ordinary course of propagation, increase to a great multitude, the monarch, finding it impossible, in his own person, to execute every office of sovereignty, in every place, must delegate his authority to inferior magistrates, who preserve peace and order in their respective districts. As experience and education have not yet refined the judgments of men to any considerable degree, the prince, who is himself unrestrained, never dreams of restraining his ministers, but delegates his full authority to every one whom he sets over any portion of the people. All general laws are attended with inconveniences, when applied to particular cases; and it requires great penetration and experience, both to perceive that these inconveniences are fewer than what result from full discretionary powers in every magistrate, and also discern what general laws are, upon the whole, attended with fewest inconveniences. This is a matter of so great difficulty, that men may have made some advances, even in the sublime arts of poetry and eloquence, where a rapidity of genius and imagination assists their progress, before they have arrived at any great refinement in their municipal laws, where frequent trials and diligent observation can alone direct their improvements. It is not, therefore, to be supposed, that a barbarous monarch, unrestrained and uninstructed, will ever become a legislator, or think of restraining his *Bashaws* in every province, or even his *Cadis* in every village.* We are told, that the late *Czar*,* though actuated with a noble genius, and smit with the love and admiration of EUROPEAN arts; yet professed an esteem for the Turkish policy in this particular, and approved of such summary decisions of causes, as are practised in that barbarous monarchy, where the judges are not restrained by any methods, forms, or laws. He did not perceive, how contrary such a practice would have been to all his other endeavours for refining his people. Arbitrary power, in all cases, is somewhat oppressive and debasing; but it is altogether ruinous and intolerable, when contracted into a small compass; and becomes still worse, when the person, who possesses it, knows that the time of his authority is limited and uncertain. *Habet subjectos tanquam suos; viles ut alienos.*[†] He governs the subjects with full authority, as if they were his own; and with negligence or tyranny, as belonging to another. A people, governed after such a manner, are slaves in the full and proper sense of the word; and it is impossible they can ever aspire to any refinements of taste or reason. They dare not so much as pretend to enjoy the necessaries of life in plenty or security.

To expect, therefore, that the arts and sciences should take their first rise in a monarchy, is to expect a contradiction. Before these refinements have taken place, the monarch is ignorant and uninstructed; and not having knowledge sufficient to make him sensible of the necessity of balancing his government upon general laws, he delegates his full power to all inferior magistrates. This barbarous policy debases the people, and for ever prevents all improvements. Were it possible, that, before science were known in the world, a monarch could possess so much wisdom as to become a legislator, and govern his people by law, not by the arbitrary will of their fellow-subjects, it might be possible for that species of government to be the first nursery of arts and sciences. But that supposition seems scarcely to be consistent or rational.

It may happen, that a republic, in its infant state, may be supported by as few laws as a barbarous monarchy, and may intrust as unlimited an authority to its magistrates or judges. But, besides that the frequent elections by the people are a considerable check upon authority; it is impossible, but in time, the necessity of restraining the magistrates, in order to preserve liberty, must at last appear, and give rise to general laws and statutes. The ROMAN Consuls, for some time, decided all causes, without being confined by any positive statutes, till the people, bearing this yoke with impatience, created the *decemvirs*, who promulgated the *twelve tables*; a body of laws which, though perhaps they were not equal in

bulk to one ENGLISH act of parliament, were almost the only
written rules, which regulated property and punishment, for
some ages, in that famous republic. They were, however,
sufficient, together with the forms of a free government, to
secure the lives and properties of the citizens; to exempt one
man from the dominion of another; and to protect every
one against the violence or tyranny of his fellow-citizens. In
such a situation, the sciences may raise their heads and
flourish; but never can have being amidst such a scene of
oppression and slavery, as always results from barbarous
monarchies, where the people alone are restrained by the
authority of the magistrates, and the magistrates are not
restrained by any law or statute. An unlimited despotism of
this nature, while it exists, effectually puts a stop to all
improvements, and keeps men from attaining that knowledge, which is requisite to instruct them in the advantages
arising from a better police, and more moderate authority.

Here then are the advantages of free states. Though a
republic should be barbarous, it necessarily, by an infallible
operation, gives rise to LAW, even before mankind have
made any considerable advances in the other sciences.
From law arises security; from security curiosity; and from
curiosity knowledge. The latter steps of this progress may be
more accidental; but the former are altogether necessary.
A republic without laws can never have any duration. On
the contrary, in a monarchical government, law arises not
necessarily from the forms of government. Monarchy, when
absolute, contains even something repugnant to law. Great
wisdom and reflection can alone reconcile them. But such a
degree of wisdom can never be expected, before the greater
refinements and improvements of human reason. These
refinements require curiosity, security, and law. The *first*
growth, therefore, of the arts and sciences, can never be
expected in despotic governments.

There are other causes, which discourage the rise of the
refined arts in despotic governments; though I take the want
of laws, and the delegation of full powers to every petty
magistrate, to be the principal. Eloquence certainly springs
up more naturally in popular governments. Emulation, too,

in every accomplishment, must there be more animated and enlivened; and genius and capacity have a fuller scope and career. All these causes render free governments the only proper *nursery* for the arts and sciences.

The next observation which I shall make on this head is, *That nothing is more favourable to the rise of politeness and learning, than a number of neighbouring and independent states, connected together by commerce and policy*. The emulation which naturally arises among those neighbouring states is an obvious source of improvement. But what I would chiefly insist on is the stop which such limited territories give both to *power* and to *authority*.

Extended governments, where a single person has great influence, soon become absolute; but small ones change naturally into commonwealths. A large government is accustomed by degrees to tyranny, because each act of violence is at first performed upon a part, which, being distant from the majority, is not taken notice of, nor excites any violent ferment. Besides, a large government, though the whole be discontented, may, by a little art, be kept in obedience; while each part, ignorant of the resolutions of the rest, is afraid to begin any commotion or insurrection: not to mention that there is a superstitious reverence for princes, which mankind naturally contract when they do not often see the sovereign, and when many of them become not acquainted with him so as to perceive his weaknesses. And as large states can afford a great expense in order to support the pomp of majesty, this is a kind of fascination on men, and naturally contributes to the enslaving of them.

In a small government any act of oppression is immediately known throughout the whole; the murmurs and discontents proceeding from it are easily communicated; and the indignation arises the higher, because the subjects are not to apprehend, in such states, that the distance is very wide between themselves and their sovereign. 'No man,' said the prince of CONDE, 'is a hero to his *Valet de Chambre*.'* It is certain that admiration and acquaintance are altogether incompatible towards any mortal creature. Sleep and love convinced even ALEXANDER himself that he was not a God.

But I suppose that such as daily attended him could easily, from the numberless weaknesses to which he was subject, have given him many still more convincing proofs of his humanity.

But the divisions into small states are favourable to learning, by stopping the progress of *authority* as well as that of *power*. Reputation is often as great a fascination upon men as sovereignty, and is equally destructive to the freedom of thought and examination. But where a number of neighbouring states have a great intercourse of arts and commerce, their mutual jealousy keeps them from receiving too lightly the law from each other, in matters of taste and of reasoning, and makes them examine every work of art with the greatest care and accuracy. The contagion of popular opinion spreads not so easily from one place to another. It readily receives a check in some state or other, where it concurs not with the prevailing prejudices. And nothing but nature and reason, or at least what bears them a strong resemblance, can force its way through all obstacles, and unite the most rival nations into an esteem and admiration of it.

GREECE was a cluster of little principalities, which soon became republics; and being united both by their near neighbourhood, and by the ties of the same language and interest, they entered into the closest intercourse of commerce and learning. There concurred a happy climate, a soil not unfertile, and a most harmonious and comprehensive language; so that every circumstance among that people seemed to favour the rise of the arts and sciences. Each city produced its several artists and philosophers, who refused to yield the preference to those of the neighbouring republics; their contention and debates sharpened the wits of men; a variety of objects was presented to the judgment, while each challenged the preference to the rest; and the sciences, not being dwarfed by the restraint of authority, were enabled to make such considerable shoots as are even at this time the objects of our admiration. After the ROMAN *christian* or *catholic* church had spread itself over the civilized world, and had engrossed all the learning of the times, being really one large state within itself, and united under one head, this variety of sects immediately disappeared, and the PERIPATETIC* philosophy was alone admitted into all the schools, to the utter depravation of every kind of learning. But mankind having at length thrown off this yoke, affairs are now returned nearly to the same situation as before, and EUROPE is at present a copy, at large, of what GREECE was formerly a pattern in miniature. We have seen the advantage of this situation in several instances. What checked the progress of the CARTESIAN philosophy,* to which the FRENCH nation showed such a strong propensity towards the end of the last century, but the opposition made to it by the other nations of EUROPE, who soon discovered the weak sides of that philosophy? The severest scrutiny which NEWTON's theory* has undergone proceeded not from his own countrymen, but from foreigners; and if it can overcome the obstacles which it meets with at present in all parts of EUROPE, it will probably go down triumphant to the latest posterity. The ENGLISH are become sensible of the scandalous licentiousness of their stage, from the example of the FRENCH decency and morals. The FRENCH are convinced that their theatre has become somewhat effeminate by too much love and gallantry, and begin to approve of the more masculine taste of some neighbouring nations.

In CHINA, there seems to be a pretty considerable stock of politeness and science, which, in the course of so many centuries, might naturally be expected to ripen into something more perfect and finished than what has yet arisen from them. But CHINA is one vast empire, speaking one language, governed by one law, and sympathizing in the same manners. The authority of any teacher, such as CONFUCIUS, was propagated easily from one corner of the empire to the other. None had courage to resist the torrent of popular opinion: and posterity was not bold enough to dispute what had been universally received by their ancestors. This seems to be one natural reason why the sciences have made so slow a progress in that mighty empire.†

If we consider the face of the globe, EUROPE, of all the

four parts of the world, is the most broken by seas, rivers, and mountains, and GREECE of all countries of EUROPE. Hence these regions were naturally divided into several distinct governments; and hence the sciences arose in GREECE, and EUROPE has been hitherto the most constant habitation of them.

I have sometimes been inclined to think, that interruptions in the periods of learning, were they not attended with such a destruction of ancient books, and the records of history, would be rather favourable to the arts and sciences, by breaking the progress of authority, and dethroning the tyrannical usurpers over human reason. In this particular, they have the same influence as interruptions in political governments and societies. Consider the blind submission of the ancient philosophers to the several masters in each school, and you will be convinced, that little good could be expected from a hundred centuries of such a servile philosophy. Even the ECLECTICS,* who arose about the age of AUGUSTUS, notwithstanding their professing to choose freely what pleased them from every different sect, were yet, in the main, as slavish and dependent as any of their brethren; since they sought for truth, not in nature, but in the several schools; where they supposed she must necessarily be found, though not united in a body, yet dispersed in parts. Upon the revival of learning, those sects of STOICS and EPICUREANS, PLATONISTS* and PYTHAGOREANS, could never regain any credit or authority; and, at the same time, by the example of their fall, kept men from submitting, with such blind deference, to those new sects, which have attempted to gain an ascendant over them.

The *third* observation, which I shall form on this head, of the rise and progress of the arts and sciences, is, *That, though the only proper* nursery *of these noble plants be a free state, yet may they be transplanted into any government; and that a republic is most favourable to the growth of the sciences, and a civilized monarchy to that of the polite arts*.

To balance a large state or society, whether monarchical or republican, on general laws, is a work of so great difficulty, that no human genius, however comprehensive, is able, by the mere dint of reason and reflection, to effect it. The judgments of many must unite in this work: experience must guide their labour: time must bring it to perfection: and the feeling of inconveniences must correct the mistakes, which they inevitably fall into, in their first trials and experiments. Hence appears the impossibility that this undertaking should be begun and carried on in any monarchy; since such a form of government, ere civilized, knows no other secret or policy, than that of intrusting unlimited powers to every governor or magistrate, and subdividing the people into so many classes and orders of slavery. From such a situation, no improvement can ever be expected in the sciences, in the liberal arts, in laws, and scarcely in the manual arts and manufactures. The same barbarism and ignorance, with which the government commences, is propagated to all posterity, and can never come to a period by the efforts or ingenuity of such unhappy slaves.

But though law, the source of all security and happiness, arises late in any government, and is the slow product of order and of liberty, it is not preserved with the same difficulty with which it is produced; but when it has once taken root, is a hardy plant, which will scarcely ever perish through the ill culture of men, or the rigour of the seasons. The arts of luxury, and much more the liberal arts, which depend on a refined taste or sentiment, are easily lost; because they are always relished by a few only, whose leisure, fortune, and genius, fit them for such amusements. But what is profitable to every mortal, and in common life, when once discovered, can scarcely fall into oblivion, but by the total subversion of society, and by such furious inundations of barbarous invaders, as obliterate all memory of former arts and civility. Imitation also is apt to transport these coarser and more useful arts from one climate to another, and to make them precede the refined arts in their progress; though, perhaps, they sprang after them in their first rise and propagation. From these causes proceed civilized monarchies, where the arts of government, first invented in free states, are preserved to the mutual advantage and security of sovereign and subject.

However perfect, therefore, the monarchical form may appear to some politicians, it owes all its perfection to the republican; nor is it possible that a pure despotism, established among a barbarous people, can ever, by its native force and energy, refine and polish itself. It must borrow its laws, and methods, and institutions, and consequently its stability and order, from free governments. These advantages are the sole growth of republics. The extensive despotism of a barbarous monarchy, by entering into the detail of the government, as well as into the principal points of administration, for ever prevents all such improvements.

In a civilized monarchy, the prince alone is unrestrained in the exercise of his authority, and possesses alone a power, which is not bounded by any thing but custom, example, and the sense of his own interest. Every minister or magistrate, however eminent, must submit to the general laws which govern the whole society, and must exert the authority delegated to him after the manner which is prescribed. The people depend on none but their sovereign for the security of their property. He is so far removed from them, and is so much exempt from private jealousies or interests, that this dependence is scarcely felt. And thus a species of government arises, to which, in a high political rant, we may give the name of *Tyranny*, but which, by a just and prudent administration, may afford tolerable security to the people, and may answer most of the ends of political society.

But though in a civilized monarchy, as well as in a republic, the people have security for the enjoyment of their property, yet in both these forms of government, those who possess the supreme authority have the disposal of many honours and advantages, which excite the ambition and avarice of mankind. The only difference is, that, in a republic, the candidates for office must look downwards to gain the suffrages of the people; in a monarchy, they must turn their attention upwards, to court the good graces and favour of the great. To be successful in the former way, it is necessary for a man to make himself *useful* by his industry, capacity, or knowledge: to be prosperous in the latter way, it is requisite for him to render himself *agreeable* by his wit, complaisance, or civility. A strong genius succeeds best in republics; a refined taste in monarchies. And, consequently, the sciences are the more natural growth of the one, and the polite arts of the other.

Not to mention, that monarchies, receiving their chief stability from a superstitious reverence to priests and princes, have commonly abridged the liberty of reasoning, with regard to religion and politics, and consequently metaphysics and morals. All these form the most considerable branches of science. Mathematics and natural philosophy, which only remain, are not half so valuable.

Among the arts of conversation, no one pleases more than mutual deference or civility, which leads us to resign our own inclinations to those of our companion, and to curb and conceal that presumption and arrogance so natural to the human mind. A good-natured man, who is well educated, practises this civility to every mortal, without premeditation or interest. But in order to render that valuable quality general among any people, it seems necessary to assist the natural disposition by some general motive. Where power rises upwards from the people to the great, as in all republics, such refinements of civility are apt to be little practised, since the whole state is, by that means, brought near to a level, and every member of it is rendered, in a great measure, independent of another. The people have the advantage, by the authority of their suffrages; the great by the superiority of their station. But in a civilized monarchy, there is a long train of dependence from the prince to the peasant, which is not great enough to render property precarious, or depress the minds of the people; but is sufficient to beget in every one an inclination to please his superiors, and to form himself upon those models which are most acceptable to people of condition and education. Politeness of manners, therefore, arises most naturally in monarchies and courts; and where that flourishes, none of the liberal arts will be altogether neglected or despised.

The republics in EUROPE are at present noted for want of politeness. *The good manners of a* SWISS *civilized in*

HOLLAND,[†] is an expression for rusticity among the FRENCH. The ENGLISH, in some degree, fall under the same censure, notwithstanding their learning and genius. And if the VENETIANS be an exception to the rule, they owe it, perhaps, to their communication with the other ITALIANS, most of whose governments beget a dependence more than sufficient for civilizing their manners.

It is difficult to pronounce any judgment concerning the refinements of the ancient republics in this particular: but I am apt to suspect, that the arts of conversation were not brought so near to perfection among them as the arts of writing and composition. The scurrility of the ancient orators, in many instances, is quite shocking, and exceeds all belief. Vanity, too, is often not a little offensive in authors of those ages;[†] as well as the common licentiousness and immodesty of their style. *Quicunque impudicus, adulter, ganeo, manu, ventre, pene, bona patria laceraverat*, says SALLUST,[*] in one of the gravest and most moral passages of his history. *Nam fuit ante Helenam Cunnus, teterrima belli causa*, is an expression of HORACE,[*] in tracing the origin of moral good and evil. OVID and LUCRETIUS[†] are almost as licentious in their style as Lord ROCHESTER; though the former were fine gentlemen and delicate writers, and the latter, from the corruptions of that court in which he lived, seems to have thrown off all regard to shame and decency. JUVENAL inculcates modesty with great zeal; but sets a very bad example of it, if we consider the impudence of his expressions.

I shall also be bold to affirm, that among the ancients, there was not much delicacy of breeding, or that polite deference and respect, which civility obliges us either to express or counterfeit towards the persons with whom we converse. CICERO was certainly one of the finest gentlemen of his age; yet, I must confess, I have frequently been shocked with the poor figure under which he represents his friend ATTICUS, in those dialogues where he himself is introduced as a speaker. That learned and virtuous ROMAN, whose dignity, though he was only a private gentleman, was inferior to that of no one in ROME, is there shown in rather a more pitiful light than PHILALETHES's friend in our modern dialogues. He is a humble admirer of the orator, pays him frequent compliments, and receives his instructions, with all the deference which a scholar owes to his master.[†] Even CATO is treated in somewhat of a cavalier manner in the dialogues *de finibus*.[*]

One of the most particular details of a real dialogue, which we meet with in antiquity, is related by POLYBIUS,[†] when PHILIP king of MACEDON, a prince of wit and parts, met with TITUS FLAMININUS, one of the politest of the ROMANS, as we learn from PLUTARCH,[†] accompanied with ambassadors from almost all the GREEK cities. The AETOLIAN ambassador very abruptly tells the king, that he talked like a fool or madman (λη‑ρεῖν). *That's evident*, says his majesty, *even to a blind man*; which was a raillery on the blindness of his excellency. Yet all this did not pass the usual bounds: for the conference was not disturbed; and FLAMININUS was very well diverted with these strokes of humour. At the end, when PHILIP craved a little time to consult with his friends, of whom he had none present, the ROMAN general, being desirous also to show his wit, as the historian says, tells him, 'That perhaps the reason why he had none of his friends with him, was because he had murdered them all;' which was actually the case. This unprovoked piece of rusticity is not condemned by the historian; caused no further resentment in PHILIP than to excite a SARDONIAN smile, or what we call a grin; and hindered him not from renewing the conference next day. PLUTARCH,[†] too, mentions this raillery amongst the witty and agreeable sayings of FLAMININUS.

Cardinal WOLSEY apologized for his famous piece of insolence, in saying, EGO ET REX MEUS, *I and my king*, by observing, that this expression was conformable to the *Latin* idiom, and that a ROMAN always named himself before the person to whom, or of whom, he spake. Yet this seems to have been an instance of want of civility among that people. The ancients made it a rule, that the person of the greatest dignity should be mentioned first in the discourse; insomuch, that we find the spring of a quarrel and jealousy between the ROMANS and AETOLIANS, to have been a poet's naming the AETOLIANS before the ROMANS in celebrating a victory gained by their united arms over the MACEDONIANS.† Thus LIVIA disgusted TIBERIUS by placing her own name before his in an inscription.†

No advantages in this world are pure and unmixed. In like manner, as modern politeness, which is naturally so ornamental, runs often into affectation and foppery, disguise and insincerity; so the ancient simplicity, which is naturally so amiable and affecting, often degenerates into rusticity and abuse, scurrility and obscenity.

If the superiority in politeness should be allowed to modern times, the modern notions of *gallantry*, the natural produce of courts and monarchies, will probably be assigned as the causes of this refinement. No one denies this invention to be modern:† but some of the more zealous partisans of the ancients have asserted it to be foppish and ridiculous, and a reproach, rather than a credit, to the present age.† It may here be proper to examine this question.

Nature has implanted in all living creatures an affection between the sexes, which, even in the fiercest and most rapacious animals, is not merely confined to the satisfaction of the bodily appetite, but begets a friendship and mutual sympathy, which runs through the whole tenor of their lives. Nay, even in those species, where nature limits the indulgence of this appetite to one season and to one object, and forms a kind of marriage or association between a single male and female, there is yet a visible complacency and benevolence, which extends further, and mutually softens the affections of the sexes towards each other. How much more must this have place in man, where the confinement of the appetite is not natural, but either is derived accidentally from some strong charm of love, or arises from reflections on duty and convenience! Nothing, therefore, can proceed less from affectation than the passion of gallantry. It is *natural* in the highest degree. Art and education, in the most elegant courts, make no more alteration on it than on all the other laudable passions. They only turn the mind more towards it; they refine it; they polish it; and give it a proper grace and expression.

But gallantry is as *generous* as it is *natural*. To correct
such gross vices as lead us to commit real injury on others,
is the part of morals, and the object of the most ordinary
education. Where *that* is not attended to in some degree, no
human society can subsist. But, in order to render conversation, and the intercourse of minds more easy and agreeable, good manners have been invented, and have carried
the matter somewhat further. Wherever nature has given
the mind a propensity to any vice, or to any passion disagreeable to others, refined breeding has taught men to
throw the bias on the opposite side, and to preserve, in
all their behaviour, the appearance of sentiments different
from those to which they naturally incline. Thus, as we
are commonly proud and selfish, and apt to assume the
preference above others, a polite man learns to behave
with deference towards his companions, and to yield the
superiority to them in all the common incidents of society.
In like manner, wherever a person's situation may naturally
beget any disagreeable suspicion in him, it is the part of
good manners to prevent it, by a studied display of sentiments, directly contrary to those of which he is apt to be
jealous. Thus, old men know their infirmities, and naturally
dread contempt from the youth: hence well-educated youth
redouble the instances of respect and deference to their
elders. Strangers and foreigners are without protection:
hence, in all polite countries, they receive the highest
civilities, and are entitled to the first place in every company.
A man is lord in his own family; and his guests are, in a
manner, subject to his authority: hence, he is always the
lowest person in the company, attentive to the wants of
every one, and giving himself all the trouble in order to
please, which may not betray too visible an affectation, or
impose too much constraint on his guests.[†] Gallantry is
nothing but an instance of the same generous attention. As
nature has given *man* the superiority above *woman*, by
endowing him with greater strength both of mind and
body, it is his part to alleviate that superiority, as much
as possible, by the generosity of his behaviour, and by a
studied deference and complaisance for all her inclinations

and opinions. Barbarous nations display this superiority, by reducing their females to the most abject slavery; by confining them, by beating them, by selling them, by killing them. But the male sex, among a polite people, discover their authority in a more generous, though not a less evident manner; by civility, by respect, by complaisance, and, in a word, by gallantry. In good company, you need not ask, who is the master of the feast? The man who sits in the lowest place, and who is always industrious in helping every one, is certainly the person. We must either condemn all such instances of generosity as foppish and affected, or admit of gallantry among the rest. The ancient Muscovites wedded their wives with a whip, instead of a ring. The same people, in their own houses, took always the precedency above foreigners, even[†] foreign ambassadors. These two instances of their generosity and politeness are much of a piece.

Gallantry is not less compatible with *wisdom* and *prudence*, than with *nature* and *generosity*; and, when under proper regulations, contributes more than any other invention to the *entertainment* and *improvement* of the youth of both sexes. Among every species of animals, nature has founded on the love between the sexes their sweetest and best enjoyment. But the satisfaction of the bodily appetite is not alone sufficient to gratify the mind; and, even among brute creatures, we find that their play and dalliance, and other expressions of fondness, form the greatest part of the entertainment. In rational beings, we must certainly admit the mind for a considerable share. Were we to rob the feast of all its garniture of reason, discourse, sympathy, friendship, and gaiety, what remains would scarcely be worth acceptance, in the judgment of the truly elegant and luxurious.

What better school for manners than the company of virtuous women, where the mutual endeavour to please must insensibly polish the mind, where the example of the female softness and modesty must communicate itself to their admirers, and where the delicacy of that sex puts every one on his guard, lest he give offence by any breach of decency?[†]

Among the ancients, the character of the fair sex was considered as altogether domestic; nor were they regarded as part of the polite world, or of good company. This, perhaps, is the true reason why the ancients have not left us one piece of pleasantry that is excellent (unless one may except the Banquet of XENOPHON, and the Dialogues of LUCIAN), though many of their serious compositions are altogether inimitable. HORACE condemns the coarse railleries and cold jests of PLAUTUS:* but, though the most easy, agreeable, and judicious writer in the world, is his own talent for ridicule very striking or refined? This, therefore, is one considerable improvement which the polite arts have received from gallantry, and from courts where it first arose.†

But to return from this digression, I shall advance it as a *fourth* observation on this subject, of the rise and progress of the arts and sciences, *That when the arts and sciences come to perfection in any state, from that moment they naturally, or rather necessarily, decline, and seldom or never revive in that nation where they formerly flourished.*

It must be confessed, that this maxim, though conformable to experience, may at first sight be esteemed contrary to reason. If the natural genius of mankind be the same in all ages, and in almost all countries (as seems to be the truth), it must very much forward and cultivate this genius, to be possessed of patterns in every art, which may regulate the taste, and fix the objects of imitation. The models left us by the ancients gave birth to all the arts about two hundred years ago, and have mightily advanced their progress in every country of EUROPE. Why had they not a like effect during the reign of TRAJAN and his successors, when they were much more entire, and were still admired and studied by the whole world? So late as the emperor JUSTINIAN, the POET, by way of distinction, was understood, among the GREEKS, to be HOMER; among the ROMANS, VIRGIL. Such admirations still remained for these divine geniuses; though no poet had appeared for many centuries, who could justly pretend to have imitated them.

A man's genius is always, in the beginning of life, as much unknown to himself as to others; and it is only after frequent trials, attended with success, that he dares think himself equal to those undertakings, in which those who have succeeded have fixed the admiration of mankind. If his own nation be already possessed of many models of eloquence, he naturally compares his own juvenile exercises with these; and, being sensible of the great disproportion, is discouraged from any further attempts, and never aims at a rivalship with those authors whom he so much admires. A noble emulation is the source of every excellence. Admiration and modesty naturally extinguish this emulation; and no one is so liable to an excess of admiration and modesty as a truly great genius.

Next to emulation, the greatest encourager of the noble arts is praise and glory. A writer is animated with new force when he hears the applauses of the world for his former productions; and, being roused by such a motive, he often reaches a pitch of perfection, which is equally surprising to himself and to his readers. But when the posts of honour are all occupied, his first attempts are but coldly received by the public; being compared to productions which are both in themselves more excellent, and have already the advantage of an established reputation. Were MOLIERE and CORNEILLE to bring upon the stage at present their early productions, which were formerly so well received, it would discourage the young poets to see the indifference and disdain of the public. The ignorance of the age alone could have given admission to the *Prince of* TYRE; but it is to that we owe *the Moor*. Had *Every Man in his humour* been rejected, we had never seen VOLPONE.*

Perhaps it may not be for the advantage of any nation to have the arts imported from their neighbours in too great perfection. This extinguishes emulation, and sinks the ardour of the generous youth. So many models of ITALIAN painting brought to ENGLAND,* instead of exciting our artists, is the cause of their small progress in that noble art. The same, perhaps, was the case of ROME when it received the arts from GREECE. That multitude of polite productions in the FRENCH language, dispersed all over GERMANY and the NORTH, hinder these nations from cultivating their own language, and keep them still dependent on their neighbours for those elegant entertainments.

It is true, the ancients had left us models in every kind of writing, which are highly worthy of admiration. But besides that they were written in languages known only to the learned; besides this, I say, the comparison is not so perfect or entire between modern wits, and those who lived in so remote an age. Had WALLER* been born in ROME, during the reign of TIBERIUS, his first productions had been despised, when compared to the finished odes of HORACE. But in this Island, the superiority of the ROMAN poet diminished nothing from the fame of the ENGLISH. We esteemed ourselves sufficiently happy that our climate and language could produce but a faint copy of so excellent an original.

In short, the arts and sciences, like some plants, require a fresh soil; and however rich the land may be, and however you may recruit it by art or care, it will never, when once exhausted, produce any thing that is perfect or finished in the kind.

THE EPICUREAN†

IT is a great mortification to the vanity of man, that his utmost art and industry can never equal the meanest of nature's productions, either for beauty or value. Art is only the under-workman, and is employed to give a few strokes of embellishment to those pieces which come from the hand of the master. Some of the drapery may be of his drawing, but he is not allowed to touch the principal figure. Art may make a suit of clothes, but nature must produce a man.

Even in those productions commonly denominated works of art, we find that the noblest of the kind are beholden for their chief beauty to the force and happy influence of nature. To the native enthusiasm of the poets we owe whatever is admirable in their productions. The greatest genius, where nature at any time fails him (for she is not equal), throws aside the lyre, and hopes not, from the rules of art, to reach that divine harmony which must proceed from her inspiration alone. How poor are those songs where a happy flow of fancy has not furnished materials for art to embellish and refine!

But of all the fruitless attempts of art, no one is so ridiculous as that which the severe philosophers have undertaken, the producing of an *artificial happiness*, and making us be pleased by rules of reason and by reflection. Why did none of them claim the reward which XERXES promised to him who should invent a new pleasure? Unless, perhaps, they invented so many pleasures for their own use, that they despised riches, and stood in no need of any enjoyments which the rewards of that monarch could produce them. I am apt, indeed, to think, that they were not willing to furnish the PERSIAN court with a new pleasure, by presenting it with so new and unusual an object of ridicule. Their speculations, when confined to theory, and gravely delivered in the schools of GREECE, might excite admiration in their ignorant pupils; but the attempting to reduce such principles to practice would soon have betrayed their absurdity.

You pretend to make me happy, by reason and by rules of art. You must then create me anew by rules of art, for on my original frame and structure does my happiness depend. But you want power to effect this, and skill too, I am afraid; nor can I entertain a less opinion of nature's wisdom than yours; and let her conduct the machine which she has so wisely framed; I find that I should only spoil it by tampering.

To what purpose should I pretend to regulate, refine, or invigorate any of those springs or principles which nature has implanted in me? Is this the road by which I must reach happiness? But happiness implies ease, contentment, repose, and pleasure; not watchfulness, care, and fatigue. The health of my body consists in the facility with which all its operations are performed. The stomach digests the aliments; the heart circulates the blood; the brain separates and refines the spirits; and all this without my concerning myself in the matter. When by my will alone I can stop the blood, as it runs with impetuosity along its canals, then may I hope to change the course of my sentiments and passions. In vain should I strain my faculties, and endeavour to receive pleasure from an object which is not fitted by nature to affect my organs with delight. I may give myself pain by my fruitless endeavours, but shall never reach any pleasure.

Away then with all those vain pretences of making ourselves happy within ourselves, of feasting on our own thoughts, of being satisfied with the consciousness of well-doing, and of despising all assistance and all supplies from external objects. This is the voice of PRIDE, not of NATURE. And it were well if even this pride could support itself, and communicate a real *inward* pleasure, however melancholy or severe. But this impotent pride can do no more than regulate the *outside*, and, with infinite pains and attention, compose the language and countenance to a philosophical dignity, in order to deceive the ignorant vulgar. The heart, meanwhile, is empty of all enjoyment, and the mind, unsupported by its proper objects, sinks into the deepest sorrow and dejection. Miserable, but vain mortal! Thy mind be happy within itself! With what resources is it endowed to fill so immense a void, and supply the place of all thy bodily senses and faculties? Can thy head subsist without thy other members? In such a situation,

> What foolish figure must it make?
> Do nothing else but *sleep* and *ake*.

Into such a lethargy, or such a melancholy, must thy mind be plunged, when deprived of foreign occupations and enjoyments.

Keep me, therefore, no longer in this violent constraint. Confine me not within myself, but point out to me those objects and pleasures which afford the chief enjoyment. But why do I apply to you, proud and ignorant sages, to show me the road to happiness? Let me consult my own passions and inclinations. In them must I read the dictates of nature, not in your frivolous discourses.

But see, propitious to my wishes, the divine, the amiable PLEASURE,[†] the supreme love of GODS and men, advances towards me. At her approach my heart beats with genial heat, and every sense and every faculty is dissolved in joy, while she pours around me all the embellishments of the spring, and all the treasures of the autumn. The melody of her voice charms my ears with the softest music, as she invites me to partake of those delicious fruits, which, with a smile that diffuses a glory on the heavens and the earth, she presents to me. The sportive CUPIDS who attend her, or fan me with their odoriferous wings, or pour on my head the most fragrant oils, or offer me their sparkling nectar in golden goblets; O! for ever let me spread my limbs on this bed of roses, and thus, thus feel the delicious moments, with soft and downy steps, glide along. But cruel chance! Whither do you fly so fast? Why do my ardent wishes, and that load of pleasures under which you labour, rather hasten than retard your unrelenting pace? Suffer me to enjoy this soft repose, after all my fatigues in search of happiness. Suffer me to satiate myself with these delicacies, after the pains of so long and so foolish an abstinence.

But it will not do. The roses have lost their hue, the fruit its flavour, and that delicious wine, whose fumes so late intoxicated all my senses with such delight, now solicits in vain the sated palate. *Pleasure* smiles at my languor. She beckons her sister, *Virtue*, to come to her assistance. The gay, the frolic *Virtue*, observes the call, and brings along the whole troop of my jovial friends. Welcome, thrice welcome, my ever dear companions, to these shady bowers, and to this luxurious repast. Your presence has restored to the rose its hue, and to the fruit its flavour. The vapours of this sprightly nectar now again ply round my heart; while you partake of my delights, and discover, in your cheerful looks, the pleasure which you receive from my happiness and satisfaction. The like do I receive from yours; and, encouraged by your joyous presence, shall again renew the feast, with which, from too much enjoyment, my senses are well-nigh sated, while the mind kept not pace with the body, nor afforded relief to her overburdened partner.

In our cheerful discourses, better than in the formal reasoning of the schools, is true wisdom to be found. In our friendly endearments, better than in the hollow debates of statesmen and pretended patriots, does true virtue display itself. Forgetful of the past, secure of the future, let us here enjoy the present; and while we yet possess a being, let us fix some good, beyond the power of fate or fortune. To-morrow will bring its own pleasures along with it: or, should it disappoint our fond wishes, we shall at least enjoy the pleasure of reflecting on the pleasures of to-day.

Fear not, my friends, that the barbarous dissonance of BACCHUS and of his revellers should break in upon this entertainment, and confound us with their turbulent and clamorous pleasures. The sprightly muses wait around, and, with their charming symphony, sufficient to soften the wolves and tigers of the savage desert, inspire a soft joy into every bosom. Peace, harmony, and concord, reign in this retreat; nor is the silence ever broken but by the music of our songs, or the cheerful accents of our friendly voices.

But hark! the favourite of the muses, the gentle DAMON* strikes the lyre; and, while he accompanies its harmonious notes with his more harmonious song, he inspires us with the same happy debauch of fancy by which he is himself transported. 'Ye happy youth,' he sings, 'Ye favoured of Heaven,† while the wanton spring pours upon you all her blooming honours, let not *glory* seduce you with her delusive blaze, to pass in perils and dangers this delicious season, this prime of life. Wisdom points out to you the road to pleasure: Nature, too, beckons you to follow her in that smooth and flowery path. Will you shut your ears to their commanding voice? Will you harden your heart to their soft allurements? Oh, deluded mortals, thus to lose your youth, thus to throw away so invaluable a present, to trifle with so perishing a blessing. Contemplate well your recompense. Consider that glory, which so allures your proud hearts, and seduces you with your own praises. It is an echo, a dream, nay the shadow of a dream, dissipated by every wind, and lost by every contrary breath of the ignorant and ill-judging multitude. You fear not that even death itself shall ravish it from you. But behold! while you are yet alive, calumny bereaves you of it; ignorance neglects it; nature enjoys it not; fancy alone, renouncing every pleasure, receives this airy recompense, empty and unstable as herself.'

Thus the hours pass unperceived along, and lead in their wanton train all the pleasures of sense, and all the joys

of harmony and friendship. Smiling *innocence* closes the
procession; and, while she presents herself to our ravished
eyes, she embellishes the whole scene, and renders the view
of these pleasures as transporting after they have passed
us, as when, with laughing countenances, they were yet
advancing towards us.

But the sun has sunk below the horizon; and darkness,
stealing silently upon us, has now buried all nature in an
universal shade. 'Rejoice, my friends, continue your repast,
or change it for soft repose. Though absent, your joy or
your tranquillity shall still be mine.' *But whither do you go?*
Or what new pleasures call you from our society? Is there
aught agreeable without your friends? And can aught please
in which we partake not? 'Yes, my friends, the joy which I
now seek admits not of your participation. Here alone I
wish your absence; and here alone can I find a sufficient
compensation for the loss of your society.'

But I have not advanced far through the shades of the
thick wood, which spreads a double night around me,
ere, methinks, I perceive through the gloom the charming
CAELIA, the mistress of my wishes, who wanders impatient
through the grove, and, preventing the appointed hour,
silently chides my tardy steps. But the joy which she receives
from my presence best pleads my excuse, and, dissipating
every anxious and every angry thought, leaves room for
nought but mutual joy and rapture. With what words, my
fair one, shall I express my tenderness, or describe the
emotions which now warm my transported bosom! Words
are too faint to describe my love; and if, alas! you feel not
the same flame within you, in vain shall I endeavour to
convey to you a just conception of it. But your every word
and every motion suffice to remove this doubt; and while
they express your passion, serve also to inflame mine. How
amiable this solitude, this silence, this darkness! No objects
now importune the ravished soul. The thought, the sense,
all full of nothing but our mutual happiness, wholly possess
the mind, and convey a pleasure which deluded mortals
vainly seek for in every other enjoyment.

But why does your bosom heave with these sighs, while

tears bathe your glowing cheeks? Why distract your heart
with such vain anxieties? Why so often ask me, *How long
my love shall yet endure*? Alas, my CAELIA, can I resolve this
question? *Do I know how long my life shall yet endure*? But
does this also disturb your tender breast? And is the image
of our frail mortality for ever present with you, to throw a
damp on your gayest hours, and poison even those joys
which love inspires! Consider rather, that if life be frail, if
youth be transitory, we should well employ the present
moment, and lose no part of so perishable an existence. Yet
a little moment, and *these* shall be no more. We shall be as
if we had never been. Not a memory of us be left upon
earth; and even the fabulous shades below will not afford us
a habitation. Our fruitless anxieties, our vain projects, our
uncertain speculations, shall all be swallowed up and lost.
Our present doubts, concerning the original cause of all
things, must never, alas! be resolved. This alone we may be
certain of, that if any governing mind preside, he must be
pleased to see us fulfil the ends of our being, and enjoy that
pleasure for which alone we were created. Let this reflection
give ease to your anxious thoughts; but render not your
joys too serious, by dwelling for ever upon it. It is sufficient
once to be acquainted with this philosophy, in order to give
an unbounded loose to love and jollity, and remove all
the scruples of a vain superstition: but while youth and
passion, my fair one, prompt our eager desires, we must
find gayer subjects of discourse to intermix with these
amorous caresses.

THE STOIC†

THERE is this obvious and material difference in the conduct of nature, with regard to man and other animals, that,
having endowed the former with a sublime celestial spirit,
and having given him an affinity with superior beings, she
allows not such noble faculties to lie lethargic or idle, but
urges him by necessity to employ, on every emergence, his

utmost *art* and *industry*. Brute creatures have many of their necessities supplied by nature, being clothed and armed by this beneficent parent of all things: and where their own *industry* is requisite on any occasion, nature, by implanting instincts, still supplies them with the *art*, and guides them to their good by her unerring precepts. But man, exposed naked and indigent to the rude elements, rises slowly from that helpless state by the care and vigilance of his parents; and, having attained his utmost growth and perfection, reaches only a capacity of subsisting by his own care and vigilance. Every thing is sold to skill and labour; and where nature furnishes the materials, they are still rude and unfinished, till industry, ever active and intelligent, refines them from their brute state, and fits them for human use and convenience.

Acknowledge, therefore, O man, the beneficence of nature; for she has given thee that intelligence which supplies all thy necessities. But let not indolence, under the false appearance of gratitude, persuade thee to rest contented with her presents. Wouldst thou return to the raw herbage for thy food, to the open sky for thy covering, and to stones and clubs for thy defence against the ravenous animals of the desert? Then return also to thy savage manners, to thy timorous superstition, to thy brutal ignorance, and sink thyself below those animals whose condition thou admirest and wouldst so fondly imitate.

Thy kind parent, nature, having given thee art and intelligence, has filled the whole globe with materials to employ these talents. Hearken to her voice, which so plainly tells thee, that thou, thyself, shouldst also be the object of thy industry, and that by art and attention alone thou canst acquire that ability which will raise thee to thy proper station in the universe. Behold this artisan who converts a rude and shapeless stone into a noble metal; and, moulding that metal by his cunning hands, creates, as it were, by magic, every weapon for his defence, and every utensil for his convenience. He has not this skill from nature: use and practice have taught it him; and if thou wouldst emulate his success, thou must follow his laborious footsteps.

But while thou *ambitiously* aspirest to perfecting thy bodily powers and faculties, wouldst thou *meanly* neglect thy mind, and, from a preposterous sloth, leave it still rude and uncultivated, as it came from the hands of nature? Far be such folly and negligence from every rational being. If nature has been frugal in her gifts and endowments, there is the more need of art to supply her defects. If she has been generous and liberal, know that she still expects industry and application on our part, and revenges herself in proportion to our negligent ingratitude. The richest genius, like the most fertile soil, when uncultivated, shoots up into the rankest weeds; and instead of vines and olives for the pleasure and use of man, produces, to its slothful owner, the most abundant crop of poisons.

The great end of all human industry, is the attainment of happiness. For this were arts invented, sciences cultivated, laws ordained, and societies modelled, by the most profound wisdom of patriots and legislators. Even the lonely savage, who lies exposed to the inclemency of the elements and the fury of wild beasts, forgets not, for a moment, this grand object of his being. Ignorant as he is of every art of life, he still keeps in view the end of all those arts, and eagerly seeks for felicity amidst that darkness with which he is environed. But as much as the wildest savage is inferior to the polished citizen, who, under the protection of laws, enjoys every convenience which industry has invented, so much is this citizen himself inferior to the man of virtue, and the true philosopher, who governs his appetites, subdues his passions, and has learned, from reason, to set a just value on every pursuit and enjoyment. For is there an art and apprenticeship necessary for every other attainment? And is there no art of life, no rule, no precepts, to direct us in this principal concern? Can no particular pleasure be attained without skill; and can the whole be regulated, without reflection or intelligence, by the blind guidance of appetite and instinct? Sure then no mistakes are ever committed in this affair; but every man, however dissolute and negligent, proceeds in the pursuit of happiness with as unerring a motion as that which the celestial bodies observe, when, conducted by the hand of the Almighty, they roll along the ethereal plains. But if mistakes be often, be inevitably committed, let us register these mistakes; let us consider their causes; let us weigh their importance; let us inquire for their remedies. When from this we have fixed all the rules of conduct, we are *philosophers*. When we have reduced these rules to practice, we are *sages*.

Like many subordinate artists, employed to form the several wheels and springs of a machine, such are those who excel in all the particular arts of life. *He* is the master workman who puts those several parts together, moves them according to just harmony and proportion, and produces true felicity as the result of their conspiring order.

While thou hast such an alluring object in view, shall that labour and attention, requisite to the attainment of thy end, ever seem burdensome and intolerable? Know, that this labour itself is the chief ingredient of the felicity to which thou aspirest, and that every enjoyment soon becomes insipid and distasteful, when not acquired by fatigue and industry. See the hardy hunters rise from their downy couches, shake off the slumbers which still weigh down their heavy eyelids, and, ere *Aurora* has yet covered the heavens with her flaming mantle, hasten to the forest. They leave behind, in their own houses, and in the neighbouring plains, animals of every kind, whose flesh furnishes the most delicious fare, and which offer themselves to the fatal stroke. Laborious man disdains so easy a purchase. He seeks for a prey, which hides itself from his search, or flies from his pursuit, or defends itself from his violence. Having exerted in the chase every passion of the mind, and every member of the body, he then finds the charms of repose, and with joy compares his pleasures to those of his engaging labours.

And can vigorous industry give pleasure to the pursuit even of the most worthless prey, which frequently escapes our toils? And cannot the same industry render the cultivating of our mind, the moderating of our passions, the enlightening of our reason, an agreeable occupation; while we are every day sensible of our progress, and behold our inward features and countenance brightening incessantly with new charms? Begin by curing yourself of this lethargic indolence; the task is not difficult: you need but taste the sweets of honest labour. Proceed to learn the just value of every pursuit; long study is not requisite. Compare, though but for once, the mind to the body, virtue to fortune, and glory to pleasure. You will then perceive the advantages of industry; you will then be sensible what are the proper objects of your industry.

In vain do you seek repose from beds of roses: in vain do you hope for enjoyment from the most delicious wines and fruits. Your indolence itself becomes a fatigue; your pleasure itself creates disgust. The mind, unexercised, finds every delight insipid and loathsome; and ere yet the body, full of noxious humours, feels the torment of its multiplied diseases, your nobler part is sensible of the invading poison, and seeks in vain to relieve its anxiety by new pleasures, which still augment the fatal malady.

I need not tell you, that, by this eager pursuit of pleasure, you more and more expose yourself to fortune and accidents, and rivet your affections on external objects, which chance may, in a moment, ravish from you. I shall suppose that your indulgent stars favour you still with the enjoyment of your riches and possessions. I prove to you, that, even in the midst of your luxurious pleasures, you are unhappy; and that, by too much indulgence, you are incapable of enjoying what prosperous fortune still allows you to possess.

But surely the instability of fortune is a consideration not to be overlooked or neglected. Happiness cannot possibly exist where there is no security; and security can have no place where fortune has any dominion. Though that unstable deity should not exert her rage against you, the dread of it would still torment you; would disturb your slumbers, haunt your dreams, and throw a damp on the jollity of your most delicious banquets.

The temple of wisdom is seated on a rock, above the rage

of the fighting elements, and inaccessible to all the malice of man. The rolling thunder breaks below; and those more terrible instruments of human fury reach not to so sublime a height. The sage, while he breathes that serene air, looks down with pleasure, mixed with compassion, on the errors of mistaken mortals, who blindly seek for the true path of life, and pursue riches, nobility, honour, or power, for genuine felicity. The greater part he beholds disappointed of their fond wishes: some lament, that having once possessed the object of their desires, it is ravished from them by envious fortune; and all complain, that even their own vows, though granted, cannot give them happiness, or relieve the anxiety of their distracted minds.

But does the sage always preserve himself in this philosophical indifference, and rest contented with lamenting the miseries of mankind, without ever employing himself for their relief? Does he constantly indulge this severe wisdom, which, by pretending to elevate him above human accidents, does in reality harden his heart, and render him careless of the interests of mankind, and of society? No; he knows that in this sullen *Apathy* neither true wisdom nor true happiness can be found. He feels too strongly the charm of the social affections, ever to counteract so sweet, so natural, so virtuous a propensity. Even when, bathed in tears, he laments the miseries of the human race, of his country, of his friends, and, unable to give succour, can only relieve them by compassion; he yet rejoices in the generous disposition, and feels a satisfaction superior to that of the most indulged sense. So engaging are the sentiments of humanity, that they brighten up the very face of sorrow, and operate like the sun, which, shining on a dusky cloud or falling rain, paints on them the most glorious colours which are to be found in the whole circle of nature.

But it is not here alone that the social virtues display their energy. With whatever ingredients you mix them, they are still predominant. As sorrow cannot overcome them, so neither can sensual pleasure obscure them. The joys of love, however tumultuous, banish not the tender sentiments of sympathy and affection. They even derive their chief influence from that generous passion: and when presented alone, afford nothing to the unhappy mind but lassitude and disgust. Behold this sprightly debauchee, who professes a contempt of all other pleasures but those of wine and jollity: separate him from his companions, like a spark from a fire, where before it contributed to the general blaze: his alacrity suddenly extinguishes; and, though surrounded with every other means of delight, he loathes the sumptuous banquet, and prefers even the most abstracted study and speculation, as more agreeable and entertaining.

But the social passions never afford such transporting pleasures, or make so glorious an appearance in the eyes both of GOD and man, as when, shaking off every earthly mixture, they associate themselves with the sentiments of virtue, and prompt us to laudable and worthy actions. As harmonious colours mutually give and receive a lustre by their friendly union, so do these ennobling sentiments of the human mind. See the triumph of nature in parental affection! What selfish passion, what sensual delight is a match for it, whether a man exults in the prosperity and virtue of his offspring, or flies to their succour through the most threatening and tremendous dangers?

Proceed still in purifying the generous passions, you will still the more admire its shining glories. What charms are there in the harmony of minds, and in a friendship founded on mutual esteem and gratitude! What satisfaction in relieving the distressed, in comforting the afflicted, in raising the fallen, and in stopping the career of cruel fortune, or of more cruel man, in their insults over the good and virtuous! But what supreme joy in the victories over vice as well as misery, when, by virtuous example or wise exhortation, our fellow-creatures are taught to govern their passions, reform their vices, and subdue their worst enemies, which inhabit within their own bosoms?

But these objects are still too limited for the human mind, which, being of celestial origin, swells with the divinest and most enlarged affections, and, carrying its attention beyond kindred and acquaintance, extends its benevolent wishes to the most distant posterity. It views liberty and laws as the source of human happiness, and devotes itself, with the utmost alacrity, to their guardianship and protection. Toils, dangers, death itself, carry their charms, when we brave them for the public good, and ennoble that being which we generously sacrifice for the interests of our country. Happy the man whom indulgent fortune allows to pay to virtue what he owes to nature, and to make a generous gift of what must otherwise be ravished from him by cruel necessity!

In the true sage and patriot are united whatever can distinguish human nature, or elevate mortal man to a resemblance with the divinity. The softest benevolence, the most undaunted resolution, the tenderest sentiments, the most sublime love of virtue, all these animate successively his transported bosom. What satisfaction, when he looks within, to find the most turbulent passions tuned to just harmony and concord, and every jarring sound banished from this enchanting music! If the contemplation, even of inanimate beauty, is so delightful; if it ravishes the senses, even when the fair form is foreign to us; what must be the effects of moral beauty? and what influence must it have, when it embellishes our own mind, and is the result of our own reflection and industry?

But where is the reward of virtue? And what recompense has nature provided for such important sacrifices as those of life and fortune, which we must often make to it? Oh, sons of earth! Are ye ignorant of the value of this celestial mistress? And do ye meanly inquire for her portion, when ye observe her genuine charms? But know, that Nature has been indulgent to human weakness, and has not left this favourite child naked and unendowed. She has provided virtue with the richest dowry; but being careful lest the allurements of interest should engage such suitors as were insensible of the native worth of so divine a beauty, she has wisely provided, that this dowry can have no charms but in the eyes of those who are already transported with the love of virtue. GLORY is the portion of virtue, the sweet reward of honourable toils, the triumphant crown which covers the thoughtful head of the disinterested patriot, or the dusty brow of the victorious warrior. Elevated by so sublime a prize, the man of virtue looks down with contempt on all the allurements of pleasure, and all the menaces of danger. Death itself loses its terrors, when he considers, that its dominion extends only over a part of him, and that, in spite of death and time, the rage of the elements, and the endless vicissitude of human affairs, he is assured of an immortal fame among all the sons of men.

There surely is a being who presides over the universe, and who, with infinite wisdom and power, has reduced the jarring elements into just order and proportion. Let the speculative reasoners dispute, how far this beneficent being extends his care, and whether he prolongs our existence beyond the grave, in order to bestow on virtue its just reward, and render it fully triumphant. The man of morals, without deciding any thing on so dubious a subject, is satisfied with the portion marked out to him by the supreme disposer of all things. Gratefully he accepts of that further reward . prepared for him; but if disappointed, he thinks not virtue an empty name; but, justly esteeming it his own reward, he gratefully acknowledges the bounty of his creator, who, by calling him into existence, has thereby afforded him an opportunity of once acquiring so invaluable a possession.

THE PLATONIST[†]

To some philosophers it appears matter of surprise, that all mankind, possessing the same nature, and being endowed with the same faculties, should yet differ so widely in their pursuits and inclinations, and that one should utterly condemn what is fondly sought after by another. To some it appears matter of still more surprise, that a man should differ so widely from himself at different times; and, after possession, reject with disdain what before was the object of all his vows and wishes. To me this feverish uncertainty and irresolution, in human conduct, seems altogether unavoidable; nor can a rational soul, made for the contemplation of the Supreme Being, and of his works, ever enjoy tranquillity or satisfaction, while detained in the ignoble pursuits of sensual pleasure or popular applause. The divinity is a boundless ocean of bliss and glory: human minds are smaller streams, which, arising at first from this ocean, seek still, amid all their wanderings, to return to it, and to lose themselves in that immensity of perfection. When checked in this natural course by vice or folly, they become furious and enraged; and, swelling to a torrent, do then spread horror and devastation on the neighbouring plains.

In vain, by pompous phrase and passionate expression, each recommends his own pursuit, and invites the credulous hearers to an imitation of his life and manners. The heart belies the countenance, and sensibly feels, even amid the highest success, the unsatisfactory nature of all those pleasures which detain it from its true object. I examine the voluptuous man before enjoyment; I measure the vehemence of his desire, and the importance of his object; I find that all his happiness proceeds only from that hurry of thought, which takes him from himself, and turns his view from his guilt and misery. I consider him a moment after; he has now enjoyed the pleasure which he fondly sought after. The sense of his guilt and misery returns upon him with double anguish: his mind tormented with fear and remorse; his body depressed with disgust and satiety.

But a more august, at least a more haughty personage, presents himself boldly to our censure; and, assuming the title of a philosopher and man of morals, offers to submit to the most rigid examination. He challenges with a visible, though concealed impatience, our approbation and applause; and seems offended, that we should hesitate a moment before we break out into admiration of his virtue. Seeing this impatience, I hesitate still more; I begin to examine the motives of his seeming virtue: but, behold! ere I can enter upon this inquiry, he flings himself from me; and, addressing his discourse to that crowd of heedless auditors, fondly amuses them by his magnificent pretensions.

O philosopher! thy wisdom is vain, and thy virtue unprofitable. Thou seekest the ignorant applauses of men, not the solid reflections of thy own conscience, or the more solid approbation of that being, who, with one regard of his all-seeing eye, penetrates the universe. Thou surely art conscious of the hollowness of thy pretended probity; whilst calling thyself a citizen, a son, a friend, thou forgettest thy higher sovereign, thy true father, thy greatest benefactor. Where is the adoration due to infinite perfection, whence every thing good and valuable is derived? Where is the gratitude owing to thy creator, who called thee forth from nothing, who placed thee in all these relations to thy fellow-creatures, and, requiring thee to fulfil the duty of each relation, forbids thee to neglect what thou owest to himself, the most perfect being, to whom thou art connected by the closest tie?

But thou art thyself thy own idol. Thou worshippest thy *imaginary* perfections; or rather, sensible of thy *real* imperfections, thou seekest only to deceive the world, and to please thy fancy, by multiplying thy ignorant admirers. Thus, not content with neglecting what is most excellent in the universe, thou desirest to substitute in his place what is most vile and contemptible.

Consider all the works of men's hands, all the inventions of human wit, in which thou affectest so nice a discernment. Thou wilt find, that the most perfect production still proceeds from the most perfect thought, and that it is MIND alone which we admire, while we bestow our applause on the graces of a well-proportioned statue, or the symmetry of a noble pile. The statuary, the architect, come still in view, and makes us reflect on the beauty of his art and contrivance, which, from a heap of unformed matter, could extract such expressions and proportions. This superior beauty of thought and intelligence thou thyself acknowledgest, while thou invitest us to contemplate, in thy conduct, the harmony of affections, the dignity of sentiments, and all those graces of a mind which chiefly merit our attention.

But why stoppest thou short? Seest thou nothing further that is valuable? Amid thy rapturous applauses of beauty and order, art thou still ignorant where is to be found the most consummate beauty, the most perfect order? Compare the works of art with those of nature. The one are but imitations of the other. The nearer art approaches to nature, the more perfect is it esteemed. But still how wide are its nearest approaches, and what an immense interval may be observed between them! Art copies only the outside of nature, leaving the inward and more admirable springs and principles as exceeding her imitation, as beyond her comprehension. Art copies only the minute productions of nature, despairing to reach that grandeur and mag-nificence which are so astonishing in the masterly works of her original. Can we then be so blind as not to discover an intelligence and a design in the exquisite and most stupendous contrivance of the universe? Can we be so stupid as not to feel the warmest raptures of worship and adoration upon the contemplation of that intelligent being, so infinitely good and wise?

The most perfect happiness surely must arise from the contemplation of the most perfect object. But what more perfect than beauty and virtue? And where is beauty to be found equal to that of the universe, or virtue which can be compared to the benevolence and justice of the Deity? If aught can diminish the pleasure of this contemplation, it must be either the narrowness of our faculties, which conceals from us the greatest part of these beauties and perfections, or the shortness of our lives, which allows not time sufficient to instruct us in them. But it is our comfort, that if we employ worthily the faculties here assigned us, they will be enlarged in another state of existence, so as to render us more suitable worshippers of our maker; and that the task, which can never be finished in time, will be the business of an eternity.

I HAVE long entertained a suspicion with regard to the decisions of philosophers upon all subjects, and found in myself a greater inclination to dispute than assent to their conclusions. There is one mistake to which they seem liable, almost without exception; they confine too much their principles, and make no account of that vast variety which nature has so much affected in all her operations. When a philosopher has once laid hold of a favourite principle, which perhaps accounts for many natural effects, he extends the same principle over the whole creation, and reduces to it every phenomenon, though by the most violent and absurd reasoning. Our own mind being narrow and contracted, we cannot extend our conception to the variety and extent of nature, but imagine that she is as much bounded in her operations as we are in our speculation.

But if ever this infirmity of philosophers is to be suspected on any occasion, it is in their reasonings concerning human life, and the methods of attaining happiness. In that case they are led astray, not only by the narrowness of their understandings, but by that also of their passions. Almost every one has a predominant inclination, to which his other desires and affections submit, and which governs him, though perhaps with some intervals, through the whole course of his life. It is difficult for him to apprehend, that any thing which appears totally indifferent to him can ever give enjoyment to any person, or can possess charms which altogether escape his observation. His own pursuits are always, in his account, the most engaging, the objects of his passion the most valuable, and the road which he pursues the only one that leads to happiness.

But would these prejudiced reasoners reflect a moment, there are many obvious instances and arguments sufficient to undeceive them, and make them enlarge their maxims and principles. Do they not see the vast variety of inclinations and pursuits among our species, where each man seems fully satisfied with his own course of life, and would esteem it the greatest unhappiness to be confined to that of his neighbour? Do they not feel in themselves, that what pleases at one time, displeases at another, by the change of inclination, and that it is not in their power, by their utmost efforts, to recall that taste or appetite which formerly bestowed charms on what now appears indifferent or disagreeable? What is the meaning, therefore, of those general preferences of the town or country life, of a life of action or one of pleasure, of retirement or society; when, besides the different inclinations of different men, every one's experience may convince him that each of these kinds of life is agreeable in its turn, and that their variety or their judicious mixture chiefly contributes to the rendering all of them agreeable?

But shall this business be allowed to go altogether at adventures? And must a man only consult his humour and inclination, in order to determine his course of life, without employing his reason to inform him what road is preferable, and leads most surely to happiness? Is there no difference, then, between one man's conduct and another?

I answer, there is a great difference. One man, following his inclination, in choosing his course of life, may employ much surer means for succeeding than another, who is led by his inclination into the same course of life, and pursues the same object. *Are riches the chief object of your desires?* Acquire skill in your profession; be diligent in the exercise of it; enlarge the circle of your friends and acquaintance; avoid pleasure and expense; and never be generous, but with a view of gaining more than you could save by frugality. *Would you acquire the public esteem?* Guard equally against the extremes of arrogance and fawning. Let it appear that you set a value upon yourself, but without despising others. If you fall into either of the extremes, you either provoke men's pride by your insolence, or teach them to despise you by your timorous submission, and by the mean opinion which you seem to entertain of yourself.

These, you say, are the maxims of common prudence and discretion; what every parent inculcates on his child, and what every man of sense pursues in the course of life which he has chosen. What is it then you desire more? Do you come to a philosopher as to a *cunning man*, to learn something by magic or witchcraft, beyond what can be known by common prudence and discretion?—Yes; we come to a philosopher to be instructed, how we shall choose our ends, more than the means for attaining these ends: we want to know what desire we shall gratify, what passion we shall comply with, what appetite we shall indulge. As to the rest, we trust to common sense, and the general maxims of the world, for our instruction.

I am sorry, then, I have pretended to be a philosopher; for I find your questions very perplexing, and am in danger, if my answer be too rigid and severe, of passing for a pedant and scholastic; if it be too easy and free, of being taken for a preacher of vice and immorality. However, to satisfy you, I shall deliver my opinion upon the matter, and shall only desire you to esteem it of as little consequence as I do myself. By that means you will neither think it worthy of your ridicule nor your anger.

If we can depend upon any principle which we learn from philosophy, this, I think, may be considered as certain and undoubted, that there is nothing, in itself, valuable or despicable, desirable or hateful, beautiful or deformed; but that these attributes arise from the particular constitution and fabric of human sentiment and affection. What seems the most delicious food to one animal, appears loathsome to another; what affects the feeling of one with delight, produces uneasiness in another. This is confessedly the case with regard to all the bodily senses. But, if we examine the matter more accurately, we shall find that the same observation holds even where the mind concurs with the body, and mingles its sentiment with the exterior appetite.

Desire this passionate lover to give you a character of his mistress: he will tell you, that he is at a loss for words to describe her charms, and will ask you very seriously, if ever you were acquainted with a goddess or an angel? If you answer that you never were, he will then say that it is impossible for you to form a conception of such divine beauties as those which his charmer possesses; so complete a shape; such well-proportioned features; so engaging an air; such sweetness of disposition; such gaiety of humour.

You can infer nothing, however, from all this discourse, but that the poor man is in love; and that the general appetite between the sexes, which nature has infused into all animals, is in him determined to a particular object by some qualities which give him pleasure. The same divine creature, not only to a different animal, but also to a different man, appears a mere mortal being, and is beheld with the utmost indifference.

Nature has given all animals a like prejudice in favour of their offspring. As soon as the helpless infant sees the light, though in every other eye it appears a despicable and a miserable creature, it is regarded by its fond parent with the utmost affection, and is preferred to every other object, however perfect and accomplished. The passion alone, arising from the original structure and formation of human nature, bestows a value on the most insignificant object.

We may push the same observation further, and may conclude that, even when the mind operates alone, and feeling the sentiment of blame or approbation, pronounces one object deformed and odious, another beautiful and amiable; I say that, even in this case, those qualities are not really in the objects, but belong entirely to the sentiment of that mind which blames or praises. I grant, that it will be more difficult to make this proposition evident, and, as it were, palpable, to negligent thinkers; because nature is more uniform in the sentiments of the mind than in most feelings of the body, and produces a nearer resemblance in the inward than in the outward part of human kind. There is something approaching to principles in mental taste; and critics can reason and dispute more plausibly than cooks or perfumers. We may observe, however, that this uniformity among human kind hinders not, but that there is a considerable diversity in the sentiments of beauty and worth, and that education, custom, prejudice, caprice, and humour, frequently vary our taste of this kind. You will never convince a man, who is not accustomed to ITALIAN music, and has not an ear to follow its intricacies, that a SCOTCH tune is not preferable. You have not even any single argument beyond your own taste, which you can employ in your behalf: and to your antagonist his particular taste will always appear a more convincing argument to the contrary. If you be wise, each of you will allow that the other may be in the right; and having many other instances of this diversity of taste, you will both confess, that beauty and worth are merely of a relative nature, and consist in an agreeable sentiment, produced by an object in a particular mind, according to the peculiar structure and constitution of that mind.

By this diversity of sentiment, observable in human kind, nature has, perhaps, intended to make us sensible of her authority, and let us see what surprising changes she could produce on the passions and desires of mankind, merely by the change of their inward fabric, without any alteration on the objects. The vulgar may even be convinced by this argument. But men, accustomed to thinking, may draw a more convincing, at least a more general argument, from the very nature of the subject.

In the operation of reasoning, the mind does nothing but run over its objects, as they are supposed to stand in reality, without adding any thing to them, or diminishing any thing from them. If I examine the PTOLEMAIC and COPERNICAN systems,* I endeavour only, by my inquiries, to know the real situation of the planets; that is, in other words, I endeavour to give them, in my conception, the same relations that they bear towards each other in the heavens. To this operation of the mind, therefore, there seems to be always a real, though often an unknown standard, in the nature of things; nor is truth or falsehood variable by the various apprehensions of mankind. Though all the human race should for ever conclude that the sun moves, and the earth remains at rest, the sun stirs not an inch from his place for all these reasonings; and such conclusions are eternally false and erroneous.

But the case is not the same with the qualities of *beautiful and deformed, desirable and odious*, as with truth and falsehood. In the former case, the mind is not content with merely surveying its objects, as they stand in themselves: it also feels a sentiment of delight or uneasiness, approbation or blame, consequent to that survey; and this sentiment determines it to affix the epithet *beautiful or deformed, desirable or odious*. Now, it is evident, that this sentiment must depend upon the particular fabric or structure of the mind, which enables such particular forms to operate in such a particular manner, and produces a sympathy or conformity between the mind and its objects. Vary the structure of the mind or inward organs, the sentiment no longer follows, though the form remains the same. The sentiment being different from the object, and arising from its operation upon the organs of the mind, an alteration upon the latter must vary the effect; nor can the same object, presented to a mind totally different, produce the same sentiment.

This conclusion every one is apt to draw of himself, without much philosophy, where the sentiment is evidently distinguishable from the object. Who is not sensible that power, and glory, and vengeance, are not desirable of themselves, but derive all their value from the structure of human passions, which begets a desire towards such particular pursuits? But with regard to beauty, either natural or moral, the case is commonly supposed to be different. The agreeable quality is thought to lie in the object, not in the sentiment; and that merely because the sentiment is not so turbulent and violent as to distinguish itself, in an evident manner, from the perception of the object.

But a little reflection suffices to distinguish them. A man may know exactly all the circles and ellipses of the COPERNICAN system, and all the irregular spirals of the PTOLEMAIC, without perceiving that the former is more beautiful than the latter. EUCLID has fully explained every quality of the circle, but has not, in any proposition, said a word of its beauty. The reason is evident. Beauty is not a quality of the circle. It lies not in any part of the line, *whose* parts are all equally distant from a common centre. It is only the effect, which that figure produces upon a mind, whose particular fabric or structure renders it susceptible of such sentiments. In vain would you look for it in the circle, or seek it, either by your senses, or by mathematical reasonings, in all the properties of that figure.

The mathematician, who took no other pleasure in reading VIRGIL, but that of examining AENEAS'S voyage by the map, might perfectly understand the meaning of every Latin word employed by that divine author; and, consequently, might have a distinct idea of the whole narration. He would even have a more distinct idea of it, than they could attain who had not studied so exactly the geography of the poem. He knew, therefore, every thing in the poem: but he was ignorant of its beauty, because the beauty, properly speaking, lies not in the poem, but in the sentiment or taste of the reader. And where a man has no such delicacy of temper as to make him feel this sentiment, he must be ignorant of the beauty, though possessed of the science and understanding of an angel.†

The inference upon the whole is, that it is not from the value or worth of the object which any person pursues, that we can determine his enjoyment, but merely from the passion with which he pursues it, and the success which he meets with in his pursuit. Objects have absolutely no worth or value in themselves. They derive their worth merely from the passion. If that be strong and steady, and successful, the person is happy. It cannot reasonably be doubted, but a little miss, dressed in a new gown for a dancing-school ball, receives as complete enjoyment as the greatest orator, who triumphs in the splendour of his eloquence, while he governs the passions and resolutions of a numerous assembly.

All the difference, therefore, between one man and another, with regard to life, consists either in the *passion*, or in the *enjoyment*: and these differences are sufficient to produce the wide extremes of happiness and misery.

To be happy, the *passion* must neither be too violent, nor too remiss. In the first case, the mind is in a perpetual hurry and tumult; in the second, it sinks into a disagreeable indolence and lethargy.

To be happy, the passion must be benign and social, not rough or fierce. The affections of the latter kind are not near so agreeable to the feeling as those of the former. Who will compare rancour and animosity, envy and revenge, to friendship, benignity, clemency, and gratitude?

To be happy, the passion must be cheerful and gay, not gloomy and melancholy. A propensity to hope and joy is real riches; one to fear and sorrow, real poverty.

Some passions or inclinations, in the *enjoyment* of their object, are not so steady or constant as others, nor convey such durable pleasure and satisfaction. *Philosophical devotion*, for instance, like the enthusiasm of a poet, is the transitory effect of high spirits, great leisure, a fine genius, and a habit of study and contemplation: but notwithstanding all these circumstances, an abstract, invisible object, like that which *natural* religion alone presents to us, cannot long actuate the mind, or be of any moment in life. To render the passion of continuance, we must find some method of affecting the senses and imagination, and must embrace some *historical* as well as *philosophical* account of the Divinity. Popular superstitions and observances are even found to be of use in this particular.

Though the tempers of men be very different, yet we may safely pronounce in general, that a life of pleasure cannot support itself so long as one of business, but is much more subject to satiety and disgust. The amusements which are the most durable, have all a mixture of application and attention in them; such as gaming and hunting. And in general, business and action fill up all the great vacancies in human life.

But where the temper is the best disposed for any *enjoyment*, the object is often wanting: and in this respect, the passions, which pursue external objects, contribute not so much to happiness as those which rest in ourselves; since we are neither so certain of attaining such objects, nor so secure in possessing them. A passion for learning is preferable, with regard to happiness, to one for riches.

Some men are possessed of great strength of mind; and even when they pursue *external* objects, are not much affected by a disappointment, but renew their application and industry with the greatest cheerfulness. Nothing contributes more to happiness than such a turn of mind.

According to this short and imperfect sketch of human life, the happiest disposition of mind is the *virtuous*; or, in other words, that which leads to action and employment, renders us sensible to the social passions, steels the heart against the assaults of fortune, reduces the affections to a just moderation, makes our own thoughts an entertainment to us, and inclines us rather to the pleasures of society and conversation than to those of the senses. This, in the mean time, must be obvious to the most careless reasoner, that all dispositions of mind are not alike favourable to happiness, and that one passion or humour may be extremely desirable, while another is equally disagreeable. And, indeed, all the difference between the conditions of life depends upon the mind; nor is there any one situation of affairs, in itself, preferable to another. Good and ill, both natural and moral, are entirely relative to human sentiment and affection. No man would ever be unhappy, could he alter his feelings. PROTEUS-like,* he would elude all attacks, by the continual alterations of his shape and form.

But of this resource nature has, in a great measure, deprived us. The fabric and constitution of our mind no more depends on our choice, than that of our body. The generality of men have not even the smallest notion that any alteration in this respect can ever be desirable. As a stream necessarily follows the several inclinations of the ground on which it runs, so are the ignorant and thoughtless part of mankind actuated by their natural propensities. Such are effectually excluded from all pretensions to philosophy, and the *medicine of the mind*, so much boasted. But even upon the wise and thoughtful, nature has a prodigious influence; nor is it always in a man's power, by the utmost art and industry, to correct his temper, and attain that virtuous character to which he aspires. The empire of philosophy extends over a few; and with regard to these, too, her authority is very weak and limited. Men may well be sensible of the value of virtue, and may desire to attain it; but it is not always certain that they will be successful in their wishes.

Whoever considers, without prejudice, the course of human actions, will find, that mankind are almost entirely guided by constitution and temper, and that general maxims have little influence, but so far as they affect our taste or sentiment. If a man have a lively sense of honour and virtue, with moderate passions, his conduct will always be conformable to the rules of morality: or if he depart from them, his return will be easy and expeditious. On the other hand, where one is born of so perverse a frame of mind, of so callous and insensible a disposition, as to have no relish for virtue and humanity, no sympathy with his fellow-creatures, no desire of esteem and applause, such a one must be allowed entirely incurable; nor is there any remedy in philosophy. He reaps no satisfaction but from low and sensual objects, or from the indulgence of malignant passions: he feels no remorse to control his vicious inclinations: he has not even that sense or taste, which is requisite to make him desire a better character. For my part, I know not how I should address myself to such a one, or by what arguments I should endeavour to reform him. Should I tell him of the inward satisfaction which results from laudable and humane actions, and delicate pleasure of disinterested love and friendship, the lasting enjoyments of a good name and an established character, he might still reply, that these were, perhaps, pleasures to such as were susceptible of them; but that, for his part, he finds himself of a quite different turn and disposition. I must repeat it, my philosophy affords no remedy in such a case; nor could I do any thing but lament this person's unhappy condition. But then I ask, If any other philosophy can afford a remedy; or if it be possible, by any system, to render all mankind virtuous, however perverse may be their natural frame of mind? Experience will soon convince us of the contrary; and I will venture to affirm, that, perhaps, the chief benefit which results from philosophy, arises in an indirect manner, and proceeds more from its secret insensible influence, than from its immediate application.

It is certain, that a serious attention to the sciences and liberal arts softens and humanizes the temper, and cherishes those fine emotions, in which true virtue and honour consists. It rarely, very rarely happens, that a man of taste and learning is not, as least, an honest man, whatever frailties may attend him. The bent of his mind to speculative studies must mortify in him the passions of interest and ambition, and must, at the same time, give him a greater sensibility of all the decencies and duties of life. He feels more fully a moral distinction in characters and manners; nor is his sense of this kind diminished, but, on the contrary, it is much increased, by speculation.

Besides such insensible changes upon the temper and disposition, it is highly probable, that others may be produced by study and application. The prodigious effects of education may convince us, that the mind is not altogether stubborn and inflexible, but will admit of many alterations from its original make and structure. Let a man propose to himself the model of a character which he approves: let him be well acquainted with those particulars in which his own character deviates from this model: let him keep a constant watch over himself, and bend his mind, by a continual effort, from the vices, towards the virtues; and I doubt not but, in time, he will find, in his temper, an alteration for the better.

Habit is another powerful means of reforming the mind, and implanting in it good dispositions and inclinations. A man, who continues in a course of sobriety and temperance, will hate riot and disorder: if he engage in business or study, indolence will seem a punishment to him: if he constrain himself to practise beneficence and affability, he will soon abhor all instances of pride and violence. Where one is thoroughly convinced that the virtuous course of life is preferable; if he have but resolution enough, for some time, to impose a violence on himself; his reformation needs not be despaired of. The misfortune is, that this conviction and this resolution never can have place, unless a man be, beforehand, tolerably virtuous.

Here then is the chief triumph of art and philosophy: it insensibly refines the temper, and it points out to us those dispositions which we should endeavour to attain, by a constant *bent* of mind, and by repeated *habit*. Beyond this I cannot acknowledge it to have great influence; and I must entertain doubts concerning all those exhortations and consolations, which are in such vogue among speculative reasoners.

We have already observed, that no objects are, in themselves, desirable or odious, valuable or despicable; but that objects acquire these qualities from the particular character and constitution of the mind which surveys them. To diminish, therefore, or augment any person's value for an object, to excite or moderate his passions, there are no direct arguments or reasons, which can be employed with any force or influence. The catching of flies, like DOMITIAN, if it give more pleasure, is preferable to the hunting of wild beasts, like WILLIAM RUFUS, or conquering of kingdoms like ALEXANDER.*

But though the value of every object can be determined only by the sentiment or passion of every individual, we may observe, that the passion, in pronouncing its verdict, considers not the object simply, as it is in itself, but surveys it with all the circumstances which attend it. A man, transported with joy on account of his possessing a diamond, confines not his view to the glittering stone before him. He also considers its rarity; and thence chiefly arises his pleasure and exultation. Here, therefore, a philosopher may step in, and suggest particular views, and considerations, and circumstances, which otherwise would have escaped us, and by that means he may either moderate or excite any particular passion.

It may seem unreasonable absolutely to deny the authority of philosophy in this respect: but it must be confessed, that there lies this strong presumption against it, that, if these views be natural and obvious, they would have occurred of themselves without the assistance of philosophy: if they be not natural, they never can have any influence on the affections. *These* are of a very delicate nature, and cannot be forced or constrained by the utmost art or industry. A consideration which we seek for on purpose, which we enter into with difficulty, which we cannot retain without care and attention, will never produce those genuine and durable movements of passion which are the result of nature, and the constitution of the mind. A man may as well pretend to cure himself of love, by viewing his mistress through the *artificial* medium of a microscope or prospect, and beholding there the coarseness of her skin, and monstrous disproportion of her features, as hope to excite or moderate any passion by the *artificial* arguments of a SENECA or an EPICTETUS. The remembrance of the natural aspect and situation of the object will, in both cases, still recur upon him. The reflections of philosophy are too subtile and distant to take place in common life, or eradicate any affection. The air is too fine to breathe in, where it is above the winds and clouds of the atmosphere.

Another defect of those refined reflections which philosophy suggests to us, is, that commonly they cannot diminish or extinguish our vicious passions, without diminishing or extinguishing such as are virtuous, and rendering the mind totally indifferent and inactive. They are, for the most part, general, and are applicable to all our affections. In vain do we hope to direct their influence only to one side. If by incessant study and meditation we have rendered them intimate and present to us, they will operate throughout, and spread an universal insensibility over the mind. When we destroy the nerves, we extinguish the sense of pleasure, together with that of pain, in the human body.

It will be easy, by one glance of the eye, to find one or other of these defects in most of those philosophical reflections, so much celebrated both in ancient and modern times. *Let not the injuries or violence of men*, say the philosophers,[†] *ever discompose you by anger or hatred. Would you be angry at the ape for its malice, or the tiger for its ferocity?* This reflection leads us into a bad opinion of human nature, and must extinguish the social affections. It tends also to prevent all remorse for a man's own crimes, when he considers that vice is as natural to mankind as the particular instincts to brute creatures.

All ills arise from the order of the universe, which is absolutely perfect. Would you wish to disturb so divine an order for the sake of your own particular interest? What if the ills I suffer arise from malice or oppression? *But the vices and imperfections of men are also comprehended in the order of the universe.*

> If plagues and earthquakes break not heaven's design,
> Why then a BORGIA or a CATILINE?[†]

Let this be allowed, and my own vices will also be a part of the same order.

To one who said that none were happy who were not above opinion, a Spartan replied, *Then none are happy but knaves and robbers.*[†]

Man is born to be miserable; and is he surprised at any particular misfortune? And can he give way to sorrow and lamentation upon account of any disaster? Yes: he very reasonably laments that he should be born to be miserable. Your consolation presents a hundred ills for one, of which you pretend to ease him.

You should always have before your eyes death, disease, poverty, blindness, exile, calumny, and infamy, as ills which are incident to human nature. If any one of these ills fall to your lot, you will bear it the better when you have reckoned upon it. I answer, if we confine ourselves to a general and distant reflection on the ills of human life, *that* can have no effect to prepare us for them. If by close and intense meditation we render them present and intimate to us, *that* is the true secret for poisoning all our pleasures, and rendering us perpetually miserable.

Your sorrow is fruitless, and will not change the course of destiny. Very true; and for that very reason I am sorry.

CICERO's consolation for deafness is somewhat curious. *How many languages are there*, says he, *which you do not understand? The* PUNIC, SPANISH, GALLIC, EGYPTIAN, *etc. With regard to all these, you are as if you were deaf, yet you are indifferent about the matter. Is it then so great a misfortune to be deaf to one language more?*[†]

I like better the repartee of ANTIPATER the CYRENAIC, when some women were condoling with him for his blindness: *What!* says he, *Do you think there are no pleasures in the dark?*[*]

Nothing can be more destructive, says FONTENELLE,[*] *to*

ambition, and the passion for conquest, than the true system of astronomy. What a poor thing is even the whole globe in comparison of the infinite extent of nature? This consideration is evidently too distant ever to have any effect; or, if it had any, would it not destroy patriotism as well as ambition? The same gallant author adds, with some reason, that the bright eyes of the ladies are the only objects which lose nothing of their lustre or value from the most extensive views of astronomy, but stand proof against every system. Would philosophers advise us to limit our affection to them?

Exile, says PLUTARCH to a friend in banishment, *is no evil: Mathematicians tell us that the whole earth is but a point, compared to the heavens. To change one's country, then, is little more than to remove from one street to another. Man is not a plant, rooted to a certain spot of earth: all soils and all climates are alike suited to him.*† These topics are admirable, could they fall only into the hands of banished persons. But what if they come also to the knowledge of those who are employed in public affairs, and destroy all their attachment to their native country? Or will they operate like the quack's medicine, which is equally good for a diabetes and a dropsy?

It is certain, were a superior being thrust into a human body, that the whole of life would to him appear so mean, contemptible, and puerile, that he never could be induced to take part in any thing, and would scarcely give attention to what passes around him. To engage him to such a condescension as to play even the part of a PHILIP with zeal and alacrity, would be much more difficult than to constrain the same PHILIP, after having been a king and a conqueror during fifty years, to mend old shoes with proper care and attention, the occupation which LUCIAN assigns him in the infernal regions.* Now, all the same topics of disdain towards human affairs, which could operate on this supposed being, occur also to a philosopher; but being, in some measure, disproportioned to human capacity, and not being fortified by the experience of any thing better, they make not a full impression on him. He sees, but he feels not sufficiently their truth; and is always a sublime philosopher when he needs not; that is, as long as nothing disturbs him, or rouses his affections. While others play, he wonders at their keenness and ardour; but he no sooner puts in his own stake, than he is commonly transported with the same passions that he had so much condemned while he remained a simple spectator.

There are two considerations chiefly to be met with in books of philosophy, from which any important effect is to be expected, and that because these considerations are drawn from common life, and occur upon the most superficial view of human affairs. When we reflect on the shortness and uncertainty of life, how despicable seem all our pursuits of happiness! And even if we would extend our concern beyond our own life, how frivolous appear our most enlarged and most generous projects, when we consider the incessant changes and revolutions of human affairs, by which laws and learning, books and governments, are hurried away by time, as by a rapid stream, and are lost in the immense ocean of matter! Such a reflection certainly tends to mortify all our passions: but does it not thereby counterwork the artifice of nature, who has happily deceived us into an opinion, that human life is of some importance? And may not such a reflection be employed with success by voluptuous reasoners, in order to lead us from the paths of action and virtue, into the flowery fields of indolence and pleasure?

We are informed by THUCYDIDES,* that, during the famous plague of ATHENS, when death seemed present to every one, a dissolute mirth and gaiety prevailed among the people, who exhorted one another to make the most of life as long as it endured. The same observation is made by BOCCACE, with regard to the plague of FLORENCE.* A like principle makes soldiers, during war, be more addicted to riot and expense, than any other race of men. Present pleasure is always of importance; and whatever diminishes the importance of all other objects, must bestow on it an additional influence and value.

The *second* philosophical consideration, which may often

have an influence on the affections, is derived from a comparison of our own condition with the condition of others. This comparison we are continually making even in common life; but the misfortune is, that we are rather apt to compare our situation with that of our superiors, than with that of our inferiors. A philosopher corrects this natural infirmity, by turning his view to the other side, in order to render himself easy in the situation to which fortune has confined him. There are few people who are not susceptible of some consolation from this reflection, though, to a very good-natured man, the view of human miseries should rather produce sorrow than comfort, and add, to his lamentations for his own misfortunes, a deep compassion for those of others. Such is the imperfection, even of the best of these philosophical topics of consolation.[†]

I shall conclude this subject with observing, that, though virtue be undoubtedly the best choice, when it is attainable, yet such is the disorder and confusion of human affairs, that no perfect or regular distribution of happiness and misery is ever in this life to be expected. Not only the goods of fortune, and the endowments of the body (both of which are important), not only these advantages, I say, are unequally divided between the virtuous and vicious, but even the mind itself partakes, in some degree, of this disorder; and the most worthy character, by the very constitution of the passions, enjoys not always the highest felicity.

It is observable, that though every bodily pain proceeds from some disorder in the part or organ, yet the pain is not always proportioned to the disorder, but is greater or less, according to the greater or less sensibility of the part upon which the noxious humours exert their influence. A *toothache* produces more violent convulsions of pain than a *phthisis* or a *dropsy*. In like manner, with regard to the economy of the mind, we may observe, that all vice is indeed pernicious; yet the disturbance or pain is not measured out by nature with exact proportion to the degrees of vice; nor is the man of highest virtue, even abstracting from external accidents, always the most happy. A gloomy and melancholy disposition is certainly, *to our sentiments*, a vice or imperfection;

but as it may be accompanied with great sense of honour and great integrity, it may be found in very worthy characters, though it is sufficient alone to embitter life, and render the person affected with it completely miserable. On the other hand, a selfish villain may possess a spring and alacrity of temper, a certain *gaiety of heart*, which is indeed a good quality, but which is rewarded much beyond its merit, and when attended with good fortune, will compensate for the uneasiness and remorse arising from all the other vices.

I shall add, as an observation to the same purpose, that, if a man be liable to a vice or imperfection, it may often happen, that a good quality, which he possesses along with it, will render him more miserable, than if he were completely vicious. A person of such imbecility of temper, as to be easily broken by affliction, is more unhappy for being endowed with a generous and friendly disposition, which gives him a lively concern for others, and exposes him the more to fortune and accidents. A sense of shame, in an imperfect character, is certainly a virtue; but produces great uneasiness and remorse, from which the abandoned villain is entirely free. A very amorous complexion, with a heart incapable of friendship, is happier than the same excess in love, with a generosity of temper, which transports a man beyond himself, and renders him a total slave to the object of his passion.

In a word, human life is more governed by fortune than by reason; is to be regarded more as a dull pastime than a serious occupation; and is more influenced by particular humour, than by general principles. Shall we engage ourselves in it with passion and anxiety? It is not worthy of so much concern. Shall we be indifferent about what happens? We lose all the pleasure of the game by our phlegm and carelessness. While we are reasoning concerning life, life is gone; and death, though *perhaps* they receive him differently, yet treats alike the fool and the philosopher. To reduce life to exact rule and method is commonly a painful, oft a fruitless occupation: and is it not also a proof, that we overvalue the prize for which we contend? Even to reason so carefully concerning it, and to fix with accuracy its just idea, would be overvaluing it, were it not that, to some tempers, this occupation is one of the most amusing in which life could possibly be employed.

OF NATIONAL CHARACTERS

THE vulgar are apt to carry all *national characters* to extremes; and, having once established it as a principle that any people are knavish, or cowardly, or ignorant, they will admit of no exception, but comprehend every individual under the same censure. Men of sense condemn these undistinguishing judgments; though, at the same time, they allow that each nation has a peculiar set of manners, and that some particular qualities are more frequently to be met with among one people than among their neighbours. The common people in SWITZERLAND have probably more honesty than those of the same rank in IRELAND; and every prudent man will, from that circumstance alone, make a difference in the trust which he reposes in each. We have reason to expect greater wit and gaiety in a FRENCHMAN than in a SPANIARD, though CERVANTES was born in SPAIN. An ENGLISHMAN will naturally be supposed to have more knowledge than a DANE, though TYCHO BRAHE was a native of DENMARK.

Different reasons are assigned for these *national characters*; while some account for them from *moral*, others from *physical* causes. By *moral* causes, I mean all circumstances which are fitted to work on the mind as motives or reasons, and which render a peculiar set of manners habitual to us. Of this kind are, the nature of the government, the revolutions of public affairs, the plenty or penury in which the people live, the situation of the nation with regard to its neighbours, and such like circumstances. By *physical* causes, I mean those qualities of the air and climate which are supposed to work insensibly on the temper, by altering the tone and habit of the body, and giving a particular complexion, which, though reflection and reason may sometimes overcome it, will yet prevail among the generality of mankind, and have an influence on their manners.

That the character of a nation will much depend on *moral* causes, must be evident to the most superficial observer; since a nation is nothing but a collection of individuals, and the manners of individuals are frequently determined by these causes. As poverty and hard labour debase the minds of the common people, and render them unfit for any science and ingenious profession, so, where any government becomes very oppressive to all its subjects, it must have a proportional effect on their temper and genius, and must banish all the liberal arts from among them.

The same principle of moral causes fixes the character of different professions, and alters even that disposition which the particular members receive from the hand of nature. A *soldier* and a *priest* are different characters, in all nations, and all ages; and this difference is founded on circumstances whose operation is eternal and unalterable.

The uncertainty of their life makes soldiers lavish and generous, as well as brave: their idleness, together with the large societies which they form in camps or garrisons, inclines them to pleasure and gallantry: by their frequent change of company, they acquire good breeding and an openness of behaviour: being employed only against a public and an open enemy, they become candid, honest, and undesigning: and as they use more the labour of the body than that of the mind, they are commonly thoughtless and ignorant.[†]

It is a trite, but not altogether a false maxim, that *priests of all religions are the same*; and though the character of the profession will not, in every instance, prevail over the personal character, yet it is sure always to predominate with the greater number. For as chemists observe, that spirits, when raised to a certain height, are all the same, from whatever materials they be extracted; so these men, being elevated above humanity, acquire a uniform character, which is entirely their own, and which, in my opinion, is, generally speaking, not the most amiable that is to be met with in human society. It is, in most points, opposite to that of a soldier; as is the way of life from which it is derived.[†]

As to *physical causes*, I am inclined to doubt altogether of their operation in this particular; nor do I think that men owe any thing of their temper or genius to the air, food, or climate. I confess, that the contrary opinion may justly, at first sight, seem probable; since we find, that these circumstances have an influence over every other animal, and that even those creatures, which are fitted to live in all climates, such as dogs, horses, etc., do not attain the same perfection in all. The courage of bull-dogs and game-cocks seems peculiar to ENGLAND. FLANDERS is remarkable for large and heavy horses: SPAIN for horses light, and of good mettle. And any breed of these creatures, transplanted from one country to another, will soon lose the qualities which they derived from their native climate. It may be asked, why not the same with men?[†]

There are few questions more curious than this, or which will oftener occur in our inquiries concerning human affairs; and therefore it may be proper to give it a full examination.

The human mind is of a very imitative nature; nor is it possible for any set of men to converse often together, without acquiring a similitude of manner, and communicating to each other their vices as well as virtues. The propensity to company and society is strong in all rational creatures; and the same disposition, which gives us this propensity, makes us enter deeply into each other's sentiments, and causes like passions and inclinations to run, as it were, by contagion, through the whole club or knot of companions. Where a number of men are united into one political body, the occasions of their intercourse must be so frequent for defence, commerce, and government, that, together with the same speech or language, they must acquire a resemblance in their manners, and have a common or national character, as well as a personal one, peculiar to each individual. Now, though nature produces all kinds of temper and understanding in great abundance, it does not follow, that she always produces them in like proportions, and that in every society the ingredients of industry and indolence, valour and cowardice, humanity and brutality, wisdom and folly, will be mixed after the same manner. In the infancy of society, if any of these dispositions be found in greater abundance than the rest, it will naturally prevail in the composition, and give a tincture to the national character. Or, should it be asserted that no species of temper can reasonably be presumed to predominate, even in those contracted societies, and that the same proportions will always be preserved in the mixture; yet surely the persons in credit and authority, being still a more contracted body, cannot always be presumed to be of the same character; and their influence on the manners of the people must, at all times, be very considerable. If, on the first establishment of a republic, a BRUTUS* should be placed in authority, and be transported with such an enthusiasm for liberty and public good, as to overlook all the ties of nature, as well as private interest, such an illustrious example will naturally have an effect on the whole society, and kindle the same passion in every bosom. Whatever it be that forms the manners of one generation, the next must imbibe a deeper tincture of the same dye; men being more susceptible of all impressions during infancy, and retaining these impressions as long as they remain in the world. I assert, then, that all national characters, where they depend not on fixed *moral* causes, proceed from such accidents as these, and that physical causes have no discernible operation on the human mind. It is a maxim in all philosophy, that causes which do not appear are to be considered as not existing.

If we run over the globe, or revolve the annals of history, we shall discover everywhere signs of a sympathy or contagion of manners, none of the influence of air or climate.

First, We may observe, that where a very extensive government has been established for many centuries, it spreads a national character over the whole empire, and communicates to every part a similarity of manners. Thus the CHINESE have the greatest uniformity of character imaginable, though the air and climate, in different parts of those vast dominions, admit of very considerable variations.

Secondly, In small governments which are contiguous, the people have, notwithstanding, a different character, and are often as distinguishable in their manners as the most distant nations. ATHENS and THEBES were but a short day's journey from each other, though the ATHENIANS were as remarkable for ingenuity, politeness, and gaiety, as the THEBANS for dulness, rusticity, and a phlegmatic temper. PLUTARCH, discoursing of the effects of air on the minds of men, observes, that the inhabitants of the PIRAEUM* possessed very different tempers from those of the higher town in ATHENS, which was distant about four miles from the former. But I believe no one attributes the difference of manners, in WAPPING and St JAMES's, to a difference of air or climate.

Thirdly, The same national character commonly follows the authority of government to a precise boundary; and upon crossing a river or passing a mountain, one finds a new set of manners, with a new government. The LANGUEDOCIANS and GASCONS are the gayest people in FRANCE; but whenever you pass the PYRENEES, you are among SPANIARDS. Is it conceivable that the qualities of the air should change exactly with the limits of an empire, which depends so much on the accidents of battles, negotiations, and marriages?

Fourthly, Where any set of men, scattered over distant nations, maintain a close society or communication together, they acquire a similitude of manners, and have but little in common with the nations amongst whom they live. Thus the JEWS in EUROPE, and the ARMENIANS in the East, have a peculiar character; and the former are as much noted for fraud as the latter for probity.† The *Jesuits*, in all *Roman catholic* countries, are also observed to have a character peculiar to themselves.

Fifthly, Where any accident, as a difference in language or religion, keeps two nations, inhabiting the same country, from mixing with each other, they will preserve, during several centuries, a distinct and even opposite set of manners. The integrity, gravity, and bravery of the TURKS, form an exact contrast to the deceit, levity, and cowardice of the modern GREEKS.

Sixthly, The same set of manners will follow a nation, and adhere to them over the whole globe, as well as the same laws and language. The SPANISH, ENGLISH, FRENCH, and DUTCH colonies, are all distinguishable even between the tropics.

Seventhly, The manners of a people change very considerably from one age to another, either by great alterations in their government, by the mixtures of new people, or by that inconstancy to which all human affairs are subject. The ingenuity, industry, and activity of the ancient GREEKS, have nothing in common with the stupidity and indolence of the present inhabitants of those regions. Candour, bravery, and love of liberty, formed the character of the ancient ROMANS, as subtilty, cowardice, and a slavish disposition, do that of the modern. The old SPANIARDS were restless, turbulent, and so addicted to war, that many of them killed themselves when deprived of their arms by the ROMANS.[†] One would find an equal difficulty at present (at least one would have found it fifty years ago) to rouse up the modern SPANIARDS to arms. The BATAVIANS were all soldiers of fortune, and hired themselves into the ROMAN armies. Their posterity make use of foreigners for the same purpose that the ROMANS did their ancestors. Though some few strokes of the FRENCH character be the same with that which CAESAR has ascribed to the GAULS; yet what comparison between the civility, humanity, and knowledge of the modern inhabitants of that country, and the ignorance, barbarity, and grossness of the ancient? Not to insist upon the great difference between the present possessors of BRITAIN, and those before the ROMAN conquest, we may observe, that our ancestors, a few centuries ago, were sunk into the most abject superstition. Last century they were inflamed with the most furious enthusiasm, and are now settled into the most cool indifference, with regard to religious matters, that is to be found in any nation of the world.

Eighthly, Where several neighbouring nations have a very close communication together, either by policy, commerce, or travelling, they acquire a similitude of manners, proportioned to the communication. Thus, all the FRANKS appear to have a uniform character to the Eastern nations. The differences among them are like the peculiar accents of different provinces, which are not distinguishable except by an ear accustomed to them, and which commonly escape a foreigner.

Ninthly, We may often remark a wonderful mixture of manners and characters in the same nation, speaking the same language, and subject to the same government: and in this particular the ENGLISH are the most remarkable of any people that perhaps ever were in the world. Nor is this to be ascribed to the mutability and uncertainty of their climate, or to any other *physical* causes, since all these causes take place in the neighbouring country of SCOTLAND, without having the same effect. Where the government of a nation is altogether republican, it is apt to beget a peculiar set of manners. Where it is altogether monarchical, it is more apt to have the same effect; the imitation of superiors spreading the national manners faster among the people. If the governing part of a state consist altogether of merchants, as in HOLLAND, their uniform way of life will fix their character. If it consists chiefly of nobles and landed gentry, like GERMANY, FRANCE, and SPAIN, the same effect follows. The genius of a particular sect or religion is also apt to mould the manners of a people. But the ENGLISH government is a mixture of monarchy, aristocracy, and democracy. The people in authority are composed of gentry and merchants. All sects of religion are to be found among them; and the great liberty and independency which every man enjoys, allows him to display the manners peculiar to him. Hence the ENGLISH, of any people in the universe, have the least of a national character, unless this very singularity may pass for such.

If the characters of men depended on the air and climate, the degrees of heat and cold should naturally be expected to have a mighty influence, since nothing has a greater effect on all plants and irrational animals. And indeed there is some reason to think, that all the nations which live beyond the polar circles or between the tropics, are inferior to the rest of the species, and are incapable of all the higher attainments of the human mind. The poverty and misery of the northern inhabitants of the globe, and the indolence of the southern, from their few necessities, may, perhaps, account for this remarkable difference, without our having recourse to *physical* causes. This, however, is certain, that the characters of nations are very promiscuous in the temperate climates, and that almost all the general observations which have been formed of the more southern or more northern people in these climates, are found to be uncertain and fallacious.[†]

Shall we say, that the neighbourhood of the sun inflames the imagination of men, and gives it a peculiar spirit and vivacity? The FRENCH, GREEKS, EGYPTIANS, and PERSIANS, are remarkable for gaiety; the SPANIARDS, TURKS, and CHINESE, are noted for gravity and a serious deportment, without any such difference of climate as to produce this difference of temper.

The GREEKS and ROMANS, who called all other nations barbarians, confined genius and a fine understanding to the more southern climates, and pronounced the northern nations incapable of all knowledge and civility. But our island has produced as great men, either for action or learning, as GREECE or ITALY has to boast of.

It is pretended, that the sentiments of men become more delicate as the country approaches nearer to the sun; and that the taste of beauty and elegance receives proportional improvements in every latitude, as we may particularly observe of the languages, of which the more southern are smooth and melodious, the northern harsh and untunable. But this observation holds not universally. The ARABIC is uncouth and disagreeable; the MUSCOVITE soft and musical. Energy, strength, and harshness, form the character of the LATIN tongue. The ITALIAN is the most liquid, smooth, and effeminate language that can possibly be imagined. Every language will depend somewhat on the manners of the people; but much more on that original stock of words and sounds which they received from their ancestors, and which remain unchangeable, even while their manners admit of the greatest alterations. Who can doubt, but the ENGLISH

are at present a more polite and knowing people than the
GREEKS were for several ages after the siege of TROY? Yet
there is no comparison between the language of MILTON and
that of HOMER. Nay, the greater are the alterations and
improvements which happen in the manners of a people, the
less can be expected in their language. A few eminent and
refined geniuses will communicate their taste and knowledge
to a whole people, and produce the greatest improvements;
but they fix the tongue by their writings, and prevent, in
some degree, its further changes.

Lord BACON has observed, that the inhabitants of the
south are, in general, more ingenious than those of the
north; but that, where the native of a cold climate has
genius, he rises to a higher pitch than can be reached by the
southern wits. This observation a late† writer confirms,
by comparing the southern wits to cucumbers, which are
commonly all good in their kind, but, at best, are an insipid
fruit; while the northern geniuses are like melons, of which
not one in fifty is good, but when it is so, it has an exquisite
relish. I believe this remark may be allowed just, when
confined to the EUROPEAN nations, and to the present
age, or rather to the preceding one. But I think it may
be accounted for from moral causes. All the sciences and
liberal arts have been imported to us from the south; and it
is easy to imagine, that, in the first order of application,
when excited by emulation and by glory, the few who were
addicted to them would carry them to the greatest height,
and stretch every nerve, and every faculty, to reach the
pinnacle of perfection. Such illustrious examples spread
knowledge everywhere, and begot an universal esteem for
the sciences; after which, it is no wonder that industry
relaxes, while men meet not with suitable encouragement,
nor arrive at such distinction by their attainments. The
universal diffusion of learning among a people, and the
entire banishment of gross ignorance and rusticity, is, therefore, seldom attended with any remarkable perfection in
particular persons. It seems to be taken for granted in the
dialogue *de Oratoribus*,* that knowledge was much more
common in VESPASIAN's age than in that of CICERO and

AUGUSTUS. QUINTILIAN also complains of the profanation of learning, by its becoming too common. 'Formerly,' says JUVENAL, 'science was confined to GREECE and ITALY. Now the whole world emulates ATHENS and ROME. Eloquent GAUL has taught BRITAIN, knowing in the laws. Even THULE entertains thoughts of hiring rhetoricians for its instruction.'[†] This state of learning is remarkable; because JUVENAL is himself the last of the ROMAN writers that possessed any degree of genius. Those who succeeded are valued for nothing but the matters of fact of which they give us information. I hope the late conversion of MUSCOVY to the study of the sciences,[*] will not prove a like prognostic to the present period of learning.

Cardinal BENTIVOGLIO gives the preference to the northern nations above the southern with regard to candour and sincerity; and mentions, on the one hand, the SPANIARDS and ITALIANS, and, on the other, the FLEMINGS and GERMANS. But I am apt to think that this has happened by accident. The ancient ROMANS seem to have been a candid, sincere people, as are the modern TURKS. But if we must needs suppose that this event has arisen from fixed causes, we may only conclude from it, that all extremes are apt to concur, and are commonly attended with the same consequences. Treachery is the usual concomitant of ignorance and barbarism; and if civilized nations ever embrace subtle and crooked politics, it is from an excess of refinement, which makes them disdain the plain direct path to power and glory.

Most conquests have gone from north to south; and it has hence been inferred, that the northern nations possess a superior degree of courage and ferocity. But it would have been juster to have said, that most conquests are made by poverty and want upon plenty and riches. The SARACENS, leaving the deserts of ARABIA, carried their conquests northwards upon all the fertile provinces of the ROMAN empire, and met the TURKS half way, who were coming southwards from the deserts of TARTARY.

An eminent writer[†] has remarked, that all courageous animals are also carnivorous, and that greater courage is to be expected in a people, such as the ENGLISH, whose food is strong and hearty, than in the half-starved commonalty of other countries. But the SWEDES, notwithstanding their disadvantages in this particular, are not inferior, in martial courage, to any nation that ever was in the world.

In general, we may observe, that courage, of all national qualities, is the most precarious; because it is exerted only at intervals, and by a few in every nation; whereas industry, knowledge, civility, may be of constant and universal use, and for several ages may become habitual to the whole people. If courage be preserved, it must be by discipline, example, and opinion. The tenth legion of CAESAR, and the regiment of PICARDY in FRANCE, were formed promiscuously from among the citizens; but having once entertained a notion that they were the best troops in the service, this very opinion really made them such.

As a proof how much courage depends on opinion, we may observe, that, of the two chief tribes of the GREEKS, the DORIANS and IONIANS, the former were always esteemed, and always appeared, more brave and manly than the latter, though the colonies of both the tribes were interspersed and intermingled throughout all the extent of GREECE, the Lesser ASIA, SICILY, ITALY, and the islands of the AEGEAN sea. The ATHENIANS were the only IONIANS that ever had any reputation for valour or military achievements, though even these were deemed inferior to the LACEDEMONIANS, the bravest of the DORIANS.

The only observation with regard to the difference of men in different climates, on which we can rest any weight, is the vulgar one, that people, in the northern regions, have a greater inclination to strong liquors, and those in the southern to love and women. One can assign a very probable *physical* cause for this difference. Wine and distilled waters warm the frozen blood in the colder climates, and fortify men against the injuries of the weather; as the genial heat of the sun, in the countries exposed to his beams, inflames the blood, and exalts the passion between the sexes.

Perhaps, too, the matter may be accounted for by *moral*

causes. All strong liquors are rarer in the north, and consequently are more coveted. DIODORUS SICULUS[†] tells us that
the GAULS, in his time, were great drunkards, and much
addicted to wine; chiefly, I suppose, from its rarity and
novelty. On the other hand, the heat in the southern climates
obliging men and women to go half naked, thereby renders
their frequent commerce more dangerous, and inflames
their mutual passion. This makes parents and husbands
more jealous and reserved, which still further inflames the
passion. Not to mention, that as women ripen sooner in the
southern regions, it is necessary to observe greater jealousy
and care in their education; it being evident, that a girl of
twelve cannot possess equal discretion to govern this passion
with one who feels not its violence till she be seventeen or
eighteen. Nothing so much encourages the passion of love
as ease and leisure, or is more destructive to it than industry
and hard labour; and as the necessities of men are evidently
fewer in the warm climates than in the cold ones, this
circumstance alone may make a considerable difference
between them.

But perhaps the fact is doubtful, that nature has, either
from moral or physical causes, distributed these respective
inclinations to the different climates. The ancient GREEKS,
though born in a warm climate, seem to have been much
addicted to the bottle; nor were their parties of pleasure
any thing but matches of drinking among men, who passed
their time altogether apart from the fair. Yet when
ALEXANDER led the GREEKS into PERSIA, a still more southern
climate, they multiplied their debauches of this kind, in
imitation of the PERSIAN manners.[†] So honourable was the
character of a drunkard among the PERSIANS, that CYRUS
the younger, soliciting the sober LACEDEMONIANS for succour
against his brother ARTAXERXES, claims it chiefly on account
of his superior endowments, as more valorous, more
bountiful, and a better drinker.[†] DARIUS HYSTASPES[*] made
it be inscribed on his tombstone, among his other virtues
and princely qualities, that no one could bear a greater
quantity of liquor. You may obtain any thing of the
NEGROES by offering them strong drink, and may easily

prevail with them to sell, not only their children, but their wives and mistresses, for a cask of brandy. In FRANCE and ITALY, few drink pure wine, except in the greatest heats of summer; and, indeed, it is then almost as necessary, in order to recruit the spirits, evaporated by heat, as it is in SWEDEN during the winter, in order to warm the bodies congealed by the rigour of the season.

If jealousy be regarded as a proof of an amorous disposition, no people were more jealous than the MUSCOVITES, before their communication with EUROPE had somewhat altered their manners in this particular.

But supposing the fact true, that nature, by physical principles, has regularly distributed these two passions, the one to the northern, the other to the southern regions, we can only infer, that the climate may affect the grosser and more bodily organs of our frame, not that it can work upon those finer organs on which the operations of the mind and understanding depend. And this is agreeable to the analogy of nature. The races of animals never degenerate when carefully attended to; and horses, in particular, always show their blood in their shape, spirit, and swiftness. But a coxcomb may beget a philosopher, as a man of virtue may leave a worthless progeny.

I shall conclude this subject with observing, that though the passion for liquor be more brutal and debasing than love, which, when properly managed, is the source of all politeness and refinement; yet this gives not so great an advantage to the southern climates as we may be apt, at first sight, to imagine. When love goes beyond a certain pitch, it renders men jealous, and cuts off the free intercourse between the sexes, on which the politeness of a nation will commonly much depend. And if we would subtilize and refine upon this point, we might observe, that the people, in very temperate climates, are the most likely to attain all sorts of improvement, their blood not being so inflamed as to render them jealous, and yet being warm enough to make them set a due value on the charms and endowments of the fair sex.

OF TRAGEDY

IT seems an unaccountable pleasure which the spectators of a well-written tragedy receive from sorrow, terror, anxiety, and other passions that are in themselves disagreeable and uneasy. The more they are touched and affected, the more are they delighted with the spectacle; and as soon as the uneasy passions cease to operate, the piece is at an end. One scene of full joy and contentment and security is the utmost that any composition of this kind can bear; and it is sure always to be the concluding one. If in the texture of the piece there be interwoven any scenes of satisfaction, they afford only faint gleams of pleasure, which are thrown in by way of variety, and in order to plunge the actors into deeper distress by means of that contrast and disappointment. The whole art of the poet is employed in rousing and supporting the compassion and indignation, the anxiety and resentment, of his audience. They are pleased in proportion as they are afflicted, and never are so happy as when they employ tears, sobs, and cries, to give vent to their sorrow, and relieve their heart, swoln with the tenderest sympathy and compassion.

The few critics who have had some tincture of philosophy have remarked this singular phenomenon, and have endeavoured to account for it.

L'Abbé Dubos, in his reflections on poetry and painting, asserts, that nothing is in general so disagreeable to the mind as the languid, listless state of indolence into which it falls upon the removal of all passion and occupation.† To get rid of this painful situation, it seeks every amusement and pursuit; business, gaming, shows, executions; whatever will rouse the passions and take its attention from itself. No matter what the passion is; let it be disagreeable, afflicting, melancholy, disordered; it is still better than that insipid languor which arises from perfect tranquillity and repose.

It is impossible not to admit this account as being, at least in part, satisfactory. You may observe, when there are several tables of gaming, that all the company run to those where the deepest play is, even though they find not there the best players. The view, or, at least, imagination of high passions, arising from great loss or gain, affects the spectator by sympathy, gives him some touches of the same passions, and serves him for a momentary entertainment. It makes the time pass the easier with him, and is some relief to that oppression under which men commonly labour when left entirely to their own thoughts and meditations.

We find that common liars always magnify, in their narrations, all kinds of danger, pain, distress, sickness, deaths, murders, and cruelties, as well as joy, beauty, mirth, and magnificence. It is an absurd secret which they have for pleasing their company, fixing their attention, and attaching them to such marvellous relation by the passions and emotions which they excite.

There is, however, a difficulty in applying to the present subject, in its full extent, this solution, however ingenious and satisfactory it may appear. It is certain that the same object of distress, which pleases in a tragedy, were it really set before us, would give the most unfeigned uneasiness, though it be then the most effectual cure to languor and indolence. Monsieur FONTENELLE seems to have been sensible of this difficulty, and accordingly attempts another solution of the phenomenon, at least makes some addition to the theory above mentioned.[†]

'Pleasure and pain,' says he, 'which are two sentiments so different in themselves, differ not so much in their cause. From the instance of tickling it appears, that the movement of pleasure, pushed a little too far, becomes pain, and that the movement of pain, a little moderate, becomes pleasure. Hence it proceeds, that there is such a thing as a sorrow, soft and agreeable: it is a pain weakened and diminished. The heart likes naturally to be moved and affected. Melancholy objects suit it, and even disastrous and sorrowful, provided they are softened by some circumstance. It is certain, that, on the theatre, the representation has almost the effect of reality; yet it has not altogether that effect. However we may be hurried away by the spectacle, whatever dominion the senses and imagination may usurp over the reason, there still lurks at the bottom a certain idea of falsehood in the whole of what we see. This idea, though weak and disguised, suffices to diminish the pain which we suffer from the misfortunes of those whom we love, and to reduce that affliction to such a pitch as converts it into a pleasure. We weep for the misfortune of a hero to whom we are attached. In the same instant we comfort ourselves by reflecting, that it is nothing but a fiction: and it is precisely that mixture of sentiments which composes an agreeable sorrow, and tears that delight us. But as that affliction which is caused by exterior and sensible objects is stronger than the consolation which arises from an internal reflection, they are the effects and symptoms of sorrow that ought to predominate in the composition.'

This solution seems just and convincing: but perhaps it wants still some new addition, in order to make it answer fully the phenomenon which we here examine. All the passions, excited by eloquence, are agreeable in the highest degree, as well as those which are moved by painting and the theatre. The epilogues of CICERO are, on this account chiefly, the delight of every reader of taste; and it is difficult to read some of them without the deepest sympathy and sorrow. His merit as an orator, no doubt, depends much on his success in this particular. When he had raised tears in his judges and all his audience, they were then the most highly delighted, and expressed the greatest satisfaction with the pleader. The pathetic description of the butchery made by VERRES of the SICILIAN captains,* is a masterpiece of this kind: but I believe none will affirm, that the being present at a melancholy scene of that nature would afford any entertainment. Neither is the sorrow here softened by fiction; for the audience were convinced of the reality of every circumstance. What is it then which in this case raises a pleasure from the bosom of uneasiness, so to speak, and a pleasure which still retains all the features and outward symptoms of distress and sorrow?

I answer: this extraordinary effect proceeds from that very eloquence with which the melancholy scene is represented. The genius required to paint objects in a lively manner, the art employed in collecting all the pathetic circumstances, the judgment displayed in disposing them; the exercise, I say, of these noble talents, together with the force of expression, and beauty of oratorial numbers, diffuse the highest satisfaction on the audience, and excite the most delightful movements. By this means, the uneasiness of the melancholy passions is not only overpowered and effaced by something stronger of an opposite kind, but the whole impulse of those passions is converted into pleasure, and swells the delight which the eloquence raises in us. The same force of oratory, employed on an uninteresting subject, would not please half so much, or rather would appear altogether ridiculous; and the mind, being left in absolute calmness and indifference, would relish none of those beauties of imagination or expression, which, if joined to passion, give it such exquisite entertainment. The impulse or vehemence arising from sorrow, compassion, indignation, receives a new direction from the sentiments of beauty. The latter, being the predominant emotion, seize the whole mind, and convert the former into themselves, at least tincture them so strongly as totally to alter their nature. And the soul being at the same time roused by passion and charmed by eloquence, feels on the whole a strong movement, which is altogether delightful.

The same principle takes place in tragedy; with this addition, that tragedy is an imitation, and imitation is always of itself agreeable. This circumstance serves still further to smooth the motions of passion, and convert the whole feeling into one uniform and strong enjoyment. Objects of the greatest terror and distress please in painting, and please more than the most beautiful objects that appear calm and indifferent.[†] The affection, rousing the mind, excites a large stock of spirit and vehemence; which is all transformed into pleasure by the force of the prevailing movement. It is thus the fiction of tragedy softens the passion, by an infusion of a new feeling, not merely by weakening or diminishing the sorrow. You may by degrees weaken a real sorrow, till it totally disappears; yet in none of its gradations will it ever give pleasure; except, perhaps, by accident, to a man sunk under lethargic indolence, whom it rouses from that languid state.

To confirm this theory, it will be sufficient to produce

other instances, where the subordinate movement is converted into the predominant, and gives force to it, though of a different, and even sometimes though of a contrary nature.

Novelty naturally rouses the mind, and attracts our attention; and the movements which it causes are always converted into any passion belonging to the object, and join their force to it. Whether an event excite joy or sorrow, pride or shame, anger or good-will, it is sure to produce a stronger affection, when new or unusual. And though novelty of itself be agreeable, it fortifies the painful, as well as agreeable passions.

Had you any intention to move a person extremely by the narration of any event, the best method of increasing its effect would be artfully to delay informing him of it, and first to excite his curiosity and impatience before you let him into the secret. This is the artifice practised by IAGO in the famous scene of SHAKSPEARE; and every spectator is sensible, that OTHELLO's jealousy acquires additional force from his preceding impatience, and that the subordinate passion is here readily transformed into the predominant one.*

Difficulties increase passions of every kind; and by rousing our attention, and exciting our active powers, they produce an emotion which nourishes the prevailing affection.

Parents commonly love that child most whose sickly infirm frame of body has occasioned them the greatest pains, trouble, and anxiety, in rearing him. The agreeable sentiment of affection here acquires force from sentiments of uneasiness.

Nothing endears so much a friend as sorrow for his death. The pleasure of his company has not so powerful an influence.

Jealousy is a painful passion; yet without some share of it, the agreeable affection of love has difficulty to subsist in its full force and violence. Absence is also a great source of complaint among lovers, and gives them the greatest uneasiness: yet nothing is more favourable to their mutual passion than short intervals of that kind. And if long intervals often prove fatal, it is only because, through time, men are accustomed to them, and they cease to give uneasiness. Jealousy and absence in love compose the *dolce peccante** of the ITALIANS, which they suppose so essential to all pleasure.

There is a fine observation of the elder PLINY,[†] which illustrates the principle here insisted on. *It is very remarkable*, says he, *that the last works of celebrated artists, which they left imperfect, are always the most prized, such as the* IRIS *of* ARISTIDES, *the* TYNDARIDES *of* NICOMACHUS, *the* MEDEA *of* TIMOMACHUS, *and the* VENUS *of* APELLES. *These are valued even above their finished productions. The broken lineaments of the piece, and the half-formed idea of the painter, are carefully studied; and our very grief for that curious hand, which had been stopped by death, is an additional increase to our pleasure.*

These instances (and many more might be collected) are sufficient to afford us some insight into the analogy of nature, and to show us, that the pleasure which poets, orators, and musicians give us, by exciting grief, sorrow, indignation, compassion, is not so extraordinary or paradoxical as it may at first sight appear. The force of imagination, the energy of expression, the power of numbers, the charms of imitation; all these are naturally, of themselves, delightful to the mind: and when the object presented lays also hold of some affection, the pleasure still rises upon us, by the conversion of this subordinate movement into that which is predominant. The passion, though perhaps naturally, and when excited by the simple appearance of a real object, it may be painful; yet is so smoothed, and softened, and mollified, when raised by the finer arts, that it affords the highest entertainment.

To confirm this reasoning, we may observe, that if the movements of the imagination be not predominant above those of the passion, a contrary effect follows; and the former, being now subordinate, is converted into the latter, and still further increases the pain and affliction of the sufferer.

Who could ever think of it as a good expedient for comforting an afflicted parent, to exaggerate, with all the force of elocution, the irreparable loss which he has met with by the death of a favourite child? The more power of imagination and expression you here employ, the more you increase his despair and affliction.

The shame, confusion, and terror of VERRES, no doubt, rose in proportion to the noble eloquence and vehemence of CICERO: so also did his pain and uneasiness. These former passions were too strong for the pleasure arising from the beauties of elocution; and operated, though from the same principle, yet in a contrary manner, to the sympathy, compassion, and indignation of the audience.

Lord CLARENDON,* when he approaches towards the catastrophe of the royal party, supposes that his narration must then become infinitely disagreeable; and he hurries over the king's death without giving us one circumstance of it. He considers it as too horrid a scene to be contemplated with any satisfaction, or even without the utmost pain and aversion. He himself, as well as the readers of that age, were too deeply concerned in the events, and felt a pain from subjects which an historian and a reader of another age would regard as the most pathetic and most interesting, and, by consequence, the most agreeable.

An action, represented in tragedy, may be too bloody and atrocious. It may excite such movements of horror as will not soften into pleasure; and the greatest energy of expression, bestowed on descriptions of that nature, serves only to augment our uneasiness. Such is that action represented in the *Ambitious Step-mother*,* where a venerable old man, raised to the height of fury and despair, rushes against a pillar, and, striking his head upon it, besmears it all over with mingled brains and gore. The English theatre abounds too much with such shocking images.

Even the common sentiments of compassion require to be softened by some agreeable affection, in order to give a thorough satisfaction to the audience. The mere suffering of plaintive virtue, under the triumphant tyranny and oppression of vice, forms a disagreeable spectacle, and is carefully avoided by all masters of the drama. In order to dismiss the audience with entire satisfaction and contentment, the virtue must either convert itself into a noble courageous despair, or the vice receive its proper punishment.

Most painters appear in this light to have been very unhappy in their subjects. As they wrought much for churches and convents, they have chiefly represented such horrible subjects as crucifixions and martyrdoms, where nothing appears but tortures, wounds, executions, and passive suffering, without any action or affection. When they turned their pencil from this ghastly mythology, they had commonly recourse to OVID, whose fictions, though passionate and agreeable, are scarcely natural or probable enough for painting.

The same inversion of that principle which is here insisted on, displays itself in common life, as in the effects of oratory and poetry. Raise so the subordinate passion that it becomes the predominant, it swallows up that affection which it before nourished and increased. Too much jealousy extinguishes love; too much difficulty renders us indifferent; too much sickness and infirmity disgusts a selfish and unkind parent.

What so disagreeable as the dismal, gloomy, disastrous stories, with which melancholy people entertain their companions? The uneasy passion being there raised alone, unaccompanied with any spirit, genius, or eloquence, conveys a pure uneasiness, and is attended with nothing that can soften it into pleasure or satisfaction.

OF THE STANDARD OF TASTE

THE great variety of Taste, as well as of opinion, which prevails in the world, is too obvious not to have fallen under every one's observation. Men of the most confined knowledge are able to remark a difference of taste in the narrow circle of their acquaintance, even where the persons have been educated under the same government, and have early imbibed the same prejudices. But those who can enlarge their view to contemplate distant nations and remote ages, are still more surprised at the great inconsistence and contrariety. We are apt to call *barbarous* whatever departs widely from our own taste and apprehension; but soon find the epithet of reproach retorted on us. And the highest arrogance and self-conceit is at last startled, on observing an equal assurance on all sides, and scruples, amidst such a contest of sentiment, to pronounce positively in its own favour.

As this variety of taste is obvious to the most careless inquirer, so will it be found, on examination, to be still greater in reality than in appearance. The sentiments of men often differ with regard to beauty and deformity of all kinds, even while their general discourse is the same. There are certain terms in every language which import blame, and others praise; and all men who use the same tongue must agree in their application of them. Every voice is united in applauding elegance, propriety, simplicity, spirit in writing; and in blaming fustian, affectation, coldness, and a false brilliancy. But when critics come to particulars, this seeming unanimity vanishes; and it is found, that they had affixed a very different meaning to their expressions. In all matters of opinion and science, the case is opposite; the difference among men is there oftener found to lie in generals than in particulars, and to be less in reality than in appearance. An explanation of the terms commonly ends the controversy: and the disputants are surprised to find that they had been quarrelling, while at bottom they agreed in their judgment.

Those who found morality on sentiment, more than on reason, are inclined to comprehend ethics under the former observation, and to maintain, that, in all questions which regard conduct and manners, the difference among men is really greater than at first sight it appears. It is indeed obvious, that writers of all nations and all ages concur in applauding justice, humanity, magnanimity, prudence, veracity; and in blaming the opposite qualities. Even poets and other authors, whose compositions are chiefly calculated to please the imagination, are yet found, from HOMER down to FENELON, to inculcate the same moral precepts, and to bestow their applause and blame on the same virtues and vices. This great unanimity is usually ascribed to the influence of plain reason, which, in all these cases, maintains similar sentiments in all men, and prevents those controversies to which the abstract sciences are so much exposed. So far as the unanimity is real, this account may be admitted as satisfactory. But we must also allow, that some part of the seeming harmony in morals may be accounted for from the very nature of language. The word *virtue*, with its equivalent in every tongue, implies praise, as that of *vice* does blame; and no one, without the most obvious and grossest impropriety, could affix reproach to a term, which in general acceptation is understood in a good sense; or bestow applause, where the idiom requires disapprobation. HOMER's general precepts, where he delivers any such, will never be controverted; but it is obvious, that, when he draws particular pictures of manners, and represents heroism in ACHILLES, and prudence in ULYSSES, he intermixes a much greater degree of ferocity in the former, and of cunning and fraud in the latter, than FENELON would admit of. The sage ULYSSES, in the GREEK poet, seems to delight in lies and fictions, and often employs them without any necessity, or even advantage. But his more scrupulous son, in the FRENCH epic writer, exposes himself to the most imminent perils, rather than depart from the most exact line of truth and veracity.

The admirers and followers of the ALCORAN* insist on the excellent moral precepts interspersed throughout that wild and absurd performance. But it is to be supposed, that the ARABIC words, which correspond to the ENGLISH, equity, justice, temperance, meekness, charity, were such as, from the constant use of that tongue, must always be taken in a good sense: and it would have argued the greatest ignorance, not of morals, but of language, to have mentioned them with any epithets, besides those of applause and approbation. But would we know, whether the pretended prophet had really attained a just sentiment of morals, let us attend to his narration, and we shall soon find, that he bestows praise on such instances of treachery, inhumanity, cruelty, revenge, bigotry, as are utterly incompatible with civilized society. No steady rule of right seems there to be attended to; and every action is blamed or praised, so far only as it is beneficial or hurtful to the true believers.

The merit of delivering true general precepts in ethics is indeed very small. Whoever recommends any moral virtues, really does no more than is implied in the terms themselves. That people who invented the word *charity*, and used it in a good sense, inculcated more clearly, and much more efficaciously, the precept, *be charitable*, than any pretended legislator or prophet, who should insert such a *maxim* in his writings. Of all expressions, those which, together with their other meaning, imply a degree either of blame or approbation, are the least liable to be perverted or mistaken.

It is natural for us to seek a *Standard of Taste*; a rule by which the various sentiments of men may be reconciled; at least a decision afforded confirming one sentiment, and condemning another.

There is a species of philosophy, which cuts off all hopes of success in such an attempt, and represents the impossibility of ever attaining any standard of taste. The difference, it is said, is very wide between judgment and sentiment. All sentiment is right; because sentiment has a reference to nothing beyond itself, and is always real, wherever a man is conscious of it. But all determinations of the understanding are not right; because they have a reference to something beyond themselves, to wit, real matter of fact; and are not always conformable to that standard. Among a thousand different opinions which different men may entertain of the same subject, there is one, and but one, that is just and true: and the only difficulty is to fix and ascertain it. On the contrary, a thousand different sentiments, excited by the same object, are all right; because no sentiment represents what is really in the object. It only marks a certain conformity or relation between the object and the organs or faculties of the mind; and if that conformity did not really exist, the sentiment could never possibly have being. Beauty is no quality in things themselves: it exists merely in the mind which contemplates them; and each mind perceives a different beauty. One person may even perceive deformity, where another is sensible of beauty; and every individual ought to acquiesce in his own sentiment, without pretending to regulate those of others. To seek the real beauty, or real deformity, is as fruitless an inquiry, as to pretend to ascertain the real sweet or real bitter. According to the disposition of the organs, the same object may be both sweet and bitter; and the proverb has justly determined it to be fruitless to dispute concerning tastes. It is very natural, and even quite necessary, to extend this axiom to mental, as well as bodily taste; and thus common sense, which is so often at variance with philosophy, especially with the sceptical kind, is found, in one instance at least, to agree in pronouncing the same decision.

But though this axiom, by passing into a proverb, seems to have attained the sanction of common sense; there is certainly a species of common sense, which opposes it, at least serves to modify and restrain it. Whoever would assert an equality of genius and elegance between OGILBY and MILTON, or BUNYAN and ADDISON, would be thought to defend no less an extravagance, than if he had maintained a mole-hill to be as high as TENERIFFE, or a pond as extensive as the ocean. Though there may be found persons, who give the preference to the former authors; no one pays attention to such a taste; and we pronounce, without scruple, the sentiment of these pretended critics to be absurd and ridiculous. The principle of the natural equality of tastes is then totally forgot, and while we admit it on some occasions, where the objects seem near an equality, it appears an extravagant paradox, or rather a palpable absurdity, where objects so disproportioned are compared together.

It is evident that none of the rules of composition are fixed by reasonings *a priori*, or can be esteemed abstract conclusions of the understanding, from comparing those habitudes and relations of ideas, which are eternal and immutable. Their foundation is the same with that of all the practical sciences, experience; nor are they any thing but general observations, concerning what has been universally

found to please in all countries and in all ages. Many of the
beauties of poetry, and even of eloquence, are founded on
falsehood and fiction, on hyperboles, metaphors, and an
abuse or perversion of terms from their natural meaning. To
check the sallies of the imagination, and to reduce every
expression to geometrical truth and exactness, would be the
most contrary to the laws of criticism; because it would
produce a work, which, by universal experience, has been
found the most insipid and disagreeable. But though poetry
can never submit to exact truth, it must be confined by
rules of art, discovered to the author either by genius or
observation. If some negligent or irregular writers have
pleased, they have not pleased by their transgressions of
rule or order, but in spite of these transgressions: they have
possessed other beauties, which were conformable to just
criticism; and the force of these beauties has been able
to overpower censure, and give the mind a satisfaction
superior to the disgust arising from the blemishes. Ariosto
pleases; but not by his monstrous and improbable fictions,
by his bizarre mixture of the serious and comic styles, by the
want of coherence in his stories, or by the continual interruptions of his narration. He charms by the force and clearness of his expression, by the readiness and variety of his
inventions, and by his natural pictures of the passions, especially those of the gay and amorous kind: and, however
his faults may diminish our satisfaction, they are not able
entirely to destroy it. Did our pleasure really arise from
those parts of his poem, which we denominate faults, this
would be no objection to criticism in general: it would only
be an objection to those particular rules of criticism, which
would establish such circumstances to be faults, and would
represent them as universally blamable. If they are found to
please, they cannot be faults, let the pleasure which they
produce be ever so unexpected and unaccountable.

But though all the general rules of art are founded only
on experience, and on the observation of the common sentiments of human nature, we must not imagine, that, on
every occasion, the feelings of men will be conformable to
these rules. Those finer emotions of the mind are of a very

tender and delicate nature, and require the concurrence of many favourable circumstances to make them play with facility and exactness, according to their general and established principles. The least exterior hindrance to such small springs, or the least internal disorder, disturbs their motion, and confounds the operations of the whole machine. When we would make an experiment of this nature, and would try the force of any beauty or deformity, we must choose with care a proper time and place, and bring the fancy to a suitable situation and disposition. A perfect serenity of mind, a recollection of thought, a due attention to the object; if any of these circumstances be wanting, our experiment will be fallacious, and we shall be unable to judge of the catholic and universal beauty. The relation, which nature has placed between the form and the sentiment, will at least be more obscure; and it will require greater accuracy to trace and discern it. We shall be able to ascertain its influence, not so much from the operation of each particular beauty, as from the durable admiration which attends those works that have survived all the caprices of mode and fashion, all the mistakes of ignorance and envy.

The same HOMER who pleased at ATHENS and ROME two thousand years ago, is still admired at PARIS and at LONDON. All the changes of climate, government, religion, and language, have not been able to obscure his glory. Authority or prejudice may give a temporary vogue to a bad poet or orator; but his reputation will never be durable or general. When his compositions are examined by posterity or by foreigners, the enchantment is dissipated, and his faults appear in their true colours. On the contrary, a real genius, the longer his works endure, and the more wide they are spread, the more sincere is the admiration which he meets with. Envy and jealousy have too much place in a narrow circle; and even familiar acquaintance with his person may diminish the applause due to his performances: but when these obstructions are removed, the beauties, which are naturally fitted to excite agreeable sentiments, immediately display their energy; and while the world endures, they maintain their authority over the minds of men.

It appears, then, that amidst all the variety and caprice of taste, there are certain general principles of approbation or blame, whose influence a careful eye may trace in all operations of the mind. Some particular forms or qualities, from the original structure of the internal fabric are calculated to please, and others to displease; and if they fail of their effect in any particular instance, it is from some apparent defect or imperfection in the organ. A man in a fever would not insist on his palate as able to decide concerning flavours; nor would one affected with the jaundice pretend to give a verdict with regard to colours. In each creature there is a sound and a defective state; and the former alone can be supposed to afford us a true standard of taste and sentiment. If, in the sound state of the organ, there be an entire or a considerable uniformity of sentiment among men, we may thence derive an idea of the perfect beauty; in like manner as the appearance of objects in daylight, to the eye of a man in health, is denominated their true and real colour, even while colour is allowed to be merely a phantasm of the senses.

Many and frequent are the defects in the internal organs, which prevent or weaken the influence of those general principles, on which depends our sentiment of beauty or deformity. Though some objects, by the structure of the mind, be naturally calculated to give pleasure, it is not to be expected that in every individual the pleasure will be equally felt. Particular incidents and situations occur, which either throw a false light on the objects, or hinder the true from conveying to the imagination the proper sentiment and perception.

One obvious cause why many feel not the proper sentiment of beauty, is the want of that *delicacy* of imagination which is requisite to convey a sensibility of those finer emotions. This delicacy every one pretends to: every one talks of it; and would reduce every kind of taste or sentiment to its standard. But as our intention in this essay is to mingle some light of the understanding with the feelings of sen-

timent, it will be proper to give a more accurate definition
of delicacy than has hitherto been attempted. And not to
draw our philosophy from too profound a source, we shall
have recourse to a noted story in DON QUIXOTE.*

It is with good reason, says SANCHO to the squire with the
great nose, that I pretend to have a judgment in wine: this is
a quality hereditary in our family. Two of my kinsmen were
once called to give their opinion of a hogshead, which was
supposed to be excellent, being old and of a good vintage.
One of them tastes it, considers it; and, after mature reflection, pronounces the wine to be good, were it not for a
small taste of leather which he perceived in it. The other,
after using the same precautions, gives also his verdict in
favour of the wine; but with the reserve of a taste of iron,
which he could easily distinguish. You cannot imagine how
much they were both ridiculed for their judgment. But who
laughed in the end? On emptying the hogshead, there was
found at the bottom an old key with a leathern thong
tied to it.

The great resemblance between mental and bodily taste
will easily teach us to apply this story. Though it be certain
that beauty and deformity, more than sweet and bitter, are
not qualities in objects, but belong entirely to the sentiment,
internal or external, it must be allowed, that there are
certain qualities in objects which are fitted by nature to
produce those particular feelings. Now, as these qualities
may be found in a small degree, or may be mixed and
confounded with each other, it often happens that the taste
is not affected with such minute qualities, or is not able to
distinguish all the particular flavours, amidst the disorder in
which they are presented. Where the organs are so fine as to
allow nothing to escape them, and at the same time so exact
as to perceive every ingredient in the composition, this we
call delicacy of taste, whether we employ these terms in the
literal or metaphorical sense. Here then the general rules of
beauty are of use, being drawn from established models,
and from the observation of what pleases or displeases,
when presented singly and in a high degree; and if the
same qualities, in a continued composition, and in a smaller

degree, affect not the organs with a sensible delight or uneasiness, we exclude the person from all pretensions to this delicacy. To produce these general rules or avowed patterns of composition, is like finding the key with the leathern thong, which justified the verdict of SANCHO's kinsmen, and confounded those pretended judges who had condemned them. Though the hogshead had never been emptied, the taste of the one was still equally delicate, and that of the other equally dull and languid; but it would have been more difficult to have proved the superiority of the former, to the conviction of every bystander. In like manner, though the beauties of writing had never been methodized, or reduced to general principles; though no excellent models had ever been acknowledged, the different degrees of taste would still have subsisted, and the judgment of one man been preferable to that of another; but it would not have been so easy to silence the bad critic, who might always insist upon his particular sentiment, and refuse to submit to his antagonist. But when we show him an avowed principle of art; when we illustrate this principle by examples, whose operation, from his own particular taste, he acknowledges to be conformable to the principle; when we prove that the same principle may be applied to the present case, where he did not perceive or feel its influence: he must conclude, upon the whole, that the fault lies in himself, and that he wants the delicacy which is requisite to make him sensible of every beauty and every blemish in any composition or discourse.

It is acknowledged to be the perfection of every sense or faculty, to perceive with exactness its most minute objects, and allow nothing to escape its notice and observation. The smaller the objects are which become sensible to the eye, the finer is that organ, and the more elaborate its make and composition. A good palate is not tried by strong flavours, but by a mixture of small ingredients, where we are still sensible of each part, notwithstanding its minuteness and its confusion with the rest. In like manner, a quick and acute perception of beauty and deformity must be the perfection of our mental taste; nor can a man be satisfied with himself while he suspects that any excellence or blemish in a discourse has passed him unobserved. In this case, the perfection of the man, and the perfection of the sense of feeling, are found to be united. A very delicate palate, on many occasions, may be a great inconvenience both to a man himself and to his friends. But a delicate taste of wit or beauty must always be a desirable quality, because it is the source of all the finest and most innocent enjoyments of which human nature is susceptible. In this decision the sentiments of all mankind are agreed. Wherever you can ascertain a delicacy of taste, it is sure to meet with approbation; and the best way of ascertaining it is, to appeal to those models and principles which have been established by the uniform consent and experience of nations and ages.

But though there be naturally a wide difference, in point of delicacy, between one person and another, nothing tends further to increase and improve this talent, than *practice* in a particular art, and the frequent survey or contemplation of a particular species of beauty. When objects of any kind are first presented to the eye or imagination, the sentiment which attends them is obscure and confused; and the mind is, in a great measure, incapable of pronouncing concerning their merits or defects. The taste cannot perceive the several excellences of the performance, much less distinguish the particular character of each excellency, and ascertain its quality and degree. If it pronounce the whole in general to be beautiful or deformed, it is the utmost that can be expected; and even this judgment, a person so unpractised will be apt to deliver with great hesitation and reserve. But allow him to acquire experience in those objects, his feeling becomes more exact and nice: he not only perceives the beauties and defects of each part, but marks the distinguishing species of each quality, and assigns it suitable praise or blame. A clear and distinct sentiment attends him through the whole survey of the objects; and he discerns that very degree and kind of approbation or displeasure which each part is naturally fitted to produce. The mist dissipates which seemed formerly to hang over the object; the organ acquires greater perfection in its operations, and can pronounce, without danger of mistake, concerning the merits of every performance. In a word, the same address and dexterity which practice gives to the execution of any work, is also acquired by the same means in the judging of it.

So advantageous is practice to the discernment of beauty, that, before we can give judgment on any work of importance, it will even be requisite that that very individual performance be more than once perused by us, and be surveyed in different lights with attention and deliberation. There is a flutter or hurry of thought which attends the first perusal of any piece, and which confounds the genuine sentiment of beauty. The relation of the parts is not discerned: the true characters of style are little distinguished. The several perfections and defects seem wrapped up in a species of confusion, and present themselves indistinctly to the imagination. Not to mention, that there is a species of beauty, which, as it is florid and superficial, pleases at first; but being found incompatible with a just expression either of reason or passion, soon palls upon the taste, and is then rejected with disdain, at least rated at a much lower value.

It is impossible to continue in the practice of contemplating any order of beauty, without being frequently obliged to form *comparisons* between the several species and degrees of excellence, and estimating their proportion to each other. A man who has had no opportunity of comparing the different kinds of beauty, is indeed totally unqualified to pronounce an opinion with regard to any object presented to him. By comparison alone we fix the epithets of praise or blame, and learn how to assign the due degree of each. The coarsest daubing contains a certain lustre of colours and exactness of imitation, which are so far beauties, and would affect the mind of a peasant or Indian with the highest admiration. The most vulgar ballads are not entirely destitute of harmony or nature; and none but a person familiarized to superior beauties would pronounce their members harsh, or narration uninteresting. A great inferiority of beauty gives pain to a person conversant in the highest excellence of the kind, and is for that reason pronounced a deformity; as the most finished object with which we are acquainted is naturally supposed to have reached the pinnacle of perfection, and to be entitled to the highest applause. One accustomed to see, and examine, and weigh the several performances, admired in different ages and nations, can alone rate the merits of a work exhibited to his view, and assign its proper rank among the productions of genius.

But to enable a critic the more fully to execute this undertaking, he must preserve his mind free from all *prejudice*, and allow nothing to enter into his consideration, but the very object which is submitted to his examination. We may observe, that every work of art, in order to produce its due effect on the mind, must be surveyed in a certain point of view, and cannot be fully relished by persons whose situation, real or imaginary, is not conformable to that which is required by the performance. An orator addresses himself to a particular audience, and must have a regard to their particular genius, interests, opinions, passions, and prejudices; otherwise he hopes in vain to govern their resolutions, and inflame their affections. Should they even have entertained some prepossessions against him, however unreasonable, he must not overlook this disadvantage: but, before he enters upon the subject, must endeavour to conciliate their affection, and acquire their good graces. A critic of a different age or nation, who should peruse this discourse, must have all these circumstances in his eye, and must place himself in the same situation as the audience, in order to form a true judgment of the oration. In like manner, when any work is addressed to the public, though I should have a friendship or enmity with the author, I must depart from this situation, and, considering myself as a man in general, forget, if possible, my individual being, and my peculiar circumstances. A person influenced by prejudice complies not with this condition, but obstinately maintains his natural position, without placing himself in that point of view which the performance supposes. If the work be addressed to persons of a different age or nation, he makes no allowance for their peculiar views and prejudices; but, full of the manners of his own age and country, rashly condemns what seemed admirable in the eyes of those for whom alone the discourse was calculated. If the work be executed for the public, he never sufficiently enlarges his comprehension, or forgets his interest as a friend or enemy, as a rival or commentator. By this means his sentiments are perverted; nor have the same beauties and blemishes the same influence upon him, as if he had imposed a proper violence on his imagination, and had forgotten himself for a moment. So far his taste evidently departs from the true standard, and of consequence loses all credit and authority.

It is well known, that, in all questions submitted to the understanding, prejudice is destructive of sound judgment, and perverts all operations of the intellectual faculties: it is no less contrary to good taste; nor has it less influence to corrupt our sentiment of beauty. It belongs to *good sense* to check its influence in both cases; and in this respect, as well as in many others, reason, if not an essential part of taste, is at least requisite to the operations of this latter faculty. In all the nobler productions of genius, there is a mutual relation and correspondence of parts; nor can either the beauties or blemishes be perceived by him whose thought is not capacious enough to comprehend all those parts, and compare them with each other, in order to perceive the consistence and uniformity of the whole. Every work of art has also a certain end or purpose for which it is calculated; and is to be deemed more or less perfect, as it is more or less fitted to attain this end. The object of eloquence is to persuade, of history to instruct, of poetry to please, by means of the passions and the imagination. These ends we must carry constantly in our view when we peruse any performance; and we must be able to judge how far the means employed are adapted to their respective purposes. Besides, every kind of composition, even the most poetical, is nothing but a chain of propositions and reasonings; not always, indeed, the justest and most exact, but still plausible and specious, however disguised by the colouring of the imagination. The persons introduced in tragedy and epic poetry must be represented as reasoning, and thinking, and concluding, and acting, suitably to their character and circumstances; and without judgment, as well as taste and invention, a poet can never hope to succeed in so delicate an undertaking. Not to mention, that the same excellence of faculties which contributes to the improvement of reason, the same clearness of conception, the same exactness of distinction, the same vivacity of apprehension, are essential to the operations of true taste, and are its infallible concomitants. It seldom or never happens, that a man of sense, who has experience in any art, cannot judge of its beauty; and it is no less rare to meet with a man who has a just taste without a sound understanding.

Thus, though the principles of taste be universal, and nearly, if not entirely, the same in all men; yet few are qualified to give judgment on any work of art, or establish their own sentiment as the standard of beauty. The organs of internal sensation are seldom so perfect as to allow the general principles their full play, and produce a feeling correspondent to those principles. They either labour under some defect, or are vitiated by some disorder; and by that means excite a sentiment, which may be pronounced erroneous. When the critic has no delicacy, he judges without any distinction, and is only affected by the grosser and more palpable qualities of the object: the finer touches pass unnoticed and disregarded. Where he is not aided by practice, his verdict is attended with confusion and hesitation. Where no comparison has been employed, the most frivolous beauties, such as rather merit the name of defects, are the object of his admiration. Where he lies under the influence of prejudice, all his natural sentiments are perverted. Where good sense is wanting, he is not qualified to discern the beauties of design and reasoning, which are the highest and most excellent. Under some or other of these imperfections, the generality of men labour, and hence a true judge in the finer arts is observed, even during the most polished ages, to be so rare a character: strong sense, united to delicate sentiment, improved by practice, perfected by comparison, and cleared of all prejudice, can alone entitle critics to this valuable character; and the joint verdict of such, wherever they are to be found, is the true standard of taste and beauty.

But where are such critics to be found? By what marks

are they to be known? How distinguish them from pretenders? These questions are embarrassing; and seem to throw us back into the same uncertainty from which, during the course of this essay, we have endeavoured to extricate ourselves.

But if we consider the matter aright, these are questions of fact, not of sentiment. Whether any particular person be endowed with good sense and a delicate imagination, free from prejudice, may often be the subject of dispute, and be liable to great discussion and inquiry: but that such a character is valuable and estimable, will be agreed in by all mankind. Where these doubts occur, men can do no more than in other disputable questions which are submitted to the understanding: they must produce the best arguments that their invention suggests to them; they must acknowledge a true and decisive standard to exist somewhere, to wit, real existence and matter of fact; and they must have indulgence to such as differ from them in their appeals to this standard. It is sufficient for our present purpose, if we have proved, that the taste of all individuals is not upon an equal footing, and that some men in general, however difficult to be particularly pitched upon, will be acknowledged by universal sentiment to have a preference above others.

But, in reality, the difficulty of finding, even in particulars, the standard of taste, is not so great as it is represented. Though in speculation we may readily avow a certain criterion in science, and deny it in sentiment, the matter is found in practice to be much more hard to ascertain in the former case than in the latter. Theories of abstract philosophy, systems of profound theology, have prevailed during one age: in a successive period these have been universally exploded: their absurdity has been detected: other theories and systems have supplied their place, which again gave place to their successors: and nothing has been experienced more liable to the revolutions of chance and fashion than these pretended decisions of science. The case is not the same with the beauties of eloquence and poetry. Just expressions of passion and nature are sure, after a little time, to gain public applause, which they maintain for ever. ARISTOTLE, and PLATO, and EPICURUS, and DESCARTES, may successively yield to each other: but TERENCE and VIRGIL maintain an universal, undisputed empire over the minds of men. The abstract philosophy of CICERO has lost its credit: the vehemence of his oratory is still the object of our admiration.

Though men of delicate taste be rare, they are easily to be distinguished in society by the soundness of their understanding, and the superiority of their faculties above the rest of mankind. The ascendant, which they acquire, gives a prevalence to that lively approbation with which they receive any productions of genius, and renders it generally predominant. Many men, when left to themselves, have but a faint and dubious perception of beauty, who yet are capable of relishing any fine stroke which is pointed out to them. Every convert to the admiration of the real poet or orator, is the cause of some new conversion. And though prejudices may prevail for a time, they never unite in celebrating any rival to the true genius, but yield at last to the force of nature and just sentiment. Thus, though a civilized nation may easily be mistaken in the choice of their admired philosopher, they never have been found long to err, in their affection for a favourite epic or tragic author.

But notwithstanding all our endeavours to fix a standard of taste, and reconcile the discordant apprehensions of men, there still remain two sources of variation, which are not sufficient indeed to confound all the boundaries of beauty and deformity, but will often serve to produce a difference in the degrees of our approbation or blame. The one is the different humours of particular men; the other, the particular manners and opinions of our age and country. The general principles of taste are uniform in human nature: where men vary in their judgments, some defect or perversion in the faculties may commonly be remarked; proceeding either from prejudice, from want of practice, or want of delicacy: and there is just reason for approving one taste, and condemning another. But where there is such a diversity in the internal frame or external situation as is entirely blameless on both sides, and leaves no room to give one the preference above the other; in that case a certain degree of diversity in judgment is unavoidable, and we seek in vain for a standard, by which we can reconcile the contrary sentiments.

A young man, whose passions are warm, will be more sensibly touched with amorous and tender images, than a man more advanced in years, who takes pleasure in wise, philosophical reflections, concerning the conduct of life, and moderation of the passions. At twenty, OVID may be the favourite author, HORACE at forty, and perhaps TACITUS at fifty. Vainly would we, in such cases, endeavour to enter into the sentiments of others, and divest ourselves of those propensities which are natural to us. We choose our favourite author as we do our friend, from a conformity of humour and disposition. Mirth or passion, sentiment or reflection; whichever of these most predominates in our temper, it gives us a peculiar sympathy with the writer who resembles us.

One person is more pleased with the sublime, another with the tender, a third with raillery. One has a strong sensibility to blemishes, and is extremely studious of correctness; another has a more lively feeling of beauties, and pardons twenty absurdities and defects for one elevated or pathetic stroke. The ear of this man is entirely turned towards conciseness and energy; that man is delighted with a copious, rich, and harmonious expression. Simplicity is affected by one; ornament by another. Comedy, tragedy, satire, odes, have each its partisans, who prefer that particular species of writing to all others. It is plainly an error in a critic, to confine his approbation to one species or style of writing, and condemn all the rest. But it is almost impossible not to feel a predilection for that which suits our particular turn and disposition. Such performances are innocent and unavoidable, and can never reasonably be the object of dispute, because there is no standard by which they can be decided.

For a like reason, we are more pleased, in the course of our reading, with pictures and characters that resemble objects which are found in our own age and country, than with those which describe a different set of customs. It is not without some effort that we reconcile ourselves to the simplicity of ancient manners, and behold princesses carrying water from the spring, and kings and heroes dressing their own victuals. We may allow in general, that the representation of such manners is no fault in the author, nor deformity in the piece; but we are not so sensibly touched with them. For this reason, comedy is not easily transferred from one age or nation to another. A FRENCHMAN or ENGLISHMAN is not pleased with the ANDRIA of TERENCE, or CLITIA of MACHIAVEL;* where the fine lady, upon whom all the play turns, never once appears to the spectators, but is always kept behind the scenes, suitably to the reserved humour of the ancient GREEKS and modern ITALIANS. A man of learning and reflection can make allowance for these peculiarities of manners; but a common audience can never divest themselves so far of their usual ideas and sentiments, as to relish pictures which nowise resemble them.

But here there occurs a reflection, which may, perhaps, be useful in examining the celebrated controversy concerning ancient and modern learning; where we often find the one side excusing any seeming absurdity in the ancients from the manners of the age, and the other refusing to admit this excuse, or at least admitting it only as an apology for the author, not for the performance. In my opinion, the proper boundaries in this subject have seldom been fixed between the contending parties. Where any innocent peculiarities of manners are represented, such as those above mentioned, they ought certainly to be admitted; and a man who is shocked with them, gives an evident proof of false delicacy and refinement. The poet's *monument more durable than brass*,* must fall to the ground like common brick or clay, were men to make no allowance for the continual revolutions of manners and customs, and would admit of nothing but what was suitable to the prevailing fashion. Must we throw aside the pictures of our ancestors, because of their ruffs and farthingales? But where the ideas of morality and decency alter from one age to another, and where vicious manners are described, without being marked with the proper characters of blame and disapprobation, this must be allowed to disfigure the poem, and to be a real deformity. I cannot, nor is it proper I should, enter into such sentiments; and however I may excuse the poet, on account of the manners of his age, I can never relish the composition. The want of humanity and of decency, so conspicuous in the characters drawn by several of the ancient poets, even sometimes by HOMER and the GREEK tragedians, diminishes considerably the merit of their noble performances, and gives modern authors an advantage over them. We are not interested in the fortunes and sentiments of such rough heroes; we are displeased to find the limits of vice and virtue so much confounded; and whatever indulgence we may give to the writer on account of his prejudices, we cannot prevail on ourselves to enter into his sentiments, or bear an affection to characters which we plainly discover to be blamable.

The case is not the same with moral principles as with speculative opinions of any kind. These are in continual flux and revolution. The son embraces a different system from the father. Nay, there scarcely is any man, who can boast of great constancy and uniformity in this particular. Whatever speculative errors may be found in the polite writings of any age or country, they detract but little from the value of those compositions. There needs but a certain turn of thought or imagination to make us enter into all the opinions which then prevailed, and relish the sentiments or conclusions derived from them. But a very violent effort is requisite to change our judgment of manners, and excite sentiments of approbation or blame, love or hatred, different from those to which the mind, from long custom, has been familiarized. And where a man is confident of the rectitude of that moral standard by which he judges, he is justly jealous of it, and will not pervert the sentiments of his heart for a moment, in complaisance to any writer whatsoever.

Of all speculative errors, those which regard religion are the most excusable in compositions of genius; nor is it ever permitted to judge of the civility or wisdom of any people, or even of single persons, by the grossness or refinement of their theological principles. The same good sense that directs men in the ordinary occurrences of life, is not hearkened to in religious matters, which are supposed to be placed altogether above the cognizance of human reason. On this account, all the absurdities of the pagan system of theology must be overlooked by every critic, who would pretend to form a just notion of ancient poetry; and our posterity, in their turn, must have the same indulgence to their forefathers. No religious principles can ever be imputed as a fault to any poet, while they remain merely principles, and take not such strong possession of his heart as to lay him under the imputation of *bigotry* or *superstition*. Where that happens, they confound the sentiments of morality, and alter the natural boundaries of vice and virtue. They are therefore eternal blemishes, according to the principle above mentioned; nor are the prejudices and false opinions of the age sufficient to justify them.

It is essential to the ROMAN catholic religion to inspire a violent hatred of every other worship, and to represent all pagans, mahometans, and heretics, as the objects of divine wrath and vengeance. Such sentiments, though they are in reality very blamable, are considered as virtues by the zealots of that communion, and are represented in their tragedies and epic poems as a kind of divine heroism. This bigotry has disfigured two very fine tragedies of the FRENCH theatre, POLIEUCTE and ATHALIA;* where an intemperate zeal for particular modes of worship is set off with all the pomp imaginable, and forms the predominant character of the heroes. 'What is this,' says the sublime JOAD to JOSABET, finding her in discourse with MATHAN the priest of BAAL, 'Does the daughter of DAVID speak to this traitor? Are you not afraid lest the earth should open, and pour forth flames to devour you both? Or lest these holy walls should fall and crush you together? What is his purpose? Why comes that enemy of God hither to poison the air, which we breathe, with his horrid presence?' Such sentiments are received with great applause on the theatre of PARIS; but at LONDON the spectators would be full as much pleased to hear ACHILLES tell AGAMEMNON, that he was a dog in his forehead, and a deer in his heart; or JUPITER threaten JUNO with a sound drubbing, if she will not be quiet.*

RELIGIOUS principles are also a blemish in any polite composition, when they rise up to superstition, and intrude themselves into every sentiment, however remote from any connection with religion. It is no excuse for the poet, that the customs of his country had burdened life with so many religious ceremonies and observances, that no part of it was exempt from that yoke. It must for ever be ridiculous in PETRARCH* to compare his mistress, LAURA, to JESUS CHRIST. Nor is it less ridiculous in that agreeable libertine, BOCCACE, very seriously to give thanks to GOD ALMIGHTY and the ladies, for their assistance in defending him against his enemies.*

OF COMMERCE

THE greater part of mankind may be divided into two classes; that of *shallow* thinkers, who fall short of the truth; and that of *abstruse* thinkers, who go beyond it. The latter class are by far the most rare; and, I may add, by far the most useful and valuable. They suggest hints at least, and start difficulties, which they want perhaps skill to pursue, but which may produce fine discoveries when handled by men who have a more just way of thinking. At worst, what they say is uncommon; and if it should cost some pains to comprehend it, one has, however, the pleasure of hearing something that is new. An author is little to be valued who tells us nothing but what we can learn from every coffee-house conversation.

All people of *shallow* thought are apt to decry even those of *solid* understanding, as *abstruse* thinkers, and metaphysicians, and refiners; and never will allow any thing to be just which is beyond their own weak conceptions. There are some cases, I own, where an extraordinary refinement affords a strong presumption of falsehood, and where no reasoning is to be trusted but what is natural and easy. When a man deliberates concerning his conduct in any *particular* affair, and forms schemes in politics, trade, economy, or any business in life, he never ought to draw his arguments too fine, or connect too long a chain of consequences together. Something is sure to happen, that will disconcert his reasoning, and produce an event different from what he expected. But when we reason upon *general* subjects, one may justly affirm, that our speculations can scarcely ever be too fine, provided they be just; and that the difference between a common man and a man of genius is chiefly seen in the shallowness or depth of the principles upon which they proceed. General reasonings seem intricate, merely because they are general; nor is it easy for the bulk of mankind to distinguish, in a great number of particulars, that common circumstance in which they all agree, or to extract it, pure and unmixed, from the other superfluous circumstances. Every judgment or conclusion with them is particular. They cannot enlarge their view to those universal propositions which comprehend under them an infinite number of individuals, and include a whole science in a single theorem. Their eye is confounded with such an extensive prospect; and the conclusions derived from it, even though clearly expressed, seem intricate and obscure. But however intricate they may seem, it is certain that general principles, if just and sound, must always prevail in the general course of things, though they may fail in particular cases; and it is the chief business of philosophers to regard the general course of things. I may add, that it is also the chief business of politicians, especially in the domestic government of the state, where the public good, which is or ought to be their object, depends on the concurrence of a multitude of causes;† not, as in foreign politics, on accidents and chances, and the caprices of a few persons. This therefore makes the difference between *particular* deliberations and *general* reasonings, and renders subtilty and refinement much more suitable to the latter than to the former.

I thought this introduction necessary before the following discourses on *commerce*, *money*, *interest*, *balance of trade*, *etc.*, where perhaps there will occur some principles which are uncommon, and which may seem too refined and subtle for such vulgar subjects. If false, let them be rejected; but no one ought to entertain a prejudice against them merely because they are out of the common road.

The greatness of a state, and the happiness of its subjects, how independent soever they may be supposed in some respects, are commonly allowed to be inseparable with regard to commerce; and as private men receive greater security, in the possession of their trade and riches, from the power of the public, so the public becomes powerful in proportion to the opulence and extensive commerce of private men. This maxim is true in general, though I cannot forbear thinking that it may possibly admit of exceptions, and that we often establish it with too little reserve and limitation. There may be some circumstances where the commerce, and riches, and luxury of individuals, instead of adding strength to the public, will serve only to thin its armies, and diminish its authority among the neighbouring nations. Man is a very variable being, and susceptible of many different opinions, principles, and rules of conduct. What may be true, while he adheres to one way of thinking, will be found false, when he has embraced an opposite set of manners and opinions.

The bulk of every state may be divided into *husbandmen* and *manufacturers*. The former are employed in the culture of the land; the latter works up the materials furnished by the former, into all the commodities which are necessary or ornamental to human life. As soon as men quit their savage state, where they live chiefly by hunting and fishing, they must fall into these two classes, though the arts of agriculture employ, *at first*, the most numerous part of the society.[†] Time and experience improve so much these arts, that the land may easily maintain a much greater number of men than those who are immediately employed in its culture, or who furnish the more necessary manufactures to such as are so employed.

If these superfluous hands apply themselves to the finer arts, which are commonly denominated the arts of *luxury*, they add to the happiness of the state, since they afford to many the opportunity of receiving enjoyments with which they would otherwise have been unacquainted. But may not another scheme be proposed for the employment of these superfluous hands? May not the sovereign lay claim to them, and employ them in fleets and armies, to increase the dominions of the state abroad, and spread its fame over distant nations? It is certain, that the fewer desires and wants are found in the proprietors and labourers of land, the fewer hands do they employ; and consequently, the superfluities of the land, instead of maintaining tradesmen and manufacturers, may support fleets and armies to a much greater extent than where a great many arts are required to minister to the luxury of particular persons. Here, therefore, seems to be a kind of opposition between the greatness of the state and the happiness of the subject. A state is never greater than when all its superfluous hands are employed in the service of the public. The ease and convenience of private persons require that these hands should be employed in their service. The one can never be satisfied but at the expense of the other. As the ambition of the sovereign must entrench on the luxury of individuals, so the luxury of individuals must diminish the force, and check the ambition, of the sovereign.

Nor is this reasoning merely chimerical, but it is founded on history and experience. The republic of SPARTA was certainly more powerful than any state now in the world, consisting of an equal number of people; and this was owing entirely to the want of commerce and luxury. The HELOTES were the labourers, the SPARTANS were the soldiers or gentlemen. It is evident that the labour of the HELOTES could not have maintained so great a number of SPARTANS, had these latter lived in ease and delicacy, and given employment to a great variety of trades and manufactures. The like policy may be remarked in ROME. And, indeed, throughout all ancient history it is observable, that the smallest republics raised and maintained greater armies than states, consisting of triple the number of inhabitants, are able to support at present. It is computed, that, in all EUROPEAN nations, the proportion between soldiers and people does not exceed one to a hundred. But we read, that the city of ROME alone, with its small territory, raised and maintained, in early times, ten legions against the LATINS. ATHENS, the whole of whose dominions was not larger than YORKSHIRE, sent to the expedition against SICILY near forty thousand men.[†] DIONYSIUS the elder, it is said, maintained a standing army of a hundred thousand foot, and ten thousand horse, besides a large fleet of four hundred sail;[†] though his territories extended no further than the city of SYRACUSE, about a third of the island of SICILY, and some sea-port towns and garrisons on the coast of ITALY and ILLYRICUM.[*] It is true, the ancient armies, in time of war, subsisted much upon plunder: but did not the enemy plunder in their turn? which was a more ruinous way of levying a tax than any other that could be devised. In short, no probable reason can be assigned for the great power of the more ancient states above the modern, but their want of commerce and luxury. Few artisans were maintained by the labour of the farmers, and therefore more soldiers might live upon it. LIVY says, that ROME, in his time, would find it difficult to raise as large an army as that which, in her early days, she sent out against the GAULS and LATINS.[†] Instead of those soldiers who fought for liberty and empire in CAMILLUS's time, there were, in AUGUSTUS's days, musicians, painters, cooks, players, and tailors; and if the land was equally cultivated at both periods, it could certainly maintain equal numbers in the one profession as in the other. They added nothing to the mere necessaries of life, in the latter period more than in the former.

It is natural on this occasion to ask, whether sovereigns may not return to the maxims of ancient policy and consult their own interest in this respect, more than the happiness of their subjects? I answer, that it appears to me almost impossible: and that because ancient policy was violent, and contrary to the more natural and usual course of things. It is well known with what peculiar laws SPARTA was governed,

and what a prodigy that republic is justly esteemed by every
one who has considered human nature, as it has displayed
itself in other nations, and other ages. Were the testimony
of history less positive and circumstantial, such a government would appear a mere philosophical whim or fiction,
and impossible ever to be reduced to practice. And though
the ROMAN and other ancient republics were supported on
principles somewhat more natural, yet was there an extraordinary concurrence of circumstances, to make them submit
to such grievous burdens. They were free states; they were
small ones; and the age being martial, all their neighbours
were continually in arms. Freedom naturally begets public
spirit, especially in small states; and this public spirit, this
amor patriae, must increase, when the public is almost in
continual alarm, and men are obliged every moment to
expose themselves to the greatest dangers for its defence. A
continual succession of wars makes every citizen a soldier:
he takes the field in his turn: and during his service he is
chiefly maintained by himself. This service is indeed equivalent to a heavy tax; yet is it less felt by a people addicted
to arms, who fight for honour and revenge more than pay,
and are unacquainted with gain and industry, as well as
pleasure.[†] Not to mention the great equality of fortunes
among the inhabitants of the ancient republics, where every
field, belonging to a different proprietor, was able to maintain a family, and rendered the numbers of citizens very
considerable, even without trade and manufactures.

But though the want of trade and manufactures among a
free and very martial people, may sometimes have no other
effect than to render the public more powerful, it is certain
that, in the common course of human affairs, it will have a
quite contrary tendency. Sovereigns must take mankind as
they find them, and cannot pretend to introduce any violent
change in their principles and ways of thinking. A long
course of time, with a variety of accidents and circumstances, are requisite to produce those great revolutions,
which so much diversify the face of human affairs. And the
less natural any set of principles are, which support a particular society, the more difficulty will a legislator meet with

in raising and cultivating them. It is his best policy to comply with the common bent of mankind, and give it all the improvements of which it is susceptible. Now, according to the most natural course of things, industry, and arts, and trade, increase the power of the sovereign, as well as the happiness of the subjects; and that policy is violent which aggrandizes the public by the poverty of individuals. This will easily appear from a few considerations, which will present to us the consequences of sloth and barbarity.

Where manufactures and mechanic arts are not cultivated, the bulk of the people must apply themselves to agriculture; and if their skill and industry increase, there must arise a great superfluity from their labour, beyond what suffices to maintain them. They have no temptation, therefore, to increase their skill and industry; since they cannot exchange that superfluity for any commodities which may serve either to their pleasure or vanity. A habit of indolence naturally prevails. The greater part of the land lies uncultivated. What is cultivated, yields not its utmost, for want of skill and assiduity in the farmers. If at any time the public exigencies require that great numbers should be employed in the public service, the labour of the people furnishes now no superfluities by which these numbers can be maintained. The labourers cannot increase their skill and industry on a sudden. Lands uncultivated cannot be brought into tillage for some years. The armies, meanwhile, must either make sudden and violent conquests, or disband for want of subsistence. A regular attack or defence, therefore, is not to be expected from such a people, and their soldiers must be as ignorant and unskilful as their farmers and manufacturers.

Every thing in the world is purchased by labour; and our passions are the only causes of labour. When a nation abounds in manufactures and mechanic arts, the proprietors of land, as well as the farmers, study agriculture as a science, and redouble their industry and attention. The superfluity which arises from their labour is not lost, but is exchanged with manufactures for those commodities which men's luxury now makes them covet. By this means, land furnishes a great deal more of the necessaries of life than what suffices for those who cultivate it. In times of peace and tranquillity, this superfluity goes to the maintenance of manufacturers, and the improvers of liberal arts. But it is easy for the public to convert many of these manufacturers into soldiers, and maintain them by that superfluity which arises from the labour of the farmers. Accordingly we find, that this is the case in all civilized governments. When the sovereign raises an army, what is the consequence? He imposes a tax. This tax obliges all the people to retrench what is least necessary to their subsistence. Those who labour in such commodities must either enlist in the troops, or turn themselves to agriculture, and thereby oblige some labourers to enlist for want of business. And to consider the matter abstractedly, manufactures increase the power of the state only as they store up so much labour, and that of a kind to which the public may lay claim, without depriving any one of the necessaries of life. The more labour, therefore, that is employed beyond mere necessaries, the more powerful is any state; since the persons engaged in that labour may easily be converted to the public service. In a state without manufactures, there may be the same number of hands; but there is not the same quantity of labour, nor of the same kind. All the labour is there bestowed upon necessaries, which can admit of little or no abatement.

Thus the greatness of the sovereign, and the happiness of the state, are in a great measure united with regard to trade and manufactures. It is a violent method, and in most cases impracticable, to oblige the labourer to toil, in order to raise from the land more than what subsists himself and family. Furnish him with manufactures and commodities, and he will do it of himself; afterwards you will find it easy to seize some part of his superfluous labour, and employ it in the public service, without giving him his wonted return. Being accustomed to industry, he will think this less grievous, than if at once you obliged him to an augmentation of labour without any reward. The case is the same with regard to the other members of the state. The greater is the stock of labour of all kinds, the greater quantity may be taken from the heap without making any sensible alteration in it.

A public granary of corn, a storehouse of cloth, a magazine of arms; all these must be allowed real riches and strength in any state. Trade and industry are really nothing but a stock of labour, which, in times of peace and tranquillity, is employed for the ease and satisfaction of individuals, but in the exigencies of state, may in part be turned to public advantage. Could we convert a city into a kind of fortified camp, and infuse into each breast so martial a genius, and such a passion for public good, as to make every one willing to undergo the greatest hardships for the sake of the public, these affections might now, as in ancient times, prove alone a sufficient spur to industry, and support the community. It would then be advantageous, as in camps, to banish all arts and luxury; and by restrictions on equipage and tables, make the provisions and forage last longer than if the army were loaded with a number of superfluous retainers. But as these principles are too disinterested, and too difficult to support, it is requisite to govern men by other passions, and animate them with a spirit of avarice and industry, art and luxury. The camp is, in this case, loaded with a superfluous retinue, but the provisions flow in proportionably larger. The harmony of the whole is still supported; and the natural bent of the mind, being more complied with, individuals, as well as the public, find their account in the observance of those maxims.

The same method of reasoning will let us see the advantage of *foreign* commerce in augmenting the power of the state, as well as the riches and happiness of the subject. It increases the stock of labour in the nation; and the sovereign may convert what share of it he finds necessary to the service of the public. Foreign trade, by its imports, furnishes materials for new manufactures; and, by its exports, it produces labour in particular commodities, which could not be consumed at home. In short, a kingdom that has a large import and export, must abound more with industry, and that employed upon delicacies and luxuries, than a kingdom which rests contented with its native commodities. It is therefore more powerful, as well as richer and happier. The individuals reap the benefit of these commodities, so far as they gratify the senses and appetites; and the public is also a gainer, while a greater stock of labour is, by this means, stored up against any public exigency; that is, a greater number of laborious men are maintained, who may be diverted to the public service, without robbing any one of the necessaries, or even the chief conveniences of life.

If we consult history, we shall find, that in most nations foreign trade has preceded any refinement in home manufactures, and given birth to domestic luxury. The temptation is stronger to make use of foreign commodities which are ready for use, and which are entirely new to us, than to make improvements on any domestic commodity, which always advance by slow degrees, and never affect us by their novelty. The profit is also very great in exporting what is superfluous at home, and what bears no price, to foreign nations whose soil or climate is not favourable to that commodity. Thus men become acquainted with the *pleasures* of luxury, and the *profits* of commerce; and their *delicacy* and *industry* being once awakened, carry them on to further improvements in every branch of domestic as well as foreign trade; and this perhaps is the chief advantage which arises from a commerce with strangers. It rouses men from their indolence; and, presenting the gayer and more opulent part of the nation with objects of luxury which they never before dreamed of, raises in them a desire of a more splendid way of life than what their ancestors enjoyed. And at the same time, the few merchants who possessed the secret of this importation and exportation, make great profits, and, becoming rivals in wealth to the ancient nobility, tempt other adventurers to become their rivals in commerce. Imitation soon diffuses all those arts, while domestic manufacturers emulate the foreign in their improvements, and work up every home commodity to the utmost perfection of which it is susceptible. Their own steel and iron, in such laborious hands, become equal to the gold and rubies of the INDIES.

When the affairs of the society are once brought to this situation, a nation may lose most of its foreign trade, and yet continue a great and powerful people. If strangers will not take any particular commodity of ours, we must cease to labour in it. The same hands will turn themselves towards some refinement in other commodities which may be wanted at home; and there must always be materials for them to work upon, till every person in the state who possesses riches, enjoys as great plenty of home commodities, and those in as great perfection, as he desires; which can never possibly happen. CHINA is represented as one of the most flourishing empires in the world, though it has very little commerce beyond its own territories.

It will not, I hope, be considered as a superfluous digression, if I here observe, that as the multitude of mechanical arts is advantageous, so is the great number of persons to whose share the productions of these arts fall. A too great disproportion among the citizens weakens any state. Every person, if possible, ought to enjoy the fruits of his labour, in a full possession of all the necessaries, and many of the conveniences of life. No one can doubt but such an equality is most suitable to human nature, and diminishes much less from the *happiness* of the rich, than it adds to that of the poor. It also augments the *power of the state*, and makes any extraordinary taxes or impositions be paid with more cheerfulness. Where the riches are engrossed by a few, these must contribute very largely to the supplying of the public necessities; but when the riches are dispersed among multitudes, the burden feels light on every shoulder, and the taxes make not a very sensible difference on any one's way of living.

Add to this, that where the riches are in few hands, these must enjoy all the power, and will readily conspire to lay the whole burden on the poor, and oppress them still further, to the discouragement of all industry.

In this circumstance consists the great advantage of ENGLAND above any nation at present in the world, or that appears in the records of any story. It is true, the ENGLISH feel some disadvantages in foreign trade by the high price of labour, which is in part the effect of the riches of their artisans, as well as of the plenty of money. But as foreign trade is not the most material circumstance, it is not to be put in competition with the happiness of so many millions; and if there were no more to endear to them that free government under which they live, this alone were sufficient. The poverty of the common people is a natural, if not an infallible effect of absolute monarchy; though I doubt whether it be always true on the other hand, that their riches are an infallible result of liberty. Liberty must be attended with particular accidents, and a certain turn of thinking, in order to produce that effect. Lord BACON, accounting for the great advantages obtained by the ENGLISH in their wars with FRANCE, ascribes them chiefly to the superior ease and plenty of the common people amongst the former; yet the government of the two kingdoms was, at that time, pretty much alike.* Where the labourers and artisans are accustomed to work for low wages, and to retain but a small part of the fruits of their labour, it is difficult for them, even in a free government, to better their condition, or conspire among themselves to heighten their wages; but even where they are accustomed to a more plentiful way of life, it is easy for the rich, in an arbitrary government, to conspire against *them*, and throw the whole burden of the taxes on their shoulders.

It may seem an odd position, that the poverty of the common people in FRANCE, ITALY, and SPAIN, is, in some measure, owing to the superior riches of the soil and happiness of climate; yet there want no reasons to justify this paradox. In such a fine mould or soil as that of those more southern regions, agriculture is an easy art; and one man, with a couple of sorry horses, will be able, in a season, to cultivate as much land as will pay a pretty considerable rent to the proprietor. All the art which the farmer knows, is to leave his ground fallow for a year, as soon as it is exhausted; and the warmth of the sun alone and temperature of the climate enrich it, and restore its fertility. Such poor peasants, therefore, require only a simple maintenance for their labour. They have no stock or riches which claim more; and at the same time they are for ever dependent on the landlord, who gives no leases, nor fears that his land will be spoiled by the ill methods of cultivation. In ENGLAND, the land is rich, but coarse; must be cultivated at a great expense; and produces slender crops when not carefully managed, and by a method which gives not the full profit but in a course of several years. A farmer, therefore, in ENGLAND must have a considerable stock, and a long lease; which beget proportional profits. The vineyards of CHAMPAGNE and BURGUNDY, that often yield to the landlord about five pounds *per* acre, are cultivated by peasants who have scarcely bread: the reason is, that peasants need no stock but their own limbs, with instruments of husbandry which they can buy for twenty shillings. The farmers are commonly in some better circumstances in those countries. But the graziers are most at their ease of all those who cultivate the land. The reason is still the same. Men must have profits proportionable to their expense and hazard. Where so considerable a number of the labouring poor, as the peasants and farmers, are in very low circumstances, all the rest must partake of their poverty, whether the government of that nation be monarchical or republican.

We may form a similar remark with regard to the general history of mankind. What is the reason why no people living between the tropics, could ever yet attain to any art of civility, or reach even any police in their government, and any military discipline, while few nations in the temperate climates have been altogether deprived of these advantages? It is probable that one cause of this phenomenon is the warmth and equality of weather in the torrid zone, which render clothes and houses less requisite for the inhabitants, and thereby remove, in part, that necessity which is the great spur to industry and invention. *Curis acuens mortalia corda.** Not to mention, that the fewer goods or possessions of this kind any people enjoy, the fewer quarrels are likely to arise amongst them, and the less necessity will there be for a settled police or regular authority, to protect and defend them from foreign enemies, or from each other.

OF REFINEMENT IN THE ARTS*

LUXURY is a word of an uncertain signification, and may be taken in a good as well as in a bad sense. In general it means great refinement in the gratification of the senses; and any degree of it may be innocent or blamable, according to the age, or country, or condition of the person. The bounds between the virtue and the vice cannot here be exactly fixed, more than in other moral subjects. To imagine, that the gratifying of any sense, or the indulging of any delicacy in meat, drink, or apparel, is of itself a vice, can never enter into a head, that is not disordered by the frenzies of enthusiasm. I have, indeed, heard of a monk abroad, who, because the windows of his cell opened upon a noble prospect, made a *covenant with his eyes* never to turn that way, or receive so sensual a gratification. And such is the crime of drinking CHAMPAGNE or BURGUNDY, preferably to small beer or porter. These indulgences are only vices, when they are pursued at the expense of some virtue, as liberality or charity; in like manner as they are follies, when for them a man ruins his fortune, and reduces himself to want and beggary. Where they entrench upon no virtue, but leave ample subject whence to provide for friends, family, and every proper object of generosity or compassion, they are entirely innocent, and have in every age been acknowledged such by almost all moralists. To be entirely occupied with the luxury of the table, for instance, without any relish for the pleasures of ambition, study, or conversation, is a mark of stupidity, and is incompatible with any vigour of temper or genius. To confine one's expense entirely to such a gratification, without regard to friends or family, is an indication of a heart destitute of humanity or benevolence. But if a man reserve time sufficient for all laudable pursuits, and money sufficient for all generous purposes, he is free from every shadow of blame or reproach.

Since luxury may be considered either as innocent or blamable, one may be surprised at those preposterous opinions which have been entertained concerning it; while men of libertine principles bestow praises even on vicious luxury, and represent it as highly advantageous to society; and, on the other hand, men of severe morals blame even the most innocent luxury, and represent it as the source of all the corruptions, disorders, and factions incident to civil government. We shall here endeavour to correct both these extremes, by proving, *first*, that the ages of refinement are both the happiest and most virtuous; *secondly*, that wherever luxury ceases to be innocent, it also ceases to be beneficial; and when carried a degree too far, is a quality pernicious, though perhaps not the most pernicious, to political society.

To prove the first point, we need but consider the effects of refinement both on *private* and on *public* life. Human happiness, according to the most received notions, seems to consist in three ingredients: action, pleasure, and indolence: and though these ingredients ought to be mixed in different proportions, according to the particular disposition of the person; yet no one ingredient can be entirely wanting, without destroying, in some measure, the relish of the whole composition. Indolence or repose, indeed, seems not of itself to contribute much to our enjoyment; but, like sleep, is requisite as an indulgence, to the weakness of human nature, which cannot support an uninterrupted course of business or pleasure. That quick march of the spirits, which takes a man from himself, and chiefly gives satisfaction, does in the end exhaust the mind, and requires some intervals of repose, which, though agreeable for a moment, yet, if prolonged, beget a languor and lethargy, that destroy all enjoyment. Education, custom, and example, have a mighty influence in turning the mind to any of these pursuits; and it must be owned that, where they promote a relish for action and pleasure, they are so far favourable to human happiness. In times when industry and the arts flourish, men are kept in perpetual occupation, and enjoy, as their reward, the occupation itself, as well as those pleasures which are the fruit of their labour. The mind acquires new vigour; enlarges its powers and faculties; and, by an assiduity in honest industry, both satisfies its natural appetites, and prevents the growth of unnatural ones, which commonly spring up, when nourished by ease and idleness. Banish those arts from society, you deprive men both of action and of pleasure; and, leaving nothing but indolence in their place, you even destroy the relish of indolence, which never is agreeable, but when it succeeds to labour, and recruits the spirits, exhausted by too much application and fatigue.

Another advantage of industry and of refinements in the mechanical arts, is, that they commonly produce some refinements in the liberal; nor can one be carried to perfection, without being accompanied, in some degree, with the other. The same age which produces great philosophers and politicians, renowned generals and poets, usually abounds with skilful weavers, and ship-carpenters. We cannot reasonably expect, that a piece of woollen cloth will be wrought to perfection in a nation which is ignorant of astronomy, or where ethics are neglected. The spirit of the age* affects all the arts, and the minds of men being once roused from their lethargy, and put into a fermentation, turn themselves on all sides, and carry improvements into every art and science. Profound ignorance is totally banished, and men enjoy the privilege of rational creatures, to think as well as to act, to cultivate the pleasures of the mind as well as those of the body.

The more these refined arts advance, the more sociable men become: nor is it possible, that, when enriched with science, and possessed of a fund of conversation, they should be contented to remain in solitude, or live with their fellow-citizens in that distant manner, which is peculiar to ignorant and barbarous nations. They flock into cities; love to receive and communicate knowledge; to show their wit or their breeding; their taste in conversation or living, in clothes or furniture. Curiosity allures the wise; vanity the foolish; and pleasure both. Particular clubs and societies are everywhere formed: both sexes meet in an easy and sociable manner; and the tempers of men, as well as their behaviour, refine apace. So that, beside the improvements which they receive from knowledge and the liberal arts, it is impossible but they must feel an increase of humanity, from the very habit of conversing together, and contributing to each other's pleasure and entertainment. Thus *industry*, *knowledge*, and *humanity*, are linked together, by an indissoluble chain, and are found, from experience as well as reason, to be peculiar to the more polished, and, what are commonly denominated, the more luxurious ages.

Nor are these advantages attended with disadvantages that bear any proportion to them. The more men refine upon pleasure, the less will they indulge in excesses of any kind; because nothing is more destructive to true pleasure than such excesses. One may safely affirm, that the TARTARS are oftener guilty of beastly gluttony, when they feast on their dead horses, than EUROPEAN courtiers with all their refinement of cookery. And if libertine love, or even infidelity to the marriage-bed, be more frequent in polite ages, when it is often regarded only as a piece of gallantry; drunkenness, on the other hand, is much less common; a vice more odious, and more pernicious, both to mind and body. And in this matter I would appeal, not only to an OVID or a PETRONIUS, but to a SENECA or a CATO. We know that CAESAR, during CATILINE's conspiracy, being necessitated to put into CATO's hands a *billet-doux*, which discovered an intrigue with SERVILIA, CATO's own sister, that stern philosopher threw it back to him with indignation; and, in the bitterness of his wrath, gave him the appellation of drunkard, as a term more opprobrious than that with which he could more justly have reproached him.*

But industry, knowledge, and humanity, are not advantageous in private life alone; they diffuse their beneficial influence on the *public*, and render the government as great and flourishing as they make individuals happy and prosperous. The increase and consumption of all the commodities, which serve to the ornament and pleasure of life, are advantages to society; because, at the same time that they multiply those innocent gratifications to individuals, they are a kind of *storehouse* of labour, which, in the exigencies of state, may be turned to the public service. In a nation where there is no demand for such superfluities, men sink into indolence, lose all enjoyment of life, and are useless to the public, which cannot maintain or support its fleets and armies from the industry of such slothful members.

The bounds of all the EUROPEAN kingdoms are, at present, nearly the same as they were two hundred years ago. But what a difference is there in the power and grandeur of those kingdoms? which can be ascribed to nothing but the increase of art and industry. When CHARLES VIII of FRANCE invaded ITALY, he carried with him about 20,000 men; yet this armament so exhausted the nation, as we learn from GUICCIARDIN,* that for some years it was not able to make so great an effort. The late king of FRANCE, in time of war, kept in pay above 400,000† men; though from Mazarine's death to his own, he was engaged in a course of wars that lasted near thirty years.*

This industry is much promoted by the knowledge inseparable from ages of art and refinement; as, on the other hand, this knowledge enables the public to make the best advantage of the industry of its subjects. Laws, order, police, discipline; these can never be carried to any degree of perfection, before human reason has refined itself by exercise, and by an application to the more vulgar arts, at least of commerce and manufacture. Can we expect that a government will be well modelled by a people, who know not how to make a spinning wheel, or to employ a loom to advantage? Not to mention, that all ignorant ages are infested with superstition, which throws the government off its bias, and disturbs men in the pursuit of their interest and happiness. Knowledge in the arts of government begets mildness and moderation, by instructing men in the advantages of humane maxims above rigour and severity, which drive subjects into rebellion, and make the return to submission impracticable, by cutting off all hopes of pardon. When the tempers of men are softened as well as their knowledge improved, this humanity appears still more conspicuous, and is the chief characteristic which distinguishes a civilized age from times of barbarity and ignorance. Factions are then less inveterate, revolutions less tragical, authority less severe, and seditions less frequent. Even foreign wars abate of their cruelty; and after the field of battle, where honour and interest steel men against compassion, as well as fear, the combatants divest themselves of the brute, and resume the man.

Nor need we fear, that men, by losing their ferocity, will lose their martial spirit, or become less undaunted and vigorous in defence of their country or their liberty. The arts have no such effect in enervating either the mind or body. On the contrary, industry, their inseparable attendant, adds new force to both. And if anger, which is said to be the whetstone of courage, loses somewhat of its asperity, by politeness and refinement; a sense of honour, which is a stronger, more constant, and more governable principle, acquires fresh vigour by that elevation of genius which arises from knowledge and a good education. Add to this, that courage can neither have any duration, nor be of any use, when not accompanied with discipline and martial skill, which are seldom found among a barbarous people. The ancients remarked, that DATAMES was the only barbarian that ever knew the art of war. And PYRRHUS, seeing the ROMANS marshal their army with some art and skill, said with surprise, *These barbarians have nothing barbarous in their discipline!* It is observable, that, as the old ROMANS, by applying themselves solely to war, were almost the only uncivilized people that ever possessed military discipline; so the modern ITALIANS are the only civilized people, among EUROPEANS, that ever wanted courage and a martial spirit. Those who would ascribe this effeminacy of the ITALIANS to their luxury, or politeness, or application to the arts, need but consider the FRENCH and ENGLISH, whose bravery is as incontestable as their love for the arts, and their assiduity in commerce. The ITALIAN historians give us a more satisfactory reason for the degeneracy of their countrymen. They show us how the sword was dropped at once by all the ITALIAN sovereigns; while the VENETIAN aristocracy was jealous of its subjects, the FLORENTINE democracy applied itself entirely to commerce; ROME was governed by priests, and NAPLES by women. War then became the business of soldiers of fortune, who spared one another, and, to the astonishment of the world, could engage a whole day in what they called a battle, and return at night to their camp without the least bloodshed.

What has chiefly induced severe moralists to declaim

against refinement in the arts, is the example of ancient ROME, which, joining to its poverty and rusticity virtue and public spirit, rose to such a surprising height of grandeur and liberty; but, having learned from its conquered provinces the ASIATIC luxury, fell into every kind of corruption; whence arose sedition and civil wars, attended at last with the total loss of liberty. All the LATIN classics, whom we peruse in our infancy, are full of these sentiments, and universally ascribe the ruin of their state to the arts and riches imported from the East; insomuch, that SALLUST represents a taste for painting as a vice, no less than lewdness and drinking.* And so popular were these sentiments, during the latter ages of the republic, that this author abounds in praises of the old rigid ROMAN virtue, though himself the most egregious instance of modern luxury and corruption; speaks contemptuously of the GRECIAN eloquence, though the most elegant writer in the world; nay, employs preposterous digressions and declamations to this purpose, though a model of taste and correctness.

But it would be easy to prove, that these writers mistook the cause of the disorders in the ROMAN state, and ascribed to luxury and the arts, what really proceeded from an ill-modelled government, and the unlimited extent of conquests. Refinement on the pleasures and conveniences of life has no natural tendency to beget venality and corruption. The value which all men put upon any particular pleasure, depends on comparison and experience; nor is a porter less greedy of money, which he spends on bacon and brandy, than a courtier, who purchases champagne and ortolans.* Riches are valuable at all times, and to all men; because they always purchase pleasures, such as men are accustomed to and desire: nor can any thing restrain or regulate the love of money, but a sense of honour and virtue; which, if it be not nearly equal at all times, will naturally abound most in ages of knowledge and refinement.

Of all EUROPEAN kingdoms POLAND seems the most defective in the arts of war as well as peace, mechanical as well as liberal; yet it is there that venality and corruption do most prevail. The nobles seem to have preserved their crown elective for no other purpose, than regularly to sell it to the highest bidder. This is almost the only species of commerce with which that people are acquainted.

The liberties of ENGLAND, so far from decaying since the improvements in the arts, have never flourished so much as during that period. And though corruption may seem to increase of late years; this is chiefly to be ascribed to our established liberty, when our princes have found the impossibility of governing without parliaments, or of terrifying parliaments by the phantom of prerogative. Not to mention, that this corruption or venality prevails much more among the electors than the elected; and therefore cannot justly be ascribed to any refinements in luxury.

If we consider the matter in a proper light, we shall find, that a progress in the arts is rather favourable to liberty, and has a natural tendency to preserve, if not produce a free government. In rude unpolished nations, where the arts are neglected, all labour is bestowed on the cultivation of the ground; and the whole society is divided into two classes, proprietors of land, and their vassals or tenants. The latter are necessarily dependent, and fitted for slavery and subjection; especially where they possess no riches, and are not valued for their knowledge in agriculture; as must always be the case where the arts are neglected. The former naturally erect themselves into petty tyrants; and must either submit to an absolute master, for the sake of peace and order; or, if they will preserve their independency, like the ancient barons, they must fall into feuds and contests among themselves, and throw the whole society into such confusion, as is perhaps worse than the most despotic government. But where luxury nourishes commerce and industry, the peasants, by a proper cultivation of the land, become rich and independent: while the tradesmen and merchants acquire a share of the property, and draw authority and consideration to that middling rank of men, who are the best and firmest basis of public liberty. These submit not to slavery, like the peasants, from poverty and meanness of spirit; and, having no hopes of tyrannizing over others, like the barons, they are not tempted, for the sake of that gratification, to submit to the tyranny of their sovereign. They covet equal laws, which may secure their property, and preserve them from monarchical, as well as aristocratical tyranny.

The lower house is the support of our popular government; and all the world acknowledges, that it owed its chief influence and consideration to the increase of commerce, which threw such a balance of property into the hands of the commons. How inconsistent, then, is it to blame so violently a refinement in the arts, and to represent it as the bane of liberty and public spirit!

To declaim against present times, and magnify the virtue of remote ancestors, is a propensity almost inherent in human nature: and as the sentiments and opinions of civilized ages alone are transmitted to posterity, hence it is that we meet with so many severe judgments pronounced against luxury, and even science; and hence it is that at present we give so ready an assent to them. But the fallacy is easily perceived, by comparing different nations that are contemporaries; where we both judge more impartially, and can better set in opposition those manners, with which we are sufficiently acquainted. Treachery and cruelty, the most pernicious and most odious of all vices, seem peculiar to uncivilized ages; and, by the refined GREEKS and ROMANS, were ascribed to all the barbarous nations which surrounded them. They might justly, therefore, have presumed, that their own ancestors, so highly celebrated, possessed no greater virtue, and were as much inferior to their posterity in honour and humanity, as in taste and science. An ancient FRANK or SAXON may be highly extolled: but I believe every man would think his life or fortune much less secure in the hands of a MOOR or TARTAR, than in those of a FRENCH or ENGLISH gentleman, the rank of men the most civilized in the most civilized nations.

We come now to the *second* position which we proposed to illustrate, to wit, that, as innocent luxury, or a refinement in the arts and conveniences of life, is advantageous to the public; so, wherever luxury ceases to be innocent, it also ceases to be beneficial; and when carried a degree further, begins to be a quality pernicious, though perhaps not the most pernicious, to political society.

Let us consider what we call vicious luxury. No gratification, however sensual, can of itself be esteemed vicious. A gratification is only vicious when it engrosses all a man's expense, and leaves no ability for such acts of duty and generosity as are required by his situation and fortune. Suppose that he correct the vice, and employ part of his expense in the education of his children, in the support of his friends, and in relieving the poor; would any prejudice result to society? On the contrary, the same consumption would arise; and that labour, which at present is employed only in producing a slender gratification to one man, would relieve the necessitous, and bestow satisfaction on hundreds. The same care and toil that raise a dish of peas at CHRISTMAS, would give bread to a whole family, during six months. To say that, without a vicious luxury, the labour would not have been employed at all, is only to say, that there is some other defect in human nature, such as indolence, selfishness, inattention to others, for which luxury, in some measure, provides a remedy; as one poison may be an antidote to another. But virtue, like wholesome food, is better than poisons, however corrected.

Suppose the same number of men that are at present in GREAT BRITAIN, with the same soil and climate; I ask, is it not possible for them to be happier, by the most perfect way of life that can be imagined, and by the greatest reformation that Omnipotence itself could work in their temper and disposition? To assert that they cannot, appears evidently ridiculous. As the land is able to maintain more than all its present inhabitants, they could never in such a UTOPIAN state, feel any other ills than those which arise from bodily sickness: and these are not the half of human miseries. All other ills spring from some vice, either in ourselves or others; and even many of our diseases proceed from the same origin. Remove the vices, and the ills follow. You must only take care to remove all the vices. If you remove part, you may render the matter worse. By banishing *vicious* luxury, without curing sloth and an indifference to others, you only diminish industry in the state, and add nothing to men's charity or their generosity. Let us, therefore, rest contented with asserting, that two opposite vices in a state may be more advantageous than either of them alone; but let us never pronounce vice in itself advantageous. It is not very inconsistent for an author to assert in one page, that moral distinctions are inventions of politicians for public interest, and in the next page maintain, that vice is advantageous to the public.[†] And indeed it seems, upon any system of morality, little less than a contradiction in terms, to talk of a vice, which is in general beneficial to society.

I thought this reasoning necessary, in order to give some light to a philosophical question, which has been much disputed in ENGLAND. I call it a *philosophical* question, not a *political* one. For whatever may be the consequence of such a miraculous transformation of mankind, as would endow them with every species of virtue, and free them from every species of vice, this concerns not the magistrate, who aims only at possibilities. He cannot cure every vice by substituting a virtue in its place. Very often he can only cure one vice by another; and in that case he ought to prefer what is least pernicious to society. Luxury, when excessive, is the source of many ills, but is in general preferable to sloth and idleness, which would commonly succeed in its place, and are more hurtful both to private persons and to the public. When sloth reigns, a mean uncultivated way of life prevails amongst individuals, without society, without enjoyment. And if the sovereign, in such a situation, demands the service of his subjects, the labour of the state suffices only to furnish the necessaries of life to the labourers, and can afford nothing to those who are employed in the public service.

OF INTEREST

NOTHING is esteemed a more certain sign of the flourishing condition of any nation than the lowness of interest: and with reason, though I believe the cause is somewhat different from what is commonly apprehended. Lowness of interest is generally ascribed to plenty of money. But money, however plentiful, has no other effect, *if fixed*, than to raise the price of labour. Silver is more common than gold, and therefore you receive a greater quantity of it for the same commodities. But do you pay less interest for it? Interest in BATAVIA and JAMAICA is at 10 *per cent*, in PORTUGAL at 6, though these places, as we may learn from the prices of every thing, abound more in gold and silver than either LONDON or AMSTERDAM.

Were all the gold in ENGLAND annihilated at once, and one and twenty shillings substituted in the place of every guinea, would money be more plentiful, or interest lower? No, surely: we should only use silver, instead of gold. Were gold rendered as common as silver, and silver as common as copper, would money be more plentiful, or interest lower? We may assuredly give the same answer. Our shillings would then be yellow, and our halfpence white; and we should have no guineas. No other difference would ever be observed; no alteration on commerce, manufactures, navigation, or interest; unless we imagine that the colour of the metal is of any consequence.

Now, what is so visible in these greater variations of scarcity or abundance in the precious metals, must hold in all inferior changes. If the multiplying of gold and silver fifteen times makes no difference, much less can the doubling or tripling them. All augmentation has no other effect than to heighten the price of labour and commodities; and even this variation is little more than that of a name. In the progress towards these changes, the augmentation may have some influence, by exciting industry; but after the prices are settled, suitably to the new abundance of gold and silver, it has no manner of influence.

An effect always holds proportion with its cause. Prices have risen near four times since the discovery of the INDIES; and it is probable gold and silver have multiplied much more: but interest has not fallen much above half. The rate of interest, therefore, is not derived from the quantity of the precious metals.

Money having chiefly a fictitious value, the greater or less plenty of it is of no consequence, if we consider a nation within itself; and the quantity of specie, when once fixed, though ever so large, has no other effect than to oblige every one to tell out a greater number of those shining bits of metal for clothes, furniture, or equipage, without increasing any one convenience of life. If a man borrow money to build a house, he then carries home a greater load; because the stone, timber, lead, glass, &c. with the labour of the masons and carpenters, are represented by a greater quantity of gold and silver. But as these metals are considered chiefly as representations, there can no alteration arise from their bulk or quantity, their weight or colour, either upon their real value or their interest. The same interest, in all cases, bears the same proportion to the sum. And if you lent me so much labour and so many commodities, by receiving five *per cent* you always receive proportional labour and commodities, however represented, whether by yellow or white coin, whether by a pound or an ounce. It is in vain, therefore, to look for the cause of the fall or rise of interest in the greater or less quantity of gold and silver, which is fixed in any nation.

High interest arises from *three* circumstances: a great demand for borrowing, little riches to supply that demand, and great profits arising from commerce: and the circumstances are a clear proof of the small advance of commerce and industry, not of the scarcity of gold and silver. Low interest, on the other hand, proceeds from the three opposite circumstances: a small demand for borrowing; great riches to supply that demand; and small profits arising from commerce: and these circumstances are all connected together, and proceed from the increase of industry and commerce, not of gold and silver. We shall endeavour to prove these points; and shall begin with the causes and the effects of a great or small demand for borrowing.

When a people have emerged ever so little from a savage state, and their numbers have increased beyond the original multitude, there must immediately arise an inequality of property; and while some possess large tracts of land, others

are confined within narrow limits, and some are entirely
without landed property. Those who possess more land than
they can labour, employ those who possess none, and agree
to receive a determinate part of the product. Thus the
landed interest is immediately established; nor is there any
settled government, however rude, in which affairs are not
on this footing. Of these proprietors of land, some must
presently discover themselves to be of different tempers
from others; and while one would willingly store up the
produce of his land for futurity, another desires to consume
at present what should suffice for many years. But as the
spending of a settled revenue is a way of life entirely without occupation; men have so much need of somewhat to fix
and engage them, that pleasures, such as they are, will be
the pursuit of the greater part of the landholders, and the
prodigals among them will always be more numerous than
the misers. In a state, therefore, where there is nothing but
a landed interest, as there is little frugality, the borrowers
must be very numerous, and the rate of interest must hold
proportion to it. The difference depends not on the quantity
of money, but on the habits and manners which prevail.
By this alone the demand for borrowing is increased or
diminished. Were money so plentiful as to make an egg be
sold for sixpence; so long as there are only landed gentry
and peasants in the state, the borrowers must be numerous,
and interest high. The rent for the same farm would be
heavier and more bulky: but the same idleness of the landlord, with the high price of commodities, would dissipate
it in the same time, and produce the same necessity and
demand for borrowing.

Nor is the case different with regard to the *second* circumstance which we proposed to consider, namely, the great or
little riches to supply the demand. This effect also depends
on the habits and way of living of the people, not on the
quantity of gold and silver. In order to have, in any state, a
great number of lenders, it is not sufficient nor requisite that
there be great abundance of the precious metals. It is only
requisite that the property or command of that quantity,
which is in the state, whether great or small, should be

collected in particular hands, so as to form considerable sums, or compose a great moneyed interest. This begets a number of lenders, and sinks the rate of usury; and this, I shall venture to affirm, depends not on the quantity of specie, but on particular manners and customs, which make the specie gather into separate sums or masses of considerable value.

For, suppose that, by miracle, every man in GREAT BRITAIN should have five pounds slipped into his pocket in one night; this would much more than double the whole money that is at present in the kingdom; yet there would not next day, nor for some time, be any more lenders, nor any variation in the interest. And were there nothing but landlords and peasants in the state, this money, however abundant, could never gather into sums, and would only serve to increase the prices of every thing, without any further consequence. The prodigal landlord dissipates it as fast as he receives it, and the beggarly peasant has no means, nor view, nor ambition of obtaining above a bare livelihood. The overplus of borrowers above that of lenders continuing still the same, there will follow no reduction of interest. That depends upon another principle; and must proceed from an increase of industry and frugality of arts and commerce.

Every thing useful to the life of man arises from the ground; but few things arise in that condition which is requisite to render them useful. There must, therefore, beside the peasants and the proprietors of land, be another rank of men, who, receiving from the former the rude materials, work them into their proper form, and retain part for their own use and subsistence. In the infancy of society, these contracts between the artisans and the peasants, and between one species of artisans and another, are commonly entered into immediately by the persons themselves, who, being neighbours, are easily acquainted with each other's necessities, and can lend their mutual assistance to supply them. But when men's industry increases, and their views enlarge, it is found, that the most remote parts of the state can assist each other as well as the more contiguous; and that this intercourse of good offices may be carried on to the greatest extent and intricacy. Hence the origin of *merchants*, one of the most useful races of men, who serve as agents between those parts of the state that are wholly unacquainted, and are ignorant of each other's necessities. Here are in a city fifty workmen in silk and linen, and a thousand customers; and these two ranks of men, so necessary to each other, can never rightly meet, till one man erects a shop, to which all the workmen and all the customers repair. In this province, grass rises in abundance: the inhabitants abound in cheese, and butter, and cattle; but want bread and corn, which, in a neighbouring province, are in too great abundance for the use of the inhabitants. One man discovers this. He brings corn from the one province, and returns with cattle; and, supplying the wants of both, he is, so far, a common benefactor. As the people increase in numbers and industry, the difficulty of their intercourse increases: the business of the agency or merchandise becomes more intricate; and divides, subdivides, compounds, and mixes to a greater variety. In all these transactions, it is necessary and reasonable, that a considerable part of the commodities and labour should belong to the merchant, to whom, in a great measure, they are owing. And these commodities he will sometimes preserve in kind, or more commonly convert into money, which is their common representation. If gold and silver have increased in the state, together with the industry, it will require a great quantity of these metals to represent a great quantity of commodities and labour. If industry alone has increased, the prices of every thing must sink, and a small quantity of specie will serve as a representation.

There is no craving or demand of the human mind more constant and insatiable than that for exercise and employment; and this desire seems the foundation of most of our passions and pursuits. Deprive a man of all business and serious occupation, he runs restless from one amusement to another; and the weight and oppression which he feels from idleness is so great, that he forgets the ruin which must follow him from his immoderate expenses. Give him a more harmless way of employing his mind or body, he is satisfied, and feels no longer that insatiable thirst after pleasure. But if the employment you give him be lucrative, especially if the profit be attached to every particular exertion of industry, he has gain so often in his eye, that he acquires, by degrees, a passion for it, and knows no such pleasure as that of seeing the daily increase of his fortune. And this is the reason why trade increases frugality, and why, among merchants, there is the same overplus of misers above prodigals, as among the possessors of land there is the contrary.

Commerce increases industry, by conveying it readily from one member of the state to another, and allowing none of it to perish or become useless. It increases frugality, by giving occupation to men, and employing them in the arts of gain, which soon engage their affection, and remove all relish for pleasure and expense. It is an infallible consequence of all industrious professions to beget frugality, and make the love of gain prevail over the love of pleasure. Among lawyers and physicians who have any practice, there are many more who live within their income, than who exceed it, or even live up to it. But lawyers and physicians beget no industry; and it is even at the expense of others they acquire their riches; so that they are sure to diminish the possessions of some of their fellow-citizens, as fast as they increase their own. Merchants, on the contrary, beget industry, by serving as canals to convey it through every corner of the state: and, at the same time, by their frugality, they acquire great power over that industry, and collect a large property in the labour and commodities, which they are the chief instruments in producing. There is no other profession, therefore, except merchandise, which can make the moneyed interest considerable; or, in other words, can increase industry, and, by also increasing frugality, give a great command of that industry to particular members of the society. Without commerce, the state must consist chiefly of landed gentry, whose prodigality and expense make a continual demand for borrowing; and of peasants, who have no sums to supply that demand. The money never gathers into large stocks or sums, which can be lent at interest. It is dispersed into numberless hands, who either squander it in idle show and magnificence, or employ it in the purchase of the common necessaries of life. Commerce alone assembles it into considerable sums; and this effect it has merely from the industry which it begets, and the frugality which it inspires, independent of that particular quantity of precious metal which may circulate in the state.

Thus an increase of commerce, by a necessary consequence, raises a great number of lenders, and by that means produces lowness of interest. We must now consider how far this increase of commerce diminishes the profits arising from that profession, and gives rise to the *third* circumstance requisite to produce lowness of interest.

It may be proper to observe on this head, that low interest and low profits of merchandise, are two events that mutually forward each other, and are both originally derived from that extensive commerce, which produces opulent merchants, and renders the moneyed interest considerable. Where merchants possess great stocks, whether represented by few or many pieces of metal, it must frequently happen, that, when they either become tired of business, or leave heirs unwilling or unfit to engage in commerce, a great proportion of these riches naturally seeks an annual and secure revenue. The plenty diminishes the price, and makes the lenders accept of a low interest. This consideration obliges many to keep their stock employed in trade, and rather be content with low profits than dispose of their money at an undervalue. On the other hand, when commerce has become extensive, and employs large stocks, there must arise rivalships among the merchants, which diminish the profits of trade, at the same time that they increase the trade itself. The low profits of merchandise induce the merchants to accept more willingly of a low interest when they leave off business, and begin to indulge themselves in ease and indolence. It is needless, therefore, to inquire, which of these circumstances, to wit, *low interest* or *low profits*, is the cause, and which the effect? They both arise from an extensive commerce, and mutually forward each other. No man will accept of low profits where he can have high interest; and no man will accept of low interest where he can have high profits. An extensive commerce, by producing large stocks, diminishes both interest and profits, and is always assisted, in its diminution of the one, by the proportional sinking of the other. I may add, that, as low profits arise from the increase of commerce and industry, they serve in their turn to its further increase, by rendering the commodities cheaper, encouraging the consumption, and heightening the industry. And thus, if we consider the whole connection of causes and effects, interest is the barometer of the state, and its lowness is a sign, almost infallible, of the flourishing condition of a people. It proves the increase of industry, and its prompt circulation, through the whole state, little inferior to a demonstration. And though, perhaps, it may not be impossible but a sudden and a great check to commerce may have a momentary effect of the same kind, by throwing so many stocks out of trade, it must be attended with such misery and want of employment in the poor, that, besides its short duration, it will not be possible to mistake the one case for the other.

Those who have asserted, that the plenty of money was the cause of low interest, seem to have taken a collateral effect for a cause, since the same industry, which sinks the interest, commonly acquires great abundance of the precious metals. A variety of fine manufactures, with vigilant enterprising merchants, will soon draw money to a state, if it be anywhere to be found in the world. The same cause, by multiplying the conveniences of life, and increasing industry, collects great riches into the hands of persons who are not proprietors of land, and produces, by that means, a lowness of interest. But though both these effects, plenty of money and low interest, naturally arise from commerce and industry, they are altogether independent of each other. For suppose a nation removed into the *Pacific* ocean, without any foreign commerce, or any knowledge of navigation: suppose that this nation possesses always the same stock of coin, but is continually increasing in its numbers and industry: it is evident that the price of every commodity must gradually diminish in that kingdom; since it is the proportion between money and any species of goods which fixes their mutual value; and, upon the present supposition, the conveniences of life become every day more abundant, without any alteration in the current specie. A less quantity of money, therefore, among this people, will make a rich man, during the times of industry, than would suffice to that purpose in ignorant and slothful ages. Less money will build a house, portion a daughter, buy an estate, support a manufactory, or maintain a family and equipage. These are the uses for which men borrow money; and therefore the greater or less quantity of it in a state has no influence on the interest. But it is evident that the greater or less stock of labour and commodities must have a great influence; since we really and in effect borrow these, when we take money upon interest. It is true, when commerce is extended all over the globe, the most industrious nations always abound most with the precious metals; so that low interest and plenty of money are in fact almost inseparable. But still it is of consequence to know the principle whence any phenomenon arises, and to distinguish between a cause and a concomitant effect. Besides that the speculation is curious, it may frequently be of use in the conduct of public affairs. At least it must be owned, that nothing can be of more use than to improve, by practice, the method of reasoning on these subjects, which of all others are the most important, though they are commonly treated in the loosest and most careless manner.

Another reason of this popular mistake with regard to the cause of low interest, seems to be the instance of some nations, where, after a sudden acquisition of money, or of the precious metals by means of foreign conquest, the interest has fallen not only among them, but in all the neighbouring states, as soon as that money was dispersed, and had insinuated itself into every corner. Thus, interest in SPAIN fell near a half immediately after the discovery of the WEST INDIES, as we are informed by GARCILASSO DE LA VEGA; and it has been ever since gradually sinking in every kingdom of EUROPE. Interest in ROME, after the conquest of EGYPT, fell from 6 to 4 *per cent*, as we learn from DION.[†]

The causes of the sinking of interest, upon such an event, seem different in the conquering country and in the neighbouring states; but in neither of them can we justly ascribe that effect merely to the increase of gold and silver.

In the conquering country, it is natural to imagine that this new acquisition of money will fall into a few hands, and be gathered into large sums, which seek a secure revenue, either by the purchase of land or by interest; and consequently the same effect follows, for a little time, as if there had been a great accession of industry and commerce. The increase of lenders above the borrowers sinks the interest, and so much the faster if those who have acquired those large sums find no industry or commerce in the state, and no method of employing their money but by lending it at interest. But after this new mass of gold and silver has been digested, and has circulated through the whole state, affairs will soon return to their former situation, while the landlords and new money-holders, living idly, squander above their income; and the former daily contract debt, and the latter encroach on their stock till its final extinction. The whole money may still be in the state, and make itself felt by the increase of prices; but not being now collected into any large masses or stocks, the disproportion between the borrowers and lenders is the same as formerly, and consequently the high interest returns.

Accordingly we find in ROME, that, so early as TIBERIUS's time, interest had again amounted to 6 *per cent*[†] though no accident had happened to drain the empire of money. In TRAJAN's time, money lent on mortgages in ITALY bore 6 *per cent*,[†] on common securities in BITHYNIA 12;[†] and if interest in SPAIN has not risen to its old pitch, this can be ascribed to nothing but the continuance of the same cause that sunk it, to wit, the large fortunes continually made in the INDIES, which come over to SPAIN from time to time, and supply the demand of the borrowers. By this accidental and extraneous cause, more money is to be lent in SPAIN, that is, more money is collected into large sums, than would otherwise be found in a state, where there are so little commerce and industry.

As to the reduction of interest which has followed in

ENGLAND, FRANCE, and other kingdoms of EUROPE that have no mines, it has been gradual, and has not proceeded from the increase of money, considered merely in itself, but from that of industry, which is the natural effect of the former increase in that interval, before it raises the price of labour and provisions; for to return to the foregoing supposition, if the industry of ENGLAND had risen as much from other causes, (and that rise might easily have happened, though the stock of money had remained the same,) must not all the same consequences have followed, which we observe at present? The same people would in that case be found in the kingdom, the same commodities, the same industry, manufactures, and commerce; and consequently the same merchants, with the same stocks, that is, with the same command over labour and commodities, only represented by a smaller number of white or yellow pieces, which, being a circumstance of no moment, would only affect the wagoner, porter, and trunk-maker. Luxury, therefore, manufactures, arts, industry, frugality, flourishing equally as at present, it is evident that interest must also have been as low, since that is the necessary result of all these circumstances, so far as they determine the profits of commerce, and the proportion between the borrowers and lenders in any state.

OF THE BALANCE OF TRADE

IT is very usual, in nations ignorant of the nature of commerce, to prohibit the exportation of commodities, and to preserve among themselves whatever they think valuable and useful. They do not consider, that in this prohibition they act directly contrary to their intention; and that the more is exported of any commodity, the more will be raised at home, of which they themselves will always have the first offer.

It is well known to the learned, that the ancient laws of ATHENS rendered the exportation of figs criminal; that being supposed a species of fruit so excellent in ATTICA, that the ATHENIANS deemed it too delicious for the palate of any foreigner; and in this ridiculous prohibition they were so much in earnest, that informers were thence called *sycophants* among them, from two GREEK words, which signify *figs* and *discoverer*.[†] There are proofs in many old acts of parliament of the same ignorance in the nature of commerce, particularly in the reign of EDWARD III; and to this day, in FRANCE, the exportation of corn is almost always prohibited, in order, as they say, to prevent famines; though it is evident that nothing contributes more to the frequent famines which so much distress that fertile country.

The same jealous fear, with regard to money, has also prevailed among several nations; and it required both reason and experience to convince any people, that these prohibitions serve to no other purpose than to raise the exchange against them, and produce a still greater exportation.

These errors, one may say, are gross and palpable; but there still prevails, even in nations well acquainted with commerce, a strong jealousy with regard to the balance of trade, and a fear that all their gold and silver may be leaving them. This seems to me, almost in every case, a groundless apprehension; and I should as soon dread, that all our springs and rivers should be exhausted, as that money should abandon a kingdom where there are people and industry. Let us carefully preserve these latter advantages, and we need never be apprehensive of losing the former.

It is easy to observe, that all calculations concerning the balance of trade are founded on very uncertain facts and suppositions. The custom-house books are allowed to be an insufficient ground of reasoning; nor is the rate of exchange much better, unless we consider it with all nations, and know also the proportions of the several sums remitted, which one may safely pronounce impossible. Every man, who has ever reasoned on this subject, has always proved his theory, whatever it was, by facts and calculations, and by an enumeration of all the commodities sent to all foreign kingdoms.

The writings of Mr Gee* struck the nation with an universal panic, when they saw it plainly demonstrated, by a detail of particulars, that the balance was against them for so considerable a sum, as must leave them without a single shilling in five or six years. But luckily, twenty years have since elapsed, with an expensive foreign war; yet it is commonly supposed that money is still more plentiful among us than in any former period.

Nothing can be more entertaining on this head than Dr Swift;* an author so quick in discerning the mistakes and absurdities of others. He says, in his *short view of the state of* IRELAND, that the whole cash of that kingdom formerly amounted but to 500,000£; that out of this the IRISH remitted every year a neat million to ENGLAND, and had scarcely any other source from which they could compensate themselves, and little other foreign trade than the importation of FRENCH wines, for which they paid ready money. The consequence of this situation, which must be owned to be disadvantageous, was, that, in a course of three years, the current money of IRELAND, from 500,000£, was reduced to less than two. And at present, I suppose, in a course of 30 years, it is absolutely nothing. Yet I know not how that opinion of the advance of riches in IRELAND, which gave the Doctor so much indignation, seems still to continue, and gain ground with everybody.

In short, this apprehension of the wrong balance of trade, appears of such a nature, that it discovers itself wherever one is out of humour with the ministry, or is in low spirits; and as it can never be refuted by a particular detail of all the exports which counterbalance the imports, it may here be proper to form a general argument, that may prove the impossibility of this event, so long as we preserve our people and our industry.

Suppose four fifths of all the money in GREAT BRITAIN to be annihilated in one night, and the nation reduced to the same condition, with regard to specie, as in the reigns of the HARRYS and EDWARDS,* what would be the consequence? Must not the price of all labour and commodities sink in proportion, and every thing be sold as cheap as they were in those ages? What nation could then dispute with us in any foreign market, or pretend to navigate or to sell manufactures at the same price, which to us would afford sufficient profit? In how little time, therefore, must this bring back the money which we had lost, and raise us to the level of all the neighbouring nations? where, after we have arrived, we immediately lose the advantage of the cheapness of labour and commodities, and the further flowing in of money is stopped by our fulness and repletion.

Again, suppose that all the money of GREAT BRITAIN were multiplied fivefold in a night, must not the contrary effect follow? Must not all labour and commodities rise to such an exorbitant height, that no neighbouring nations could afford to buy from us; while their commodities, on the other hand, became comparatively so cheap, that, in spite of all the laws which could be formed, they would be run in upon us, and our money flow out; till we fall to a level with foreigners, and lose that great superiority of riches, which had laid us under such disadvantages?

Now, it is evident, that the same causes which would correct these exorbitant inequalities, were they to happen miraculously, must prevent their happening in the common course of nature, and must forever, in all neighbouring nations, preserve money nearly proportionable to the art and industry of each nation. All water, wherever it communicates, remains always at a level. Ask naturalists the reason; they tell you, that, were it to be raised in any one place, the superior gravity of that part not being balanced, must depress it, till it meets a counterpoise; and that the same cause, which redresses the inequality when it happens, must forever prevent it, without some violent external operation.[†]

Can one imagine that it had ever been possible, by any laws, or even by any art or industry, to have kept all the money in SPAIN, which the galleons have brought from the INDIES? Or that all commodities could be sold in FRANCE for a tenth of the price which they would yield on the other side of the PYRENEES, without finding their way thither, and draining from that immense treasure? What other reason, indeed, is there, why all nations at present gain in their trade with SPAIN and PORTUGAL, but because it is impossible to heap up money, more than any fluid, beyond its proper level? The sovereigns of these countries have shown, that they wanted not inclination to keep their gold and silver to themselves, had it been in any degree practicable.

But as any body of water may be raised above the level of the surrounding element, if the former has no communication with the latter; so in money, if the communication be cut off, by any material or physical impediment (for all laws alone are ineffectual), there may, in such a case, be a very great inequality of money. Thus the immense distance of CHINA, together with the monopolies of our INDIA companies* obstructing the communication, preserve in EUROPE the gold and silver, especially the latter, in much greater plenty than they are found in that kingdom. But, notwithstanding this great obstruction, the force of the causes above mentioned is still evident. The skill and ingenuity of EUROPE in general surpasses perhaps that of CHINA, with regard to manual arts and manufactures, yet are we never able to trade thither without great disadvantage. And were it not for the continual recruits which we receive from AMERICA, money would soon sink in EUROPE, and rise in CHINA, till it came nearly to a level in both places. Nor can any reasonable man doubt, but that industrious nation, were they as near as POLAND or BARBARY, would drain us of the overplus of our specie, and draw to themselves a larger share of the WEST INDIAN treasures. We need not have recourse to a physical attraction, in order to explain the necessity of this operation. There is a moral attraction, arising from the interests and passions of men, which is full as potent and infallible.

How is the balance kept in the provinces of every kingdom among themselves, but by the force of this principle, which makes it impossible for money to lose its level, and either to rise or sink beyond the proportion of the labour and commodities which are in each province? Did not long experience make people easy on this head, what a fund of gloomy reflections might calculations afford to a melancholy YORKSHIREMAN, while he computed and magnified the sums drawn to LONDON by taxes, absentees, commodities, and found on comparison the opposite articles so much inferior! And no doubt, had the *Heptarchy** subsisted in ENGLAND, the legislature of each state had been continually alarmed by the fear of a wrong balance; and as it is probable that the mutual hatred of these states would have been extremely violent on account of their close neighbourhood, they would have loaded and oppressed all commerce, by a jealous and superfluous caution. Since the union has removed the barriers between SCOTLAND and ENGLAND, which of these nations gains from the other by this free commerce? Or if the former kingdom has received any increase of riches, can it reasonably be accounted for by any thing but the increase of its art and industry? It was a common apprehension in ENGLAND before the union, as we learn from L'Abbé DU BOS,[†] that SCOTLAND would soon drain them of their treasures, were an open trade allowed; and on the other side of the TWEED a contrary apprehension prevailed: with what justice in both, time has shown.

What happens in small portions of mankind must take place in greater. The provinces of the ROMAN empire, no doubt, kept their balance with each other, and with ITALY, independent of the legislature; as much as the several counties of GREAT BRITAIN, or the several parishes of each county. And any man who travels over EUROPE at this day, may see, by the prices of commodities, that money, in spite of the absurd jealousy of princes and states, has brought itself nearly to a level; and that the difference between one kingdom and another is not greater in this respect, than it is often between different provinces of the same kingdom. Men naturally flock to capital cities, seaports, and navigable rivers. There we find more men, more industry, more commodities, and consequently more money, but still the latter difference holds proportion with the former, and the level is preserved.[†]

Our jealousy and our hatred of FRANCE are without bounds; and the former sentiment, at least, must be acknowledged reasonable and wellgrounded. These passions have occasioned innumerable barriers and obstructions upon commerce, where we are accused of being commonly the aggressors. But what have we gained by the bargain? We lost the FRENCH market for our woollen manufactures, and transferred the commerce of wine to SPAIN and PORTUGAL, where we buy worse liquor at a higher price. There are few ENGLISHMEN who would not think their country absolutely ruined, were FRENCH wines sold in ENGLAND so cheap and in such abundance as to supplant, in some measure, all ale and home-brewed liquors: but would we lay aside prejudice, it would not be difficult to prove, that nothing could be more innocent, perhaps advantageous. Each new acre of vineyard planted in FRANCE, in order to supply ENGLAND with wine, would make it requisite for the FRENCH to take the produce of an ENGLISH acre, sown in wheat or barley, in order to subsist themselves; and it is evident that we should thereby get command of the better commodity.

There are many edicts of the FRENCH king, prohibiting the planting of new vineyards, and ordering all those which are lately planted to be grubbed up; so sensible are they, in that country, of the superior value of corn above every other product.

Mareschal VAUBAN* complains often, and with reason, of the absurd duties which load the entry of those wines of LANGUEDOC, GUIENNE, and other southern provinces, that are imported into BRITANNY and NORMANDY. He entertained no doubt but these latter provinces could preserve their balance, notwithstanding the open commerce which he recommends. And it is evident, that a few leagues more navigation to ENGLAND would make no difference; or if it did, that it must operate alike on the commodities of both kingdoms.

There is indeed one expedient by which it is possible to sink, and another by which we may raise money beyond its natural level in any kingdom; but these cases, when examined, will be found to resolve into our general theory, and to bring additional authority to it.

I scarcely know any method of sinking money below its level, but those institutions of banks, funds, and paper credit, which are so much practised in this kingdom. These render paper equivalent to money, circulate it throughout the whole state, make it supply the place of gold and silver, raise proportionably the price of labour and commodities, and by that means either banish a great part of those precious metals, or prevent their further increase. What can be more short-sighted than our reasonings on this head? We fancy, because an individual would be much richer, were his stock of money doubled, that the same good effect would follow, were the money of every one increased; not considering that this would raise as much the price of every commodity, and reduce every man in time to the same condition as before. It is only in our public negotiations and transactions with foreigners, that a greater stock of money is advantageous; and as our paper is there absolutely insignificant, we feel, by its means, all the ill effects arising from a great abundance of money, without reaping any of the advantages.†

Suppose that there are 12 millions of paper, which circulate in the kingdom as money (for we are not to imagine that all our enormous funds are employed in that shape), and suppose the real cash of the kingdom to be 18 millions: here is a state which is found by experience to be able to hold a stock of 30 millions. I say, if it be able to hold it, it must of necessity have acquired it in gold and silver, had we not obstructed the entrance of these metals by this new invention of paper. *Whence would it have acquired that sum?* From all the kingdoms of the world. *But why?* Because, if you remove these 12 millions, money in this state is below its level, compared with our neighbours; and we must immediately draw from all of them, till we be full and saturate, so to speak, and can hold no more. By our present politics, we are as careful to stuff the nation with this fine commodity of bank-bills and chequer notes, as if we were afraid of being overburdened with the precious metals.

It is not to be doubted, but the great plenty of bullion in FRANCE is, in a great measure, owing to the want of paper-credit. The FRENCH have no banks: merchants' bills do not circulate as with us: usury, or lending on interest, is not directly permitted; so that many have large sums in their coffers: great quantities of plate are used in private houses; and all the churches are full of it. By this means, provisions and labour still remain cheaper among them, than in nations that are not half so rich in gold and silver. The advantages of this situation, in point of trade, as well as in great public emergencies, are too evident to be disputed.

The same fashion a few years ago prevailed in GENOA, which still has place in ENGLAND and HOLLAND, of using services of CHINA-ware instead of plate; but the senate, foreseeing the consequence, prohibited the use of that brittle commodity beyond a certain extent; while the use of silver plate was left unlimited. And I suppose, in their late distresses, they felt the good effect of this ordinance. Our tax on plate is, perhaps, in this view, somewhat impolitic.

Before the introduction of paper-money into our colonies, they had gold and silver sufficient for their circulation. Since the introduction of that commodity, the least inconveniency that has followed is the total banishment of the precious metals. And after the abolition of paper, can it be doubted but money will return, while those colonies possess manufactures and commodities, the only thing valuable in commerce, and for whose sake alone all men desire money?

What pity LYCURGUS* did not think of paper-credit, when he wanted to banish gold and silver from SPARTA! It would have served his purpose better than the lumps of iron he made use of as money; and would also have prevented more effectually all commerce with strangers, as not being of so much real and intrinsic value.

It must, however, be confessed, that, as all these questions of trade and money are extremely complicated, there are certain lights in which this subject may be placed, so as to represent the advantages of paper-credit and banks to be superior to their disadvantages. That they banish specie and bullion from a state, is undoubtedly true; and whoever looks no further than this circumstance, does well to condemn them; but specie and bullion are not of so great consequence as not to admit of a compensation, and even an overbalance from the increase of industry and of credit, which may be promoted by the right use of paper-money. It is well known of what advantage it is to a merchant to be able to discount his bills upon occasion; and every thing that facilitates this species of traffic is favourable to the general commerce of a state. But private bankers are enabled to give such credit by the credit they receive from the depositing of money in their shops; and the bank of ENGLAND, in the same manner, from the liberty it has to issue its notes in all payments. There was an invention of this kind which was fallen upon some years ago by the banks of EDINBURGH, and which, as it is one of the most ingenious ideas that has been executed in commerce, has also been thought advantageous to SCOTLAND. It is there called a BANK CREDIT, and is of this nature. A man goes to the bank, and finds surety to the amount, we shall suppose, of a thousand pounds. This money, or any part of it, he has the liberty of drawing out whenever he pleases, and he pays only the ordinary interest for it while it is in his hands. He may, when he pleases, repay any sum so small as twenty pounds, and the interest is discounted from the very day of the repayment. The advantages resulting from this contrivance are manifold. As a man may find surety nearly to the amount of his substance, and his bank credit is equivalent to ready money, a merchant does hereby in a manner coin his houses, his household furniture, the goods in his warehouse, the foreign debts due to him, his ships at sea; and can, upon occasion, employ them in all payments, as if they were the current money of the country. If a man borrow a thousand pounds from a private hand, besides that it is not always to be found when required, he pays interest for it whether he be using it or not: his bank credit costs him nothing except during the very moment in which it is of service to him: and this circumstance is of equal advantage as if he had borrowed money at much lower interest. Merchants likewise, from this invention, acquire a great facility in supporting each other's credit, which is a considerable security against bankruptcies. A man, when his own bank credit is exhausted, goes to any of his neighbours who is not in the same condition, and he gets the money, which he replaces at his convenience.

After this practice had taken place during some years at

EDINBURGH, several companies of merchants at GLASGOW carried the matter further. They associated themselves into different banks, and issued notes so low as ten shillings, which they used in all payments for goods, manufactures, tradesmen's labour of all kinds; and these notes, from the established credit of the companies, passed as money in all payments throughout the country. By this means, a stock of five thousand pounds was able to perform the same operations as if it were six or seven; and merchants were thereby enabled to trade to a greater extent, and to require less profit in all their transactions. But whatever other advantages result from these inventions, it must still be allowed, that, besides giving too great facility to credit, which is dangerous, they banish the precious metals: and nothing can be a more evident proof of it than a comparison of the past and present condition of SCOTLAND in that particular. It was found, upon the recoinage made after the union, that there was near a million of specie in that country: but notwithstanding the great increase of riches, commerce, and manufactures of all kinds, it is thought, that, even where there is no extraordinary drain made by ENGLAND, the current specie will not now amount to a third of that sum.

But as our projects of paper-credit are almost the only expedient by which we can sink money below its level, so, in my opinion, the only expedient by which we can raise money above it, is a practice which we should all exclaim against as destructive, namely, the gathering of large sums into a public treasure, locking them up, and absolutely preventing their circulation. The fluid, not communicating with the neighbouring element, may, by such an artifice, be raised to what height we please. To prove this, we need only return to our first supposition, of annihilating the half or any part of our cash; where we found, that the immediate consequence of such an event would be the attraction of an equal sum from all the neighbouring kingdoms. Nor does there seem to be any necessary bounds set, by the nature of things, to this practice of hoarding. A small city like GENEVA, continuing this policy for ages, might engross nine tenths of the money of EUROPE. There seems, indeed, in the nature of man, an invincible obstacle to that immense growth of riches. A weak state, with an enormous treasure, will soon become a prey to some of its poorer, but more powerful neighbours. A great state would dissipate its wealth in dangerous and ill-concerted projects, and probably destroy, with it, what is much more valuable, the industry, morals, and numbers of its people. The fluid, in this case, raised to too great a height, bursts and destroys the vessel that contains it; and, mixing itself with the surrounding element, soon falls to its proper level.

So little are we commonly acquainted with this principle, that, though all historians agree in relating uniformly so recent an event as the immense treasure amassed by HARRY VII (which they make amount to 2,700,000 pounds), we rather reject their concurring testimony than admit of a fact which agrees so ill with our inveterate prejudices. It is indeed probable that this sum might be three fourths of all the money in ENGLAND. But where is the difficulty in conceiving that such a sum might be amassed in twenty years by a cunning, rapacious, frugal, and almost absolute monarch? Nor is it probable that the diminution of circulating money was ever sensibly felt by the people, or ever did them any prejudice. The sinking of the prices of all commodities would immediately replace it, by giving ENGLAND the advantage in its commerce with the neighbouring kingdoms.

Have we not an instance in the small republic of ATHENS with its allies, who, in about fifty years between the MEDIAN and PELOPONNESIAN wars, amassed a sum not much inferior to that of HARRY VII? For all the GREEK historians and orators agree,[†] that the ATHENIANS collected in the citadel more than 10,000 talents, which they afterwards dissipated to their own ruin, in rash and imprudent enterprises. But when this money was set a running, and began to communicate with the surrounding fluid, what was the consequence? Did it remain in the state? No. For we find, by the memorable *census* mentioned by DEMOSTHENES and POLYBIUS,[†] that, in about fifty years afterwards, the whole value of the republic, comprehending lands, houses, commodities, slaves, and money, was less than 6,000 talents.

What an ambitious high-spirited people was this, to collect and keep in their treasury, with a view to conquests, a sum, which it was every day in the power of the citizens, by a single vote, to distribute among themselves, and which would have gone near to triple the riches of every individual! For we must observe, that the numbers and private riches of the ATHENIANS are said, by ancient writers, to have been no greater at the beginning of the PELOPONNESIAN war, than at the beginning of the MACEDONIAN.

Money was little more plentiful in GREECE during the age of PHILIP and PERSEUS, than in ENGLAND during that of HARRY VII: yet these two monarchs in thirty years[†] collected from the small kingdom of MACEDON, a larger treasure than that of the English monarch. PAULUS AEMILIUS brought to ROME about 1,700,000 pounds *Sterling*. Pliny says, 2,400,000.[†] And that was but a part of the MACEDONIAN treasure. The rest was dissipated by the resistance and flight of PERSEUS.

We may learn from STANIAN, that the canton of BERNE had 300,000 pounds lent at interest, and had about six times as much in their treasury. Here then is a sum hoarded of 1,800,000 pounds *Sterling*, which is at least quadruple what should naturally circulate in such a petty state; and yet no one, who travels in the PAIS DE VAUX, or any part of that canton, observes any want of money more than could be supposed in a country of that extent, soil, and situation. On the contrary, there are scarce any inland provinces in the continent of FRANCE or GERMANY, where the inhabitants are at this time so opulent, though that canton has vastly increased its treasure since 1714, the time when STANIAN wrote his judicious account of SWITZERLAND.[†]

The account given by APPIAN[†] of the treasure of the PTOLEMIES, is so prodigious, that one cannot admit of it; and so much the less, because the historian says, that the other successors of ALEXANDER were also frugal, and had many of them treasures not much inferior. For this saving humour of the neighbouring princes must necessarily have checked the frugality of the EGYPTIAN monarchs, according to the foregoing theory. The sum he mentions is 740,000 talents, or

191,166,666 pounds 13 shillings and 4 pence, according to Dr ARBUTHNOT's* computation. And yet APPIAN says, that he extracted his account from the public records; and he was himself a native of ALEXANDRIA.

From these principles we may learn what judgment we ought to form of those numberless bars, obstructions, and imposts, which all nations of EUROPE, and none more than ENGLAND, have put upon trade, from an exorbitant desire of amassing money, which never will heap up beyond its level, while it circulates; or from an ill-grounded apprehension of losing their specie, which never will sink below it. Could any thing scatter our riches, it would be such impolitic contrivances. But this general ill effect, however, results from them, that they deprive neighbouring nations of that free communication and exchange which the Author of the world has intended, by giving them soils, climates, and geniuses, so different from each other.

Our modern politics embrace the only method of banishing money, the using of paper-credit; they reject the only method of amassing it, the practice of hoarding; and they adopt a hundred contrivances, which serve to no purpose but to check industry, and rob ourselves and our neighbours of the common benefits of art and nature.

All taxes, however, upon foreign commodities, are not to be regarded as prejudicial or useless, but those only which are founded on the jealousy above mentioned. A tax on GERMAN linen encourages home manufactures, and thereby multiplies our people and industry. A tax on brandy increases the sale of rum, and supports our southern colonies. And as it is necessary that imposts should be levied for the support of government, it may be thought more convenient to lay them on foreign commodities, which can easily be intercepted at the port, and subjected to the impost. We ought, however, always to remember the maxim of Dr SWIFT,* that, in the arithmetic of the customs, two and two make not four, but often make only one. It can scarcely be doubted, but if the duties on wine were lowered to a third, they would yield much more to the government than at present; our people might thereby afford to drink commonly a better and more wholesome liquor; and no prejudice would ensue to the balance of trade, of which we are so jealous. The manufacture of ale beyond the agriculture is but inconsiderable, and gives employment to few hands. The transport of wine and corn would not be much inferior.

But are there not frequent instances, you will say, of states and kingdoms, which were formerly rich and opulent, and are now poor and beggarly? Has not the money left them, with which they formerly abounded? I answer, if they lose their trade, industry, and people, they cannot expect to keep their gold and silver: for these precious metals will hold proportion to the former advantages. When LISBON and AMSTERDAM got the EAST INDIA trade from VENICE and GENOA, they also got the profits and money which arose from it. Where the seat of government is transferred, where expensive armies are maintained at a distance, where great funds are possessed by foreigners; there naturally follows from these causes a diminution of the specie. But these, we may observe, are violent and forcible methods of carrying away money, and are in time commonly attended with the transport of people and industry. But where these remain, and the drain is not continued, the money always finds its way back again, by a hundred canals, of which we have no notion or suspicion. What immense treasures have been spent, by so many nations, in FLANDERS, since the revolution,* in the course of three long wars? More money perhaps than the half of what is at present in EUROPE. But what has now become of it? Is it in the narrow compass of the AUSTRIAN provinces? No, surely: it has most of it returned to the several countries whence it came, and has followed that art and industry by which at first it was acquired. For above a thousand years, the money of EUROPE has been flowing to ROME, by an open and sensible current; but it has been emptied by many secret and insensible canals: and the want of industry and commerce renders at present the papal dominions the poorest territory in all ITALY.

In short, a government has great reason to preserve with care its people and its manufactures. Its money, it may safely trust to the course of human affairs, without fear or jealousy. Or, if it ever give attention to this latter circumstance, it ought only to be so far as it affects the former.

OF PUBLIC CREDIT

IT appears to have been the common practice of antiquity, to make provision, during peace, for the necessities of war, and to hoard up treasures beforehand as the instruments either of conquest or defence; without trusting to extraordinary impositions, much less to borrowing in times of disorder and confusion. Besides the immense sums above mentioned,[†] which were amassed by ATHENS, and by the PTOLEMIES, and other successors of ALEXANDER; we learn from PLATO,[f] that the frugal LACEDEMONIANS had also collected a great treasure; and ARRIAN[†] and PLUTARCH[†] take notice of the riches which ALEXANDER got possession of on the conquest of SUSA and ECBATANA, and which were reserved, some of them, from the time of CYRUS. If I remember right, the scripture also mentions the treasure of HEZEKIAH and the JEWISH princes;[*] as profane history does that of PHILIP and PERSEUS, kings of MACEDON. The ancient republics of GAUL had commonly large sums in reserve.[†] Every one knows the treasure seized in ROME by JULIUS CAESAR,[*] during the civil wars: and we find afterwards, that the wiser emperors, AUGUSTUS, TIBERIUS, VESPASIAN, SEVERUS, etc. always discovered the prudent foresight of saving great sums against any public exigency.

On the contrary, our modern expedient, which has become very general, is to mortgage the public revenues, and to trust that posterity will pay off the incumbrances contracted by their ancestors: and they, having before their eyes so good an example of their wise fathers, have the same prudent reliance on *their* posterity; who, at last, from necessity more than choice, are obliged to place the same confidence in a new posterity. But not to waste time in declaiming against a practice which appears ruinous beyond all controversy, it seems pretty apparent, that the ancient maxims are, in this respect, more prudent than the modern; even though the latter had been confined within some reasonable bounds, and had ever, in any instance, been attended with such frugality, in time of peace, as to discharge the debts incurred by an expensive war. For why should the case be so different between the public and an individual, as to make us establish different maxims of conduct for each? If the funds of the former be greater, its necessary expenses are proportionably larger; if its resources be more numerous, they are not infinite; and as its frame should be calculated for a much longer duration than the date of a single life, or even of a family, it should embrace maxims, large, durable, and generous, agreeably to the supposed extent of its existence. To trust to chances and temporary expedients, is, indeed, what the necessity of human affairs frequently renders unavoidable; but whoever voluntarily depend on such resources, have not necessity, but their own folly to accuse for their misfortunes, when any such befall them.

If the abuses of treasures be dangerous, either by engaging the state in rash enterprises, or making it neglect military discipline, in confidence of its riches; the abuses of mortgaging are more certain and inevitable; poverty, impotence, and subjection to foreign powers.

According to the modern policy, war is attended with every destructive circumstance; loss of men, increase of taxes, decay of commerce, dissipation of money, devastation by sea and land. According to ancient maxims, the opening of the public treasure, as it produced an uncommon affluence of gold and silver, served as a temporary encouragement to industry, and atoned, in some degree, for the inevitable calamities of war.

It is very tempting to a minister to employ such an expedient, as enables him to make a great figure during his administration, without overburdening the people with taxes, or exciting any immediate clamours against himself. The practice, therefore, of contracting debt, will almost infallibly be abused in every government. It would scarcely be more imprudent to give a prodigal son a credit in every banker's shop in London, than to empower a statesman to draw bills, in this manner, upon posterity.

What, then, shall we say to the new paradox, that public incumbrances are, of themselves, advantageous, independent of the necessity of contracting them; and that any state, even though it were not pressed by a foreign enemy, could not possibly have embraced a wiser expedient for promoting commerce and riches, than to create funds, and debts, and taxes, without limitation? Reasonings such as these might naturally have passed for trials of wit among rhetoricians, like the panegyrics on folly and fever, on BUSIRIS and NERO, had we not seen such absurd maxims patronized by great ministers, and by a whole party among us.

Let us examine the consequences of public debts, both in our domestic management, by their influence on commerce and industry; and in our foreign transactions, by their effect on wars and negotiations.†

Public securities are with us become a kind of money, and pass as readily at the current price as gold or silver. Wherever any profitable undertaking offers itself, how expensive however, there are never wanting hands enough to embrace it; nor need a trader, who has sums in the public stocks, fear to launch out into the most extensive trade; since he is possessed of funds which will answer the most sudden demand that can be made upon him. No merchant thinks it necessary to keep by him any considerable cash. Bank stock, or India bonds, especially the latter, serve all the same purposes; because he can dispose of them, or pledge them to a banker, in a quarter of an hour; and at the same time they are not idle, even when in his scrutoire,* but bring him in a constant revenue. In short our national debts furnish merchants with a species of money that is continually multiplying in their hands, and produces sure gain, besides the profits of their commerce. This must enable them to trade upon less profit. The small profit of the merchant renders the commodity cheaper, causes a greater consumption, quickens the labour of the common people, and helps to spread arts and industry throughout the whole society.

There are also, we may observe, in ENGLAND and in all states which have both commerce and public debts, a set of men, who are half merchants, half stockholders, and may be supposed willing to trade for small profits; because commerce is not their principal or sole support, and their revenues in the funds are a sure resource for themselves and their families. Were there no funds, great merchants would have no expedient for realizing or securing any part of their profit, but by making purchases of land; and land has many disadvantages in comparison of funds. Requiring more care and inspection, it divides the time and attention of the merchant: upon any tempting offer or extraordinary accident in trade, it is not so easily converted into money; and as it attracts too much, both by the many natural pleasures it affords, and the authority it gives, it soon converts the citizen into the country gentleman. More men, therefore, with large stocks and incomes, may naturally be supposed to continue in trade, where there are public debts; and this, it must be owned, is of some advantage to commerce, by diminishing its profits, promoting circulation, and encouraging industry.

But, in opposition to these two favourable circumstances, perhaps of no very great importance, weigh the many disadvantages which attend our public debts in the whole *interior* economy of the state: you will find no comparison between the ill and the good which result from them.

First, It is certain that national debts cause a mighty confluence of people and riches to the capital, by the great sums levied in the provinces to pay the interest, and perhaps, too, by the advantages in trade above mentioned, which they give the merchants in the capital above the rest of the kingdom. The question is, whether, in our case, it be for the public interest that so many privileges should be conferred on LONDON, which has already arrived at such an enormous size, and seems still increasing? Some men are apprehensive of the consequences. For my own part, I cannot forbear thinking, that, though the head is undoubtedly too large for the body, yet that great city is so happily situated, that its excessive bulk causes less inconvenience than even a smaller capital to a greater kingdom. There is more difference between the prices of all provisions in PARIS and LANGUEDOC, than between those in LONDON and YORKSHIRE. The immense greatness, indeed, of LONDON, under a government which admits not of discretionary power, renders the people factious, mutinous, seditious, and even perhaps rebellious. But to this evil the national debts themselves tend to provide a remedy. The first visible eruption, or even immediate danger of public disorders, must alarm all the stockholders, whose property is the most precarious of any; and will make them fly to the support of government, whether menaced by Jacobitish violence,* or democratical frenzy.

Secondly, Public stocks, being a kind of paper-credit, have all the disadvantages attending that species of money. They banish gold and silver from the most considerable commerce of the state, reduce them to common circulation, and by that means render all provisions and labour dearer than otherwise they would be.

Thirdly, The taxes which are levied to pay the interest of these debts are apt either to heighten the price of labour, or to be an oppression on the poorer sort.

Fourthly, As foreigners possess a great share of our national funds, they render the public in a manner tributary to them, and may in time occasion the transport of our people and our industry.

Fifthly, The greater part of the public stock being always in the hands of idle people, who live on their revenue, our funds, in that view, give great encouragement to an useless and inactive life.

But though the injury that arises to commerce and industry from our public funds will appear, upon balancing the whole, not inconsiderable, it is trivial in comparison of the prejudice that results to a state considered as a body politic, which must support itself in the society of nations, and have various transactions with other states in wars and negotiations. The ill there is pure and unmixed, without any favourable circumstance to atone for it; and it is an ill too of a nature the highest and most important.

We have indeed been told,* that the public is no weaker on account of its debts, since they are mostly due among ourselves, and bring as much property to one as they take from another. It is like transferring money from the right hand to the left, which leaves the person neither richer nor poorer than before. Such loose reasoning and specious comparisons will always pass where we judge not upon principles. I ask, Is it possible, in the nature of things, to overburden a nation with taxes, even where the sovereign resides among them? The very doubt seems extravagant, since it is requisite, in every community, that there be a certain proportion observed between the laborious and the idle part of it. But if all our present taxes be mortgaged, must we not invent new ones? And may not this matter be carried to a length that is ruinous and destructive?

In every nation there are always some methods of levying money more easy than others, agreeably to the way of living of the people, and the commodities they make use of. In GREAT BRITAIN, the excises upon malt and beer afford a large revenue, because the operations of malting and brewing are tedious, and are impossible to be concealed; and, at the same time, these commodities are not so absolutely necessary to life as that the raising of their price would very much affect the poorer sort. These taxes being all mortgaged, what difficulty to find new ones! what vexation and ruin of the poor!

Duties upon consumptions are more equal and easy than those upon possessions. What a loss to the public that the former are all exhausted, and that we must have recourse to the more grievous method of levying taxes!

Were all the proprietors of land only stewards to the public, must not necessity force them to practise all the arts of oppression used by stewards, where the absence or negligence of the proprietor render them secure against injury?

It will scarcely be asserted, that no bounds ought ever to be set to national debts, and that the public would be no weaker were twelve or fifteen shillings in the pound, land-tax, mortgaged, with all the present customs and excises.

There is something, therefore, in the case, beside the mere transferring of property from the one hand to another. In five hundred years, the posterity of those now in the coaches, and of those upon the boxes, will probably have changed places, without affecting the public by these revolutions.

Suppose the public once fairly brought to that condition to which it is hastening with such amazing rapidity; suppose the land to be taxed eighteen or nineteen shillings in the pound, for it can never bear the whole twenty; suppose all the excises and customs to be screwed up to the utmost which the nation can bear, without entirely losing its commerce and industry; and suppose that all those funds are mortgaged to perpetuity, and that the invention and wit of all our projectors can find no new imposition which may serve as the foundation of a new loan; and let us consider the necessary consequences of this situation. Though the imperfect state of our political knowledge, and the narrow capacities of men, make it difficult to fortell the effects which will result from any untried measure, the seeds of ruin are here scattered with such profusion as not to escape the eye of the most careless observer.

In this unnatural state of society, the only persons who possess any revenue beyond the immediate effects of their industry, are the stockholders, who draw almost all the rent of the land and houses, besides the produce of all the customs and excises. These are men who have no connections with the state, who can enjoy their revenue in any part of the globe in which they choose to reside, who will naturally bury themselves in the capital, or in great cities, and who will sink into the lethargy of a stupid and pampered luxury, without spirit, ambition, or enjoyment. Adieu to all ideas of nobility, gentry, and family. The stocks can be transferred in an instant; and, being in such a fluctuating state, will seldom be transmitted during three generations from father to son. Or were they to remain ever so long in one family, they convey no hereditary authority or credit to the possessor; and by this means the several ranks of men, which form a kind of independent magistracy in a state, instituted by the hand of nature, are entirely lost; and every man in authority derives his influence from the commission alone of the sovereign. No expedient remains for preventing or suppressing insurrections but mercenary armies: no expedient at all remains for resisting tyranny: elections are swayed by bribery and corruption alone: and the middle power between king and people being totally removed, a grievous despotism must infallibly prevail. The landholders, despised for their poverty, and hated for their oppressions, will be utterly unable to make any opposition to it.

Though a resolution should be formed by the legislature never to impose any tax which hurts commerce and discourages industry, it will be impossible for men, in subjects of such extreme delicacy, to reason so justly as never to be mistaken, or, amidst difficulties so urgent, never to be seduced from their resolution. The continual fluctuations in commerce require continual alterations in the nature of the taxes, which exposes the legislature every moment to the danger both of wilful and involuntary error. And any great blow given to trade, whether by injudicious taxes or by other accidents, throws the whole system of government into confusion.

But what expedient can the public now employ, even supposing trade to continue in the most flourishing condition, in order to support its foreign wars and enterprises, and to defend its own honour and interest, or those of its allies? I do not ask how the public is to exert such a prodigious power as it has maintained during our late wars; where we have so much exceeded, not only our own natural strength, but even that of the greatest empires. This extravagance is the abuse complained of, as the source of all the dangers to which we are at present exposed. But since we must still suppose great commerce and opulence to remain, even after every fund is mortgaged; these riches must be defended by proportional power; and whence is the public to derive the revenue which supports it? It must plainly be from a continual taxation of the annuitants, or, which is the same thing, from mortgaging anew, on every exigency, a certain part of their annuities;* and thus making them contribute to their own defence, and to that of the nation. But the difficulties attending this system of policy will easily appear, whether we suppose the king to have become absolute master, or to be still controlled by national councils, in which the annuitants themselves must necessarily bear the principal sway.

If the prince has become absolute, as may naturally be expected from this situation of affairs, it is so easy for him to increase his exactions upon the annuitants, which amount only to the retaining of money in his own hands, that this species of property would soon lose all its credit, and the whole income of every individual in the state must lie entirely at the mercy of the sovereign; a degree of despotism which no oriental monarchy has ever yet attained. If, on the contrary, the consent of the annuitants be requisite for every taxation, they will never be persuaded to contribute sufficiently even to the support of government; as the diminution of their revenue must in that case be very sensible, it would not be disguised under the appearance of a branch of excise of customs, and would not be shared by any other order of the state, who are already supposed to be taxed to the utmost. There are instances, in some republics, of a hundredth penny, and sometimes of the fiftieth, being given to the support of the state; but this is always an extraordinary exertion of power, and can never become the foundation of a constant national defence. We have always found, where a government has mortgaged all its revenues, that it necessarily sinks into a state of languor, inactivity, and impotence.

Such are the inconveniences which may reasonably be foreseen of this situation to which GREAT BRITAIN is visibly tending. Not to mention the numberless inconveniences, which cannot be foreseen, and which must result from so monstrous a situation as that of making the public the chief or sole proprietor of land, besides investing it with every branch of customs and excise, which the fertile imagination of ministers and projectors have been able to invent.

I must confess that there has a strange supineness, from long custom, creeped into all ranks of men, with regard to public debts, not unlike what divines so vehemently complain of with regard to their religious doctrines. We all own that the most sanguine imagination cannot hope, either that this or any future ministry will be possessed of such rigid and steady frugality, as to make a considerable progress in the payment of our debts; or that the situation of foreign affairs will, for any long time, allow them leisure and tranquillity for such an undertaking. *What then is to become of us?* Were we ever so good Christians, and ever so resigned to Providence; this, methinks, were a curious question, even considered as a speculative one, and what it might not be altogether impossible to form some conjectural solution of. The events here will depend little upon the contingencies of battles, negotiations, intrigues, and factions. There seems to be a natural progress of things which may guide our reasoning. As it would have required but a moderate share of prudence, when we first began this practice of mortgaging, to have foretold, from the nature of men and of ministers, that things would necessarily be carried to the length we see; so now, that they have at last happily reached it, it may not be difficult to guess at the consequences. It must, indeed, be one of these two events; either the nation must destroy public credit, or public credit will destroy the nation. It is impossible that they can both subsist, after the manner they have been hitherto managed, in this, as well as in some other countries.

There was, indeed, a scheme for the payment of our debts, which was proposed by an excellent citizen, Mr HUTCHINSON,* about thirty years ago, and which was much approved of by some men of sense, but never was likely to take effect. He asserted that there was a fallacy in imagining that the public owed this debt; for that really every individual owed a proportional share of it, and paid, in his taxes, a proportional share of the interest, beside the expense of levying these taxes. Had we not better, then, says he, make a distribution of the debt among ourselves, and each of us contribute a sum suitable to his property, and by that means discharge at once all our funds and public mortgages? He seems not to have considered that the laborious poor pay a considerable part of the taxes by their annual consumptions, though they could not advance, at once, a proportional part of the sum required. Not to mention, that property in money and stock in trade might easily be concealed or disguised; and that visible property in lands and houses would really at last answer for the whole; an inequality and oppression which never would be submitted to. But though this project is not likely to take place, it is not altogether improbable, that when the nation becomes heartily sick of their debts, and is cruelly oppressed by them, some daring projector may arise with visionary schemes for their discharge. And as public credit will begin, by that time, to be a little frail, the least touch will destroy it, as happened in FRANCE during the regency;* and in this manner it will *die of the doctor.*

But it is more probable, that the breach of national faith will be the necessary effect of wars, defeats, misfortunes, and public calamities, or even perhaps of victories and conquests. I must confess when I see princes and states fighting and quarrelling, amidst their debts, funds, and public mortgages, it always brings to my mind a match of cudgel-playing fought in a *China* shop. How can it be expected, that sovereigns will spare a species of property, which is pernicious to themselves and to the public, when they have so little compassion on lives and properties that are useful to both? Let the time come (and surely it will come) when the new funds, created for the exigencies of the year, are not subscribed to, and raise not the money projected. Suppose either that the cash of the nation is exhausted; or that our faith, which has hitherto been so ample, begins to fail us. Suppose that, in this distress, the nation is threatened with an invasion; a rebellion is suspected or broken out at home; a squadron cannot be equipped for want of pay, victuals, or repairs; or even a foreign subsidy cannot be advanced. What must a prince or minister do in such an emergence? The right of self-preservation is unalienable in every individual, much more in every community. And the folly of our statesmen must then be greater than the folly of those who first contracted debt; or what is more, than that of those who trusted, or continue to trust this security, if these statesmen have the means of safety in their hands, and do not employ them. The funds, created and mortgaged, will by that time bring in a large yearly revenue, sufficient for the defence and security of the nation: money is perhaps lying in the exchequer, ready for the discharge of the quarterly interest: necessity calls, fear urges, reason exhorts, compassion alone exclaims: the money will immediately be seized for the current service, under the most solemn protestations, perhaps of being immediately replaced. But no more is requisite. The whole fabric, already tottering, falls to the ground, and buries thousands in its ruins. And this, I think, may be called the *natural death* of public credit; for to this period it tends as naturally as an animal body to its dissolution and destruction.

So great dupes are the generality of mankind, that notwithstanding such a violent shock to public credit, as a voluntary bankruptcy in ENGLAND would occasion, it would not probably be long ere credit would again revive in as flourishing a condition as before. The present king of FRANCE, during the late war,* borrowed money at a lower interest than ever his grandfather did; and as low as the BRITISH parliament, comparing the natural rate of interest in both kingdoms. And though men are commonly more governed by what they have seen, than by what they foresee, with whatever certainty; yet promises, protestations, fair appearances, with the allurements of present interest, have such powerful influence as few are able to resist. Mankind are, in all ages, caught by the same baits: the same tricks played over and over again, still trepan them. The heights of popularity and patriotism are still the beaten road to power and tyranny; flattery, to treachery; standing armies to arbitrary government; and the glory of God to the temporal interest of the clergy. The fear of an everlasting destruction of credit, allowing it to be an evil, is a needless bugbear. A prudent man, in reality, would rather lend to the public immediately after we had taken a spunge to our debts, than at present; as much as an opulent knave, even though one could not force him to pay, is a preferable debtor to an honest bankrupt: for the former, in order to carry on business, may find it his interest to discharge his debts, where they are not exorbitant: the latter has it not in his power. The reasoning of TACITUS, as it is eternally true, is very applicable to our present case. *Sed vulgus ad magnitudinem beneficiorum aderat: stultissimus* quisque pecuniis mercabatur: apud sapientes cassa habebantur, quae neque dari neque accipi, salva republica, poterant.*[†] The public is a debtor, whom no man can oblige to pay. The only check which the creditors have upon her, is the interest of preserving credit; an interest which may easily be over-balanced by a great debt, and by a difficult and extraordinary emergence, even supposing that credit irrecoverable. Not to mention, that a present necessity often forces states into measures, which are, strictly speaking, against their interest.

These two events supposed above, are calamitous, but not the most calamitous. Thousands are thereby sacrificed to the safety of millions. But we are not without danger, that the contrary event may take place, and that millions may be sacrificed for ever to the temporary safety of thousands.[†] Our popular government, perhaps, will render it difficult or dangerous for a minister to venture on so desperate an expedient as that of a voluntary bankruptcy. And though the house of Lords be altogether composed of proprietors of land, and the house of Commons chiefly; and consequently neither of them can be supposed to have great property in the funds: yet the connections of the members may be so great with the proprietors, as to render them more tenacious of public faith than prudence, policy, or even justice, strictly speaking, requires. And perhaps, too, our foreign enemies may be so politic as to discover, that our safety lies in despair, and may not therefore show the danger, open and barefaced, till it be inevitable. The balance of power in EUROPE, our grandfathers, our fathers, and we, have all deemed too unequal to be preserved without our attention and assistance. But our children, weary of the struggle, and fettered with incumbrances, may sit down secure, and see their neighbours oppressed and conquered; till, at last, they themselves and their creditors lie both at the mercy of the conqueror. And this may properly enough be denominated the *violent death* of our public credit.

These seem to be the events, which are not very remote, and which reason foresees as clearly almost as she can do any thing that lies in the womb of time. And though the ancients maintained, that in order to reach the gift of prophecy, a certain divine fury or madness was requisite, one may safely affirm, that in order to deliver such prophecies as these, no more is necessary than merely to be in one's senses, free from the influence of popular madness and delusion.

OF SOME REMARKABLE CUSTOMS

I SHALL observe three remarkable customs in three celebrated governments; and shall conclude from the whole, that all general maxims in politics ought to be established with great caution; and that irregular and extraordinary appearances are frequently discovered in the moral, as well as in the physical world. The former, perhaps, we can better account for after they happen, from springs and principles, of which every one has, within himself, or from observation, the strongest assurance and conviction: but it is often fully as impossible for human prudence, beforehand, to foresee and foretell them.

I. One would think it essential to every supreme council or assembly which debates, that entire liberty of speech should be granted to every member, and that all motions or reasonings should be received, which can any way tend to illustrate the point under deliberation. One would conclude, with still greater assurance, that after a motion was made, which was voted and approved by that assembly in which the legislative power is lodged, the member who made the motion must for ever be exempted from future trial or inquiry. But no political maxim can, at first sight, appear more indisputable, than that he must, at least, be secured from all inferior jurisdiction; and that nothing less than the same supreme legislative assembly in their subsequent meetings, could make him accountable for those motions and harangues, to which they had before given their approbation. But these axioms, however irrefragable they may appear, have all failed in the ATHENIAN government, from causes and principles too, which appear almost inevitable.

By the γραφὴ παρανόμων, or *indictment of illegality*, (though it has not been remarked by antiquaries or commentators,) any man was tried and punished in a common court of judicature, for any law which had passed upon his motion, in the assembly of the people, if that law appeared to the court unjust, or prejudicial to the public. Thus DEMOSTHENES, finding that ship-money was levied irregularly, and that the poor bore the same burden as the rich in equipping the galleys, corrected this inequality by a very useful law, which proportioned the expense to the revenue and income of each individual. He moved for this law in the assembly; he proved its advantages;[†] he convinced the people, the only legislature in ATHENS; the law passed, and was carried into execution: yet was he tried in a criminal court for that law, upon the complaint of the rich, who resented the alteration that he had introduced into the finances.[†] He was indeed acquitted, upon proving anew the usefulness of his law.

CTESIPHON moved in the assembly of the people, that particular honours should be conferred on DEMOSTHENES, as on a citizen affectionate and useful to the commonwealth: the people, convinced of this truth, voted those honours: yet was CTESIPHON tried by the γραφὴ παρανόμων. It was asserted, among other topics, that DEMOSTHENES was not a good citizen, nor affectionate to the commonwealth: and the orator was called upon to defend his friend, and consequently himself; which he executed by that sublime piece of eloquence that has ever since been the admiration of mankind.

After the battle of CHAERONEA, a law was passed upon the motion of HYPERIDES, giving liberty to slaves, and enrolling them in the troops.[†] On account of this law, the orator was afterwards tried by the indictment above mentioned, and defended himself, among other topics, by that stroke celebrated by PLUTARCH and LONGINUS. *It was not I,* said he, *that moved for this law: it was the necessities of war; it was the battle of* CHAERONEA. The orations of DEMOSTHENES abound with many instances of trials of this nature, and prove clearly, that nothing was more commonly practised.

The ATHENIAN Democracy was such a tumultuous government as we can scarcely form a notion of in the present age of the world. The whole collective body of the people voted in every law, without any limitation of property, without any distinction of rank, without control from any magistracy or senate;[†] and consequently without regard to order, justice, or prudence. The ATHENIANS soon became sensible of the mischiefs attending this constitution: but being averse to checking themselves by any rule or restriction, they resolved, at least to check their demagogues or counsellors, by the fear of future punishment and inquiry. They accordingly instituted this remarkable law, a law esteemed so essential to their form of government, that AESCHINES insisted on it as a known truth, that were it abolished or neglected, it were impossible for the Democracy to subsist.[†]

The people feared not any ill consequence to liberty from the authority of the criminal courts, because these were nothing but very numerous juries, chosen by lot from among the people. And they justly considered themselves as in a state of perpetual pupilage, where they had an authority, after they came to the use of reason, not only to retract and control whatever had been determined, but to punish any guardian for measures which they had embraced by his persuasion. The same law had place in THEBES,[†] and for the same reason.

It appears to have been a usual practice in ATHENS, on the establishment of any law esteemed very useful or popular, to prohibit for ever its abrogation and repeal. Thus the demagogue, who diverted all the public revenues to the support of shows and spectacles, made it criminal so much as to move for a repeal of this law.[†] Thus LEPTINES moved for a law, not only to recall all the immunities formerly granted, but to deprive the people for the future of the

power of granting any more.† Thus all bills of attainder†
were forbid, or laws that affected one ATHENIAN, without
extending to the whole commonwealth. These absurd
clauses, by which the legislature vainly attempted to bind
itself for ever, proceeded from an universal sense in the
people of their own levity and inconstancy.

II. A wheel within a wheel, such as we observe in the
GERMAN empire, is considered by Lord SHAFTESBURY† as an
absurdity in politics: but what must we say to two equal
wheels, which govern the same political machine, without any mutual check, control, or subordination, and yet
preserve the greatest harmony and concord? To establish
two distinct legislatures, each of which possesses full and
absolute authority within itself, and stands in no need of the
other's assistance, in order to give validity to its acts; this
may appear, beforehand, altogether impracticable, as long
as men are actuated by the passions of ambition, emulation,
and avarice, which have hitherto been their chief governing
principles. And should I assert, that the state I have in my
eye was divided into two distinct factions, each of which
predominated in a distinct legislature, and yet produced no
clashing in these independent powers, the supposition may
appear incredible. And if, to augment the paradox, I should
affirm, that this disjointed, irregular government, was the
most active, triumphant, and illustrious commonwealth that
ever yet appeared; I should certainly be told, that such a
political chimera was as absurd as any vision of priests or
poets. But there is no need for searching long, in order to
prove the reality of the foregoing suppositions: for this was
actually the case with the ROMAN republic.

The legislative power was there lodged in the *comitia
centuriata* and *comitia tributa*.* In the former, it is well
known, the people voted according to their *census*, so that
when the first class was unanimous, though it contained not
perhaps the hundredth part of the commonwealth, it determined the whole; and, with the authority of the senate,
established a law. In the latter every vote was equal; and as
the authority of the senate was not there requisite, the lower
people entirely prevailed, and gave law to the whole state.

In all party divisions, at first between the PATRICIANS and PLEBEIANS, afterwards between the nobles and the people, the interest of the aristocracy was predominant in the first legislature, that of the democracy in the second: the one could always destroy what the other had established: nay, the one by a sudden and unforeseen motion, might take the start of the other, and totally annihilate its rival by a vote, which, from the nature of the constitution, had the full authority of a law. But no such contest is observed in the history of ROME: no instance of a quarrel between these two legislatures, though many between the parties that governed in each. Whence arose this concord, which may seem so extraordinary?

The legislature established in ROME, by the authority of SERVIUS TULLIUS, was the *comitia centuriata*, which, after the expulsion of the kings, rendered the government for some time very aristocratical. But the people, having numbers and force on their side, and being elated with frequent conquests and victories in their foreign wars, always prevailed when pushed to extremity, and first extorted from the senate the magistracy of the tribunes, and next the legislative power of the *comitia tributa*. It then behoved the nobles to be more careful than ever not to provoke the people. For beside the force which the latter were always possessed of, they had now got possession of legal authority, and could instantly break in pieces any order or institution which directly opposed them. By intrigue, by influence, by money, by combination, and by the respect paid to their character, the nobles might often prevail, and direct the whole machine of government: but had they openly set their *comitia centuriata* in opposition to the *tributa*, they had soon lost the advantage of that institution, together with their consuls, praetors, ediles, and all the magistrates elected by it. But the *comitia tributa*, not having the same reason for respecting the *centuriata*, frequently repealed laws favourable to the aristocracy: they limited the authority of the nobles, protected the people from oppression, and controlled the actions of the senate and magistracy. The *centuriata* found it convenient always to submit; and though equal in authority, yet being inferior in power, durst never directly give any shock to the other legislature, either by repealing its laws, or establishing laws which it foresaw would soon be repealed by it.

No instance is found of any opposition or struggle between these *comitia*, except one slight attempt of this kind, mentioned by APPIAN in the third book of his civil wars.* MARK ANTONY, resolving to deprive DECIMUS BRUTUS of the government of CISALPINE GAUL, railed in the *Forum*, and called one of the *comitia*, in order to prevent the meeting of the other, which had been ordered by the senate. But affairs were then fallen into such confusion, and the ROMAN constitution was so near its final dissolution, that no inference can be drawn from such an expedient. This contest, besides, was founded more on form than party. It was the senate who ordered the *comitia tributa*, that they might obstruct the meeting of the *centuriata*, which, by the constitution, or at least forms of the government, could alone dispose of provinces.

CICERO was recalled by the *comitia centuriata*, though banished by the *tributa*, that is, by a *plebiscitum*. But his banishment, we may observe, never was considered as a legal deed, arising from the free choice and inclination of the people. It was always ascribed to the violence alone of CLODIUS, and to the disorders introduced by him into the government.

III. The *third* custom which we purpose to remark regards ENGLAND, and, though it be not so important as those which we have pointed out in ATHENS and ROME, is no less singular and unexpected. It is a maxim in politics, which we readily admit as undisputed and universal, that a power, however great, when granted by law to an eminent magistrate, is not so dangerous to liberty as an authority, however inconsiderable, which he acquires from violence and usurpation. For besides that the law always limits every power which it bestows, the very receiving it as a concession establishes the authority whence it is derived, and preserves the harmony of the constitution. By the same right that one prerogative is assumed without law, another may also be claimed, and another, with still greater facility; while the first usurpations both serve as precedents to the following, and give force to maintain them. Hence the heroism of HAMPDEN's conduct,* who sustained the whole violence of royal prosecution, rather than pay a tax of twenty shillings not imposed by parliament; hence the care of all ENGLISH patriots to guard against the first encroachments of the crown; and hence alone the existence, at this day, of ENGLISH liberty.

There is, however, one occasion where the Parliament has departed from this maxim; and that is, in the *pressing of seamen.** The exercise of an irregular power is here tacitly permitted in the crown; and though it has frequently been under deliberation how that power might be rendered legal, and granted, under proper restrictions, to the sovereign, no safe expedient could ever be proposed for that purpose; and the danger to liberty always appeared greater from law than from usurpation. When this power is exercised to no other end than to man the navy, men willingly submit to it from a sense of its use and necessity; and the sailors, who are alone affected by it, find nobody to support them in claiming the rights and privileges which the law grants, without distinction, to all ENGLISH subjects. But were this power, on any occasion, made an instrument of faction or ministerial tyranny, the opposite faction, and indeed all lovers of their country, would immediately take the alarm, and support the injured party; the liberty of ENGLISHMEN would be asserted; juries would be implacable; and the tools of tyranny, acting both against law and equity, would meet with the severest vengeance. On the other hand, were the parliament to grant such an authority, they would probably fall into one of these two inconveniences. They would either bestow it under so many restrictions as would make it lose its effect, by cramping the authority of the crown; or they would render it so large and comprehensive as might give occasion to great abuses, for which we could, in that case, have no remedy. The very irregularity of the practice at present prevents its abuses, by affording so easy a remedy against them.

I pretend not, by this reasoning, to exclude all possibility of contriving a register for seamen, which might man the navy without being dangerous to liberty. I only observe, that no satisfactory scheme of that nature has yet been proposed. Rather than adopt any project hitherto invented, we continue a practice seemingly the most absurd and unaccountable. Authority, in times of full internal peace and concord, is armed against law. A continued violence is permitted in the crown, amidst the greatest jealousy and watchfulness in the people; nay, proceeding from those very principles. Liberty, in a country of the highest liberty, is left entirely to its own defence, without any countenance or protection. The wild state of nature is renewed in one of the most civilized societies of mankind, and great violence and disorder are committed with impunity; while the one party pleads obedience to the supreme magistrate, the other the sanction of fundamental laws.

OF THE POPULOUSNESS OF ANCIENT NATIONS

THERE is very little ground, either from reason or observation, to conclude the world eternal or incorruptible. The continual and rapid motion of matter, the violent revolutions with which every part is agitated, the changes remarked in the heavens, the plain traces as well as traditions of an universal deluge, or general convulsion of the elements; all these prove strongly the mortality of this fabric of the world, and its passage, by corruption or dissolution, from one state or order to another. It must therefore, as well as each individual form which it contains, have its infancy, youth, manhood, and old age; and it is probable, that, in all these variations, man, equally with every animal and vegetable, will partake. In the flourishing age of the world it may be expected, that the human species should possess greater vigour both of mind and body, more prosperous health, higher spirits, longer life, and a stronger inclination and power of generation. But if the general system of things, and human society of course, have any such gradual revolutions, they are too slow to be discernible in that short period which is comprehended by history and tradition. Stature and force of body, length of life, even courage and extent of genius, seem hitherto to have been naturally, in all ages, pretty much the same. The arts and sciences, indeed, have flourished in one period, and have decayed in another; but we may observe, that at the time when they rose to greatest perfection among one people, they were perhaps totally unknown to all the neighbouring nations; and though they universally decayed in one age, yet in a succeeding generation they again revived, and diffused themselves over the world. As far, therefore, as observation reaches, there is no universal difference discernible in the human species; and though it were allowed, that the universe, like an animal body, had a natural progress from infancy to old age, yet as it must still be uncertain, whether, at present, it be advancing to its point of perfection, or declining from it, we cannot thence presuppose any decay in human nature.[†] To prove, therefore, or account for that superior populousness of antiquity, which is commonly supposed, by the imaginary youth or vigour of the world, will scarcely be admitted by any just reasoner. These *general physical* causes ought entirely to be excluded from this question.

There are indeed some more *particular physical* causes of importance. Diseases are mentioned in antiquity, which are almost unknown to modern medicine; and new diseases have arisen and propagated themselves, of which there are no traces in ancient history. In this particular we may observe, upon comparison, that the disadvantage is much on the side of the moderns. Not to mention some others of less moment, the smallpox commits such ravages, as would almost alone account for the great superiority ascribed to ancient times. The tenth or the twelfth part of mankind destroyed, every generation should make a vast difference, it may be thought, in the numbers of the people; and when joined to venereal distempers, a new plague diffused everywhere, this disease is perhaps equivalent, by its constant operation, to the three great scourges of mankind, war, pestilence, and famine. Were it certain, therefore, that ancient times were more populous than the present, and could no moral causes be assigned for so great a change, these physical causes alone, in the opinion of many, would be sufficient to give us satisfaction on that head.

But is it certain that antiquity was so much more populous, as is pretended? The extravagances of VOSSIUS,* with regard to this subject, are well known. But an author of much greater genius and discernment† has ventured to affirm, that according to the best computations which these subjects will admit of, there are not now, on the face of the earth, the fiftieth part of mankind, which existed in the time of JULIUS CAESAR. It may easily be observed, that the comparison in this case must be imperfect, even though we confine ourselves to the scene of ancient history; EUROPE, and the nations round the MEDITERRANEAN. We know not exactly the numbers of any EUROPEAN kingdom, or even city, at present: how can we pretend to calculate those of ancient cities and states, where historians have left us such imperfect traces? For my part, the matter appears to me so uncertain, that, as I intend to throw together some reflections on that head, I shall intermingle the inquiry concerning *causes* with that concerning *facts*; which ought never to be admitted, where the facts can be ascertained with any tolerable assurance. We shall, *first*, consider whether it be probable, from what we know of the situation of society in both periods, that antiquity must have been more populous; *secondly*, whether in reality it was so. If I can make it appear, that the conclusion is not so certain as is pretended, in favour of antiquity, it is all I aspire to.

In general, we may observe, that the question with regard to the comparative populousness of ages or kingdoms, implies important consequences, and commonly determines concerning the preference of their whole police, their manners, and the constitution of their government. For as there is in all men, both male and female, a desire and power of generation, more active than is ever universally exerted, the restraints which they lie under must proceed from some difficulties in their situation, which it belongs to a wise legislature carefully to observe and remove. Almost every man, who thinks he can maintain a family, will have one; and the human species, at this rate of propagation, would more than double every generation. How fast do mankind multiply in every colony or new settlement, where it is an easy matter to provide for a family, and where men are nowise straitened or confined as in long established governments? History tells us frequently of plagues which have swept away the third or fourth part of a people; yet in a generation or two, the destruction was not perceived, and the society had again acquired their former number. The lands which were cultivated, the houses built, the commodities raised, the riches acquired, enabled the people, who escaped, immediately to marry and to rear families, which supplied the place of those who had perished.[†] And, for a like reason, every wise, just, and mild government, by rendering the condition of its subjects easy and secure, will always abound most in people, as well as in commodities and riches. A country, indeed, whose climate and soil are fitted for vines, will naturally be more populous than one which produces corn only, and that more populous than one which is only fitted for pasturage. In general, warm climates, as the necessities of the inhabitants are there fewer, and vegetation more powerful, are likely to be most populous: but if every thing else be equal, it seems natural to expect that, wherever there are most happiness and virtue, and the wisest institutions, there will also be most people.

The question, therefore, concerning the populousness of ancient and modern times, being allowed of great importance, it will be requisite, if we would bring it to some determination, to compare both the *domestic* and *political* situation of these two periods, in order to judge of the facts by their moral causes; which is the *first* view in which we proposed to consider them.

The chief difference between the *domestic* economy of the ancients and that of the moderns, consists in the practice of slavery, which prevailed among the former, and which has been abolished for some centuries throughout the greater part of Europe. Some passionate admirers of the ancients, and zealous partisans of civil liberty, (for these sentiments, as they are both of them in the main extremely just, are found to be almost inseparable,) cannot forbear regretting the loss of this institution; and whilst they brand all submission to the government of a single person with the harsh denomination of slavery, they would gladly reduce the greater part of mankind to real slavery and subjection. But to one who considers coolly on the subject, it will appear that human nature, in general, really enjoys more liberty at present, in the most arbitrary government of EUROPE, than it ever did during the most flourishing period of ancient times. As much as submission to a petty prince, whose dominions extend not beyond a single city, is more grievous than obedience to a great monarch; so much is domestic slavery more cruel and oppressive than any civil subjection whatsoever. The more the master is removed from us in place and rank, the greater liberty we enjoy, the less are our actions inspected and controlled, and the fainter that cruel comparison becomes between our own subjection, and the freedom, and even dominion of another. The remains which are found of domestic slavery, in the AMERICAN colonies, and among some EUROPEAN nations, would never surely create a desire of rendering it more universal. The little humanity commonly observed in persons accustomed, from their infancy, to exercise so great authority over their fellow-creatures, and to trample upon human nature, were sufficient alone to disgust us with that unbounded dominion. Nor can a more probable reason be assigned for the severe, I might say, barbarous manners of ancient times, than the practice of domestic slavery; by which every man of rank was rendered a petty tyrant, and educated amidst the flattery, submission, and low debasement of his slaves.

According to ancient practice, all checks were on the inferior, to restrain him to the duty of submission; none on the superior, to engage him to the reciprocal duties of gentleness and humanity. In modern times, a bad servant finds not easily a good master, nor a bad master a good servant; and the checks are mutual, suitably to the inviolable and eternal laws of reason and equity.

The custom of exposing old, useless, or sick slaves in an island of the TYBER, there to starve, seems to have been pretty common in ROME; and whoever recovered, after having been so exposed, had his liberty given him by an edict of the Emperor CLAUDIUS; in which it was likewise forbidden to kill any slave merely for old age or sickness.[†] But supposing that this edict was strictly obeyed, would it better the domestic treatment of slaves, or render their lives much more comfortable? We may imagine what others would practise, when it was the professed maxim of the elder CATO, to sell his superannuated slaves for any price, rather than maintain what he esteemed a useless burden.[†]

The *ergastula*, or dungeons, where slaves in chains were forced to work, were very common all over ITALY. COLUMELLA advises, that they be always built underground; and recommends[†] it as the duty of a careful overseer, to call over every day the names of these slaves, like the mustering of a regiment or ship's company, in order to know presently when any of them had deserted; a proof of the frequency of these *ergastula*, and of the greater number of slaves usually confined in them.

A chained slave for a porter was usual in ROME, as appears from OVID,[†] and other authors.[†] Had not these people shaken off all sense of compassion towards that unhappy part of their species, would they have presented their friends, at the first entrance, with such an image of the severity of the master and misery of the slave?

Nothing so common in all trials, even of civil causes, as to call for the evidence of slaves; which was always extorted by the most exquisite torments. DEMOSTHENES[†] says, that, where it was possible to produce, for the same fact, either freemen or slaves, as witnesses, the judges always preferred the torturing of slaves as a more certain evidence.[†]

SENECA draws a picture of that disorderly luxury which changes day into night, and night into day, and inverts every stated hour of every office in life. Among other circumstances, such as displacing the meals and times of bathing, he mentions, that, regularly about the third hour of the night, the neighbours of one, who indulges this false refinement, hear the noise of whips and lashes; and, upon inquiry, find that he is then taking an account of the conduct of his servants, and giving them due correction and discipline. This is not remarked as an instance of cruelty, but only of disorder, which, even in actions the most usual and methodical, changes the fixed hours that an established custom had assigned for them.[†]

But our present business is only to consider the influence of slavery on the populousness of a state. It is pretended, that, in this particular, the ancient practice had infinitely the advantage, and was the chief cause of that extreme populousness which is supposed in those times. At present, all masters discourage the marrying of their male servants, and admit not by any means the marriage of the female, who are then supposed altogether incapacitated for their service. But where the property of the servants is lodged in the master, their marriage forms his riches, and brings him a succession of slaves, that supply the place of those whom age and infirmity have disabled. He encourages, therefore, their propagation as much as that of his cattle, rears the young with the same care, and educates them to some art or calling, which may render them more useful or valuable to him. The opulent are, by this policy, interested in the being at least, though not in the well-being, of the poor; and enrich themselves by increasing the number and industry of those who are subjected to them. Each man, being a sovereign in his own family, has the same interest with regard to it as the prince with regard to the state, and has not, like the prince, any opposite motives of ambition or vainglory, which may lead him to depopulate his little sovereignty. All of it is, at all times, under his eye; and he has leisure to inspect the most minute detail of the marriage and education of his subjects.[†]

Such are the consequences of domestic slavery, according to the first aspect and appearance of things: but if we enter more deeply into the subject, we shall perhaps find reason to retract our hasty determinations. The comparison is shocking between the management of human creatures and that of cattle; but being extremely just, when applied to the present subject, it may be proper to trace the consequences of it. At the capital, near all great cities, in all populous, rich, industrious provinces, few cattle are bred. Provisions, lodging, attendance, labour, are there dear; and men find their account better in buying the cattle, after they come to a certain stage, from the remoter and cheaper countries. These are consequently the only breeding countries for cattle; and, by a parity of reason, for men too, when the latter are put on the same footing with the former. To rear a child in LONDON till he could be serviceable, would cost much dearer than to buy one of the same age from SCOTLAND or IRELAND, where he had been bred in a cottage, covered with rags, and fed on oatmeal or potatoes. Those who had slaves, therefore, in all the richer and more populous countries, would discourage the pregnancy of the females, and either prevent or destroy the birth. The human species would perish in those places where it ought to increase the fastest, and a perpetual recruit be wanted from the poorer and more desert provinces. Such a continued drain would tend mightily to depopulate the state, and render great cities ten times more destructive than with us; where every man is master of himself, and provides for his children from the powerful instinct of nature, not the calculations of sordid interest. If LONDON at present, without much increasing, needs a yearly recruit from the country of 5,000 people, as is usually computed, what must it require if the greater part of the tradesmen and common people were slaves, and were hindered from breeding by their avaricious masters?

All ancient authors tell us, that there was a perpetual flux of slaves to ITALY, from the remoter provinces, particularly SYRIA, CILICIA,[†] CAPPADOCIA, and the Lesser ASIA, THRACE, and EGYPT: yet the number of people did not increase in ITALY; and writers complain of the continual decay of industry and agriculture.[*] Where then is that extreme fertility of the ROMAN slaves, which is commonly supposed? So far from multiplying, they could not, it seems, so much as keep up the stock without immense recruits. And though great numbers were continually manumitted and converted into

ROMAN citizens, the numbers even of these did not increase,[†] till the freedom of the city was communicated to foreign provinces.

The term for a slave, born and bred in the family, was *verna*;[†] and these slaves seem to have been entitled by custom to privileges and indulgences beyond others; a sufficient reason why the masters would not be fond of rearing many of that kind.[†] Whoever is acquainted with the maxims of our planters, will acknowledge the justness of this observation.[†]

ATTICUS is much praised by his historian for the care which he took in recruiting his family from the slaves born in it.[†] May we not thence infer, that this practice was not then very common?

The names of slaves in the GREEK comedies, SYRUS, MYSUS, GETA, THRAX, DAVUS, LYDUS, PHRYX, etc., afford a presumption, that, at ATHENS at least, most of the slaves were imported from foreign countries. The ATHENIANS, says STRABO,[†] gave to their slaves either the names of the nations whence they were bought, as LYDUS, SYRUS, or the names that were most common among those nations, as MANES or MIDAS to a PHRYGIAN, TIBIAS to a PAPHLAGONIAN.

DEMOSTHENES,[†] having mentioned a law which forbade any man to strike the slave of another, praises the humanity of this law; and adds, that if the barbarians, from whom the slaves were bought, had information that their countrymen met with such gentle treatment, they would entertain a great esteem for the ATHENIANS. ISOCRATES,[†] too, insinuates that the slaves of the GREEKS were generally or very commonly barbarians. ARISTOTLE in his Politics,[†] plainly supposes, that a slave is always a foreigner. The ancient comic writers represented the slaves as speaking a barbarous language.[†] This was an imitation of nature.

It is well known that DEMOSTHENES, in his nonage, had been defrauded of a large fortune by his tutors, and that afterwards he recovered, by a prosecution at law, the value of his patrimony. His orations, on that occasion, still remain, and contain an exact detail of the whole substance left by his father,[†] in money, merchandise, houses, and slaves, together with the value of each particular. Among the rest were 52 slaves, handicraftsmen, namely, 32 sword-cutlers, and 20 cabinet-makers,[†] all males; not a word of any wives, children, or family, which they certainly would have had, had it been a common practice at ATHENS to breed from the slaves; and the value of the whole must have much depended on that circumstance. No female slaves are even so much as mentioned, except some housemaids, who belonged to his mother. This argument has great force, if it be not altogether conclusive.

Consider this passage of PLUTARCH,[†] speaking of the Elder CATO: 'He had a great number of slaves, whom he took care to buy at the sales of prisoners of war; and he chose them young, that they might easily be accustomed to any diet or manner of life, and be instructed in any business or labour, as men teach any thing to young dogs or horses. And esteeming love the chief source of all disorders, he allowed the male slaves to have a commerce with the female in his family, upon paying a certain sum for this privilege: but he strictly prohibited all intrigues out of his family.' Are there any symptoms in this narration of that care which is supposed in the ancients of the marriage and propagation of their slaves? If that was a common practice founded on general interest, it would surely have been embraced by CATO, who was a great economist, and lived in times when the ancient frugality and simplicity of manners were still in credit and reputation.

It is expressly remarked by the writers of the ROMAN law, that scarcely any ever purchased slaves with a view of breeding from them.[†]

Our lackeys and housemaids, I own, do not serve much to multiply their species: but the ancients, besides those who attended on their person, had almost all their labour performed, and even manufactures executed by slaves, who lived, many of them, in their family; and some great men possessed to the number of 10,000. If there be any suspicion, therefore, that this institution was unfavourable to propagation (and the same reason, at least in part, holds with regard to ancient slaves as modern servants), how destructive must slavery have proved!

History mentions a ROMAN nobleman who had 400 slaves under the same roof with him: and having been assassinated at home by the furious revenge of one of them, the law was executed with rigour, and all without exception were put to death.[†] Many other ROMAN noblemen had families equally, or more numerous; and I believe every one will allow, that this would scarcely be practicable, were we to suppose all the slaves married, and the females to be breeders.[†]

So early as the poet HESIOD,[†] married slaves, whether male or female, were esteemed inconvenient. How much more, where families had increased to such an enormous size as in Rome, and where the ancient simplicity of manners was banished from all ranks of people!

XENOPHON in his Oeconomics, where he gives directions for the management of a farm, recommends a strict care and attention of laying the male and the female slaves at a distance from each other. He seems not to suppose that they are ever married. The only slaves among the GREEKS that appear to have continued their own race, were the HELOTES, who had houses apart, and were more the slaves of the public than of individuals.[†]

The same author[†] tells us, that NICIAS's overseer, by agreement with his master, was obliged to pay him an obolus a day for each slave, besides maintaining them and keeping up the number. Had the ancient slaves been all breeders, this last circumstance of the contract had been superfluous.

The ancients talk so frequently of a fixed, stated portion of provisions assigned to each slave,[†] that we are naturally led to conclude, that slaves lived almost all single, and received that portion as a kind of board-wages.

The practice, indeed, of marrying slaves, seems not to have been very common, even among the country labourers, where it is more naturally to be expected. CATO,[†] enumerating the slaves requisite to labour a vineyard of a hundred acres, makes them amount to 15; the overseer and his wife, *villicus* and *villica*, and 13 male slaves; for an olive plantation of 240 acres, the overseer and his wife, and 11 male slaves; and so in proportion to a greater or less plantation or vineyard.

VARRO,[†] quoting this passage of CATO, allows his computation to be just in every respect except the last. For as it is requisite, says he, to have an overseer and his wife, whether the vineyard or plantation be great or small, this must alter the exactness of the proportion. Had CATO's computation been erroneous in any other respect, it had certainly been corrected by VARRO, who seems fond of discovering so trivial an error.

The same author,[†] as well as COLUMELLA,[†] recommends it as requisite to give a wife to the overseer, in order to attach him the more strongly to his master's service. This was therefore a peculiar indulgence granted to a slave, in whom so great confidence was reposed.

In the same place, VARRO mentions it as an useful precaution, not to buy too many slaves from the same nation, lest they beget factions and seditions in the family; a presumption, that in ITALY the greater part even of the country slaves (for he speaks of no other) were bought from the remoter provinces. All the world knows, that the family slaves in ROME, who were instruments of show and luxury, were commonly imported from the East. *Hoc profecere*, says PLINY, speaking of the jealous care of masters, *mancipiorum legiones, et in domo turba externa ac servorum quoque causa nomenclator adhibendus.*[†]

It is indeed recommended by VARRO[†] to propagate young shepherds in the family from the old ones. For as grazing farms were commonly in remote and cheap places, and each shepherd lived in a cottage apart, his marriage and increase were not liable to the same inconvenience as in dearer places, and where many servants lived in the family, which was universally the case in such of the ROMAN farms as produced wine or corn. If we consider this exception with regard to shepherds, and weigh the reasons of it, it will serve for a strong confirmation of all our foregoing suspicions.[†]

COLUMELLA,[†] I own, advises the master to give a reward, and even liberty to a female slave, that had reared him above three children; a proof that sometimes the ancients propagated from their slaves, which indeed cannot be denied. Were it otherwise, the practice of slavery, being so common in antiquity, must have been destructive to a degree which no expedient could repair. All I pretend to infer from these reasonings is, that slavery is in general disadvantageous both to the happiness and populousness of mankind, and that its place is much better supplied by the practice of hired servants.

The laws, or, as some writers call them, the seditions of the GRACCHI, were occasioned by their observing the increase of slaves all over ITALY, and the diminution of free citizens. APPIAN[†] ascribes this increase to the propagation of the slaves: PLUTARCH[†] to the purchasing of barbarians, who were chained and imprisoned, βαρβαρικα δεσμωτηρια.[†] It is to be presumed that both causes concurred.

SICILY, says FLORUS,[†] was full of *ergastula*, and was cultivated by labourers in chains. EUNUS and ATHENIO excited the servile war, by breaking up these monstrous prisons, and giving liberty to 60,000 slaves. The younger POMPEY augmented his army in SPAIN by the same expedient.[†] If the country labourers throughout the ROMAN empire, were so generally in this situation, and if it was difficult or impossible to find separate lodgings for the families of the city servants, how unfavourable to propagation, as well as to humanity, must the institution of domestic slavery be esteemed?

CONSTANTINOPLE, at present, requires the same recruits of slaves from all the provinces that ROME did of old; and these provinces are of consequence far from being populous.

EGYPT, according to Mons. MAILLET,[*] sends continual colonies of black slaves to the other parts of the TURKISH empire, and receives annually an equal return of white: the one brought from the inland parts of AFRICA, the other from MINGRELIA, CIRCASSIA, and TARTARY.

Our modern convents are, no doubt, bad institutions: but there is reason to suspect, that anciently every great family in ITALY, and probably in other parts of the world, was a species of convent. And though we have reason to condemn all those popish institutions as nurseries of superstition, burdensome to the public, and oppressive to the poor prisoners, male as well as female, yet may it be questioned whether they be so destructive to the populousness of a state, as is commonly imagined. Were the land which belongs to a convent bestowed on a nobleman, he would spend its revenue on dogs, horses, grooms, footmen, cooks, and housemaids, and his family would not furnish many more citizens than the convent.

The common reason why any parent thrusts his daughters into nunneries, is, that he may not be overburdened with too numerous a family; but the ancients had a method almost as innocent, and more effectual to that purpose, to wit, exposing their children in early infancy. This practice was very common, and is not spoken of by any author of those times with the horror it deserves, or scarcely[†] even with disapprobation. PLUTARCH,[†] the humane good-natured PLUTARCH, mentions it as a merit in ATTALUS, king of PERGAMUS, that he murdered, or, if you will, exposed all his own children, in order to leave his crown to the son of his brother EUMENES; signalizing in this manner his gratitude and affection to EUMENES, who had left him his heir, preferably to that son. It was SOLON, the most celebrated of the sages of GREECE, that gave parents permission by law to kill their children.[†]

Shall we then allow these two circumstances to compensate each other, to wit, monastic vows and the exposing of children, and to be unfavourable, in equal degrees, to the propagation of mankind? I doubt the advantage is here on the side of antiquity. Perhaps, by an odd connection of causes, the barbarous practice of the ancients might rather render those times more populous. By removing the terrors of too numerous a family, it would engage many people in marriage; and such is the force of natural affection, that very few, in comparison, would have resolution enough, when it came to the push, to carry into execution their former intentions.

CHINA, the only country where this practice of exposing children prevails at present, is the most populous country we know of, and every man is married before he is twenty. Such early marriages could scarcely be general, had not men the prospect of so easy a method of getting rid of their children. I own that PLUTARCH speaks of it as a very general maxim of the poor to expose their children; and as the rich were then averse to marriage, on account of the courtship they met with from those who expected legacies from them, the public must have been in a bad situation between them.[†]

Of all sciences, there is none where first appearances are more deceitful than in politics. Hospitals for foundlings seem favourable to the increase of numbers, and perhaps may be so, when kept under proper restrictions. But when they open the door to every one without distinction, they have probably a contrary effect, and are pernicious to the state. It is computed, that every ninth child born in PARIS is sent to the hospital; though it seems certain, according to the common course of human affairs, that it is not a hundredth child whose parents are altogether incapacitated to rear and educate him. The great difference, for health, industry, and morals, between an education in an hospital and that in a private family, should induce us not to make the entrance into the former too easy and engaging. To kill one's own child is shocking to nature, and must therefore be somewhat unusual; but to turn over the care of him upon others, is very tempting to the natural indolence of mankind.

Having considered the domestic life and manners of the ancients, compared to those of the moderns, where, in the main, we seem rather superior, so far as the present question is concerned, we shall now examine the *political* customs and institutions of both ages, and weigh their influence in retarding or forwarding the propagation of mankind.

Before the increase of the ROMAN power, or rather till its full establishment, almost all the nations, which are the scene of ancient history, were divided into small territories or petty commonwealths, where of course a great equality of fortune prevailed; and the centre of the government was always very near its frontiers.

This was the situation of affairs not only in GREECE and ITALY, but also in SPAIN, GAUL, GERMANY, AFRICA, and a great part of the Lesser ASIA: and it must be owned, that no institution could be more favourable to the propagation of mankind. For though a man of an overgrown fortune, not being able to consume more than another, must share it with those who serve and attend him, yet their possession being precarious, they have not the same encouragement to marry as if each had a small fortune, secure and independent. Enormous cities are, besides, destructive to society, beget vice and disorder of all kinds, starve the remoter provinces, and even starve themselves, by the prices to which they raise all provisions. Where each man had his little house and field to himself, and each county had its capital, free and independent, what a happy situation of mankind! how favourable to industry and agriculture, to marriage and propagation! The prolific virtue of men, were it to act in its full extent, without that restraint which poverty and necessity impose on it, would double the number every generation: and nothing surely can give it more liberty than such small commonwealths, and such an equality of fortune among the citizens. All small states naturally produce equality of fortune, because they afford no opportunities of great increase; but small commonwealths much more, by that division of power and authority which is essential to them.

When XENOPHON[†] returned after the famous expedition with CYRUS, he hired himself and 6,000 of the GREEKS into the service of SEUTHES, a prince of THRACE; and the articles of his agreement were, that each soldier should receive a *daric* a month, each captain two *darics*, and he himself, as general, four; a regulation of pay which would not a little surprise our modern officers.

DEMOSTHENES and AESCHINES, with eight more, were sent ambassadors[†] to PHILIP of MACEDON, and their appointments for above four months were a thousand *drachmas*, which is less than a *drachma* a day for each ambassador. But a *drachma* a day, nay, sometimes two,[†] was the pay of a common foot soldier.

A centurion among the ROMANS had only double pay to a private man in POLYBIUS's time,[†] and we accordingly find the gratuities after a triumph regulated by that proportion.[†] But MARK ANTONY and the triumvirate gave the centurions five times the reward of the other;* so much had the increase of the commonwealth increased the inequality among the citizens.†

It must be owned, that the situation of affairs in modern times, with regard to civil liberty, as well as equality of fortune, is not near so favourable either to the propagation or happiness of mankind. EUROPE is shared out mostly into great monarchies; and such parts of it as are divided into small territories are commonly governed by absolute princes, who ruin their people by a mimicry of the great monarchs, in the splendour of their court, and number of their forces. SWISSERLAND alone, and HOLLAND, resembles the ancient republics; and though the former is far from possessing any advantage, either of soil, climate, or commerce, yet the numbers of people with which it abounds, notwithstanding their enlisting themselves into every service in EUROPE, prove sufficiently the advantages of their political institutions.

The ancient republics derived their chief or only security from the numbers of their citizens. The TRACHINIANS having lost great numbers of their people, the remainder, instead of enriching themselves by the inheritance of their fellow-citizens, applied to SPARTA, their metropolis, for a new stock of inhabitants. The SPARTANS immediately collected ten thousand men, among whom the old citizens divided the lands of which the former proprietors had perished.†

After TIMOLEON had banished DIONYSIUS from SYRACUSE, and had settled the affairs of SICILY, finding the cities of SYRACUSE and SELINUNTUM extremely depopulated by tyranny, war, and faction, he invited over from GREECE some new inhabitants to repeople them.† Immediately forty thousand men (PLUTARCH† says sixty thousand) offered themselves; and he distributed so many lots of land among them, to the great satisfaction of the ancient inhabitants; a proof at once of the maxims of ancient policy, which affected populousness more than riches, and of the good effects of these maxims, in the extreme populousness of that small country, GREECE, which could at once supply so great a colony. The case was not much different with the ROMANS in early times. He is a pernicious citizen, said M'. CURIUS, who cannot be content with seven acres.[†] Such ideas of equality could not fail of producing great numbers of people.

We must now consider what disadvantages the ancients lay under with regard to populousness, and what checks they received from their political maxims and institutions. There are commonly compensations in every human condition; and though these compensations be not always perfectly equal, yet they serve, at least, to restrain the prevailing principle. To compare them, and estimate their influence, is indeed difficult, even where they take place in the same age, and in neighbouring countries: but where several ages have intervened, and only scattered lights are afforded us by ancient authors; what can we do but amuse ourselves by talking *pro* and *con* on an interesting subject, and thereby correcting all hasty and violent determinations?

First, We may observe, that the ancient republics were almost in perpetual war; a natural effect of their martial spirit, their love of liberty, their mutual emulation, and that hatred which generally prevails among nations that live in close neighbourhood. Now, war in a small state is much more destructive than in a great one; both because all the inhabitants, in the former case, must serve in the armies, and because the whole state is frontier, and is all exposed to the inroads of the enemy.

The maxims of ancient war were much more destructive than those of modern, chiefly by that distribution of plunder, in which the soldiers were indulged. The private men in our armies are such a low set of people, that we find any abundance, beyond their simple pay, breeds confusion and disorder among them, and a total dissolution of discipline. The very wretchedness and meanness of those who fill the modern armies, render them less destructive to the countries which they invade; one instance, among many, of the deceitfulness of first appearances in all political reasonings.[†]

Ancient battles were much more bloody, by the very nature of the weapons employed in them. The ancients drew up their men 16 or 20, sometimes 50 men deep, which made a narrow front; and it was not difficult to find a field, in which both armies might be marshalled, and might engage with each other. Even where any body of the troops was kept off by hedges, hillocks, woods, or hollow ways, the battle was not so soon decided between the contending parties, but that the others had time to overcome the difficulties which opposed them, and take part in the engagement. And as the whole army was thus engaged, and each man closely buckled to his antagonist, the battles were commonly very bloody, and great slaughter was made on both sides, especially on the vanquished. The long thin lines, required by fire-arms, and the quick decision of the fray, render our modern engagements but partial rencounters, and enable the general, who is foiled in the beginning of the day, to draw off the greater part of his army, sound and entire.

The battles of antiquity, both by their duration and their resemblance to single combats, were wrought up to a degree of fury quite unknown to later ages. Nothing could then engage the combatants to give quarter, but the hopes of profit, by making slaves of their prisoners. In civil wars, as we learn from TACITUS,* the battles were the most bloody, because the prisoners were not slaves.

What a stout resistance must be made, where the vanquished expected so hard a fate! How inveterate the rage, where the maxims of war were, in every respect, so bloody and severe!

Instances are frequent, in ancient history, of cities besieged, whose inhabitants, rather than open their gates, murdered their wives and children, and rushed themselves on a voluntary death, sweetened perhaps by a little prospect of revenge upon the enemy. GREEKS,† as well as BARBARIANS, have often been wrought up to this degree of fury. And the same determined spirit and cruelty must, in other instances less remarkable, have been destructive to human society, in those petty commonwealths which lived in close neighbourhood, and were engaged in perpetual wars and contentions.

Sometimes the wars in GREECE, says PLUTARCH,† were carried on entirely by inroads, and robberies, and piracies.

Such a method of war must be more destructive in small states, than the bloodiest battles and sieges.

By the laws of the twelve tables, possession during two years formed a prescription for land; one year for movables; an indication, that there was not in ITALY, at that time, much more order, tranquillity, and settled police, than there is at present among the TARTARS.

The only cartel I remember in ancient history, is that between DEMETRIUS POLIORCETES and the RHODIANS; when it was agreed, that a free citizen should be restored for 1,000 *drachmas*, a slave bearing arms for 500.[†]

But, *secondly*, It appears that ancient manners were more unfavourable than the modern, not only in times of war, but also in those of peace; and that too in every respect, except the love of civil liberty and of equality, which is, I own, of considerable importance. To exclude faction from a free government, is very difficult, if not altogether impracticable; but such inveterate rage between the factions, and such bloody maxims are found, in modern times, amongst religious parties alone. In ancient history we may always observe, where one party prevailed, whether the nobles or people (for I can observe no difference in this respect),[†] that they immediately butchered all of the opposite party who fell into their hands, and banished such as had been so fortunate as to escape their fury. No form of process, no law, no trial, no pardon. A fourth, a third, perhaps near half of the city was slaughtered, or expelled, every revolution; and the exiles always joined foreign enemies, and did all the mischief possible to their fellow-citizens, till fortune put it in their power to take full revenge by a new revolution. And as these were frequent in such violent governments, the disorder, diffidence, jealousy, enmity, which must prevail, are not easy for us to imagine in this age of the world.

There are only two revolutions I can recollect in ancient history, which passed without great severity, and great effusion of blood in massacres and assassinations, namely, the restoration of the ATHENIAN democracy by THRASYBULUS, and the subduing of the ROMAN republic by CAESAR. We learn from ancient history, that THRASYBULUS passed a general amnesty for all past offences; and first introduced that word, as well as practice, into GREECE.[†] It appears, however, from many orations of LYSIAS,[†] that the chief, and even some of the subaltern offenders, in the preceding tyranny, were tried and capitally punished. And as to CAESAR's clemency, though much celebrated, it would not gain great applause in the present age. He butchered, for instance, all CATO's senate, when he became master of UTICA;[†] and these, we may readily believe, were not the most worthless of the party. All those who had borne arms against that usurper were attainted, and by HIRTIUS's law declared incapable of all public offices.

These people were extremely fond of liberty, but seem not to have understood it very well. When the thirty tyrants first established their dominion at ATHENS, they began with seizing all the sycophants and informers, who had been so troublesome during the democracy, and putting them to death by an arbitrary sentence and execution. *Every man*, says SALLUST[†] and LYSIAS,[†] *rejoiced at these punishments*; not considering that liberty was from that moment annihilated.

The utmost energy of the nervous style of THUCYDIDES, and the copiousness and expression of the GREEK language, seem to sink under that historian, when he attempts to describe the disorders which arose from faction throughout all the GRECIAN commonwealths. You would imagine that he still labours with a thought greater than he can find words to communicate. And he concludes his pathetic description with an observation, which is at once refined and solid: 'In these contests,' says he, 'those who were the dullest and most stupid, and had the least foresight, commonly prevailed. For being conscious of this weakness, and dreading to be overreached by those of greater penetration, they went to work hastily, without premeditation, by the sword and poniard, and thereby got the start of their antagonists, who were forming fine schemes and projects for their destruction.'[†]

Not to mention DIONYSIUS[†] the elder, who is computed to have butchered in cold blood above 10,000 of his fellow-citizens; or AGATHOCLES,[†] NABIS,[†] and others, still more bloody than he; the transactions, even in free governments, were extremely violent and destructive. At ATHENS, the thirty tyrants and the nobles, in a twelvemonth, murdered without trial, about 1,200 of the people, and banished above the half of the citizens that remained.[†] In ARGOS, near the same time, the people killed 1,200 of the nobles; and afterwards their own demagogues, because they had refused to carry their prosecutions farther.[†] The people also in CORCYRA killed 1,500 of the nobles, and banished a thousand.[†] These numbers will appear the more surprising, if we consider the extreme smallness of these states; but all ancient history is full of such instances.[†]

When ALEXANDER ordered all the exiles to be restored throughout all the cities, it was found, that the whole amounted to 20,000 men;[†] the remains probably of still greater slaughters and massacres. What an astonishing multitude in so narrow a country as ancient GREECE! And what domestic confusion, jealousy, partiality, revenge, heart-burnings, must have torn those cities, where factions were wrought up to such a degree of fury and despair!

It would be easier, says ISOCRATES to PHILIP, to raise an army in GREECE at present from the vagabonds than from the cities.[*]

Even when affairs came not to such extremities (which they failed not to do almost in every city twice or thrice every century), property was rendered very precarious by the maxims of ancient government. XENOPHON, in the Banquet of SOCRATES, gives us a natural unaffected description of the tyranny of the ATHENIAN people. 'In my poverty,' says CHARMIDES, 'I am much more happy than I ever was while possessed of riches: as much as it is happier to be in security than in terrors, free than a slave, to receive than to pay court, to be trusted than suspected. Formerly I was obliged to caress every informer; some imposition was continually laid upon me; and it was never allowed me to travel, or be absent from the city. At present, when I am poor, I look big, and threaten others. The rich are afraid of me, and show me every kind of civility and respect; and I am become a kind of tyrant in the city.'[†]

In one of the pleadings of Lysias,[†] the orator very coolly speaks of it, by the by, as a maxim of the ATHENIAN people, that whenever they wanted money, they put to death some of the rich citizens as well as strangers, for the sake of the forfeiture. In mentioning this, he seems not to have any intention of blaming them, still less of provoking them, who were his audience and judges.

Whether a man was a citizen or a stranger among that people, it seemed indeed requisite, either that he should impoverish himself, or that the people would impoverish him, and perhaps kill him into the bargain. The orator last mentioned gives a pleasant account of an estate laid out in the public service;[†] that is, above the third of it in raree-shows and figured dances.

I need not insist on the GREEK tyrannies, which were altogether horrible. Even the mixed monarchies, by which most of the ancient states of GREECE were governed, before the introduction of republics, were very unsettled. Scarcely any city, but ATHENS, says ISOCRATES, could show a succession of kings for four or five generations.[†]

Besides many other obvious reasons for the instability of ancient monarchies, the equal division of property among the brothers of private families, must, by a necessary consequence, contribute to unsettle and disturb the state. The universal preference given to the elder by modern laws, though it increases the inequality of fortunes, has, however, this good effect, that it accustoms men to the same idea in public succession, and cuts off all claim and pretension of the younger.

The new settled colony of HERACLEA, falling immediately into faction, applied to SPARTA, who sent HERIPIDAS with full authority to quiet their dissensions. This man, not provoked by any opposition, not inflamed by party rage, knew no better expedient than immediately putting to death about 500 of the citizens;[*] a strong proof how deeply rooted these violent maxims of government were throughout all GREECE.

If such was the disposition of men's minds among that refined people, what may be expected in the commonwealths of ITALY, AFRICA, SPAIN, and GAUL, which were denominated barbarous? Why otherwise did the GREEKS so much value themselves on their humanity, gentleness, and moderation, above all other nations? This reasoning seems very natural. But unluckily the history of the ROMAN commonwealth, in its earlier times, if we give credit to the received accounts, presents an opposite conclusion. No blood was ever shed in any sedition at ROME till the murder of the GRACCHI. DIONYSIUS HALICARNASSAEUS,* observing the singular humanity of the ROMAN people in this particular, makes use of it as an argument that they were originally of GRECIAN extraction: whence we may conclude, that the factions and revolutions in the barbarous republics were usually more violent than even those of GREECE above mentioned.

If the ROMANS were so late in coming to blows, they made ample compensation after they had once entered upon the bloody scene; and APPIAN'S history of their civil wars contains the most frightful picture of massacres, proscriptions, and forfeitures, that ever was presented to the world. What pleases most, in that historian, is, that he seems to feel a proper resentment of these barbarous proceedings; and talks not with that provoking coolness and indifference which custom had produced in many of the GREEK historians.†

The maxims of ancient politics contain, in general, so little humanity and moderation, that it seems superfluous to give any particular reason for the acts of violence committed at any particular period. Yet I cannot forbear observing, that the laws, in the later period of the ROMAN commonwealth, were so absurdly contrived, that they obliged the heads of parties to have recourse to these extremities. All capital punishments were abolished: however criminal, or, what is more, however dangerous any citizen might be, he could not regularly be punished otherwise than by banishment: and it became necessary, in the revolutions of party, to draw the sword of private vengeance; nor was it easy, when laws were once violated, to set bounds to these sanguinary proceedings. Had BRUTUS himself prevailed over the *triumvirate*; could he, in common prudence, have allowed OCTAVIUS and ANTONY to live, and have contented himself with banishing them to RHODES or MARSEILLES, where they might still have plotted new commotions and rebellions? His executing C. ANTONIUS, brother to the *triumvir*, shows evidently his sense of the matter. Did not CICERO, with the approbation of all the wise and virtuous of ROME, arbitrarily put to death CATILINE'S accomplices, contrary to law, and without any trial or form of process? and if he moderated his executions, did it not proceed, either from the clemency of his temper, or the conjunctures of the times? A wretched security in a government which pretends to laws and liberty!

Thus one extreme produces another. In the same manner as excessive severity in the laws is apt to beget great relaxation in their execution; so their excessive lenity naturally produces cruelty and barbarity. It is dangerous to force us, in any case, to pass their sacred boundaries.

One general cause of the disorders, so frequent in all ancient governments, seems to have consisted in the great difficulty of establishing any aristocracy in those ages, and the perpetual discontents and seditions of the people, whenever even the meanest and most beggarly were excluded from the legislature and from public offices. The very quality of *freemen* gave such a rank, being opposed to that of slave, that it seemed to entitle the possessor to every power and privilege of the commonwealth. SOLON's[†] laws excluded no freemen from votes or elections, but confined some magistracies to a particular *census*; yet were the people never satisfied till those laws were repealed. By the treaty with ANTIPATER,[†] no ATHENIAN was allowed a vote whose *census* was less than 2,000 *drachmas* (about 60*l.* sterling). And though such a government would to us appear sufficiently democratical, it was so disagreeable to that people, that above two thirds of them immediately left their country. CASSANDER reduced that *census* to the half; yet still the government was considered as an oligarchical tyranny, and the effect of foreign violence.

SERVIUS TULLIUS's[†] laws seem equal and reasonable, by fixing the power in proportion to the property; yet the ROMAN people could never be brought quietly to submit to them.

In those days there was no medium between a severe, jealous aristocracy, ruling over discontented subjects, and a turbulent, factious, tyrannical democracy. At present, there is not one republic in EUROPE, from one extremity of it to the other, that is not remarkable for justice, lenity, and stability, equal to, or even beyond MARSEILLES, RHODES, or the most celebrated in antiquity. Almost all of them are well tempered aristocracies.

But *thirdly*, There are many other circumstances in which ancient nations seem inferior to the modern, both for the happiness and increase of mankind. Trade, manufactures, industry, were nowhere, in former ages, so flourishing as they are at present in EUROPE. The only garb of the ancients, both for males and females, seems to have been a kind of flannel, which they wore, commonly white or grey, and which they scoured as often as it became dirty. TYRE, which carried on, after CARTHAGE, the greatest commerce of any city in the MEDITERRANEAN, before it was destroyed by ALEXANDER, was no mighty city, if we credit ARRIAN'S account of its inhabitants.[†] ATHENS is commonly supposed to have been a trading city; but it was as populous before the MEDIAN war as at any time after it, according to HERODOTUS;[†] yet its commerce at that time was so inconsiderable, that, as the same historian observes,[†] even the neighbouring coasts of ASIA were as little frequented by the GREEKS as the pillars of HERCULES, for beyond these he conceived nothing.

Great interest of money, and great profits of trade, are an infallible indication, that industry and commerce are but in their infancy. We read in LYSIAS[†] of 100 *per cent* profit made on a cargo of two talents, sent to no greater distance than from ATHENS to the ADRIATIC; nor is this mentioned as an instance of extraordinary profit. ANTIDORUS, says DEMOSTHENES,[†] paid three talents and a half for a house, which he let at a talent a year; and the orator blames his own tutors for not employing his money to like advantage. My fortune, says he, in eleven years' minority, ought to have been tripled. The value of 20 of the slaves left by his father, he computes at 40 minas, and the yearly profit of their labour at 12.[†] The most moderate interest at ATHENS (for there was higher often paid), was 12 *per cent*,[†] and that paid monthly. Not to insist upon the high interest to which the vast sums distributed in elections had raised money[†] at ROME, we find, that VERRES, before that factious period, stated 24 *per cent* for money which he left in the hands of the publicans; and though CICERO exclaims against this article, it is not on account of the extravagant usury, but because it had never been customary to state any interest on such occasions.[†] Interest, indeed, sunk at ROME, after the settlement of the empire; but it never remained any considerable time so low as in the commercial states of modern times.[†]

Among the other inconveniences which the ATHENIANS felt from the fortifying of DECELIA by the LACEDEMONIANS, it is represented by THUCYDIDES,[†] as one of the most considerable, that they could not bring over their corn from EUBOEA by land, passing by OROPUS, but were obliged to embark it, and to sail round the promontory of SUNIUM; a surprising instance of the imperfection of ancient navigation, for the water-carriage is not here above double the land.

I do not remember a passage in any ancient author, where the growth of a city is ascribed to the establishment of a manufacture. The commerce, which is said to flourish, is chiefly the exchange of those commodities, for which different soils and climates were suited. The sale of wine and oil into AFRICA, according to DIODORUS SICULUS,[†] was the foundation of the riches of AGRIGENTUM. The situation of the city of SYBARIS, according to the same author,[†] was the cause of its immense populousness, being built near the two rivers CRATHIS and SYBARIS. But these two rivers, we may observe, are not navigable, and could only produce some fertile valleys for agriculture and tillage; an advantage so inconsiderable, that a modern writer would scarcely have taken notice of it.

The barbarity of the ancient tyrants, together with the extreme love of liberty which animated those ages, must have banished every merchant and manufacturer, and have quite depopulated the state, had it subsisted upon industry and commerce. While the cruel and suspicious DIONYSIUS was carrying on his butcheries, who, that was not detained by his landed property, and could have carried with him any art or skill to procure a subsistence in other countries, would have remained exposed to such implacable barbarity? The persecutions of PHILIP II and LOUIS XIV filled all EUROPE with the manufactures of FLANDERS and of FRANCE.*

I grant, that agriculture is the species of industry chiefly requisite to the subsistence of multitudes; and it is possible that this industry may flourish, even where manufactures and other arts are unknown and neglected. SWISSERLAND is at present a remarkable instance, where we find, at once, the most skilful husbandmen, and the most bungling tradesmen, that are to be met with in EUROPE. That agriculture flourished in GREECE and ITALY, at least in some parts of them, and at some periods, we have reason to presume; and whether the mechanical arts had reached the same degree of perfection, may not be esteemed so material, especially if we consider the great equality of riches in the ancient republics, where each family was obliged to cultivate, with the greatest care and industry, its own little field, in order to its subsistence.

But is it just reasoning, because agriculture may, in some instances, flourish without trade or manufactures, to conclude, that, in any great extent of country, and for any great tract of time, it would subsist alone? The most natural way, surely, of encouraging husbandry, is, first, to excite other kinds of industry, and thereby afford the labourer a ready market for his commodities, and a return for such goods as may contribute to his pleasure and enjoyment. This method is infallible and universal; and, as it prevails more in modern governments than in the ancient, it affords a presumption of the superior populousness of the former.

Every man, says XENOPHON,[†] may be a farmer: no art or skill is requisite: all consists in industry, and in attention to the execution; a strong proof, as COLUMELLA hints, that agriculture was but little known in the age of XENOPHON.

All our later improvements and refinements, have they done nothing towards the easy subsistence of men, and consequently towards their propagation and increase? Our superior skill in mechanics; the discovery of new worlds, by which commerce has been so much enlarged; the establishment of posts; and the use of bills of exchange: these seem all extremely useful to the encouragement of art, industry, and populousness. Were we to strike off these, what a check should we give to every kind of business and labour, and what multitudes of families would immediately perish from want and hunger? And it seems not probable, that we could supply the place of these new inventions by any other regulation or institution.

Have we reason to think, that the police of ancient states was anywise comparable to that of modern, or that men had then equal security, either at home, or in their journeys by land or water? I question not, but every impartial examiner would give us the preference in this particular.[†]

Thus, upon comparing the whole, it seems impossible to assign any just reason, why the world should have been more populous in ancient than in modern times. The equality of property among the ancients, liberty, and the small divisions of their states, were indeed circumstances favourable to the propagation of mankind: but their wars were more bloody and destructive, their governments more factious and unsettled, commerce and manufactures more feeble and languishing, and the general police more loose and irregular. These latter disadvantages seem to form a sufficient counterbalance to the former advantages; and rather favour the opposite opinion to that which commonly prevails with regard to this subject.

But there is no reasoning, it may be said, against matter of fact. If it appear that the world was then more populous than at present, we may be assured that our conjectures are false, and that we have overlooked some material circumstance in the comparison. This I readily own: all our preceding reasonings I acknowledge to be mere trifling, or, at least, small skirmishes and frivolous rencounters, which decide nothing. But unluckily the main combat, where we compare facts, cannot be rendered much more decisive. The facts delivered by ancient authors are either so uncertain or so imperfect as to afford us nothing positive in this matter. How indeed could it be otherwise? The very facts which we must oppose to them, in computing the populousness of modern states, are far from being either certain or complete. Many grounds of calculation proceeded on by celebrated writers are little better than those of the Emperor HELIOGABALUS, who formed an estimate of the immense greatness of ROME from ten thousand pounds weight of cobwebs which had been found in that city.[†]

It is to be remarked, that all kinds of numbers are uncertain in ancient manuscripts, and have been subject to much greater corruptions than any other part of the text, and that for an obvious reason. Any alteration in other places commonly affects the sense of grammar, and is more readily perceived by the reader and transcriber.

Few enumerations of inhabitants have been made of any tract of country by any ancient author of good authority, so as to afford us a large enough view for comparison.

It is probable that there was formerly a good foundation for the number of citizens assigned to any free city, because they entered for a share in the government, and there were exact registers kept of them. But as the number of slaves is seldom mentioned, this leaves us in as great uncertainty as ever with regard to the populousness even of single cities.

The first page of THUCYDIDES is, in my opinion, the commencement of real history. All preceding narrations are so intermixed with fable, that philosophers ought to abandon them, in a great measure, to the embellishment of poets and orators.[†]

With regard to remoter times, the numbers of people assigned are often ridiculous, and lose all credit and authority. The free citizens of SYBARIS, able to bear arms, and actually drawn out in battle, were 300,000. They encountered at SAGRA with 100,000 citizens of CROTONA, another GREEK city contiguous to them, and were defeated.—This is DIODORUS SICULUS'S[†] account, and is very seriously insisted on by that historian. STRABO[*] also mentions the same number of SYBARITES.

DIODORUS SICULUS,[†] enumerating the inhabitants of

AGRIGENTUM, when it was destroyed by the CARTHAGINIANS, says that they amounted to 20,000 citizens, 200,000 strangers, besides slaves, who in so opulent a city as he represents it, would probably be at least as numerous. We must remark, that the women and the children are not included; and that, therefore, upon the whole, this city must have contained near two millions of inhabitants.[†] And what was the reason of so immense an increase? They were industrious in cultivating the neighbouring fields, not exceeding a small ENGLISH county; and they traded with their wine and oil to AFRICA, which at that time produced none of these commodities.

PTOLEMY, says THEOCRITUS,[†] commands 33,333 cities. I suppose the singularity of the number was the reason of assigning it. DIODORUS SICULUS[†] assigns three millions of inhabitants to EGYPT, a small number: but then he makes the number of cities amount to 18,000; an evident contradiction.

He says, the people were formerly seven millions. Thus remote times are always most envied and admired.

That XERXES's army was extremely numerous, I can readily believe; both from the great extent of his empire, and from the practice among the eastern nations of encumbering their camp with a superfluous multitude: but will any rational man cite HERODOTUS's wonderful narrations as any authority? There is something very rational, I own, in LYSIAS's[†] argument upon this subject. Had not XERXES's army been incredibly numerous, says he, he had never made a bridge over the HELLESPONT: it had been much easier to have transported his men over so short a passage with the numerous shipping of which he was master.

POLYBIUS[†] says that the ROMANS, between the first and second PUNIC wars, being threatened with an invasion from the GAULS, mustered all their own forces, and those of their allies, and found them amount to seven hundred thousand men able to bear arms; a great number surely, and which, when joined to the slaves, is probably not less, if not rather more, than that extent of country affords at present.[†] The enumeration too seems to have been made with some exactness; and POLYBIUS gives us the detail of the particulars. But might not the number be magnified, in order to encourage the people?

DIODORUS SICULUS[†] makes the same enumeration amount to near a million. These variations are suspicious. He plainly too supposes, that ITALY, in his time, was not so populous; another suspicious circumstance. For who can believe that the inhabitants of that country diminished from the time of the first PUNIC war to that of the *triumvirate?*

JULIUS CAESAR, according to APPIAN,[†] encountered four millions of GAULS, killed one million, and made another million prisoners.[†] Supposing the number of the enemy's army and that of the slain could be exactly assigned, which never is possible, how could it be known how often the same man returned into the armies, or how distinguish the new from the old levied soldiers? No attention ought ever to be given to such loose, exaggerated calculations, especially where the author does not tell us the mediums upon which the calculations were founded.

PATERCULUS[†] makes the number of GAULS killed by CAESAR amount only to 400,000; a more probable account, and more easily reconciled to the history of these wars given by that conqueror himself in his Commentaries.[†] The most bloody of his battles were fought against the HELVETII and the GERMANS.

One would imagine that every circumstance of the life and actions of DIONYSIUS the elder might be regarded as authentic, and free from all fabulous exaggeration, both because he lived at a time when letters flourished most in GREECE, and because his chief historian was PHILISTUS, a man allowed to be of great genius, and who was a courtier and minister of that prince. But can we admit that he had a standing army of 100,000 foot, 10,000 horse, and a fleet of 400 galleys?[†] These, we may observe, were mercenary forces, and subsisted upon pay, like our armies in EUROPE, for the citizens were all disarmed; and when DION afterwards invaded SICILY, and called on his countrymen to vindicate their liberty, he was obliged to bring arms along with him, which he distributed among those who joined him.[†] In a state where agriculture alone flourishes, there may be many inhabitants; and if these be all armed and disciplined, a great force may be called out upon occasion: but great bodies of mercenary troops can never be maintained without either great trade and numerous manufactures, or extensive dominions. The United Provinces never were masters of such a force by sea and land as that which is said to belong to DIONYSIUS; yet they possess as large a territory, perfectly well cultivated, and have much more resources from their commerce and industry. DIODORUS SICULUS allows, that, even in his time, the army of DIONYSIUS appeared incredible; that is, as I interpret it, was entirely a fiction; and the opinion arose from the exaggerated flattery of the courtiers, and perhaps from the vanity and policy of the tyrant himself.

It is a usual fallacy to consider all the ages of antiquity as one period, and to compute the numbers contained in the great cities mentioned by ancient authors as if these cities had been all contemporary. The GREEK colonies flourished extremely in SICILY during the age of ALEXANDER; but in AUGUSTUS's time they were so decayed, that almost all the produce of that fertile island was consumed in ITALY.[†]

Let us now examine the numbers of the inhabitants assigned to particular cities in antiquity; and, omitting the numbers of NINEVEH, BABYLON, and the EGYPTIAN THEBES, let us confine ourselves to the sphere of real history, to the GRECIAN and ROMAN states. I must own, the more I consider this subject, the more am I inclined to scepticism with regard to the great populousness ascribed to ancient times.

ATHENS is said by PLATO[†] to be a very great city; and it was surely the greatest of all the GREEK[†] cities except SYRACUSE, which was nearly about the same size in THUCYDIDES's time,[†] and afterwards increased beyond it. For CICERO[†] mentions it as the greatest of all the GREEK cities in his time, not comprehending, I suppose, either ANTIOCH or ALEXANDRIA under that denomination. ATHENAEUS[†] says, that, by the enumeration of DEMETRIUS PHALEREUS, there were in ATHENS 21,000 citizens, 10,000 strangers, and 400,000 slaves. This number is much insisted on by those

whose opinion I call in question, and is esteemed a fundamental fact to their purpose: but, in my opinion, there is no
point of criticism more certain than that ATHENAEUS and
CTESICLES, whom he quotes, are here mistaken, and that the
number of slaves is at least augmented by a whole cipher,
and ought not to be regarded as more than 40,000.

First, When the number of citizens are said to be 21,000
by ATHENAEUS,[†] men of full age are only understood. For,
1. HERODOTUS says,[†] that ARISTAGORAS, ambassador from
the IONIANS, found it harder to deceive one SPARTAN than
30,000 ATHENIANS; meaning, in a loose way, the whole
state, supposed to be met in one popular assembly, excluding
the women and children. 2. THUCYDIDES[†] says, that, making
allowance for all the absentees in the fleet, army, garrisons,
and for people employed in their private affairs, the
ATHENIAN assembly never rose to five thousand. 3. The
forces enumerated by the same historian[†] being all citizens,
and amounting to 13,000 heavy-armed infantry, prove the
same method of calculation; as also the whole tenor of the
GREEK historians, who always understand men of full age
when they assign the number of citizens in any republic.
Now, these being but the fourth of the inhabitants, the free
ATHENIANS were by this account 84,000; the strangers
40,000; and the slaves, calculating by the smaller number,
and allowing that they married and propagated at the
same rate with freemen, were 160,000; and the whole of
the inhabitants 284,000; a number surely large enough.
The other number, 1,720,000, makes ATHENS larger than
LONDON and PARIS united.

Secondly, There were but 10,000 houses in ATHENS.[†]

Thirdly, Though the extent of the walls, as given us by
THUCYDIDES,[†] be great (to wit, eighteen miles, beside the
sea-coast), yet XENOPHON[†] says there was much waste ground
within the walls. They seem indeed to have joined four
distinct and separate cities.[†]

Fourthly, No insurrection of the slaves, or suspicion of
insurrection, is ever mentioned by historians, except one
commotion of the miners.[†]

Fifthly, The treatment of slaves by the ATHENIANS is said

by XENOPHON,[†] and DEMOSTHENES,[†] and PLAUTUS,[†] to have been extremely gentle and indulgent; which could never have been the case, had the disproportion been twenty to one. The disproportion is not so great in any of our colonies; yet we are obliged to exercise a rigorous and military government over the negroes.

Sixthly, No man is ever esteemed rich for possessing what may be reckoned an equal distribution of property in any country, or even triple or quadruple that wealth. Thus, every person in ENGLAND is computed by some to spend sixpence a day; yet he is esteemed but poor who has five times that sum. Now, TIMARCHUS is said by AESCHINES[†] to have been left in easy circumstances; but he was master of only ten slaves employed in manufactures. LYSIAS and his brother, two strangers, were proscribed by the thirty for their great riches, though they had but sixty apiece. DEMOSTHENES[†] was left very rich by his father, yet he had no more than fifty-two slaves.[†] His workhouse of twenty cabinet-makers is said to be a very considerable manufactory.

Seventhly, During the DECELIAN war, as the GREEK historians call it, 20,000 slaves deserted, and brought the ATHENIANS to great distress, as we learn from THUCYDIDES.[†] This could not have happened had they been only the twentieth part. The best slaves would not desert.

Eighthly, XENOPHON[†] proposes a scheme for maintaining by the public 10,000 slaves: and that so great a number may possibly be supported, any one will be convinced, says he, who considers the numbers we possessed before the DECELIAN war; a way of speaking altogether incompatible with the larger number of ATHENAEUS.

Ninthly, The whole *census* of the state of ATHENS was less than 6,000 talents. And though numbers in ancient manuscripts be often suspected by critics, yet this is unexceptionable; both because DEMOSTHENES,[†] who gives it, gives also the detail, which checks him; and because POLYBIUS[†] assigns the same number, and reasons upon it. Now, the most vulgar slave could yield by his labour an *obolus* a day, over and above his maintenance, as we learn from XENOPHON,[†] who says, that NICIAS's overseer paid his master so much for slaves, whom he employed in mines. If you will take the pains to estimate an *obolus* a day, and the slaves at 400,000, computing only at four years' purchase, you will find the sum above 12,000 talents; even though allowance be made for the great number of holidays in ATHENS. Besides, many of the slaves would have a much greater value from their art. The lowest that DEMOSTHENES[†] estimates any of his father's slaves is two minas a head. And upon this supposition, it is a little difficult, I confess, to reconcile even the number of 40,000 slaves with the *census* of 6,000 talents.

Tenthly, CHIOS is said by THUCYDIDES,[†] to contain more slaves than any GREEK city, except SPARTA. SPARTA then had more than ATHENS, in proportion to the number of citizens. The SPARTANS were 9,000 in the town, 30,000 in the country.[†] The male slaves, therefore, of full age, must have been more than 780,000; the whole more than 3,120,000; a number impossible to be maintained in a narrow barren country, such as LACONIA, which had no trade. Had the HELOTES been so very numerous, the murder of 2,000, mentioned by THUCYDIDES,[†] would have irritated them, without weakening them.

Besides, we are to consider, that the number assigned by ATHENAEUS,[†] whatever it is, comprehends all the inhabitants of ATTICA, as well as those of Athens. The ATHENIANS affected much a country life, as we learn from THUCYDIDES,[†] and when they were all chased into town, by the invasion of their territory during the PELOPONNESIAN war, the city was not able to contain them; and they were obliged to lie in the porticos, temples, and even streets, for want of lodging.[†]

The same remark is to be extended to all the other GREEK cities; and when the number of citizens is assigned, we must always understand it to comprehend the inhabitants of the neighbouring country, as well as of the city. Yet even with this allowance, it must be confessed that GREECE was a populous country, and exceeded what we could imagine concerning so narrow a territory, naturally not very fertile, and which drew no supplies of corn from other places. For, excepting ATHENS, which traded to PONTUS for that commodity, the other cities seem to have subsisted chiefly from their neighbouring territory.[†]

RHODES is well known to have been a city of extensive commerce, and of great fame and splendour; yet it contained only 6,000 citizens able to bear arms when it was besieged by DEMETRIUS.[†]

THEBES was always one of the capital cities of GREECE;[†] but the number of its citizens exceeded not those of RHODES.[†] PHLIASIA is said to be a small city by XENOPHON,[†] yet we find that it contained 6,000 citizens.[†] I pretend not to reconcile these two facts. Perhaps XENOPHON calls PHLIASIA a small town, because it made but a small figure in GREECE, and maintained only a subordinate alliance with SPARTA; or perhaps the country belonging to it was extensive, and most of the citizens were employed in the cultivation of it, and dwelt in the neighbouring villages.

MANTINEA was equal to any city in ARCADIA.[†] Consequently it was equal to MEGALOPOLIS, which was fifty stadia, or six miles and a quarter in circumference.[†] But MANTINEA had only 3,000 citizens.[†] The GREEK cities, therefore, contained only fields and gardens, together with the houses; and we cannot judge of them by the extent of their walls. ATHENS contained no more than 10,000 houses; yet its walls, with the sea-coast, were above twenty miles in extent. SYRACUSE was twenty-two miles in circumference; yet was scarcely ever spoken of by the ancients as more populous than ATHENS. BABYLON was a square of fifteen miles, or sixty miles in circuit; but it contained large cultivated fields and inclosures, as we learn from PLINY. Though AURELIAN'S wall was fifty miles in circumference,[†] the circuit of all the thirteen divisions of ROME, taken apart, according to PUBLIUS VICTOR, was only about forty-three miles. When an enemy invaded the country, all the inhabitants retired within the walls of the ancient cities, with their cattle and furniture, and instruments of husbandry: and the great height to which the walls were raised, enabled a small number to defend them with facility.

SPARTA, says XENOPHON,[†] is one of the cities of GREECE that has the fewest inhabitants. Yet POLYBIUS[†] says that it was forty-eight stadia in circumference, and was round.

All the AETOLIANS able to bear arms in ANTIPATER'S time, deducting some few garrisons, were but 10,000 men.[†]

POLYBIUS[†] tells us, that the ACHAEAN league might, without any inconvenience, march 30 or 40,000 men: and this account seems probable; for that league comprehended the greater part of PELOPONNESUS. Yet PAUSANIAS,[†] speaking of the same period, says, that all the ACHAEANS able to bear arms, even when several manumitted slaves were joined to them, did not amount to 15,000.

The THESSALIANS, till their final conquest by the ROMANS, were, in all ages, turbulent, factious, seditious, disorderly.[†] It is not therefore natural to suppose that this part of GREECE abounded much in people.

We are told by THUCYDIDES,[†] that the part of PELOPONNESUS, adjoining to PYLOS, was desert and uncultivated. HERODOTUS says,[†] that MACEDONIA was full of lions and wild bulls; animals which can only inhabit vast unpeopled forests. These were the two extremities of GREECE.

All the inhabitants of EPIRUS, of all ages, sexes, and conditions, who were sold by PAULUS AEMILIUS, amounted only to 150,000.[†] Yet EPIRUS might be double the extent of YORKSHIRE.

JUSTIN[†] tells us, that when PHILIP of MACEDON was declared head of the GREEK confederacy, he called a congress of all the states, except the LACEDEMONIANS, who refused to concur; and he found the force of the whole, upon computation, to amount to 200,000 infantry and 15,000 cavalry. This must be understood to be all the citizens capable of bearing arms. For as the GREEK republics maintained no mercenary forces, and had no militia distinct from the whole body of the citizens, it is not conceivable what other medium there could be of computation. That such an army could ever, by GREECE, be brought into the field, and be maintained there, is contrary to all history. Upon this supposition, therefore, we may thus reason. The free GREEKS of all ages and sexes were 860,000. The slaves, estimating them by the number of

ATHENIAN slaves as above, who seldom married or had families, were double the male citizens of full age, to wit, 430,000. And all the inhabitants of ancient GREECE, excepting LACONIA, were about one million two hundred and ninety thousand; no mighty number, nor exceeding what may be found at present in SCOTLAND, a country of not much greater extent, and very indifferently peopled.

We may now consider the numbers of people in ROME and ITALY, and collect all the lights afforded us by scattered passages in ancient authors. We shall find, upon the whole, a great difficulty in fixing any opinion on that head; and no reason to support those exaggerated calculations, so much insisted on by modern writers.

DIONYSIUS HALICARNASSAEUS[†] says, that the ancient walls of ROME were nearly of the same compass with those of ATHENS, but that the suburbs ran out to a great extent; and it was difficult to tell where the town ended, or the country began. In some places of ROME, it appears, from the same author,[†] from JUVENAL,[†] and from other ancient writers,[†] that the houses were high, and families lived in separate stories, one above another: but is it probable that these were only the poorer citizens, and only in some few streets? If we may judge from the younger PLINY's[†] account of his own house, and from BARTOLI's plans of ancient buildings, the men of quality had very spacious palaces: and their buildings were like the CHINESE houses at this day, where each apartment is separated from the rest, and rises no higher than a single story. To which if we add, that the ROMAN nobility much affected extensive porticos, and even woods[†] in town, we may perhaps allow VOSSIUS (though there is no manner of reason for it), to read the famous passage of the elder PLINY[†] his own way, without admitting the extravagant consequences which he draws from it.

The number of citizens who received corn by the public distribution in the time of AUGUSTUS were two hundred thousand.[†] This one would esteem a pretty certain ground of calculation; yet it is attended with such circumstances as to throw us back into doubt and uncertainty.

Did the poorer citizens only receive the distribution? It

was calculated, to be sure, chiefly for their benefit. But it appears from a passage in CICERO[†] that the rich might also take their portion, and that it was esteemed no reproach in them to apply for it.

To whom was the corn given; whether only to heads of families, or to every man, woman, and child? The portion every month was five *modii* to each[†] (about five-sixths of a bushel). This was too little for a family, and too much for an individual. A very accurate antiquary,[†] therefore, infers, that it was given to every man of full age: but he allows the matter to be uncertain.

Was it strictly inquired, whether the claimant lived within the precincts of ROME? or was it sufficient that he presented himself at the monthly distribution? This last seems more probable.[†]

Were there no false claimants? We are told,[†] that CAESAR struck off at once 170,000, who had creeped in without a just title; and it is very little probable that he remedied all abuses.

But, lastly, what proportion of slaves must we assign to these citizens? This is the most material question, and the most uncertain. It is very doubtful whether ATHENS can be established as a rule for ROME. Perhaps the ATHENIANS had more slaves, because they employed them in manufactures, for which a capital city, like ROME, seems not so proper. Perhaps, on the other hand, the ROMANS had more slaves on account of their superior luxury and riches.

There were exact bills of mortality kept at ROME; but no ancient author has given us the number of burials, except SUETONIUS,[†] who tells us, that in one season there were 30,000 names carried to the temple of LIBITINA: but this was during a plague, which can afford no certain foundation for any inference.

The public corn, though distributed only to 200,000 citizens, affected very considerably the whole agriculture of ITALY;[†] a fact nowise reconcilable to some modern exaggerations with regard to the inhabitants of that country.

The best ground of conjecture I can find concerning the greatness of ancient ROME is this: we are told by

HERODIAN,[†] that ANTIOCH and ALEXANDRIA were very little inferior to ROME. It appears from DIODORUS SICULUS[†] that one straight street of ALEXANDRIA, reaching from gate to gate, was five miles long; and as ALEXANDRIA was much more extended in length than breadth, it seems to have been a city nearly of the bulk of PARIS;[†] and ROME might be about the size of LONDON.

There lived in ALEXANDRIA, in DIODORUS SICULUS's time,[†] 300,000 free people, comprehending, I suppose, women and children.[†] But what number of slaves? Had we any just ground to fix these at an equal number with the free inhabitants, it would favour the foregoing computation.

There is a passage in HERODIAN which is a little surprising. He says positively, that the palace of the Emperor was as large as all the rest of the city.[†] This was NERO's golden house, which is indeed represented by SUETONIUS[†] and PLINY as of an enormous extent;[†] but no power of imagination can make us conceive it to bear any proportion to such a city as LONDON.

We may observe, had the historian been relating NERO's extravagance, and had he made use of such an expression, it would have had much less weight; these rhetorical exaggerations being apt to creep into an author's style, even when the most chaste and correct. But it is mentioned by HERODIAN only by the by, in relating the quarrels between GETA and CARACALLA.

It appears from the same historian,[†] that there was then much land uncultivated, and put to no manner of use; and he ascribes it as a great praise to PERTINAX, that he allowed every one to take such land, either in ITALY or elsewhere, and cultivate it as he pleased, without paying any taxes. *Lands uncultivated, and put to no manner of use!* This is not heard of in any part of CHRISTENDOM, except in some remote parts of HUNGARY, as I have been informed: and it surely corresponds very ill with that idea of the extreme populousness of antiquity so much insisted on.

We learn from VOPISCUS,[†] that there was even in ETRURIA much fertile land uncultivated, which the emperor AURELIAN intended to convert into vineyards, in order to furnish the

ROMAN people with a gratuitous distribution of wine; a very proper expedient for depopulating still further that capital, and all the neighbouring territories.

It may not be amiss to take notice of the account which POLYBIUS[†] gives of the great herds of swine to be met with in TUSCANY and LOMBARDY, as well as in GREECE, and of the method of feeding them which was then practised. 'There are great herds of swine,' says he, 'throughout all ITALY, particularly in former times, through ETRURIA, and CISALPINE GAUL; and a herd frequently consists of a thousand or more swine. When one of these herds in feeding meets with another, they mix together; and the swine-herds have no other expedient for separating them than to go to different quarters, where they sound their horn; and these animals, being accustomed to that signal, run immediately each to the horn of his own keeper. Whereas in GREECE, if the herds of swine happen to mix in the forests, he who has the greater flock takes cunningly the opportunity of driving all away. And thieves are very apt to purloin the straggling hogs, which have wandered to a great distance from their keeper in search of food.'

May we not infer, from this account, that the north of ITALY, as well as GREECE, was then much less peopled, and worse cultivated than at present? How could these vast herds be fed in a country so full of inclosures, so improved by agriculture, so divided by farms, so planted with vines and corn intermingled together? I must confess, that POLYBIUS's relation has more the air of that economy which is to be met with in our AMERICAN colonies, than the management of an EUROPEAN country.

We meet with a reflection in ARISTOTLE's[†] Ethics, which seems unaccountable on any supposition, and, by proving too much in favour of our present reasoning, may be thought really to prove nothing. That philosopher, treating of friendship, and observing, that this relation ought neither to be contracted to a very few, nor extended over a great multitude, illustrates his opinion by the following argument: 'In like manner,' says he, 'as a city cannot subsist, if it either have so few inhabitants as ten, or so many as a hundred thousand; so is there mediocrity required in the number of friends; and you destroy the essence of friendship by running into either extreme.' What! impossible that a city can contain a hundred thousand inhabitants! Had ARISTOTLE never seen nor heard of a city so populous? This, I must own, passes my comprehension.

PLINY[†] tells us, that SELEUCIA, the seat of the GREEK empire in the East, was reported to contain 600,000 people. CARTHAGE is said by STRABO[†] to have contained 700,000. The inhabitants of PEKIN are not much more numerous. LONDON, PARIS, and CONSTANTINOPLE, may admit of nearly the same computation; at least, the two latter cities do not exceed it. ROME, ALEXANDRIA, ANTIOCH, we have already spoken of. From the experience of past and present ages, one might conjecture that there is a kind of impossibility that any city could ever rise much beyond this proportion. Whether the grandeur of a city be founded on commerce or on empire, there seem to be invincible obstacles which prevent its further progress. The seats of vast monarchies, by introducing extravagant luxury, irregular expense, idleness, dependence, and false ideas of rank and superiority, are improper for commerce. Extensive commerce checks itself, by raising the price of all labour and commodities. When a great court engages the attendance of a numerous nobility, possessed of overgrown fortunes, the middling gentry remain in their provincial towns, where they can make a figure on a moderate income. And if the dominions of a state arrive at an enormous size, there necessarily arise many capitals, in the remoter provinces, whither all the inhabitants, except a few courtiers, repair for education, fortune, and amusement.[†] LONDON, by uniting extensive commerce and middling empire, has perhaps arrived at a greatness which no city will ever be able to exceed.

Choose DOVER or CALAIS for a centre: draw a circle of two hundred miles radius: you comprehend LONDON, PARIS, the NETHERLANDS, the UNITED PROVINCES, and some of the best cultivated parts of FRANCE and ENGLAND. It may safely, I think, be affirmed, that no spot of ground can be found, in antiquity, of equal extent, which contained near so many great and populous cities, and was so stocked with riches and inhabitants. To balance, in both periods, the states which possessed most art, knowledge, civility, and the best police, seems the truest method of comparison.

It is an observation of L'ABBÉ DU BOS,[†] that ITALY is warmer at present than it was in ancient times. 'The annals of ROME tell us,' says he, 'that in the year 480 *ab* U. C. the winter was so severe that it destroyed the trees. The TYBER froze in ROME, and the ground was covered with snow for forty days. When JUVENAL describes a superstitious woman, he represents her as breaking the ice of the TYBER, that she might perform her ablutions:

> *Hibernum fracta glacie descendet in amnem,*
> *Ter matutino Tiberi mergetur.*[†]

He speaks of that river's freezing as a common event. Many passages of HORACE suppose the streets of Rome full of snow and ice. We should have more certainty with regard to this point, had the ancients known the use of thermometers; but their writers, without intending it, give us information sufficient to convince us, that the winters are now much more temperate at ROME than formerly. At present, the TYBER no more freezes at ROME than the NILE at CAIRO. The ROMANS esteem the winters very rigorous if the snow lie two days, and if one see for eight-and-forty hours a few icicles hang from a fountain that has a north exposure.'

The observation of this ingenious critic may be extended to other EUROPEAN climates. Who could discover the mild climate of FRANCE in DIODORUS SICULUS's[†] description of GAUL? 'As it is a northern climate,' says he, 'it is infested with cold to an extreme degree. In cloudy weather, instead of rain there fall great snows; and in clear weather, it there freezes so excessive hard, that the rivers acquire bridges of their own substance; over which, not only single travellers may pass, but large armies, accompanied with all their baggage and loaded wagons. And there being many rivers in GAUL, the RHONE, the RHINE, etc., almost all of them are frozen over; and it is usual, in order to prevent falling, to cover the ice with chaff and straw at the places where

the road passes.' *Colder than a* GALLIC *Winter*, is used by
PETRONIUS as a proverbial expression. ARISTOTLE says, that
GAUL is so cold a climate that an ass could not live in it.[†]

North of the CEVENNES, says STRABO,[†] GAUL produces not
figs and olives: and the vines, which have been planted, bear
not grapes that will ripen.

OVID[†] positively maintains, with all the serious affirmation
of prose, that the EUXINE sea was frozen over every winter
in his time; and he appeals to ROMAN governors, whom he
names, for the truth of his assertion. This seldom or never
happens at present in the latitude of TOMI, whither OVID
was banished. All the complaints of the same poet seem to
mark a rigour of the seasons, which is scarcely experienced
at present in PETERSBURGH or STOCKHOLM.

TOURNEFORT, a *Provençal*, who had travelled into the
same country, observes, that there is not a finer climate
in the world: and he asserts, that nothing but OVID's
melancholy could have given him such dismal ideas of it.
But the facts mentioned by that poet are too circumstantial
to bear any such interpretation.

POLYBIUS[†] says, that the climate in ARCADIA was very
cold, and the air moist.

'ITALY,' says VARRO,[†] 'is the most temperate climate in
EUROPE. The inland parts,' (GAUL, GERMANY, and PANNONIA,
no doubt,) 'have almost perpetual winter.'

The northern parts of SPAIN, according to STRABO,[*] are
but ill inhabited, because of the great cold.

Allowing, therefore, this remark to be just, that EUROPE
is become warmer than formerly; how can we account for
it? Plainly by no other method than by supposing, that the
land is at present much better cultivated, and that the woods
are cleared, which formerly threw a shade upon the earth,
and kept the rays of the sun from penetrating to it. Our
northern colonies in AMERICA become more temperate in
proportion as the woods are felled;[†] but, in general, every
one may remark, that cold is still much more severely felt,
both in North and South AMERICA, than in places under the
same latitude in EUROPE.

SASERNA, quoted by COLUMELLA,[†] affirmed, that the disposition of the heavens was altered before his time, and that the air had become much milder and warmer; as appears hence, says he, that many places now abound with vineyards and olive plantations, which formerly, by reason of the rigour of the climate, could raise none of these productions. Such a change, if real, will be allowed an evident sign of the better cultivation and peopling of countries before the age of SASERNA;[†] and if it be continued to the present times, is a proof that these advantages have been continually increasing throughout this part of the world.

Let us now cast our eye over all the countries which are the scene of ancient and modern history, and compare their past and present situation: we shall not, perhaps, find such foundation for the complaint of the present emptiness and desolation of the world. EGYPT is represented by MAILLET, to whom we owe the best account of it,[*] as extremely populous, though he esteems the number of its inhabitants to be diminished. SYRIA and the Lesser ASIA, as well as the coast of BARBARY, I can readily own to be desert in comparison of their ancient condition. The depopulation of GREECE is also obvious. But whether the country now called TURKEY in EUROPE may not, in general, contain more inhabitants than during the flourishing period of GREECE, may be a little doubtful. The THRACIANS seem then to have lived like the TARTARS at present, by pasturage and plunder.[†] The GETES were still more uncivilized,[†] and the ILLYRIANS were no better.[†] These occupy nine tenths of that country: and though the government of the TURKS be not very favourable to industry and propagation, yet it preserves at least peace and order among the inhabitants, and is preferable to that barbarous, unsettled condition in which they anciently lived.

POLAND and MUSCOVY in EUROPE are not populous, but are certainly much more so than the ancient SARMATIA and SCYTHIA, where no husbandry or tillage was ever heard of, and pasturage was the sole art by which the people were maintained. The like observation may be extended to DENMARK and SWEDEN. No one ought to esteem the immense swarms of people which formerly came from the

North, and overran all EUROPE, to be any objection to this opinion. Where a whole nation, or even half of it, remove their seat, it is easy to imagine what a prodigious multitude they must form, with what desperate valour they must make their attacks, and how the terror they strike into the invaded nations will make these magnify, in their imagination, both the courage and multitude of the invaders! SCOTLAND is neither extensive nor populous; but were the half of its inhabitants to seek new seats, they would form a colony as numerous as the TEUTONS and CIMBRI, and would shake all EUROPE, supposing it in no better condition for defence than formerly.

GERMANY has surely at present twenty times more inhabitants than in ancient times, when they cultivated no ground, and each tribe valued itself on the extensive desolation which it spread around, as we learn from CAESAR,[†] and TACITUS,[†] and STRABO;[†] a proof that the division into small republics will not alone render a nation populous, unless attended with the spirit of peace, order, and industry.

The barbarous condition of BRITAIN in former times is well known; and the thinness of its inhabitants may easily be conjectured, both from their barbarity, and from a circumstance mentioned by HERODIAN,[†] that all BRITAIN was marshy, even in SEVERUS's time, after the ROMANS had been fully settled in it above a century.

It is not easily imagined, that the GAULS were anciently much more advanced in the arts of life than their northern neighbours, since they travelled to this island for their education in the mysteries of the religion and philosophy of the DRUIDS.[†] I cannot, therefore, think that GAUL was then near so populous as FRANCE is at present.

Were we to believe, indeed, and join together, the testimony of APPIAN, and that of DIODORUS SICULUS, we must admit of an incredible populousness in GAUL. The former historian[†] says, that there were 400 nations in that country; the latter[†] affirms, that the largest of the GALLIC nations consisted of 200,000 men, besides women and children, and the least of 50,000. Calculating, therefore, at a medium, we must admit of near 200,000,000 of people in a country which we esteem populous at present, though supposed to contain little more than twenty.[†] Such calculations, therefore, by their extravagance, lose all manner of authority. We may observe, that the equality of property, to which the populousness of antiquity may be ascribed, had no place among the GAULS.[†] Their intestine wars also, before CAESAR'S time, were almost perpetual. And STRABO[†] observes, that though all GAUL was cultivated, yet was it not cultivated with any skill or care; the genius of the inhabitants leading them less to arts than arms, till their slavery under ROME produced peace among themselves.

CAESAR[†] enumerates very particularly the great forces which were levied in BELGIUM to oppose his conquests; and makes them amount to 208,000. These were not the whole people able to bear arms; for the same historian tells us, that the BELLOVACI could have brought a hundred thousand men into the field, though they engaged only for sixty. Taking the whole, therefore, in this proportion of ten to six, the sum of fighting men in all the states of BELGIUM was about 350,000; all the inhabitants a million and a half. And BELGIUM being about a fourth of GAUL, that country might contain six millions, which is not near the third of its present inhabitants.[†] We are informed by CAESAR, that the GAULS had no fixed property in land; but that the chieftains, when any death happened in a family, made a new division of all the lands among the several members of the family. This is the custom of *Tanistry*, which so long prevailed in IRELAND, and which retained that country in a state of misery, barbarism, and desolation.

The ancient HELVETIA was 250 miles in length, and 180 in breadth, according to the same author;[†] yet contained only 360,000 inhabitants. The canton of BERNE alone has, at present, as many people.

After this computation of APPIAN and DIODORUS SICULUS, I know not whether I dare affirm that the modern DUTCH are more numerous than the ancient BATAVI.

SPAIN is perhaps decayed from what it was three centuries ago; but if we step backward two thousand years, and consider the restless, turbulent, unsettled condition of its inhabitants, we may probably be inclined to think that it is now much more populous. Many SPANIARDS killed themselves when deprived of their arms by the ROMANS.[†] It appears from PLUTARCH,[†] that robbery and plunder were esteemed honourable among the SPANIARDS. HIRTIUS[†] represents, in the same light, the situation of that country in CAESAR'S time; and he says, that every man was obliged to live in castles and walled towns for his security. It was not till its final conquest under AUGUSTUS that these disorders were repressed.[†] The account which STRABO[†] and JUSTIN[†] give of SPAIN corresponds exactly with those above mentioned. How much, therefore, must it diminish from our idea of the populousness of antiquity, when we find that TULLY, comparing ITALY, AFRICA, GAUL, GREECE, and SPAIN, mentions the great number of inhabitants as the peculiar circumstance which rendered this latter country formidable?[†]

ITALY, however, it is probable, has decayed: but how many great cities does it still contain? VENICE, GENOA, PAVIA, TURIN, MILAN, NAPLES, FLORENCE, LEGHORN, which either subsisted not in ancient times, or were then very inconsiderable? If we reflect on this, we shall not be apt to carry matters to so great an extreme as is usual with regard to this subject.

When the ROMAN authors complain that ITALY, which formerly exported corn, became dependent on all the provinces for its daily bread, they never ascribe this alteration to the increase of its inhabitants, but to the neglect of tillage and agriculture;[†] a natural effect of that pernicious practice of importing corn, in order to distribute it *gratis* among the ROMAN citizens, and a very bad means of multiplying the inhabitants of any country.[†] The *sportula*, so much talked of by MARTIAL and JUVENAL, being presents regularly made by the great lords to their smaller clients, must have had a like tendency to produce idleness, debauchery, and a continual decay among the people. The parish rates have at present the same bad consequences in ENGLAND.

Were I to assign a period when I imagined this part of the world might possibly contain more inhabitants than at present, I should pitch upon the age of TRAJAN and the

ANTONINES; the great extent of the ROMAN empire being then civilized and cultivated, settled almost in a profound peace, both foreign and domestic, and living under the same regular police and government.[†] But we are told that all extensive governments, especially absolute monarchies, are pernicious to population, and contain a secret vice and poison, which destroy the effect of all these promising appearances.[†] To confirm this, there is a passage cited from PLUTARCH,[†] which, being somewhat singular, we shall here examine it.

That author, endeavouring to account for the silence of many of the oracles, says, that it may be ascribed to the present desolation of the world, proceeding from former wars and factions; which common calamity, he adds, has fallen heavier upon GREECE than on any other country, insomuch that the whole could scarcely at present furnish three thousand warriors; a number which, in the time of the MEDIAN war, was supplied by the single city of MEGARA. The gods, therefore, who affect works of dignity and importance, have suppressed many of their oracles, and deign not to use so many interpreters of their will to so diminutive a people.

I must confess, that this passage contains so many difficulties, that I know not what to make of it. You may observe, that PLUTARCH assigns, for a cause of the decay of mankind, not the extensive dominion of the ROMANS, but the former wars and factions of the several states, all which were quieted by the ROMAN arms. PLUTARCH's reasoning, therefore, is directly contrary to the inference which is drawn from the fact he advances.

POLYBIUS supposes that GREECE had become more prosperous and flourishing after the establishment of the ROMAN yoke;[†] and though that historian wrote before these conquerors had degenerated, from being the patrons to be the plunderers of mankind, yet as we find from TACITUS,[†] that the severity of the emperors afterwards corrected the license of the governors, we have no reason to think that extensive monarchy so destructive as it is often represented.

We learn from STRABO[†] that the ROMANS, from their

regard to the GREEKS, maintained, to his time, most of the privileges and liberties of that celebrated nation; and NERO afterwards rather increased them.[†] How, therefore, can we imagine that the ROMAN yoke was so burdensome over that part of the world? The oppression of the proconsuls was checked; and the magistracies in GREECE being all bestowed, in the several cities, by the free votes of the people, there was no necessity for the competitors to attend the emperor's court. If great numbers went to seek their fortunes in ROME, and advance themselves by learning or eloquence, the commodities of their native country, many of them would return with the fortunes which they had acquired, and thereby enrich the GRECIAN commonwealths.

But PLUTARCH says that the general depopulation had been more sensibly felt in GREECE than in any other country. How is this reconcilable to its superior privileges and advantages?

Besides, this passage, by proving too much, really proves nothing. *Only three thousand men able to bear arms in all* GREECE! Who can admit so strange a proposition, especially if we consider the great number of GREEK cities, whose names still remain in history, and which are mentioned by writers long after the age of PLUTARCH? There are there surely ten times more people at present, when there scarcely remains a city in all the bounds of ancient GREECE. That country is still tolerably cultivated, and furnishes a sure supply of corn, in case of any scarcity in SPAIN, ITALY, or the south of FRANCE.

We may observe, that the ancient frugality of the GREEKS, and their equality of property, still subsisted during the age of PLUTARCH, as appears from LUCIAN.[†] Nor is there any ground to imagine, that the country was possessed by a few masters, and a great number of slaves.

It is probable, indeed, that military discipline, being entirely useless, was extremely neglected in GREECE after the establishment of the ROMAN empire; and if these commonwealths, formerly so warlike and ambitious, maintained each of them a small city guard, to prevent mobbish disorders, it is all they had occasion for; and these, perhaps, did not amount to 3,000 men throughout all GREECE. I own, that if PLUTARCH had this fact in his eye, he is here guilty of a gross paralogism, and assigns causes nowise proportioned to the effects. But is it so great a prodigy that an author should fall into a mistake of this nature?[†]

But whatever force may remain in this passage of PLUTARCH, we shall endeavour to counterbalance it by as remarkable a passage in DIODORUS SICULUS, where the historian, after mentioning NINUS's army of 1,700,000 foot, and 200,000 horse, endeavours to support the credibility of this account by some posterior facts; and adds, that we must not form a notion of the ancient populousness of mankind from the present emptiness and depopulation which is spread over the world.[†] Thus an author, who lived at that very period of antiquity which is represented as most populous,[†] complains of the desolation which then prevailed, gives the preference to former times, and has recourse to ancient fables as a foundation for his opinion. The humour of blaming the present, and admiring the past, is strongly rooted in human nature, and has an influence even on persons endued with the profoundest judgment and most extensive learning.

OF THE ORIGINAL CONTRACT

AS no party, in the present age, can well support itself without a philosophical or speculative system of principles annexed to its political or practical one, we accordingly find, that each of the factions into which this nation is divided has reared up a fabric of the former kind, in order to protect and cover that scheme of actions which it pursues. The people being commonly very rude builders, especially in this speculative way, and more especially still when actuated by party zeal, it is natural to imagine that their workmanship must be a little unshapely, and discover evident marks of that violence and hurry in which it was raised. The one party, by tracing up government to the DEITY, endeavour to render it so sacred and inviolate, that it must be little less than sacrilege, however tyrannical it may become, to touch or invade it in the smallest article. The other party, by founding government altogether on the consent of the PEOPLE, suppose that there is a kind of *original contract*, by which the subjects have tacitly reserved the power of resisting their sovereign, whenever they find themselves aggrieved by that authority with which they have, for certain purposes, voluntarily intrusted him. These are the speculative principles of the two parties, and these, too, are the practical consequences deduced from them.

I shall venture to affirm, *That both these* systems *of speculative principles are just, though not in the sense intended by the parties:* and, *That both the* schemes *of practical consequences are prudent, though not in the extremes to which each party, in opposition to the other, has commonly endeavoured to carry them.*

That the DEITY is the ultimate author of all government, will never be denied by any, who admit a general providence, and allow, that all events in the universe are conducted by an uniform plan, and directed to wise purposes. As it is impossible for the human race to subsist, at least in any comfortable or secure state, without the protection of government, this institution must certainly have been intended by that beneficent Being, who means the good of all his creatures: and as it has universally, in fact, taken place in all countries, and all ages, we may conclude, with still greater certainty, that it was intended by that omniscient Being, who can never be deceived by any event or operation. But since he gave rise to it, not by any particular or miraculous interposition, but by his concealed and universal efficacy, a sovereign cannot, properly speaking, be called his vicegerent in any other sense than every power or force, being derived from him, may be said to act by his commission. Whatever actually happens is comprehended in the general plan or intention of providence; nor has the greatest and most lawful prince any more reason, upon that account, to plead a peculiar sacredness or inviolable authority, than an inferior magistrate, or even an usurper, or even a robber and a pirate. The same divine superintendent, who, for wise purposes, invested a TITUS or a TRAJAN with authority, did also, for purposes no doubt equally wise, though unknown, bestow power on a BORGIA* or an ANGRIA. The same causes, which gave rise to the sovereign power in every state, established likewise every petty jurisdiction in it, and every limited authority. A constable, therefore, no less than a king, acts by a divine commission, and possesses an indefeasible right.

When we consider how nearly equal all men are in their bodily force, and even in their mental powers and faculties, till cultivated by education, we must necessarily allow, that nothing but their own consent could at first associate them together, and subject them to any authority. The people, if we trace government to its first origin in the woods and deserts, are the source of all power and jurisdiction, and voluntarily, for the sake of peace and order, abandoned their native liberty, and received laws from their equal and companion. The conditions upon which they were willing to submit, were either expressed, or were so clear and obvious, that it might well be esteemed superfluous to express them. If this, then, be meant by the *original contract*, it cannot be denied, that all government is, at first, founded on a contract, and that the most ancient rude combinations of mankind were formed chiefly by that principle. In vain are we asked in what records this charter of our liberties is registered. It was not written on parchment, nor yet on leaves or barks of trees. It preceded the use of writing, and all the other civilized arts of life. But we trace it plainly in the nature of man, and in the equality, or something approaching equality, which we find in all the individuals of that species. The force, which now prevails, and which is founded on fleets and armies, is plainly political, and derived from authority, the effect of established government. A man's natural force consists only in the vigour of his limbs, and the firmness of his courage; which could never subject multitudes to the command of one. Nothing but their own consent, and their sense of the advantages resulting from peace and order, could have had that influence.

Yet even this consent was long very imperfect, and could not be the basis of a regular administration. The chieftain, who had probably acquired his influence during the continuance of war, ruled more by persuasion than command; and till he could employ force to reduce the refractory and disobedient, the society could scarcely be said to have attained a state of civil government. No compact or agreement, it is evident, was expressly formed for general submission; an idea far beyond the comprehension of savages: each exertion of authority in the chieftain must have been particular, and called forth by the present exigencies of the case: the sensible utility, resulting from his interposition, made these exertions become daily more frequent; and their frequency gradually produced an habitual, and, if you please to call it so, a voluntary, and therefore precarious, acquiescence in the people.

But philosophers who have embraced a party (if that be not a contradiction in terms), are not contended with these concessions. They assert, not only that government in its earliest infancy arose from consent, or rather the voluntary acquiescence of the people; but also that, even at present, when it has attained its full maturity, it rests on no other foundation. They affirm, that all men are still born equal, and owe allegiance to no prince or government, unless bound by the obligation and sanction of a *promise*. And as no man, without some equivalent, would forego the advantages of his native liberty, and subject himself to the will of another, this promise is always understood to be conditional, and imposes on him no obligation, unless he meet with justice and protection from his sovereign. These advantages the sovereign promises him in return; and if he fail in the execution, he has broken, on his part, the articles of engagement, and has thereby freed his subject from all obligations to allegiance. Such, according to these philosophers, is the foundation of authority in every government, and such the right of resistance possessed by every subject.

But would these reasoners look abroad into the world, they would meet with nothing that, in the least, corresponds to their ideas, or can warrant so refined and philosophical a system. On the contrary, we find everywhere princes who claim their subjects as their property, and assert their independent right of sovereignty, from conquest or succession. We find also everywhere subjects who acknowledge this right in their prince, and suppose themselves born under obligations of obedience to a certain sovereign, as much as under the ties of reverence and duty to certain parents. These connections are always conceived to be equally independent of our consent, in PERSIA and CHINA, in FRANCE and SPAIN, and even in HOLLAND and ENGLAND, wherever the doctrines above mentioned have not been carefully inculcated. Obedience or subjection becomes so familiar, that most men never make any inquiry about its origin or cause, more than about the principle of gravity, resistance, or the most universal laws of nature. Or if curiosity ever move them, as soon as they learn that they themselves and their ancestors have, for several ages, or from time immemorial, been subject to such a form of government or such a family, they immediately acquiesce, and acknowledge their obligation to allegiance. Were you to preach, in most parts of the world, that political connections are founded altogether on voluntary consent or a mutual promise, the magistrate would soon imprison you as seditious for loosening the ties of obedience; if your friends did not before shut you up as delirious, for advancing such absurdities. It is strange that an act of the mind, which every individual is supposed to have formed, and after he came to the use of reason too, otherwise it could have no authority; that this act, I say, should be so much unknown to all of them, that over the face of the whole earth, there scarcely remain any traces or memory of it.

But the contract, on which government is founded, is said to be the *original contract*; and consequently may be supposed too old to fall under the knowledge of the present generation. If the agreement, by which savage men first associated and conjoined their force, be here meant, this is acknowledged to be real; but being so ancient, and being obliterated by a thousand changes of government and princes, it cannot now be supposed to retain any authority.

If we would say any thing to the purpose, we must assert, that every particular government which is lawful, and which imposes any duty of allegiance on the subject, was, at first, founded on consent and a voluntary compact. But, besides that this supposes the consent of the fathers to bind the children, even to the most remote generations (which republican writers will never allow), besides this, I say, it is not justified by history or experience in any age or country of the world.

Almost all the governments which exist at present, or of which there remains any record in story, have been founded originally, either on usurpation or conquest, or both, without any pretence of a fair consent or voluntary subjection of the people. When an artful and bold man is placed at the head of an army or faction, it is often easy for him, by employing, sometimes violence, sometimes false pretences, to establish his dominion over a people a hundred times more numerous than his partisans. He allows no such open communication, that his enemies can know, with certainty, their number or force. He gives them no leisure to assemble together in a body to oppose him. Even all those who are the instruments of his usurpation may wish his fall; but their ignorance of each other's intention keeps them in awe, and is the sole cause of his security. By such arts as these many governments have been established; and this is all the *original contract* which they have to boast of.

The face of the earth is continually changing, by the increase of small kingdoms into great empires, by the dissolution of great empires into smaller kingdoms, by the planting of colonies, by the migration of tribes. Is there any thing discoverable in all these events but force and violence? Where is the mutual agreement or voluntary association so much talked of?

Even the smoothest way by which a nation may receive a foreign master, by marriage or a will, is not extremely honourable for the people; but supposes them to be disposed of like a dowry or a legacy, according to the pleasure or interest of their rulers.

But where no force interposes, and election takes place;

what is this election so highly vaunted? It is either the combination of a few great men, who decide for the whole, and will allow of no opposition; or it is the fury of a multitude, that follow a seditious ringleader, who is not known, perhaps, to a dozen among them, and who owes his advancement merely to his own impudence, or to the momentary caprice of his fellows.

Are these disorderly elections, which are rare too, of such mighty authority as to be the only lawful foundation of all government and allegiance?

In reality there is not a more terrible event than a total dissolution of government, which gives liberty to the multitude, and makes the determination or choice of a new establishment depend upon a number, which nearly approaches to that of the body of the people: for it never comes entirely to the whole body of them. Every wise man then wishes to see, at the head of a powerful and obedient army, a general who may speedily seize the prize, and give to the people a master which they are so unfit to choose for themselves; so little correspondent is fact and reality to those philosophical notions.

Let not the establishment at the *Revolution* deceive us, or make us so much in love with a philosophical origin to government, as to imagine all others monstrous and irregular. Even that event was far from corresponding to these refined ideas. It was only the succession, and that only in the regal part of the government, which was then changed: and it was only the majority of seven hundred,* who determined that change for near ten millions. I doubt not, indeed, but the bulk of those ten millions acquiesced willingly in the determination: but was the matter left, in the least, to their choice? Was it not justly supposed to be, from that moment, decided, and every man punished, who refused to submit to the new sovereign? How otherwise could the matter have ever been brought to any issue or conclusion?

The republic of ATHENS was, I believe, the most extensive democracy that we read of in history: yet if we make the requisite allowances for the women, the slaves, and the strangers, we shall find, that that establishment was not at first made, nor any law ever voted, by a tenth part of those who were bound to pay obedience to it; not to mention the islands and foreign dominions, which the ATHENIANS claimed as theirs by right of conquest. And as it is well known that popular assemblies in that city were always full of license and disorder, notwithstanding the institutions and laws by which they were checked; how much more disorderly must they prove, where they form not the established constitution, but meet tumultuously on the dissolution of the ancient government, in order to give rise to a new one? How chimerical must it be to talk of a choice in such circumstances?

The ACHAEANS enjoyed the freest and most perfect democracy of all antiquity; yet they employed force to oblige some cities to enter into their league, as we learn from POLYBIUS.[†]

HARRY IV and HARRY VII* of ENGLAND, had really no title to the throne but a parliamentary election; yet they never would acknowledge it, lest they should thereby weaken their authority. Strange, if the only real foundation of all authority be consent and promise?

It is in vain to say that all governments are, or should be, at first founded on popular consent, as much as the necessity of human affairs will admit. This favours entirely my pretension. I maintain, that human affairs will never admit of this consent, seldom of the appearance of it; but that conquest or usurpation, that is, in plain terms, force, by dissolving the ancient governments, is the origin of almost all the new ones which were ever established in the world. And that in the few cases where consent may seem to have taken place, it was commonly so irregular, so confined, or so much intermixed either with fraud or violence, that it cannot have any great authority.

My intention here is not to exclude the consent of the people from being one just foundation of government. Where it has place, it is surely the best and most sacred of any. I only contend, that it has very seldom had place in any degree, and never almost in its full extent; and that, therefore, some other foundation of government must also be admitted.

Were all men possessed of so inflexible a regard to justice, that of themselves they would totally abstain from the properties of others; they had for ever remained in a state of absolute liberty, without subjection to any magistrate or political society: but this is a state of perfection of which human nature is justly deemed incapable. Again, were all men possessed of so perfect an understanding as always to know their own interests, no form of government had ever been submitted to but what was established on consent, and was fully canvassed by every member of the society: but this state of perfection is likewise much superior to human nature. Reason, history, and experience show us, that all political societies have had an origin much less accurate and regular; and were one to choose a period of time when the people's consent was the least regarded in public transactions, it would be precisely on the establishment of a new government. In a settled constitution their inclinations are often consulted; but during the fury of revolutions, conquests, and public convulsions, military force or political craft usually decides the controversy.

When a new government is established, by whatever means, the people are commonly dissatisfied with it, and pay obedience more from fear and necessity, than from any idea of allegiance or of moral obligation. The prince is watchful and jealous, and must carefully guard against every beginning or appearance of insurrection. Time, by degrees, removes all these difficulties, and accustoms the nation to regard, as their lawful or native princes, that family which at first they considered as usurpers or foreign conquerors. In order to found this opinion, they have no recourse to any notion of voluntary consent or promise, which, they know, never was, in this case, either expected or demanded. The original establishment was formed by violence, and submitted to from necessity. The subsequent administration is also supported by power, and acquiesced in by the people, not as a matter of choice, but of obligation. They imagine not that their consent gives their prince a title: but they willingly consent, because they think, that, from long possession, he has acquired a title, independent of their choice or inclination.

Should it be said, that, by living under the dominion of a prince which one might leave, every individual has given a *tacit* consent to his authority, and promised him obedience; it may be answered, that such an implied consent can only have place where a man imagines that the matter depends on his choice. But where he thinks (as all mankind do who are born under established governments) that, by his birth, he owes allegiance to a certain prince or certain form of government; it would be absurd to infer a consent or choice, which he expressly, in this case, renounces and disclaims.

Can we seriously say, that a poor peasant or artisan has a free choice to leave his country, when he knows no foreign language or manners, and lives, from day to day, by the small wages which he acquires? We may as well assert that a man, by remaining in a vessel, freely consents to the dominion of the master; though he was carried on board while asleep, and must leap into the ocean and perish, the moment he leaves her.

What if the prince forbid his subjects to quit his dominions; as in TIBERIUS'S time, it was regarded as a crime in a ROMAN knight that he had attempted to fly to the PARTHIANS, in order to escape the tyranny of that emperor?[†] Or as the ancient MUSCOVITES prohibited all travelling under pain of death? And did a prince observe, that many of his subjects were seized with the frenzy of migrating to foreign countries, he would, doubtless, with great reason and justice, restrain them, in order to prevent the depopulation of his own kingdom. Would he forfeit the allegiance of all his subjects by so wise and reasonable a law? Yet the freedom of their choice is surely, in that case, ravished from them.

A company of men, who should leave their native country, in order to people some uninhabited region, might dream of recovering their native freedom, but they would soon find, that their prince still laid claim to them, and called them his subjects, even in their new settlement. And in this he would but act conformably to the common ideas of mankind.

The truest *tacit* consent of this kind that is ever observed, is when a foreigner settles in any country, and is beforehand acquainted with the prince, and government, and laws, to which he must submit: yet is his allegiance, though more voluntary, much less expected or depended on, than that of a natural born subject. On the contrary, his native prince still asserts a claim to him. And if he punish not the renegade, when he seizes him in war with his new prince's commission; this clemency is not founded on the municipal law, which in all countries condemns the prisoner; but on the consent of princes, who have agreed to this indulgence, in order to prevent reprisals.

Did one generation of men go off the stage at once, and another succeed, as is the case with silkworms and butterflies, the new race, if they had sense enough to choose their government, which surely is never the case with men, might voluntarily, and by general consent, establish their own form of civil polity, without any regard to the laws or precedents which prevailed among their ancestors. But as human society is in perpetual flux, one man every hour going out of the world, another coming into it, it is necessary, in order to preserve stability in government, that the new brood should conform themselves to the established constitution, and nearly follow the path which their fathers, treading in the footsteps of theirs, had marked out to them. Some innovations must necessarily have place in every human institution; and it is happy where the enlightened genius of the age give these a direction to the side of reason, liberty, and justice: but violent innovations no individual is entitled to make: they are even dangerous to be attempted by the legislature: more ill than good is ever to be expected from them: and if history affords examples to the contrary, they are not to be drawn into precedent, and are only to be regarded as proofs, that the science of politics affords few rules, which will not admit of some exception, and which may not sometimes be controlled by fortune and accident. The violent innovations in the reign of HENRY VIII proceeded from an imperious monarch, seconded by the appearance of legislative authority: those in the reign of CHARLES I were derived from faction and fanaticism; and both of them have proved happy in the issue. But even the former were long the source of many disorders, and still more dangers; and if the measures of allegiance were to be taken from the latter, a total anarchy must have place in human society, and a final period at once be put to every government.

Suppose that an usurper, after having banished his lawful prince and royal family, should establish his dominion for ten or a dozen years in any country, and should preserve so exact a discipline in his troops, and so regular a disposition in his garrisons that no insurrection had ever been raised, or even murmur heard against his administration: can it be asserted that the people, who in their hearts abhor his treason, have tacitly consented to his authority, and promised him allegiance, merely because, from necessity, they live under his dominion? Suppose again their native prince restored, by means of an army, which he levies in foreign countries: they receive him with joy and exultation, and show plainly with what reluctance they had submitted to any other yoke. I may now ask, upon what foundation the prince's title stands? Not on popular consent surely: for though the people willingly acquiesce in his authority, they never imagine that their consent made him sovereign. They consent, because they apprehend him to be already by birth, their lawful sovereign. And as to tacit consent, which may now be inferred from their living under his dominion, this is no more than what they formerly gave to the tyrant and usurper.

When we assert that all lawful government arises from the consent of the people, we certainly do them a great deal more honour than they deserve, or even expect and desire from us. After the ROMAN dominions became too unwieldy for the republic to govern them, the people over the whole world were extremely grateful to AUGUSTUS for that authority which, by violence, he had established over them; and they showed an equal disposition to submit to the successor whom he left them by his last will and testament. It was afterwards their misfortune, that there never was, in one family, any long regular succession; but that their line of princes was continually broken, either by private assassinations or public rebellions. The *praetorian* bands, on the failure of every family, set up one emperor; the legions in the East a second; those in GERMANY, perhaps, a third; and the sword alone could decide the controversy. The condition of the people in that mighty monarchy was to be lamented, not because the choice of the emperor was never left to them, for that was impracticable, but because they never fell under any succession of masters who might regularly follow each other. As to the violence, and wars, and bloodshed, occasioned by every new settlement, these were not blamable, because they were inevitable.

The house of LANCASTER ruled in this island about sixty years; yet the partisans of the white rose seemed daily to multiply in ENGLAND. The present establishment has taken place during a still longer period. Have all views of right in another family been utterly extinguished, even though scarce any man now alive had arrived at the years of discretion when it was expelled, or could have consented to its dominion, or have promised it allegiance?—a sufficient indication, surely, of the general sentiment of mankind on this head. For we blame not the partisans of the abdicated family merely on account of the long time during which they have preserved their imaginary loyalty. We blame them for adhering to a family which we affirm has been justly expelled, and which, from the moment the new settlement took place, had forfeited all title to authority.

But would we have a more regular, at least a more philosophical refutation of this principle of an original contract, or popular consent, perhaps the following observations may suffice.

All *moral* duties may be divided into two kinds. The *first* are those to which men are impelled by a natural instinct or immediate propensity which operates on them, independent of all ideas of obligation, and of all views either to public or private utility. Of this nature are love of children, gratitude to benefactors, pity to the unfortunate. When we reflect on the advantage which results to society from such humane instincts, we pay them the just tribute of moral approbation and esteem: but the person actuated by them feels their power and influence antecedent to any such reflection.

The *second* kind of moral duties are such as are not supported by any original instinct of nature, but are performed entirely from a sense of obligation, when we consider the necessities of human society, and the impossibility of supporting it, if these duties were neglected. It is thus *justice*, or a regard to the property of others, *fidelity*, or the observance of promises, become obligatory, and acquire an authority over mankind. For as it is evident that every man loves himself better than any other person, he is naturally impelled to extend his acquisitions as much as possible; and nothing can restrain him in this propensity but reflection and experience, by which he learns the pernicious effects of that license, and the total dissolution of society which must ensue from it. His original inclination, therefore, or instinct, is here checked and restrained by a subsequent judgment or observation.

The case is precisely the same with the political or civil duty of *allegiance* as with the natural duties of justice and fidelity. Our primary instincts lead us either to indulge ourselves in unlimited freedom, or to seek dominion over others; and it is reflection only which engages us to sacrifice such strong passions to the interests of peace and public order. A small degree of experience and observation suffices to teach us, that society cannot possibly be maintained without the authority of magistrates, and that this authority must soon fall into contempt where exact obedience is not paid to it. The observation of these general and obvious interests is the source of all allegiance, and of that moral obligation which we attribute to it.

What necessity, therefore, is there to found the duty of *allegiance*, or obedience to magistrates, on that of *fidelity*, or a regard to promises, and to suppose that it is the consent of each individual which subjects him to government, when it appears that both allegiance and fidelity stand precisely on the same foundation, and are both submitted to by mankind, on account of the apparent interests and necessities of human society? We are bound to obey our sovereign, it is said, because we have given a tacit promise to that purpose. But why are we bound to observe our promise? It must here be asserted, that the commerce and intercourse of mankind, which are of such mighty advantage, can have no security where men pay no regard to their engagements. In like manner may it be said that men could not live at all in society, at least in a civilized society, without laws, and magistrates, and judges, to prevent the encroachments of the strong upon the weak, of the violent upon the just and equitable. The obligation to allegiance being of like force and authority with the obligation to fidelity, we gain nothing by resolving the one into the other. The general interests or necessities of society are sufficient to establish both.

If the reason be asked of that obedience which we are bound to pay to government, I readily answer, *because society could not otherwise subsist*; and this answer is clear and intelligible to all mankind. Your answer is, *because we should keep our word*. But besides that nobody, till trained in a philosophical system, can either comprehend or relish this answer; besides this, I say, you find yourself embarrassed when it is asked, *why we are bound to keep our word?* Nor can you give any answer but what would immediately, without any circuit, have accounted for our obligation to allegiance.

But *to whom is allegiance due, and who is our lawful sovereign?* This question is often the most difficult of any, and liable to infinite discussions. When people are so happy that they can answer, *Our present sovereign, who inherits, in a direct line, from ancestors that have governed us for many ages*, this answer admits of no reply, even though historians, in tracing up to the remotest antiquity the origin of that royal family, may find, as commonly happens, that its first authority was derived from usurpation and violence. It is confessed that private justice, or the abstinence from the properties of others, is a most cardinal virtue. Yet reason tells us that there is no property in durable objects, such as land or houses, when carefully examined in passing from hand to hand, but must, in some period, have been founded on fraud and injustice. The necessities of human society, neither in private nor public life, will allow of such an accurate inquiry; and there is no virtue or moral duty but what may, with facility, be refined away, if we indulge a false philosophy in sifting and scrutinizing it, by every captious rule of logic, in every light or position in which it may be placed.

The questions with regard to private property have filled infinite volumes of law and philosophy, if in both we add the commentators to the original text; and in the end we may safely pronounce, that many of the rules there established are uncertain, ambiguous, and arbitrary. The like opinion may be formed with regard to the succession and rights of princes, and forms of government. Several cases no doubt occur, especially in the infancy of any constitution, which admit of no determination from the laws of justice and equity; and our historian RAPIN pretends, that the controversy between EDWARD the Third and PHILIP DE VALOIS* was of this nature, and could be decided only by an appeal to heaven, that is, by war and violence.

Who shall tell me, whether GERMANICUS or DRUSUS ought to have succeeded to TIBERIUS,* had he died while they were both alive, without naming any of them for his successor? Ought the right of adoption to be received as equivalent to that of blood, in a nation where it had the same effect in private families, and had already, in two instances, taken place in the public? Ought GERMANICUS to be esteemed the elder son, because he was born before DRUSUS; or the younger, because he was adopted after the birth of his brother? Ought the right of the elder to be regarded in a nation, where he had no advantage in the succession of private families? Ought the ROMAN empire at that time to be deemed hereditary, because of two examples; or ought it even so early, to be regarded as belonging to the stronger, or to the present possessor, as being founded on so recent an usurpation?

COMMODUS mounted the throne after a pretty long succession of excellent emperors, who had acquired their title, not by birth, or public election, but by the fictitious rite of adoption. The bloody debauchee being murdered by a conspiracy, suddenly formed between his wench and her gallant, who happened at that time to be *Praetorian Praefect*, these immediately deliberated about choosing a master to the human kind, to speak in the style of those ages; and they cast their eyes on PERTINAX. Before the tyrant's death was known, the *Praefect* went secretly to that senator, who, on the appearance of the soldiers, imagined that his execution had been ordered by COMMODUS. He was immediately saluted emperor by the officer and his attendants, cheerfully proclaimed by the populace, unwillingly submitted to by the guards, formally recognized by the senate, and passively received by the provinces and armies of the empire.

The discontent of the *Praetorian* bands broke out in a sudden sedition, which occasioned the murder of that excellent prince; and the world being now without a master, and without government, the guards thought proper to set the empire formally to sale. JULIAN, the purchaser, was proclaimed by the soldiers, recognized by the senate, and submitted to by the people; and must also have been submitted to by the provinces, had not the envy of the legions begotten opposition and resistance. PESCENNIUS NIGER in SYRIA elected himself emperor, gained the tumultuary consent of his army, and was attended with the secret goodwill of the senate and people of ROME. ALBINUS in BRITAIN found an equal right to set up his claim; but SEVERUS, who governed PANNONIA, prevailed in the end above both of them. That able politician and warrior, finding his own birth and dignity too much inferior to the imperial crown, professed, at first, an intention only of revenging the death of PERTINAX. He marched as general into ITALY, defeated JULIAN, and, without our being able to fix any precise commencement even of the soldiers' consent, he was from necessity acknowledged emperor by the senate and people, and fully established in his violent authority, by subduing NIGER and ALBINUS.[†]

Inter haec Gordianus CAESAR (says CAPITOLINUS, speaking of another period) *sublatus a militibus*. Imperator *est appellatus, quia non erat alius in praesenti*.[*] It is to be remarked, that GORDIAN was a boy of fourteen years of age.

Frequent instances of a like nature occur in the history of the emperors; in that of ALEXANDER'S successors;* and of many other countries: nor can any thing be more unhappy than a despotic government of this kind; where the succession is disjointed and irregular, and must be determined on every vacancy by force or election. In a free government, the matter is often unavoidable, and is also much less dangerous. The interests of liberty may there frequently lead the people, in their own defence, to alter the succession of the crown. And the constitution, being compounded of parts, may still maintain a sufficient stability, by resting on the aristocratical or democratical members, though the monarchical be altered, from time to time, in order to accommodate it to the former.

In an absolute government, when there is no legal prince who has a title to the throne, it may safely be determined to belong to the first occupant. Instances of this kind are but too frequent, especially in the eastern monarchies. When any race of princes expires, the will or destination of the last sovereign will be regarded as a title. Thus the edict of LOUIS XIV, who called the bastard princes to the succession in case of the failure of all the legitimate princes, would, in such an event, have some authority.† Thus the will of CHARLES the Second disposed of the whole SPANISH monarchy. The cession of the ancient proprietor, especially when joined to conquest, is likewise deemed a good title. The general obligation, which binds us to government, is the interest and necessities of society; and this obligation is very strong. The determination of it to this or that particular prince, or form of government, is frequently more uncertain and dubious. Present possession has considerable authority in these cases, and greater than in private property; because of the disorders which attend all revolutions and changes of government.

We shall only observe, before we conclude, that though an appeal to general opinion may justly, in the speculative sciences of metaphysics, natural philosophy, or astronomy, be deemed unfair and inconclusive, yet in all questions with regard to morals, as well as criticism, there is really no other standard, by which any controversy can ever be decided. And nothing is a clearer proof, that a theory of this kind is erroneous, than to find, that it leads to paradoxes repugnant to the common sentiments of mankind, and to the practice and opinion of all nations and all ages. The doctrine, which founds all lawful government on an *original contract*, or consent of the people, is plainly of this kind; nor has the most noted of its partisans, in prosecution of it, scrupled to affirm, *that absolute monarchy is inconsistent with civil society, and so can be no form of civil government at all;*† and *that the supreme power in a state cannot take from any man, by taxes and impositions, any part of his property, without his own consent or that of his representatives.*† What authority any moral reasoning can have, which leads into opinions so wide of the general practice of mankind, in every place but this single kingdom, it is easy to determine.

The only passage I meet with in antiquity, where the obligation of obedience to government is ascribed to a promise, is in PLATO'S *Crito*; where SOCRATES refuses to escape from prison, because he had tacitly promised to obey the laws.* Thus he builds a *tory* consequence of passive obedience on a *whig* foundation of the original contract.

New discoveries are not to be expected in these matters. If scarce any man, till very lately, ever imagined that government was founded on compact, it is certain that it cannot, in general, have any such foundation.

The crime of rebellion among the ancients was commonly expressed by the terms νεωτερίζειν, *novas res moliri.**

OF THE PROTESTANT SUCCESSION

I SUPPOSE, that if a member of parliament, in the reign of King WILLIAM or Queen ANNE, while the establishment of the *Protestant Succession* was yet uncertain, were deliberating concerning the party he would choose in that important question, and weighing, with impartiality, the advantages and disadvantages on each side, I believe the following particulars would have entered into his consideration.

He would easily perceive the great advantage resulting from the restoration of the STUART family, by which we should preserve the succession clear and undisputed, free from a pretender, with such a specious title as that of blood, which, with the multitude, is always the claim the strongest and most easily comprehended. It is in vain to say, as many have done, that the question with regard to *governors*, independent of *government*, is frivolous, and little worth disputing, much less fighting about. The generality of mankind never will enter into these sentiments; and it is much happier, I believe, for society, that they do not, but rather continue in their natural prepossessions. How could stability be preserved in any monarchical government (which, though perhaps not the best, is, and always has been, the most common of any), unless men had so passionate a regard for the true heir of their royal family; and even though he be weak in understanding, or infirm in years, gave him so sensible a preference above persons the most accomplished in shining talents, or celebrated for great achievements? Would not every popular leader put in his claim at every vacancy, or even without any vacancy, and the kingdom become the theatre of perpetual wars and convulsions? The condition of the ROMAN empire, surely, was not in this respect much to be envied; nor is that of the *Eastern* nations, who pay little regard to the titles of their sovereign, but sacrifice them every day, to the caprice or momentary humour of the populace or soldiery. It is but a foolish wisdom, which is so carefully displayed in undervaluing princes, and placing them on a level with the meanest of mankind. To be sure, an anatomist finds no more in the greatest monarch than in the lowest peasant or day-labourer; and a moralist may, perhaps, frequently find less. But what do all these reflections tend to? We all of us still retain these prejudices in favour of birth and family; and neither in our serious occupations, nor most careless amusements, can we ever get entirely rid of them. A tragedy that should represent the adventures of sailors, or porters, or even of private gentlemen, would presently disgust us; but one that introduces kings and princes, acquires in our eyes an air of importance and dignity. Or should a man be able, by his superior wisdom, to get entirely above such prepossessions, he would soon, by means of the same wisdom, again bring himself down to them for the sake of society, whose welfare he would perceive to be intimately connected with them. Far from endeavouring to undeceive the people in this particular, he would cherish such sentiments of reverence to their princes, as requisite to preserve a due subordination in society. And though the lives of twenty thousand men be often sacrificed to maintain a king in possession of his throne, or preserve the right of succession undisturbed, he entertains no indignation at the loss, on pretence that every individual of these was, perhaps, in himself, as valuable as the prince he served. He considers the consequences of violating the hereditary right of kings; consequences which may be felt for many centuries, while the loss of several thousand men brings so little prejudice to a large kingdom, that it may not be perceived a few years after.

The advantages of the HANOVER succession are of an opposite nature, and arise from this very circumstance, that it violates hereditary right, and places on the throne a prince to whom birth gave no title to that dignity. It is evident, from the history of this island, that the privileges of the people have, during near two centuries, been continually upon the increase, by the division of the church lands, by the alienations of the barons' estates, by the progress of trade, and above all by the happiness of our situation, which, for a long time, gave us sufficient security, without any standing army or military establishment. On the contrary, public liberty has, almost in every other nation of EUROPE, been, during the same period, extremely on the decline; while the people were disgusted at the hardships of the old feudal militia, and rather chose to intrust their prince with mercenary armies, which he easily turned against themselves. It was nothing extraordinary, therefore, that some of our BRITISH sovereigns mistook the nature of the constitution, at least the genius of the people; and as they embraced all the favourable precedents left them by their ancestors, they overlooked all those which were contrary, and which supposed a limitation in our government. They were encouraged in this mistake, by the example of all the neighbouring princes, who, bearing the same title or appellation, and being adorned with the same ensigns of authority, naturally led them to claim the same powers and prerogatives. It appears from the speeches and proclamations of JAMES I, and the whole train of that prince's actions, as well as his son's, that he regarded the ENGLISH government as a simple monarchy, and never imagined that any considerable part of his subjects entertained a contrary idea. This opinion made those monarchs discover their pretensions, without preparing any force to support them; and even without reserve or disguise, which are always employed by those who enter upon any new project, or endeavour to innovate in any government. The flattery of courtiers further confirmed their prejudices; and, above all, that of the clergy, who, from several passages of *scripture*, and these wrested too, had erected a regular and avowed system of arbitrary power. The only method of destroying, at once, all these high claims and pretensions, was to depart from the true hereditary line, and choose a prince, who, being plainly a creature of the public, and receiving the crown on conditions, expressed and avowed, found his authority established on the same bottom with the privileges of the people. By electing him in the royal line, we cut off all hopes of ambitious subjects, who might, in future emergencies, disturb the government by their cabals and pretensions: by rendering the crown hereditary in his family, we avoided all the inconveniences of elective monarchy: and by excluding the lineal heir, we secured all our constitutional limitations, and rendered our government uniform, and of a piece. The people cherish monarchy, because protected by it: the monarch favours liberty, because created by it: and thus every advantage is obtained by the new establishment, as far as human skill and wisdom can extend itself.

These are the separate advantages of fixing the succession, either in the house of STUART, or in that of HANOVER. There are also disadvantages in each establishment, which an impartial patriot would ponder and examine, in order to form a just judgment upon the whole.

The disadvantages of the protestant succession consist in

the foreign dominions which are possessed by the princes of the HANOVER line, and which, it might be supposed, would engage us in the intrigues and wars of the continent, and lose us, in some measure, the inestimable advantage we possess, of being surrounded and guarded by the sea, which we command. The disadvantages of recalling the abdicated family consist chiefly in their religion, which is more prejudicial to society than that established among us; is contrary to it, and affords no toleration, or peace, or security, to any other communion.

It appears to me, that these advantages and disadvantages are allowed on both sides; at least, by every one who is at all susceptible of argument or reasoning. No subject, however loyal, pretends to deny, that the disputed title and foreign dominions of the present royal family are a loss. Nor is there any partisan of the STUARTS but will confess, that the claim of hereditary, indefeasible right, and the Roman Catholic religion, are also disadvantages in that family. It belongs, therefore, to a philosopher alone, who is of neither party, to put all the circumstances in the scale, and assign to each of them its proper poise and influence. Such a one will readily at first acknowledge, that all political questions are infinitely complicated, and that there scarcely ever occurs in any deliberation, a choice which is either purely good, or purely ill. Consequences, mixed and varied, may be foreseen to flow from every measure: and many consequences, unforeseen, do always, in fact, result from every one. Hesitation, and reserve, and suspense, are therefore the only sentiments be brings to this essay or trial. Or, if he indulges any passion, it is that of derision against the ignorant multitude, who are always clamorous and dogmatical, even in the nicest questions, of which, from want of temper, perhaps still more than of understanding, they are altogether unfit judges.

But to say something more determinate on this head, the following reflections will, I hope, show the temper, if not the understanding, of a philosopher.

Were we to judge merely by first appearances, and by past experience, we must allow that the advantages of a parliamentary title in the house of HANOVER are greater than those of an undisputed hereditary title in the house of STUART, and that our fathers acted wisely in preferring the former to the latter. So long as the house of STUART ruled in GREAT BRITAIN, which, with some interruption, was above eighty years, the government was kept in a continual fever, by the contention between the privileges of the people and the prerogatives of the crown. If arms were dropped, the noise of disputes continued: or if these were silenced, jealousy still corroded the heart, and threw the nation into an unnatural ferment and disorder. And while we were thus occupied in domestic disputes, a foreign power, dangerous to public liberty, erected itself in EUROPE, without any opposition from us, and even sometimes with our assistance.

But during these last sixty years, when a parliamentary establishment has taken place; whatever factions may have prevailed, either among the people or in public assemblies, the whole force of our constitution has always fallen to one side, and an uninterrupted harmony has been preserved between our princes and our parliaments. Public liberty, with internal peace and order, has flourished almost without interruption: trade and manufactures, and agriculture, have increased: the arts, and sciences, and philosophy, have been cultivated. Even religious parties have been necessitated to lay aside their mutual rancour; and the glory of the nation has spread itself all over EUROPE; derived equally from our progress in the arts of peace, and from valour and success in war. So long and so glorious a period no nation almost can boast of: nor is there another instance in the whole history of mankind, that so many millions of people have, during such a space of time, been held together, in a manner so free, so rational, and so suitable to the dignity of human nature.

But though this recent experience seems clearly to decide in favour of the present establishment, there are some circumstances to be thrown into the other scale; and it is dangerous to regulate our judgment by one event or example.

We have had two rebellions* during the flourishing period above mentioned, besides plots and conspiracies without number. And if none of these have produced any very fatal event, we may ascribe our escape chiefly to the narrow genius of those princes who disputed our establishment; and we may esteem ourselves so far fortunate. But the claims of the banished family, I fear, are not yet antiquated; and who can foretell, that their future attempts will produce no greater disorder?

The disputes between privilege and prerogative may easily be composed by laws, and votes, and conferences, and concessions, where there is tolerable temper or prudence on both sides, or on either side. Among contending titles, the question can only be determined by the sword, and by devastation, and by civil war.

A prince, who fills the throne with a disputed title, dares not arm his subjects; the only method of securing a people fully, both against domestic oppression and foreign conquest.

Notwithstanding our riches and renown, what a critical escape did we make, by the late peace, from dangers, which were owing not so much to bad conduct and ill success in war, as to the pernicious practice of mortgaging our finances, and the still more pernicious maxim of never paying off our incumbrances? Such fatal measures would not probably have been embraced, had it not been to secure a precarious establishment.

But to convince us, that an hereditary title is to be embraced rather than a parliamentary one, which is not supported by any other views or motives, a man needs only transport himself back to the era of the restoration, and suppose that he had had a seat in that parliament which recalled the royal family, and put a period to the greatest disorders that ever arose from the opposite pretensions of prince and people. What would have been thought of one that had proposed, at that time, to set aside CHARLES II and settle the crown on the Duke of YORK or GLOUCESTER, merely in order to exclude all high claims, like those of their father and grandfather? Would not such a one have been regarded as an extravagant projector, who loved dangerous remedies, and could tamper and play with a government and national constitution, like a quack with a sickly patient?

In reality, the reason assigned by the nation for excluding the race of STUART, and so many other branches of the royal family, is not on account of their hereditary title, (a reason which would, to vulgar apprehensions, have appeared altogether absurd,) but on account of their religion, which leads us to compare the disadvantages above mentioned in each establishment.

I confess that, considering the matter in general, it were much to be wished that our prince had no foreign dominions, and could confine all his attention to the government of the island. For not to mention some real inconveniences that may result from territories on the continent, they afford such a handle for calumny and defamation, as is greedily seized by the people, always disposed to think ill of their superiors. It must, however, be acknowledged, that HANOVER is, perhaps, the spot of ground in EUROPE the least inconvenient for a King of ENGLAND. It lies in the heart of GERMANY, at a distance from the great powers, which are our natural rivals: it is protected by the laws of the empire, as well as by the arms of its own sovereign: and it serves only to connect us more closely with the house of AUSTRIA, our natural ally.*

The religious persuasion of the house of STUART is an inconvenience of a much deeper die, and would threaten us with much more dismal consequences. The Roman Catholic religion, with its train of priests and friars, is more expensive than ours; even though unaccompanied with its natural attendants of inquisitors, and stakes, and gibbets, it is less tolerating: and, not content with dividing the sacerdotal from the regal office (which must be prejudicial to any state), it bestows the former on a foreigner, who has always a separate interest from that of the public, and may often have an opposite one.

But were this religion ever so advantageous to society, it is contrary to that which is established among us, and which is likely to keep possession, for a long time, of the minds of the people. And though it is much to be hoped, that the progress of reason will, by degrees, abate the acrimony of opposite religions all over EUROPE, yet the spirit of moderation has, as yet, made too slow advances to be entirely trusted.

Thus, upon the whole, the advantages of the settlement in the family of STUART, which frees us from a disputed title, seem to bear some proportion with those of the settlement in the family of HANOVER, which frees us from the claims of prerogative; but, at the same time, its disadvantages, by placing on the throne a Roman Catholic, are greater than those of the other establishment, in settling the crown on a foreign prince. What party an impartial patriot, in the reign of K. WILLIAM or Q. ANNE, would have chosen amidst these opposite views, may perhaps to some appear hard to determine.

But the settlement in the house of HANOVER has actually taken place. The princes of that family, without intrigue, without cabal, without solicitation on their part, have been called to mount our throne, by the united voice of the whole legislative body. They have, since their accession, displayed, in all their actions, the utmost mildness, equity, and regard to the laws and constitution. Our own ministers, our own parliaments, ourselves, have governed us; and if aught ill has befallen us, we can only blame fortune or ourselves. What a reproach must we become among nations, if, disgusted with a settlement so deliberately made, and whose conditions have been so religiously observed, we should throw every thing again into confusion, and, by our levity and rebellious disposition, prove ourselves totally unfit for any state but that of absolute slavery and subjection?

The greatest inconvenience attending a disputed title is, that it brings us in danger of civil wars and rebellions. What wise man, to avoid this inconvenience, would run directly into a civil war and rebellion? Not to mention, that so long possession, secured by so many laws, must, ere this time, in the apprehension of a great part of the nation, have begotten a title in the house of HANOVER, independent of their present possession: so that now we should not, even by a revolution, obtain the end of avoiding a disputed title.

No revolution made by national forces will ever be able, without some other great necessity, to abolish our debts and incumbrances, in which the interest of so many persons is concerned. And a revolution made by foreign forces is a conquest, a calamity with which the precarious balance of power threatens us, and which our civil dissensions are likely, above all other circumstances, to bring upon us.

IDEA OF A PERFECT COMMONWEALTH

It is not[†] with forms of government, as with other artificial contrivances, where an old engine may be rejected, if we can discover another more accurate and commodious, or where trials may safely be made, even though the success be doubtful. An established government has an infinite advantage, by that very circumstance, of its being established; the bulk of mankind being governed by authority, not reason, and never attributing authority to any thing that has not the recommendation of antiquity.

To tamper, therefore, in this affair, or try experiments merely upon the credit of supposed argument and philosophy, can never be the part of a wise magistrate, who will bear a reverence to what carries the marks of age; and though he may attempt some improvements for the public good, yet will he adjust his innovations as much as possible to the ancient fabric, and preserve entire the chief pillars and supports of the constitution.

The mathematicians in EUROPE have been much divided concerning that figure of a ship which is the most commodious for sailing; and HUYGENS, who at last determined the controversy, is justly thought to have obliged the learned as well as commercial world, though COLUMBUS had sailed to AMERICA, and Sir FRANCIS DRAKE made the tour of the world, without any such discovery. As one form of government must be allowed more perfect than another, independent of the manners and humours of particular men, why may we not inquire what is the most perfect of all, though the common botched and inaccurate governments seem to serve the purposes of society, and though it be not so easy to establish a new system of government, as to build a vessel upon a new construction? The subject is surely the most worthy of curiosity of any the wit of man can possibly devise. And who knows, if this controversy were fixed by the universal consent of the wise and learned, but, in some future age, an opportunity might be afforded of reducing the theory to practice, either by a dissolution of some old government, or by the combination of men to form a new one, in some distant part of the world? In all cases, it must be advantageous to know what is the most perfect in the kind, that we may be able to bring any real constitution or form of government as near it as possible, by such gentle alterations and innovations as may not give too great disturbance to society.

All I pretend to in the present Essay is, to revive this subject of speculation; and therefore I shall deliver my sentiments in as few words as possible. A long dissertation on that head would not, I apprehend, be very acceptable to the public, who will be apt to regard such disquisitions both as useless and chimerical.

All plans of government, which suppose great reformation in the manners of mankind, are plainly imaginary. Of this nature, are the *Republic* of PLATO, and the *Utopia* of Sir THOMAS MORE. The *OCEANA** is the only valuable model of a commonwealth that has yet been offered to the public.

The chief defects of the *OCEANA* seem to be these: *First*, Its rotation is inconvenient, by throwing men, of whatever abilites, by intervals, out of public employment. *Secondly*, Its *Agrarian* is impracticable. Men will soon learn the art which was practised in ancient ROME, of concealing their possessions under other people's names, till at last the abuse will become so common, that they will throw off even the appearance of restraint. *Thirdly*, The *OCEANA* provides not a sufficient security for liberty, or the redress of grievances. The senate must propose, and the people consent, by which means the senate have not only a negative upon the people, but, what is of much greater consequence, their negative goes before the votes of the people. Were the King's negative of the same nature in the ENGLISH constitution, and could he prevent any bill from coming into parliament, he would be an absolute monarch. As his negative follows the votes of the houses, it is of little consequence, such a difference is there in the manner of placing the same thing. When a popular bill has been debated in parliament, is brought to maturity, all its conveniences and inconveniences weighed and balanced, if afterwards it be presented for the royal assent, few princes will venture to reject the unanimous desire of the people. But could the King crush a disagreeable bill in embryo (as was the case for some time in the SCOTTISH parliament, by means of the lords of the articles),* the BRITISH government would have no balance, nor would grievances ever be redressed; and it is certain, that exorbitant power proceeds not in any government from new laws, so much as from neglecting to remedy the abuses which frequently rise from the old ones. A government, says MACHIAVEL,* must often be brought back to its original principles. It appears then, that in the *OCEANA*, the whole legislature may be said to rest in the senate, which HARRINGTON would own to be an inconvenient form of government, especially after the *Agrarian* is abolished.

Here is a form of government, to which I cannot, in theory, discover any considerable objection.

Let GREAT BRITAIN and IRELAND, or any territory of equal extent, be divided into 100 counties, and each county into 100 parishes, making in all 10,000. If the country proposed to be erected into a commonwealth be of more narrow extent, we may diminish the number of counties; but never bring them below thirty. If it be of greater extent, it were better to enlarge the parishes, or throw more parishes into a county, than increase the number of counties.

Let all the freeholders of twenty pounds a year in the county, and all the householders worth 500 pounds in the town parishes, meet annually in the parish church, and choose by ballot, some freeholder of the county for their member, whom we shall call the *county representative*.

Let the 100 county representatives, two days after their election, meet in the county town, and choose by ballot, from their own body, ten county *magistrates*, and one *senator*. There are, therefore, in the whole commonwealth, 100 senators, 1,100 county magistrates, and 10,000 county representatives; for we shall bestow on all senators the authority of county magistrates, and on all county magistrates the authority of county representatives.

Let the senators meet in the capital, and be endowed with the whole executive power of the commonwealth; the power of peace and war, of giving orders to generals, admirals, and ambassadors; and, in short, all the prerogatives of a BRITISH King, except his negative.

Let the county representatives meet in their particular counties, and possess the whole legislative power of the commonwealth, the greater number of counties deciding the question; and where these are equal, let the senate have the casting vote.

Every new law must first be debated in the senate; and though rejected by it, if ten senators insist and protest, it must be sent down to the counties. The senate, if they please, may join to the copy of the law their reasons for receiving or rejecting it.

Because it would be troublesome to assemble all the county representatives for every trivial law that may be requisite, the senate have their choice of sending down the law either to the county magistrates or county representatives.

The magistrates, though the law be referred to them, may, if they please, call the representatives, and submit the affair to their determination.

Whether the law be referred by the senate to the county magistrates or representatives, a copy of it, and of the senate's reasons, must be sent to every representative eight days before the day appointed for the assembling, in order to deliberate concerning it. And though the determination be, by the senate, referred to the magistrates, if five representatives of the county order the magistrates to assemble the whole court of representatives, and submit the affair to their determination, they must obey.

Either the county magistrates or representatives may give,

to the senator of the county, the copy of a law to be proposed to the senate; and if five counties concur in the same order, the law, though refused by the senate, must come either to the county magistrates or representatives, as is contained in the order of the five counties.

Any twenty counties, by a vote either of their magistrates or representatives, may throw any man out of all public offices for a year. Thirty counties for three years.

The senate has a power of throwing out any member or number of members of its own body, not to be reëlected for that year. The senate cannot throw out twice in a year the senator of the same county.

The power of the old senate continues for three weeks after the annual election of the county representatives. Then all the new senators are shut up in a conclave like the cardinals; and by an intricate ballot, such as that of VENICE or MALTA,* they choose the following magistrates; a protector, who represents the dignity of the commonwealth, and presides in the senate; two secretaries of state: these six councils, a council of state, a council of religion and learning, a council of trade, a council of laws, a council of war, a council of the admiralty, each council consisting of five persons; together with six commissioners of the treasury, and a first commissioner. All these must be senators. The senate also names all the ambassadors to foreign courts, who may either be senators or not.

The senate may continue any or all of these, but must reëlect them every year.

The protector and two secretaries have session and suffrage in the council of state. The business of that council is all foreign politics. The council of state has session and suffrage in all the other councils.

The council of religion and learning inspects the universities and clergy. That of trade inspects every thing that may affect commerce. That of laws inspects all the abuses of law by the inferior magistrates, and examines what improvements may be made of the municipal law. That of war inspects the militia and its discipline, magazines, stores, etc.; and when the republic is in war, examines into the proper orders for generals. The council of admiralty has the same power with regard to the navy, together with the nomination of the captains and all inferior officers.

None of these councils can give orders themselves, except where they receive such powers from the senate. In other cases, they must communicate every thing to the senate.

When the senate is under adjournment, any of the councils may assemble it before the day appointed for its meeting.

Besides these councils or courts, there is another called the court of *competitors*; which is thus constituted. If any candidates for the office of senator have more votes than a third of the representatives, that candidate who has most votes, next to the senator elected, becomes incapable for one year of all public offices, even of being a magistrate or representative; but he takes his seat in the court of competitors. Here then is a court which may sometimes consist of a hundred members, sometimes have no members at all; and by that means be for a year abolished.

The court of competitors has no power in the commonwealth. It has only the inspection of public accounts, and the accusing of any man before the senate. If the senate acquit him, the court of competitors may, if they please, appeal to the people, either magistrates or representatives. Upon that appeal, the magistrates or representatives meet on the day appointed by the court of competitors, and choose in each county three persons, from which number every senator is excluded. These, to the number of 300, meet in the capital, and bring the person accused to a new trial.

The court of competitors may propose any law to the senate; and if refused, may appeal to the people, that is, to the magistrates or representatives, who examine it in their counties. Every senator, who is thrown out of the senate by a vote of the court, takes his seat in the court of competitors.

The senate possesses all the judicative authority of the House of Lords, that is, all the appeals from the inferior courts. It likewise appoints the Lord Chancellor and all the officers of the law.

Every county is a kind of republic within itself, and the representatives may make by-laws, which have no authority till three months after they are voted. A copy of the law is sent to the senate, and to every other county. The senate, or any single county, may at any time annul any by-law of another county.

The representatives have all the authority of the BRITISH justices of the peace in trials, commitments, etc.

The magistrates have the appointment of all the officers of the revenue in each county. All causes with regard to the revenue are carried ultimately by appeal before the magistrates. They pass the accounts of all the officers; but must have their own accounts examined and passed at the end of the year by the representatives.

The magistrates name rectors or ministers to all the parishes.

The Presbyterian government is established; and the highest ecclesiastical court is an assembly or synod of all the presbyters of the county. The magistrates may take any cause from this court, and determine it themselves.

The magistrates may try, and depose or suspend any presbyter.

The militia is established in imitation of that of SWISSERLAND,* which being well known, we shall not insist upon it. It will only be proper to make this addition, that an army of 20,000 men be annually drawn out by rotation, paid and encamped during six weeks in summer, that the duty of a camp may not be altogether unknown.

The magistrates appoint all the colonels, and downwards. The senate all upwards. During war, the general appoints the colonel and downwards, and his commission is good for a twelvemonth. But after that, it must be confirmed by the magistrates of the county to which the regiment belongs. The magistrates may break any officer in the county regiment; and the senate may do the same to any officer in the service. If the magistrates do not think proper to confirm the general's choice, they may appoint another officer in the place of him they reject.

All crimes are tried within the county by the magistrates

and a jury; but the senate can stop any trial, and bring it before themselves.

Any county may indict any man before the senate for any crime.

The protector, the two secretaries, the council of state, with any five or more that the senate appoints, are possessed, on extraordinary emergencies, of *dictatorial* power for six months.

The protector may pardon any person condemned by the inferior courts.

In time of war, no officer of the army that is in the field can have any civil office in the commonwealth.

The capital, which we shall call LONDON, may be allowed four members in the senate. It may therefore be divided into four counties. The representatives of each of these choose one senator and ten magistrates. There are therefore in the city four senators, forty-four magistrates, and four hundred representatives. The magistrates have the same authority as in the counties. The representatives also have the same authority; but they never meet in one general court: they give their votes in their particular county or division of hundreds.

When they enact any by-law, the greater number of counties or divisions determines the matter. And where these are equal, the magistrates have the casting vote.

The magistrates choose the mayor, sheriff, recorder, and other officers of the city.

In the commonwealth, no representative, magistrate, or senator as such, has any salary. The protector, secretaries, councils, and ambassadors, have salaries.

The first year in every century is set apart for correcting all inequalities which time may have produced in the representative. This must be done by the legislature.

The following political aphorisms may explain the reason of these orders.

The lower sort of people and small proprietors are good enough judges of one not very distant from them in rank or habitation; and therefore, in their parochial meetings, will probably choose the best, or nearly the best representative:

but they are wholly unfit for country meetings, and for electing into the higher offices of the republic. Their ignorance gives the grandees an opportunity of deceiving them.

Ten thousand, even though they were not annually elected, are a basis large enough for any free government. It is true, the nobles in POLAND are more than 10,000, and yet these oppress the people. But as power always continues there in the same persons and families, this makes them in a manner a different nation from the people. Besides, the nobles are there united under a few heads of families.

All free governments must consist of two councils, a lesser and a greater, or, in other words, of a senate and people. The people, as HARRINGTON observes, would want wisdom without the senate: the senate, without the people, would want honesty.

A large assembly of 1,000, for instance, to represent the people, if allowed to debate, would fall into disorder. If not allowed to debate, the senate has a negative upon them, and the worst kind of negative, that before resolution.

Here, therefore, is an inconvenience which no government has yet fully remedied, but which is the easiest to be remedied in the world. If the people debate, all is confusion: if they do not debate, they can only resolve; and then the senate carves for them. Divide the people into many separate bodies, and then they may debate with safety, and every inconvenience seems to be prevented.

Cardinal de RETZ* says, that all numerous assemblies, however composed, are mere mob, and swayed in their debates by the least motive. This we find confirmed by daily experience. When an absurdity strikes a member, he conveys it to his neighbour, and so on till the whole be infected. Separate this great body; and though every member be only of middling sense, it is not probable that any thing but reason can prevail over the whole. Influence and example being removed, good sense will always get the better of bad among a number of people.

There are two things to be guarded against in every *senate*, its combination and its division. Its combination is most dangerous; and against this inconvenience we have provided the following remedies: 1. The great dependence of the senators on the people by annual elections; and that not by an undistinguished rabble, like the ENGLISH electors, but by men of fortune and education. 2. The small power they are allowed. They have few offices to dispose of. Almost all are given by the magistrates in the counties. 3. The court of competitors, which, being composed of men that are their rivals next to them in interest, and uneasy in their present situation, will be sure to take all advantages against them.

The division of the senate is prevented, 1. By the small-ness of their number. 2. As faction supposes a combination in a separate interest, it is prevented by their dependence on the people. 3. They have a power of expelling any factious member. It is true, when another member of the same spirit comes from the county, they have no power of expelling him: nor is it fit they should, for that shows the humour to be in the people, and may possibly arise from some ill conduct in public affairs. 4. Almost any man, in a senate so regularly chosen by the people, may be supposed fit for any civil office. It would be proper, therefore, for the senate to form some *general* resolutions with regard to the disposing of offices among the members: which resolutions would not confine them in critical times, when extraordinary parts on the one hand, or extraordinary stupidity on the other, appears in any senator; but they would be sufficient to prevent intrigue and faction, by making the disposal of the offices a thing of course. For instance, let it be a resolution, That no man shall enjoy any office till he has sat four years in the senate: that, except ambassadors, no man shall be in office two years following: that no man shall attain the higher offices but through the lower: that no man shall be protector twice, etc. The senate of VENICE govern them-selves by such resolutions.

In foreign politics the interest of the senate can scarcely ever be divided from that of the people; and therefore it is fit to make the senate absolute with regard to them, other-wise there could be no secrecy or refined policy. Besides, without money no alliance can be executed, and the senate is still sufficiently dependent. Not to mention, that the legislative power, being always superior to the executive, the magistrates or representatives may interpose whenever they think proper.

The chief support of the BRITISH government is the opposition of interest: but that, though in the main serviceable, breeds endless factions. In the foregoing plan, it does all the good without any of the harm. The *competitors* have no power of controlling the senate: they have only the power of accusing, and appealing to the people.

It is necessary, likewise, to prevent both combination and division in the thousand magistrates. This is done sufficiently by the separation of places and interests.

But, lest that should not be sufficient, their dependence on the 10,000 for their elections serves to the same purpose.

Nor is that all; for the 10,000 may resume the power whenever they please, and not only when they all please, but when any five of a hundred please, which will happen upon the very first suspicion of a separate interest.

The 10,000 are too large a body either to unite or divide, except when they meet in one place, and fall under the guidance of ambitious leaders. Not to mention their annual election, by the whole body of the people, that are of any consideration.

A small commonwealth is the happiest government in the world within itself, because every thing lies under the eye of the rulers: but it may be subdued by great force from without. This scheme seems to have all the advantages both of a great and a little commonwealth.

Every county law may be annulled either by the senate or another county, because that shows an opposition of interest: in which case no part ought to decide for itself. The matter must be referred to the whole, which will best determine what agrees with general interest.

As to the clergy and militia, the reasons of these orders are obvious. Without the dependence of the clergy on the civil magistrates, and without a militia, it is in vain to think that any free government will ever have security or stability.

In many governments, the inferior magistrates have no rewards but what arise from their ambition, vanity, or public spirit. The salaries of the FRENCH judges amount not to the interest of the sums they pay for their offices. The DUTCH burgomasters have little more immediate profit than the ENGLISH justices of peace, or the members of the house of commons formerly. But lest any should suspect that this would beget negligence in the administration (which is little to be feared, considering the natural ambition of mankind), let the magistrates have competent salaries. The senators have access to so many honourable and lucrative offices, that their attendance needs not be bought. There is little attendance required of the representatives.

That the foregoing plan of government is practicable, no one can doubt who considers the resemblance that it bears to the commonwealth of the United Provinces, a wise and renowned government. The alterations in the present scheme seem all evidently for the better. 1. The representation is more equal. 2. The unlimited power of the burgo-masters in the towns, which forms a perfect aristocracy in the DUTCH commonwealth, is corrected by a well-tempered democracy, in giving to the people the annual election of the county representatives. 3. The negative, which every province and town has upon the whole body of the DUTCH republic, with regard to alliances, peace and war, and the imposition of taxes, is here removed. 4. The counties, in the present plan, are not so independent of each other, nor do they form separate bodies so much as the seven provinces, where the jealousy and envy of the smaller provinces and towns against the greater, particularly HOLLAND and AMSTERDAM, have frequently disturbed the government. 5. Larger powers, though of the safest kind, are intrusted to the senate than the States-General possess; by which means the former may become more expeditious and secret in their resolutions than it is possible for the latter.

The chief alterations that could be made on the BRITISH government, in order to bring it to the most perfect model of limited monarchy, seem to be the following. *First*, The plan of CROMWELL'S parliament ought to be restored, by making the representation equal, and by allowing none to vote in the county elections who possess not a property of

200*l*. value. *Secondly*, As such a house of Commons would be too weighty for a frail house of Lords, like the present, the Bishops, and SCOTCH Peers, ought to be removed: the number of the upper house ought to be raised to three or four hundred: the seats not hereditary, but during life: they ought to have the election of their own members: and no commoner should be allowed to refuse a seat that was offered him. By this means the house of Lords would consist entirely of the men of chief credit, abilities, and interest in the nation; and every turbulent leader in the house of Commons might be taken off, and connected by interest with the house of Peers. Such an aristocracy would be an excellent barrier both to the monarchy and against it. At present, the balance of our government depends in some measure on the abilities and behaviour of the sovereign; which are variable and uncertain circumstances.

This plan of limited monarchy, however corrected, seems still liable to three great inconveniences. *First*, It removes not entirely, though it may soften the parties of *court* and *country*. *Secondly*, The king's personal character must still have great influence on the government. *Thirdly*, The sword is in the hands of a single person, who will always neglect to discipline the militia, in order to have a pretence for keeping up a standing army.

We shall conclude this subject, with observing the falsehood of the common opinion, that no large state, such as FRANCE or GREAT BRITAIN, could ever be modelled into a commonwealth, but that such a form of government can only take place in a city or small territory. The contrary seems probable. Though it is more difficult to form a republican government in an extensive country than in a city, there is more facility when once it is formed, of preserving it steady and uniform, without tumult and faction. It is not easy for the distant parts of a large state to combine in any plan of free government; but they easily conspire in the esteem and reverence for a single person, who, by means of this popular favour, may seize the power, and forcing the more obstinate to submit, may establish a monarchical government. On the other hand, a city readily concurs in the same notions of government, the natural equality of property favours liberty, and the nearness of habitation enables the citizens mutually to assist each other. Even under absolute princes, the subordinate government of cities is commonly republican; while that of counties and provinces is monarchical. But these same circumstances, which facilitate the erection of commonwealths in cities, render their constitution more frail and uncertain. Democracies are turbulent. For, however the people may be separated or divided into small parties, either in their votes or elections, their near habitation in a city will always make the force of popular tides and currents very sensible. Aristocracies are better adapted for peace and order, and accordingly were most admired by ancient writers; but they are jealous and oppressive. In a large government, which is modelled with masterly skill, there is compass and room enough to refine the democracy, from the lower people who may be admitted into the first elections, or first concoction of the commonwealth, to the higher magistrates who direct all the movements. At the same time, the parts are so distant and remote, that it is very difficult, either by intrigue, prejudice, or passion, to hurry them into any measures against the public interest.

It is needless to inquire, whether such a government would be immortal. I allow the justness of the poet's exclamation on the endless projects of human race, *Man and for ever!* * The world itself probably is not immortal. Such consuming plagues may arise as would leave even a perfect government a weak prey to its neighbours. We know not to what length enthusiasm, or other extraordinary movements of the human mind, may transport men to the neglect of all order and public good. Where difference of interest is removed, whimsical unaccountable factions often arise, from personal favour or enmity. Perhaps rust may grow to the springs of the most accurate political machine, and disorder its motions. Lastly, extensive conquests, when pursued, must be the ruin of every free government; and of the more perfect governments sooner than of the imperfect; because of the very advantages which the former possess above the latter. And though such a state ought to establish a fundamental law against conquests, yet republics have ambition as well as individuals, and present interest makes men forgetful of their posterity. It is a sufficient incitement to human endeavours, that such a government would flourish for many ages; without pretending to bestow, on any work of man, that immortality which the Almighty seems to have refused to his own productions.

ON SUICIDE

ONE considerable advantage that arises from philosophy, consists in the sovereign antidote which it affords to superstition and false religion. All other remedies against that pestilent distemper are vain, or at least uncertain. Plain good sense, and the practice of the world, which alone serve most purposes of life, are here found ineffectual: history, as well as daily experience, furnish instances of men endowed with the strongest capacity for business and affairs, who have all their lives crouched under slavery to the grossest superstition. Even gaiety and sweetness of temper, which infuse a balm into every other wound, afford no remedy to so virulent a poison, as we may particularly observe of the fair sex, who, though commonly possessed of these rich presents of nature, feel many of their joys blasted by this importunate intruder. But when sound philosophy has once gained possession of the mind, superstition is effectually excluded; and one may fairly affirm, that her triumph over this enemy is more complete than over most of the vices and imperfections incident to human nature. Love or anger, ambition or avarice, have their root in the temper and affections, which the soundest reason is scarce ever able fully to correct; but superstition being founded on false opinion, must immediately vanish when true philosophy has inspired juster sentiments of superior powers. The contest is here more equal between the distemper and the medicine; and nothing can hinder the latter from proving effectual, but its being false and sophisticated.

It will here be superfluous to magnify the merits of Philosophy by displaying the pernicious tendency of that vice of which it cures the human mind. The superstitious man, says *Tully*,[†] is miserable in every scene, in every incident of life. Even sleep itself, which banishes all other cares of unhappy mortals, affords to him matter of new terror, while he examines his dreams, and finds in those visions of the night prognostications of future calamities. I may add, that though death alone can put a full period to his misery, he dares not fly to this refuge, but still prolongs a miserable existence, from a vain fear lest he offend his maker, by using the power with which that beneficent being has endowed him. The presents of God and Nature are ravished from us by this cruel enemy; and notwithstanding that one step would remove us from the regions of pain and sorrow, her menaces still chain us down to a hated being, which she herself chiefly contributes to render miserable.

It is observed by such as have been reduced by the calamities of life to the necessity of employing this fatal remedy, that if the unseasonable care of their friends deprive them of that species of death which they proposed to themselves, they seldom venture upon any other, or can summon up so much resolution a second time, as to execute their purpose. So great is our horror of death, that when it presents itself under any form besides that to which a man has endeavoured to reconcile his imagination, it acquires new terrors, and overcomes his feeble courage: but when the menaces of superstition are joined to this natural timidity, no wonder it quite deprives men of all power over their lives, since even many pleasures and enjoyments, to which we are carried by a strong propensity, are torn from us by this inhuman tyrant. Let us here endeavour to restore men to their native liberty, by examining all the common arguments against Suicide, and showing that that action may be free from every imputation of guilt or blame, according to the sentiments of all the ancient philosophers.

If suicide be criminal, it must be a transgression of our duty either to God, our neighbour, or ourselves.

To prove that Suicide is no transgression of our duty to God, the following considerations may perhaps suffice. In order to govern the material world, the almighty creator has established general and immutable laws, by which all bodies, from the greatest planet to the smallest particle of matter, are maintained in their proper sphere and function. To govern the animal world, he has endowed all living creatures with bodily and mental powers; with senses, passions, appetites, memory, and judgment, by which they are impelled or regulated in that course of life to which they are destined. These two distinct principles of the material and animal world continually encroach upon each other, and mutually retard or forward each other's operation. The powers of men and of all other animals are restrained and directed by the nature and qualities of the surrounding bodies; and the modifications and actions of these bodies are incessantly altered by the operation of all animals. Man is stopped by rivers in his passage over the surface of the earth; and rivers, when properly directed, lend their force to the motion of machines, which serve to the use of man. But though the provinces of the material and animal powers are not kept entirely separate, there results from thence no discord or disorder in the creation; on the contrary, from the mixture, union, and contrast of all the various powers of inanimate bodies and living creatures, arises that surprizing harmony, and proportion, which affords the surest argument of supreme wisdom.

The providence of the deity appears not immediately in any operation, but governs every thing by those general and immutable laws which have been established from the beginning of time. All events, in one sense, may be pronounced the action of the almighty; they all proceed from those powers with which he has endowed his creatures. A house which falls by its own weight, is not brought to ruin by his providence, more than one destroyed by the hands of men; nor are the human faculties less his workmanship than the laws of motion and gravitation. When the passions play, when the judgment dictates, when the limbs obey; this is all the operation of God; and upon these animate principles, as well as upon the inanimate, has he established the government of the universe.

Every event is alike important in the eyes of that infinite Being, who takes in at one glance the most distant regions of space, and remotest periods of time. There is no event, however important to us, which he has exempted from the general laws that govern the universe, or which he has peculiarly reserved for his own immediate action and operation. The revolution of states and empires depends upon the smallest caprice or passion of single men; and the lives of men are shortened or extended by the smallest accident of air or diet, sunshine or tempest. Nature still continues her progress and operation; and if general laws be ever broke by particular volitions of the deity, it is after a manner which entirely escapes human observation. As, on the one hand, the elements and other inanimate parts of the creation carry on their action without regard to the particular interest and situation of men; so men are intrusted to their own judgment and discretion in the various shocks of matter, and may employ every faculty with which they are endowed, in order to provide for their ease, happiness, or preservation.

What is the meaning then of that principle, that a man, who, tired of life, and hunted by pain and misery, bravely overcomes all the natural terrors of death, and makes his escape from this cruel scene; that such a man, I say, has incurred the indignation of his creator, by encroaching on the office of divine providence, and disturbing the order of the universe? Shall we assert, that the Almighty has reserved to himself, in any peculiar manner, the disposal of the lives of men, and has not submitted that event, in common with others, to the general laws by which the universe is governed? This is plainly false: the lives of men depend upon the same laws as the lives of all other animals; and these are subjected to the general laws of matter and motion. The fall of a tower, or the infusion of a poison, will destroy a man equally with the meanest creature; an inundation sweeps away every thing without distinction that comes within the reach of its fury. Since therefore the lives of men are for ever dependent on the general laws of matter and motion, is a man's disposing of his life criminal, because in every case it is criminal to encroach upon these laws, or disturb their operation? But this seems absurd: all animals are intrusted to their own prudence and skill for their conduct in the world; and have full authority, as far as their power extends, to alter all the operations of nature. Without the exercise of this authority, they could not subsist a moment; every action, every motion of a man, innovates on the order of some parts of matter, and diverts from their ordinary course the general laws of motion. Putting together therefore these conclusions, we find *that* human life depends upon the general laws of matter and motion, and *that* it is no encroachment on the office of providence to disturb or alter these general laws: has not every one of consequence the free disposal of his own life? And may he not lawfully employ that power with which nature has endowed him?

In order to destroy the evidence of this conclusion, we must show a reason why this particular case is excepted. Is it because human life is of such great importance, that it is a presumption for human prudence to dispose of it? But the life of a man is of no greater importance to the universe than that of an oyster: and were it of ever so great importance, the order of human nature has actually submitted it to human prudence, and reduced us to a necessity, in every incident, of determining concerning it.

Were the disposal of human life so much reserved as the peculiar province of the Almighty, that it were an encroachment on his right for men to dispose of their own lives, it would be equally criminal to act for the preservation of life as for its destruction. If I turn aside a stone which is falling upon my head, I disturb the course of nature; and I invade the peculiar province of the Almighty, by lengthening out my life beyond the period, which, by the general laws of matter and motion, he has assigned it.

A hair, a fly, an insect, is able to destroy this mighty being whose life is of such importance. Is it an absurdity to suppose that human prudence may lawfully dispose of what depends on such insignificant causes?

It would be no crime in me to divert the *Nile* or *Danube* from its course, were I able to effect such purposes. Where then is the crime of turning a few ounces of blood from their natural channels!

Do you imagine that I repine at Providence, or curse my creation, because I go out of life, and put a period to a being which, were it to continue, would render me miserable? Far be such sentiments from me. I am only convinced of a matter of fact which you yourself acknowledge possible, that human life may be unhappy; and that my existence, if further prolonged, would become ineligible: but I thank providence, both for the good which I have already enjoyed, and for the power with which I am endowed of escaping the ills that threaten me.† To you it belongs to repine at providence, who foolishly imagine that you have no such power; and who must still prolong a hated life, though loaded with pain and sickness, with shame and poverty.

Do not you teach, that when any ill befalls me, though by the malice of my enemies, I ought to be resigned to providence; and that the actions of men are the operations of the Almighty, as much as the actions of inanimate beings? When I fall upon my own sword, therefore, I receive my death equally from the hands of the deity as if it had proceeded from a lion, a precipice, or a fever.

The submission which you require to providence, in every calamity that befalls me, excludes not human skill and industry, if possibly by their means I can avoid or escape the calamity. And why may I not employ one remedy as well as another?

If my life be not my own, it were criminal for me to put it in danger, as well as to dispose of it; nor could one man deserve the apellation of *Hero*, whom glory or friendship transports into the greatest dangers; and another merit the reproach of *Wretch* or *Miscreant*, who puts a period to his life from the same or like motives.

There is no being which possesses any power or faculty, that it receives not from its creator; nor is there any one, which by ever so irregular an action, can encroach upon the plan of his providence, or disorder the universe. Its operations are his works equally with that chain of events which it invades; and whichever principle prevails, we may for that very reason conclude it to be most favoured by him. Be it animate or inanimate; rational or irrational; it is all the same case: its power is still derived from the supreme creator, and is alike comprehended in the order of his providence. When the horror of pain prevails over the love of life; when a voluntary action anticipates the effects of blind causes; it is only in consequence of those powers and principles which he has implanted in his creatures. Divine providence is still inviolate, and placed far beyond the reach of human injuries.

It is impious, says the old *Roman* superstition,* to divert rivers from their course, or invade the prerogatives of nature. It is impious, says the *French* superstition, to inoculate for the smallpox, or usurp the business of providence, by voluntarily producing distempers and maladies. It is impious, says the modern *European* superstition, to put a period to our own life, and thereby rebel against our creator: and why not impious, say I, to build houses, cultivate the ground, or sail upon the ocean? In all these actions we employ our powers of mind and body to produce some innovation in the course of nature; and in none of them do we any more. They are all of them therefore equally innocent, or equally criminal.

But you are placed by providence, like a sentinel, in a particular station; and when you desert it without being recalled, you are equally guilty of rebellion against your Almighty Sovereign, and have incurred his displeasure. I ask, Why do you conclude that Providence has placed me in this station? For my part, I find that I owe my birth to a long chain of causes, of which many depended upon voluntary actions of men. *But Providence guided all these causes, and nothing happens in the universe without its consent and coöperation.* If so, then neither does my death, however voluntary, happen without its consent; and whenever pain or sorrow so far overcome my patience, as to make me tired of life, I may conclude that I am recalled from my station in the clearest and most express terms.

It is providence surely that has placed me at this present

moment in this chamber: but may I not leave it when I think proper, without being liable to the imputation of having deserted my post or station? When I shall be dead, the principles of which I am composed will still perform their part in the universe, and will be equally useful in the grand fabric, as when they composed this individual creature. The difference to the whole will be no greater than betwixt my being in a chamber and in the open air. The one change is of more importance to me than the other; but not more so to the universe.

It is a kind of blasphemy to imagine that any created being can disturb the order of the world, or invade the business of providence! It supposes, that that being possesses powers and faculties which it received not from its creator, and which are not subordinate to his government and authority. A man may disturb society, no doubt, and thereby incur the displeasure of the almighty: but the government of the world is placed far beyond his reach and violence. And how does it appear that the almighty is displeased with those actions that disturb society? By the principles which he has implanted in human nature, and which inspire us with a sentiment of remorse if we ourselves have been guilty of such actions, and with that of blame and disapprobation, if we ever observe them in others. Let us now examine, according to the method proposed, whether Suicide be of this kind of actions, and be a breach of our duty to our *neighbour* and to society.

A man who retires from life does no harm to society: he only ceases to do good; which, if it is an injury, is of the lowest kind.

All our obligations to do good to society seem to imply something reciprocal. I receive the benefits of society, and therefore ought to promote its interests; but when I withdraw myself altogether from society, can I be bound any longer?

But allowing that our obligations to do good were perpetual, they have certainly some bounds; I am not obliged to do a small good to society at the expense of a great harm to myself: why then should I prolong a miserable existence, because of some frivolous advantage which the public may perhaps receive from me? If upon account of age and infirmities, I may lawfully resign any office, and employ my time altogether in fencing against these calamities, and alleviating as much as possible the miseries of my future life; why may I not cut short these miseries at once by an action which is no more prejudicial to society?

But suppose that it is no longer in my power to promote the interest of the public; suppose that I am a burden to it; suppose that my life hinders some person from being much more useful to the public: in such cases, my resignation of life must not only be innocent, but laudable. And most people who lie under any temptation to abandon existence, are in some such situation; those who have health, or power, or authority, have commonly better reason to be in humour with the world.

A man is engaged in a conspiracy for the public interest; is seized upon suspicion; is threatened with the rack; and knows from his own weakness that the secret will be extorted from him: could such a one consult the public interest better than by putting a quick period to a miserable life? This was the case of the famous and brave *Strozzi of Florence*.

Again, suppose a malefactor is justly condemned to a shameful death; can any reason be imagined why he may not anticipate his punishment, and save himself all the anguish of thinking on its dreadful approaches? He invades the business of Providence no more than the magistrate did who ordered his execution; and his voluntary death is equally advantageous to society, by ridding it of a pernicious member.

That Suicide may often be consistent with interest and with our duty to *ourselves*, no one can question, who allows that age, sickness, or misfortune, may render life a burden, and make it worse even than annihilation. I believe that no man ever threw away life while it was worth keeping. For such is our natural horror of death, that small motives will never be able to reconcile us to it; and though perhaps the situation of a man's health or fortune did not seem to require this remedy, we may at least be assured, that any one who, without apparent reason, has had recourse to it, was cursed with such an incurable depravity or gloominess of temper as must poison all enjoyment, and render him equally miserable as if he had been loaded with the most grievous misfortune.

If Suicide be supposed a crime, it is only cowardice can impel us to it. If it be no crime, both prudence and courage should engage us to rid ourselves at once of existence when it becomes a burden. It is the only way that we can then be useful to society, by setting an example, which, if imitated, would preserve to every one his chance for happiness in life, and would effectually free him from all danger or misery.[†]

ON THE IMMORTALITY OF THE SOUL

By the mere light of reason it seems difficult to prove the Immortality of the Soul; the arguments for it are commonly derived either from *metaphysical* topics, or *moral*, or *physical*. But in reality it is the gospel, and the gospel alone, that has brought life and immortality to light.

I. Metaphysical topics suppose that the soul is immaterial, and that it is impossible for thought to belong to a material substance.

But just metaphysics teach us, that the notion of substance is wholly confused and imperfect; and that we have no other idea of any substance, than as an aggregate of particular qualities inhering in an unknown something. Matter, therefore, and spirit, are at bottom equally unknown; and we cannot determine what qualities inhere in the one or in the other.

They likewise teach us, that nothing can be decided *a priori* concerning any cause or effect; and that experience, being the only source of our judgments of this nature, we cannot know from any other principle, whether matter, by its structure or arrangement, may not be the cause of thought. Abstract reasonings cannot decide any question of fact or existence.

But admitting a spiritual substance to be dispersed throughout the universe, like the ethereal fire of the Stoics, and to be the only inherent subject of thought, we have reason to conclude from *analogy*, that nature uses it after the manner she does the other substance, matter. She employs it as a kind of paste or clay; modifies it into a variety of forms and existences; dissolves after a time each modification, and from its substance erects a new form. As the same material substance may successively compose the bodies of all animals, the same spiritual substance may compose their minds: their consciousness, or that system of thought which they formed during life, may be continually dissolved by death, and nothing interests them in the new modification. The most positive assertors of the mortality of the soul never denied the immortality of its substance; and that an immaterial substance, as well as a material, may lose its memory or consciousness, appears in part from experience, if the soul be immaterial.

Reasoning from the common course of nature, and without supposing any *new* interposition of the supreme cause, which ought always to be excluded from philosophy, what is incorruptible must also be ingenerable. The soul therefore, if immortal, existed before our birth; and if the former existence noways concerned us, neither will the latter. Animals undoubtedly feel, think, love, hate, will, and even reason, though in a more imperfect manner than men: are their souls also immaterial and immortal?

II. Let us now consider the *moral* arguments, chiefly those derived from the justice of God, which is supposed to be further interested in the future punishment of the vicious and reward of the virtuous.

But these arguments are grounded on the supposition that God has attributes beyond what he has exerted in this universe, with which alone we are acquainted. Whence do we infer the existence of these attributes?

It is very safe for us to affirm, that whatever we know the Deity to have actually done is best; but it is very dangerous to affirm that he must always do what to us seems best. In how many instances would this reasoning fail us with regard to the present world?

But if any purpose of nature be clear, we may affirm, that the whole scope and intention of man's creation, so far as we can judge by natural reason, is limited to the present life. With how weak a concern from the original inherent structure of the mind and passions, does he ever look further? What comparison either for steadiness or efficacy, betwixt so floating an idea and the most doubtful persuasion of any matter of fact that occurs in common life.

There arise indeed in some minds some unaccountable terrors with regard to futurity; but these would quickly vanish were they not artificially fostered by precept and education. And those who foster them, what is their motive? Only to gain a livelihood, and to acquire power and riches in this world. Their very zeal and industry, therefore, are an argument against them.

What cruelty, what iniquity, what injustice in nature, to confine all our concern, as well as all our knowledge, to the present life, if there be another scene still waiting us of infinitely greater consequence? Ought this barbarous deceit to be ascribed to a beneficent and wise being?

Observe with what exact proportion the task to be performed, and the performing powers, are adjusted throughout all nature. If the reason of man gives him great superiority above other animals, his necessities are proportionably multiplied upon him: his whole time, his whole capacity, activity, courage, and passion, find sufficient employment in fencing against the miseries of his present condition; and frequently, nay, almost always, are too slender for the business assigned them.

A pair of shoes, perhaps, was never yet wrought to the highest degree of perfection which that commodity is capable of attaining; yet it is necessary, at least very useful, that there should be some politicians and moralists, even some geometers, poets, and philosophers among mankind.

The powers of men are no more superior to their wants, considered merely in this life, than those of foxes and hares are, compared to *their* wants and to *their* period of existence. The inference from parity of reason is therefore obvious.

On the theory of the soul's mortality, the inferiority of women's capacity is easily accounted for. Their domestic life requires no higher faculties either of mind or body. This circumstance vanishes and becomes absolutely insignificant on the religious theory: the one sex has an equal task to perform as the other; their powers of reason and resolution ought also to have been equal, and both of them infinitely greater than at present.

As every effect implies a cause, and that another, till we reach the first cause of all, which is the *Deity*; every thing that happens is ordained by him, and nothing can be the object of his punishment or vengeance.

By what rule are punishments and rewards distributed? What is the divine standard of merit and demerit? Shall we suppose that human sentiments have place in the deity? However bold that hypothesis, we have no conception of any other sentiments.

According to human sentiments, sense, courage, good-manners, industry, prudence, genius, etc., are essential parts of personal merits. Shall we therefore erect an elysium for poets and heroes like that of ancient mythology? Why confine all rewards to one species of virtue?

Punishment, without any proper end or purpose, is inconsistent with *our* ideas of goodness and justice; and no end can be served by it after the whole scene is closed.

Punishment, according to *our* conception, should bear some proportion to the offence. Why then eternal punishment for the temporary offences of so frail a creature as man? Can any one approve of *Alexander's* rage, who intended to exterminate a whole nation because they had seized his favourite horse *Bucephalus*?*

Heaven and hell suppose two distinct species of men, the good and the bad; but the greatest part of mankind float betwixt vice and virtue.

Were one to go round the world with an intention of giving a good supper to the righteous and a sound drubbing to the wicked, he would frequently be embarrassed in his choice, and would find the merits and demerits of most men and women scarcely amount to the value of either.

To suppose measures of approbation and blame different from the human confounds every thing. Whence do we learn that there is such a thing as moral distinctions, but from our own sentiments?

What man who has not met with personal provocation (or what good-natured man who has) could inflict on crimes, from the sense of blame alone, even the common, legal, frivolous punishments? And does any thing steel the breast of judges and juries against the sentiments of humanity but reflection on necessity and public interest?

By the Roman law, those who had been guilty of parricide, and confessed their crime, were put into a sack along with an ape, a dog, and a serpent, and thrown into the river. Death alone was the punishment of those who denied their guilt, however fully proved. A criminal was tried before *Augustus*, and condemned after a full conviction; but the humane emperor, when he put the last interrogatory, gave it such a turn as to lead the wretch into a denial of his guilt. *You surely*, said the prince, *did not kill your father.*[†] This lenity suits our natural ideas of RIGHT even towards the greatest of all criminals, and even though it prevents so inconsiderable a sufferance. Nay, even the most bigoted priest would naturally without reflection approve of it, provided the crime was not heresy or infidelity; for as these crimes hurt himself in his *temporal* interest and advantages, perhaps he may not be altogether so indulgent to them.

The chief source of moral ideas is the reflection on the interests of human society. Ought these interests, so short, so frivolous, to be guarded by punishments eternal and infinite? The damnation of one man is an infinitely greater evil in the universe than the subversion of a thousand millions of kingdoms.

Nature has rendered human infancy peculiarly frail and mortal, as it were on purpose to refute the notion of a probationary state; the half of mankind die before they are rational creatures.

III. The *physical* arguments from the analogy of nature are strong for the mortality of the soul; and are really the only philosophical arguments which ought to be admitted with regard to this question, or indeed any question of fact.

Where any two objects are so closely connected that all alterations which we have ever seen in the one are attended with proportionable alterations in the other; we ought to conclude, by all rules of analogy, that, when there are still greater alterations produced in the former, and it is totally dissolved, there follows a total dissolution of the latter.

Sleep, a very small effect on the body, is attended with a temporary extinction, at least a great confusion in the soul.

The weakness of the body and that of the mind in infancy are exactly proportioned; their vigour in manhood, their sympathetic disorder in sickness, their common gradual decay in old age. The step further seems unavoidable; their common dissolution in death.

The last symptoms which the mind discovers, are disorder, weakness, insensibility, and stupidity; the forerunners of its annihilation. The further progress of the same causes increasing, the same effects totally extinguish it.

Judging by the usual analogy of nature, no form can continue when transferred to a condition of life very different from the original one in which it was placed. Trees perish in the water, fishes in the air, animals in the earth. Even so small a difference as that of climate is often fatal. What reason then to imagine, that an immense alteration, such as is made on the soul by the dissolution of its body, and all its organs of thought and sensation, can be effected without the dissolution of the whole?

Every thing is in common betwixt soul and body. The organs of the one are all of them the organs of the other; the existence, therefore, of the one must be dependent on the other.

The souls of animals are allowed to be mortal; and these bear so near a resemblance to the souls of men, that the analogy from one to the other forms a very strong argument. Their bodies are not more resembling, yet no one rejects the argument drawn from comparative anatomy. The *Metempsychosis* is therefore the only system of this kind that philosophy can hearken to.

Nothing in this world is perpetual; every thing, however

seemingly firm, is in continual flux and change: The world itself gives symptoms of frailty and dissolution: How contrary to analogy, therefore, to imagine that one single form, seeming the frailest of any, and subject to the greatest disorders, is immortal and indissoluble? What theory is that! How lightly, not to say how rashly, entertained!

How to dispose of the infinite number of posthumous existences ought also to embarrass the religious theory. Every planet in every solar system, we are at liberty to imagine peopled with intelligent mortal beings, at least we can fix on no other supposition. For these then a new universe must every generation be created beyond the bounds of the present universe, or one must have been created at first so prodigiously wide as to admit of this continual influx of beings. Ought such bold suppositions to be received by any philosophy, and that merely on the pretext of a bare possibility?

When it is asked, whether *Agamemnon*, *Thersites*, *Hannibal*, *Nero*, and every stupid clown that ever existed in *Italy*, *Scythia*, *Bactria*, or *Guinea*, are now alive; can any man think, that a scrutiny of nature will furnish arguments strong enough to answer so strange a question in the affirmative? The want of argument without revelation sufficiently establishes the negative. *Quanto facilius*, says Pliny,* *certiusque sibi quemque credere, ac specimen securitatis antiquae tali sumere experimento*. Our insensibility before the composition of the body seems to natural reason a proof of a like state after dissolution.

Were our horrors of annihilation an original passion, not the effect of our general love of happiness, it would rather prove the mortality of the soul: for as nature does nothing in vain, she would never give us a horror against an impossible event. She may give us a horror against an unavoidable event, provided our endeavours, as in the present case, may often remove it to some distance. Death is in the end unavoidable; yet the human species could not be preserved had not nature inspired us with an aversion towards it.

All doctrines are to be suspected which are favoured by

our passions; and the hopes and fears which gave rise to this doctrine are very obvious.

It is an infinite advantage in every controversy to defend the negative. If the question be out of the common experienced course of nature, this circumstance is almost if not altogether decisive. By what arguments or analogies can we prove any state of existence, which no one ever saw, and which no way resembles any that ever was seen? Who will repose such trust in any pretended philosophy as to admit upon its testimony the reality of so marvellous a scene? Some new species of logic is requisite for that purpose, and some new faculties of the mind, that they may enable us to comprehend that logic.

Nothing could set in a fuller light the infinite obligations which mankind have to Divine revelation, since we find that no other medium could ascertain this great and important truth.

our passions and the hopes and fears which gave rise to this doctrine are very obvious.

It is an infinite advantage in every controversy to defend the negative. If the question be out of the common experienced course of nature, this circumstance is almost if not altogether decisive. By what arguments or analogies can we prove any state of existence, which no one ever saw, and which no way resembles any that ever was seen? Who will repose such trust in any pretended philosophy as to admit upon its testimony the reality of so marvellous a scene? Some new species of logic is requisite for that purpose, and some new faculties of the mind, that they may enable us to comprehend that logic.

Nothing could set in a fuller light the infinite obligations which mankind have to Divine revelation, since we find that no other medium could ascertain this great and important truth.

EDITORS' NOTES

OF ESSAY WRITING

This essay only appeared in the edition of 1742.

1. *Stunn'd . . . did that?*: the source of this couplet has not been located. In his edition of the *Essays* Eugene Miller has suggested that it may belong to the same author or poem as the couplet quoted in 'The Epicurean'.

2. *belles lettres*: polite literature.

   chimerical: fancifully or fantastically conceived.

4. *pretends*: claims.

   complexion: Hume's phrasing here harks back to the medical theory of the humours.

OF THE MIDDLE STATION OF LIFE

This essay only appeared in the edition of 1742.

5. *Agur's prayer*: see Proverbs 30: 7–9.

8. *the Czar*: i.e. Peter the Great.

   Kouli-Kan: the European name for the Persian Emperor Nadir Shah (who ruled between 1736 and 1747).

9. *Homer . . . Italians*: this canon of writers reflects typical eighteenth-century literary judgements—with the possible exception of the inclusion of the controversial figure of Voltaire, and the choice of Tasso and Ariosto over Dante.

OF THE DELICACY OF TASTE AND PASSION

12. *fondly*: foolishly.

    Ingenuas . . . feros: Ovid, *Letters from Pontus*, 2. 9. 47–8: 'A faithful study of the liberal arts humanizes character and allows it not to be cruel.'

    very nice: finely discriminating.

THAT POLITICS MAY BE REDUCED TO
A SCIENCE

14. *Henry III/IV*: Henry III's reign (1574–89) was marked by civil and religious strife, which was largely calmed during Henry IV's famously pragmatic reign (1589–1610), which saw a (temporary) end to the persecution of the Huguenots.

15. *Campus Martius*: site of public meetings and commerce in Rome.

   Venetian . . . Polish: Venice is often cited by Hume and others in the period as an example both of civic, political, artistic and commercial success and of the dangers of luxury and corruption. Poland is usually presented as an example of the dangers of weak government.

   a priori: by reason alone.

18. *Verres*: Cicero first came to prominence in 70 BC by his conduct of the prosecution of Gaius Verres, a notoriously corrupt Roman governor of Sicily.

   Pais conquis: 'conquered lands'.

   Machiavel: see Machiavelli, *The Prince*, ch. 4.

20. *bank of St George*: the bank was originally set up to pay off Genoa's war debts with revenue from the custom-house. It eventually grew to administer most towns and cities under Genoese dominion, which were assigned to it as securities for loans to Genoa.

23. *Revolution and Accession*: the revolution of 1688/9 deposed James II and led to the accession of his daughter, Mary, and her husband William. He ruled alone after her death, and was succeeded by James's second daughter, Anne, before the line of succession was fixed in the house of Hanover on her death in 1714.

   Cato and Brutus: i.e. Marcus Porcius Cato (95–46 BC) and Marcus Junius Brutus (85–42 BC).

24. *pro aris et focis*: 'in defence of our altars and our hearths'.

OF THE FIRST PRINCIPLES OF GOVERNMENT

   soldan: sultan.

25. *mamalukes or praetorian bands*: the Mamelukes seized power in Egypt in 1254 and continued to form the ruling class in the

eighteenth century. The Praetorian guard was the bodyguard of the Roman emperors.

25. *A noted author*: probably James Harrington, author of *Oceana*.

27. *reign of king William*: in 1698–1701 the Tory House of Commons opposed William III's measures to secure Europe against the threat posed by Louis XIV of France. Popular feeling supported the king, particularly when petitioners to the Commons of the parties of Great Britain from Kent were arrested.

34. *Gustavus Vasa*: after the Swedish war of independence against Denmark and Norway Gustavus Eriksson Vasa confiscated the property of the Catholic church and established a Lutheran state church, as well as making the monarchy a hereditary institution.

Louvestein faction: after 1559 the stadtholders of the Dutch republic came from the House of Orange. They favoured the Calvinist faction over the Arminians. In 1610 Prince Maurice of Orange contrived the execution of the advocate of Holland and the imprisonment of some of his supporters in the castle of Louvestein. From then on, the opponents of the House of Orange were known as the Louvestein faction.

the great rebellion: i.e. the English Civil War of 1642–52.

36. *the revolution*: i.e. the Revolution of 1688/9.

OF SUPERSTITION AND ENTHUSIASM

41. *Scotland*: the Quakers, founded by George Fox in the mid-seventeenth century, emphasized inward witness and simplicity of manners, and conducted services without a minister. The Independents, or Congregationalists, emerged in England in the sixteenth century, and insisted on the independence of congregations from other civil and ecclesiastical organizations. The Presbyterians, followers of John Calvin, made congregations subject to larger assemblies, the presbyteries. The Anabaptists were widely persecuted in Europe for their insistence on the complete separation of Church and State, and refusal to swear civil oaths. The Camisards were French Calvinists who revolted in 1703 against Louis XIV's 1685 revocation of the Edict of Nantes, which had granted tolerance to French Protestants. The Levellers were radical egalitarians in the Civil War and Commonwealth period. The Scottish

Covenanters defended presbyterian church government against episcopacy until they were forcibly put down in the 1660s.

42. *sectaries*: followers of a particular sect.

   deists: a widely used generic term in the eighteenth century for those who believed in one god, and based their belief on reason rather than revealed religion.

   disputes: the conflict between seventeenth-century Molinists and Jansenists centred on the place of free will and predestination. Hume's view of the suppression of liberty in Catholic absolutist France is typical of British writings of the period.

OF CIVIL LIBERTY

49. *Prince*: Machiavelli, *The Prince*, ch. 23. The correct translation of the original should be 'imprudent' rather than 'weak'.

50. *two maritime powers*: i.e. Holland and England.

51. *Longinus*: *On the Sublime*, 44.

   Hamburg: at the time of Rubens Antwerp was Catholic and loyal to the Spanish king. In the early eighteenth century Dresden was dominated by the Catholic Elector of Saxony. Amsterdam and Hamburg were free and Protestant. For a survey of eighteenth-century discussions of the connection between artistic production and political liberty see Michael Meehan, *Liberty and Poetics in Eighteenth Century England* (Croom Helm, London/Beckenham, 1986).

52. *Sed . . . ruris*: Horace, *Epistles*, 2. 1. 160: 'yet for many a year traces of our rustic past lived on, and still live on.'

OF THE RISE AND PROGRESS OF THE ARTS AND SCIENCES

58. *Charles Quint*: Charles V, Holy Roman Emperor 1519–56, was also Charles I of Spain from 1516.

59. *Scit . . . ater*: Horace, *Epistles*, 2. 2. 187–9: 'the Genius alone knows, that companion who rules our star of birth, the god of human nature, though mortal for each single life, and changing in countenance, white or black.'

60. *village*: 'Bashaw' means head or chief; 'Cadis' are town or village judges.

   Czar: i.e. Peter I (the Great).

63. *valet de chambre*: this remark has been attributed to a number of people.

65. *Peripatetic*: the Aristotelian school of philosophy.

   Cartesian philosophy: the philosophy of René Descartes and his followers.

   Newton's theory: Sir Isaac Newton's theory of nature, based on laws of motion, and expressed in mathematical form.

66. *Eclectics*: the Alexandrian Neoplatonic school of philosophy is often known as the Eclectic school because of its attempts to incorporate features of all other systems.

   Stoics and Epicureans, Platonists: see discussion of Hume's essays on these topics in the Introduction.

70. *Sallust*: *War with Catiline*, 124. 2: 'Whatever wanton, glutton, or gamester had wasted his patrimony in play, feasting, or debauchery.'

   Horace: *Satires*, 1. 3. 107: 'before Helen's day a woman was the most dreadful cause of war.'

71. *de finibus*: Cato speaks for Stoic ethics in Cicero, *De Finibus Bonorum et Malorum*.

75. *Plautus*: see Horace, *Ars Poetica*, 270–4.

76. *Prince of Tyre . . . Volpone*: i.e. Shakespeare's (presumed early) *Pericles, Prince of Tyre* and later *Othello, The Moor of Venice*; and early and later plays by Ben Jonson.

   England: see Iain Pears, *The Discovery of Painting: The Growth of Interest in the Arts in England, 1680–1768* (Yale UP, New Haven, Conn., 1988).

77. *Waller*: Edmund Waller was valued in the eighteenth century for (in Dr Johnson's words) the 'elegance and gaiety' of his verse, even if Johnson also regretted his lack of seriousness and scope. For two characteristic judgements from the period see *Tatler*, No. 163, and Samuel Johnson, *Lives of the Poets*, Life of Waller.

THE EPICUREAN

81. *Damon*: a familiar name in pastoral poetry. See Virgil, *Eclogues*, 8.

THE SCEPTIC

99. *Ptolemaic and Copernican systems*: Ptolemy taught in the second century AD that the earth is immobile at the centre of the planetary system. His model held sway for a long period, and was not significantly challenged until Nicholas Copernicus proposed in the sixteenth century that the earth rotates and moves around the sun.

103. *Proteus-like*: the Greek sea-god Proteus had the power to change his shape at will.

106. *Domitian . . . Rufus . . . Alexander*: the Roman emperor Domitian reputedly spent much of his leisure time killing flies; William Rufus, the second Norman king of England, was addicted to hunting, and was killed while on a hunt; Alexander the Great's fame derived from his extensive conquests.

108. *in the dark*: Cicero, *Tusculan Disputations* 5. 38.

Fontenelle: *Conversations on the Plurality of Worlds*.

109. *infernal regions*: see Lucian, *Menippus*, § 17.

110. *Thucydides*: *The Peloponnesian War*, 2. 53.

plague of Florence: Boccaccio, *Decameron*, 'Introduction'.

OF NATIONAL CHARACTERS

116. *a Brutus*: i.e. Lucius Junius Brutus.

117. *Piraeum*: Piraeus, the port of Athens.

121. *de Oratoribus*: i.e. Tacitus, *Dialogue on Oratory*.

122. *study of the sciences*: during his reign Peter the Great made strenuous efforts to introduce European ideas and patterns of behaviour to Russia.

124. *Darius Hystaspes*: i.e. Darius I of Persia.

OF TRAGEDY

128. *Sicilian captains*: see Cicero, *Second Speech against Gaius Verres*, 5. 118–38.

130. *predominant one*: *Othello*, III. iii.

131. *dolce peccante*: sweet sinning.

132. *Lord Clarendon*: see Clarendon, *The True Historical Narrative of the Rebellion and Civil Wars in England* (1702–4).

132. *Ambitious Step-mother*: tragedy by Nicholas Rowe, performed in 1700.

OF THE STANDARD OF TASTE

133. This essay was originally published in 1757, along with 'The Natural History of Religion', 'Of the Passions' and 'Of Tragedy', under the title *Four Dissertations*. 'Of the Standard of Taste' was included in place of 'Of Suicide' and 'Of the Immortality of the Soul'.

135. *Alcoran*: i.e. the Koran, the holy book of Islam.

141. *Don Quixote*: Cervantes, *Don Quixote*, part 2, ch. 13.

151. *Terence . . . Machiavel*: in Terence's *Andria* Glycerium, the central female character, says nothing: in Machiavelli's *Clizia* (1525), Clizia does not appear.

   monument more durable than brass: see Horace, *Odes*, 3. 30. 1.

153. *Polieucte and Athalia*: *Polyeucte* (1642), by Corneille, and *Athalie* (1691), by Racine, are tragedies on religious subjects. *Athalie* is based on Biblical narrative (found in 2 Kings 11 and 2 Chronicles 22–3). The scene described by Hume is *Athalie* III. v.

154. *will not be quiet*: see Homer, *Iliad*, 1. 225, and 1. 56–67 for these exchanges.

   Petrarch: the love poems of Francesco Petrarca were enormously influential in establishing the conventions of theme and address of English Elizabethan sonnets.

   Boccace . . . enemies: Boccaccio, *Decameron*, introduction to 'The Fourth Day'.

OF COMMERCE

158. *Illyricum*: an area on the west coast of the Adriatic.

165. *pretty much alike*: Bacon, *Essays*, 29: 'Of the True Greatness of Kingdoms and Estates'.

166. *Curis . . . corda*: Virgil, *Georgics*, 1. 123: 'Sharpening men's wits by care.'

OF REFINEMENT IN THE ARTS

167. In some editions (1742–58) this essay is entitled 'Of Luxury'.

169. *spirit of the age*: this phrase had widespread currency in writings of the Romantic period in England and in Germany.

170. *reproached him*: the incident involving Caesar and Cato is narrated in Plutarch's *Lives*, Life of the Younger Cato.

171. *Guicciardin*: see Guicciardini, *Storia d'Italia*, books 1–3.

   lasted . . . thirty years: Louis XIV died in 1715. He had assumed absolute power on the death of Louis XIII's chief minister, Cardinal Mazarin, in 1661, and thereafter conducted a series of lengthy wars in Europe.

172. *Pyrrhus . . . discipline*: for this incident see Plutarch, *Lives*, Life of Pyrrhus, 16.

173. *lewdness and drinking*: Sallust, *War With Catiline*, 1–6.

   ortolans: small edible birds.

OF THE BALANCE OF TRADE

189. *Mr Gee*: see Gee, *The Trade and Navigation of Great Britain Considered* (1729). Gee argues in part against the importation of foreign commodities if they can be produced at home.

190. *Dr Swift*: see Swift, *A Short View of the State of Ireland* (1727–8).

   the Harrys and Edwards: i.e. the period from *c*.1100 to *c*.1550.

192. *India companies*: the various European East India companies imported a variety of commodities into Europe from the Orient, and in return exported large amounts of European silver coin and bullion.

193. *Heptarchy*: the independent Anglo-Saxon kingdoms of England.

194. *Mareschal Vauban*: see Vauban, *Projet d'une dixme royale* (1707).

196. *Lycurgus*: (the ruler of Sparta) ordained that gold and silver coinage be replaced with iron. For details, see Plutarch, *Lives*, Life of Lycurgus, 9.

201. *Dr Arbuthnot's*: John Arbuthnot's *Tables of the Grecian, Roman and Jewish Measures Weights and Coins* (*c*.1705) was expanded and reissued as *Tables of Ancient Coins, Weights, and Measures* in 1727.

   Dr Swift: see Swift, *An Answer to a Paper Called A Memorial*

of the Poor Inhabitants, Tradesmen and Labourers of the
Kingdom of Ireland (1728).

202. *since the revolution*: between 1688 and 1752 Flanders was the
scene of a series of wars in pursuit of rival claims by England,
Holland, France, Spain, and the Holy Roman Empire.

OF PUBLIC CREDIT

203. *Jewish princes*: see 2 Kings 18: 15, and 2 Chronicles 32: 27–9.

Julius Caesar: see Plutarch, *Lives*, Life of Caesar, § 35, for an
account of his seizure of the state treasure of Rome at the
start of the civil war of 49–45 BC.

205. *scrutoire*: large cabinet or desk.

207. *Jacobitish violence*: Jacobite supporters of the Stuarts after
the 1688 revolution staged revolts in 1715 and 1745.

208. *been told*: see Melon, *Essai politique sur le commerce*, ch. 23.

210. *annuities*: Adam Smith discusses forms of government
borrowing in *Wealth of Nations*, book 5, ch. 3.

212. *Mr Hutchinson*: see Archibald Hutcheson, *A Collection of
Treatises Relating to the National Debts and Funds* (1721).

213. *the regency*: in the early 1720s, during the minority of Louis
XV, when Orléans was Regent, John Law's Mississippi
scheme led to frenetic investment and eventual financial
collapse.

214. *the late war*: i.e. Louis XV and the War of Austrian
Succession.

OF SOME REMARKABLE CUSTOMS

219. *comitia centuriata and comitia tributa*: assemblies of the
people called to consider matters presented to them by the
magistrates. In the former voting was by social class, with
the wealthiest classes outweighing the poorer in influence; in
the latter it was by electoral division or 'tribe', with the
country divisions easily outweighing the representatives of the
city of Rome.

221. *civil wars*: see Appian, *Roman History: The Civil Wars*, 3. 27–
30. Decimus Brutus refused to surrender Cisalpine Gaul to
Mark Antony after the death of Julius Caesar.

222. *Hampden's conduct*: the seventeenth-century MP John Hampden's refusal to pay 'ship money', and his subsequent trial, was seen by contemporaries as an important act of resistance to the extension of royal prerogative in the period immediately before the English Civil War.

 pressing of seamen: the royal power of pressing men into the navy against their consent survived from medieval times until the early nineteenth century.

OF THE POPULOUSNESS OF ANCIENT NATIONS

225. *Vossius*: see Vossius, *Variarum Observationum Liber* (1685), 1–68.

230. *industry and agriculture*: Columella, *On Agriculture*, 1. Proem, 2, 7; Varro, *On Agriculture*, 3. 1; Horace, *Odes*, 2. 15; Tacitus, *Annals*, 3. 54; Suetonius, *Life of Augustus*, 42; Pliny, *Natural History*, 18. 4.

235. *Maillet*: *Description de l'Égypte* (1735), and *Idée du gouvernement ancien et moderne de l'Égypte* (1743).

239. *reward of the other*: Appian, *The Civil Wars*, 4. 120.

241. *Tacitus*: *History*, 2. 44.

244. *cities*: Isocrates, *To Philip*, 96.

245. *500 of the citizens*: Diodorus Siculus, 14. 38.

246. *Dionysius of Halicarnassaeus*: *The Roman Antiquities*, 1. 89.

250. *Flanders and of France*: Philip II's wars were waged against the inhabitants of the Spanish Netherlands; Louis XIV's persecution of the Huguenots led to extensive emigration, particularly to the Netherlands and Britain.

252. *Strabo*: see *Geography*, 6. 1. 13.

267. *Strabo*: 3. 1. 2.

268. *best account of it*: see Maillet, *Description de l'Égypte* (1735).

OF THE ORIGINAL CONTRACT

276. *Borgia*: Cesare Borgia's ruthless approach to government is described in chapter 7 of Machiavelli's *The Prince*.

280. *seven hundred*: the numbers in the English and Scottish

Parliamentary conventions which approved the transfer of the English crown to William and Mary after the 1689 revolution.

281. *Harry IV . . . VII*: Henry IV succeeded to the English throne after the deposition and murder of Richard II: Henry VII after the defeat of Richard III.

289. *Philip de Valois*: Edward III of England and Philip of Valois were rival claimants for the French throne in 1328.

Tiberius: the claims arose because Germanicus was the nephew and adopted son of Tiberius: Drusus was Tiberius' son.

290. *Inter . . . praesenti*: Julius Capitolinus, *Maximus and Balbinus*, 14, in *Historia Augusta*: ['In the meantime Gordian Caesar was lifted up by the soldiers and hailed emperor, there being no one else at hand.'] This event occurred in AD 238, after the deaths of his grandfather and uncle (both emperors named Gordian), and the murder of Maximus and Balbinus, who had succeeded them.

291. *Alexander's successors*: after Alexander the Great's death in 323 BC struggles between his generals for control of his empire lasted until 306, by which time it had been divided into three—Macedon, Egypt, and the Seleucid Empire.

292. *laws*: Plato, *Crito*, 50c ff.

novas res moliri: to make innovations.

OF THE PROTESTANT SUCCESSION

This essay was prepared for, but excluded from, the 1748 edition of Hume's *Essays*, because of the proximity of the 1745 Jacobite rising. Although Hume ultimately defends the Hanoverian succession, his initial exposition of the case for the Stuart line might have been read as provocative in this context. The essay was revised considerably in different editions.

298. *two rebellions*: i.e. the Jacobite rebellions of 1715 and 1745.

299. *our natural ally*: in a series of eighteenth-century conflicts including the wars of Spanish Succession and Austrian Succession Britain fought in a variety of alliances with Austria and against France.

IDEA OF A PERFECT COMMONWEALTH

302. *Oceana*: by James Harrington.

303. *lords of the articles*: a committee of the three estates in the ancient Scottish parliament, in effect dominated by the king.

Machiavel: see Machiavelli, *Discourses*, book 3, ch. 1.

305. *Venice or Malta*: the complex electoral procedure of the Great Council of Venice was adopted as a model by Harrington in *Oceana*.

307. *Swisserland*: the militias of the Swiss cantons, made up of all able-bodied males, were pledged to mutual defence, and were notably successful. They were taken as a useful model by writers in the civic humanist tradition. Debates about the relative merits of militias and standing armies are central to the Scottish Enlightenment.

309. *Cardinal de Retz*: see de Retz, *Mémoirs* (1717).

314. *Man and for ever*: Eugene Miller suggests that this may be a paraphrase of Horace, *Satires*, 2.8.62, or Lucretius, *De Rerum Natura*, 2.76 or 5.1430.

ON SUICIDE

315. Although 'On Suicide' and 'Of the Immortality of the Soul' were probably written in 1755, the prospect of ecclesiastical condemnation and possible prosecution induced Hume to withdraw them from publication. They were first published posthumously in 1777, under the title *Two Essays*.

321. *superstition*: Tacitus, *Annals*, 1.79.

ON THE IMMORTALITY OF THE SOUL

324. This essay was published with 'Of Suicide' in 1777.

327. *Bucephalus*: Quintus Curtis, *History of Alexander*, 6.5.

330. *Pliny*: *Natural History*, 7.56. ['How much easier and safer for each to trust in himself, and for us to derive our idea of future tranquillity from our experience of it before birth!']

SELECTED ORIGINAL NOTES AND TEXTUAL VARIANTS BY HUME

OF THE DELICACY OF TASTE AND PASSION

11. *luxury can afford*: earlier editions (1741–70) add: 'How far delicacy of taste, and that of passion, are connected together in the original frame of the mind, it is hard to determine. To me there appears a very considerable connexion between them. For we may observe that women, who have more delicate passions than men, have also a more delicate taste of the ornaments of life, of dress, equipage, and the ordinary decencies of behaviour. Any excellency in these hits their taste much sooner than ours; and when you please their taste, you soon engage their affections.'

13. *French author*: Mons. FONTENELLE, *Pluralité des Mondes*, Soir 6. ['Conversations on the Plurality of Worlds', Evening 6.]

THAT POLITICS MAY BE REDUCED TO A SCIENCE

It is a question . . . administered: *For forms of government let fools contest / Whate'er is best administer'd is best.* ESSAY on Man, book 3. [The quotation is from Pope's *Essay on Man* (pub. 1732–4), iii. 303. The doctrine derives ultimately from Aristotle's *Politics*. Pope's contemporary editor Warburton notes that the poet felt the need to defend himself against the suggestion that the lines imply that there is no distinction between different forms of government—which they pretty obviously do.]

18. *Tacitus informs us*: *Annals*, 1.8.

Domitian: Suetonius, *Lives of the Caesars*, Life of Domitian, 8.

In Tiberius's time: *Egregium resumendae liberati tempus, si ipsi florentes, quam inops* ITALIA, *quam imbellis urbana plebs, nihil validum in exercitibus nisi quod externum cogitarent.* [Tacitus, *Annals*, 3. 40: 'It was an unequalled opportunity for regaining their independence: they had only to look from their own resources to the poverty of Italy, the unwarlike city population, the feebleness of the armies except for their foreign components.']

18. *Polybius: Histories*, 1. 72.

19. *every undertaking*: I have taken it for granted, according to the supposition of MACHIAVEL, that the ancient PERSIANS had no nobility; though there is reason to suspect, that the FLORENTINE secretary, who seems to have been better acquainted with the ROMAN than the GREEK authors, was mistaken in this particular. The more ancient PERSIANS, whose manners are described by XENOPHON, were a free people, and had nobility. Their ὁμότιμοι [chief nobles] were preserved even after the extending of their conquests and the consequent change of their government. ARRIAN mentions them in DARIUS's time [*Expedition of Alexander*, 2]. Historians also speak often of the persons in command as men of family. TYGRANES, who was general of the MEDES under XERXES, was of the race of ACHMAENES [Herodotus, *History*, 7. 62]. ARTACHAEAS, who directed the cutting of the canal about mount ATHOS, was of the same family [ibid. 7. 117]. MEGABYZUS was one of the seven eminent PERSIANS who conspired against the MAGI. His son, ZOPYRUS, was in the highest command under DARIUS, and delivered BABYLON to him. His grandson, MEGABYZUS, commanded the army, defeated at MARATHON. His great-grandson, ZOPYRUS, was also eminent, and was banished PERSIA [Herodotus, 3. 160; Thucydides, *History of the Peloponnesian War*, 1. 109]. ROSACES, who commanded an army in EGYPT under ARTAXERXES, was also descended from one of the seven conspirators [Diodorus Siculus, *Library of History*, 16. 47]. AGESILAUS, in XENOPHON [*Hellenica*, 4. 1], being desirous of making a marriage betwixt king COTYS his ally, and the daughter of SPITHRIDATES, a PERSIAN of rank, who had descerted him, first asks COTYS what family SPITHRIDATES is of. One of the most considerable in PERSIA, says COTYS. ARLAEUS, when offered the sovereignty by CLEARCHUS and the ten thousand GREEKS, refused it as of too low a rank, and said, that so many eminent PERSIANS would never endure his rule [*Expedition of Cyrus*, 2]. Some of the families descended from the seven PERSIANS above-mentioned remained during all ALEXANDER's successors; and MITHRIDATES, in ANTIOCHUS's time, is said by POLYBIUS to be descended from one of them [5. 43]. ARTABAZUS was esteemed, as ARRIAN says, ἐν τοῖς πρώτοις Περσῶν ['among

the highest of the Persians', 3. 23]. And when Alexander married in one day 80 of his captains to PERSIAN women, his intention plainly was to ally the MACEDONIANS with the most eminent PERSIAN families [ibid. 7. 4]. DIODORUS SICULUS says they were of the most noble birth in PERSIA [17. 107]. The government of PERSIA was despotic, and conducted in many respects, after the eastern manner, but was not carried so far as to extirpate all nobility, and confound all ranks and orders. It left men who were still great, by themselves and their family, independent of their office and commission. And the reason why the MACEDONIANS kept so easily dominion over them was owing to other causes easy to be found in the historians; though it must be owned that MACHIAVEL'S reasoning is, in itself, just, however doubtful its application to the present case.

20. *integrity and wisdom*: *Essempio veramente raro, & da Filosofi intante loro imaginate & vedute Republiche mai non trovato, vedere dentro ad un medesimo cerchio, fra medesimi cittadini, la liberta & la tirannide, la vita civile & la corotta, la giustitia & la licenza; perche quello ordine solo mantiere quella citta piena di costumi antichi & venerabili. E s'egli auvenisse (che col tempo in ogni modo auverrà) que SAN GIORGIO tutta quella città occupasse, sarrebbe quella una Republica piu dalla VENETIANA memorabile.* [Machiavelli, *History of Florence*, book 8: 'A truly rare example, and one never found by the philosophers in all their dreamed of republics, to see in the same circle, among the same citizens, liberty and tyranny, the civil and the corrupt life, justice and licence, because that order alone keeps that city full of ancient and venerable customs. And should it happen, as it will in time anyway, that St George will occupy all that city, it will be a republic more memorable than the Venetian one.']

21. *three thousand*: Livy, *History of Rome*, 40. 43. [The three Punic wars between Rome and Carthage began in 264 BC and ended in 146 BC with the destruction of Carthage. The tribunes were elected by the Plebeians (commoners) to represent their interests against the Patricians (nobility). A Praetor was a high judicial officer or provincial governor.]

worse instance: ibid. 8. 18.

choice of tyrants: *L'Aigle contre L'Aigle, ROMAINS contre ROMAINS, / Combatans seulement pour le choix de tyrans.* Corneille. [Lines adapted from Corneille, *Cinna*, I. iii: 'Eagle against Eagle, Romans against Romans, / Fighting only for the choice of tyrants.' The period referred to runs from the formation of the first Triumvirate of Julius Caesar, Pompey and Crassus in 60 BC to the end of the second, of Octavian Mark Antony, and Lepidus, in 31 BC.]

23. *that noble fabric . . . blood*: *Dissertation on Parties*, Letter 10 [by Bolingbroke. The *Dissertation* originally appeared in the opposition newspaper, *The Craftsman*.]

24. *malevolence or of flattery*: earlier editions of the *Essays* (1748–68) appended a 'Character of Sir Robert Walpole' as a footnote.

OF THE FIRST PRINCIPLES OF GOVERNMENT

28. *novelties*: earlier editions (1741–60) conclude with a note on 'the present political controversy, with regard to instructions' (mandation of the votes of MPs).

OF THE PARTIES OF GREAT BRITAIN

32. *Court and Country*: earlier editions (1741–68) add a note: 'These words have become of general use, and therefore I shall employ them, without intending to express by them an universal blame of the one party, or approbation of the other. The court-party may, no doubt, on some occasions consult the best interest of the country, and the country-party oppose it. In like manner, the ROMAN parties were denominated *Optimates* and *Populares*; and CICERO, like a true party man, defines the *Optimates* to be such as, in all public conduct, regulated themselves by the sentiments of the best and worthiest of the ROMANS. [*Pro Sextio*, 45.] The term *Country-party* may afford a favourable definition or etymology of the same kind. But it would be folly to draw any argument from that head, and I have regard to it in employing these terms.'

33. *by the former*: earlier editions (1741–68) add: 'I must be understood to mean this of persons who have motives for taking party on any side. For, to tell the truth, the greatest part are commonly men who associate themselves they know not why; from example, from passion, from idleness. But still it is requisite, that there be some source of division, either in principle or interest; otherwise such persons would not find parties. to which they could associate themselves.'

33. *priests . . . ememies to liberty*: earlier editions (1742–68) add a note: 'This proposition is true, notwithstanding, that in the early times of the ENGLISH government, the clergy were the great and principal opposers of the crown. But at that time, their possessions were so immensely great, that they composed a considerable part of the proprietors of ENGLAND, and in many contests were direct rivals of the crown.'

34. *princes*: Judaei sibi ipsi reges imposuere; qui mobilitate vulgi expulsi, resumpta per arma dominatione; fugas civium, urbium eversiones, fratrum, conjugum, parentum neces, aliaque solita regibus ausi, superstitionem fovebant; quia honor sacerdotii firmamentum potentiae assumebatur. [Tacitus, *Histories*, 5. 8: 'The Jews selected their own kings. These were expelled by the fickle mob; but recovering their throne by force, they banished citizens, destroyed towns, killed brothers, wives and parents, and dared every other kind of royal crime without hesitation. But they fostered the national superstition, for they had assumed the priesthood to support their civil authority.']

   superiors: Populi imperium juxta libertatem: paucorum dominatio regiae libidini proprior est. [Tacitus, *Annals*, 6. 42: 'Supremacy of the people is similar to freedom: the distance is small between the domination of a minority and the whim of a monarch.']

37. *Protestant line*: in earlier editions (1741–68) Hume reinforces this claim with a footnote in which he insists that there is a 'real distinction' between Whigs and Tories.

38. *parties*: Some of the opinions delivered in these Essays, with regard to the public transactions of the last century, the Author, on more accurate examination, found reason to retract in his *History* of GREAT BRITAIN. And as he would not enslave himself to the systems of either party, neither would he fetter his judgment by his own preconceived opinions and principles; nor is he ashamed to acknowledge his mistakes. These mistakes were indeed, at that time, almost universal in this kingdom. [In place of the last paragraph of this edition of the essay, editions to 1768 offer various versions of an extended discussion of the differences between Whigs and Tories in England and Scotland since the Revolution. The editions of 1741 and 1742 end with a discussion of why 'the *Jacobite* Party is almost entirely vanish'd from among us'—a passage removed after the 1745 Jacobite rebellion.]

OF SUPERSTITION AND ENTHUSIASM

40. *Priests*: earlier editions (1748–60) add a footnote: 'By *Priests*, I here mean only the pretenders to power and dominion, and to a superior sanctity of character, distinct from virtue and good morals. These are very different from *clergymen*, who are set apart *by the laws*, to the care of sacred matters, and to the conducting our public devotions with greater decency and order. There is no rank of men more to be respected than the latter.'

   priesthood: earlier editions (1748–68) add a footnote, in part reading: 'Modern Judaism and popery, (especially the latter) being the most unphilosophical and absurd superstitions which have yet been known in the world, are the most enslaved by their priests. As the church of ENGLAND may justly be said to retain some mixture of Popish superstition, it partakes also, in its original constitution, of a propensity to priestly power and dominion; particularly in the respect it exacts to the sacerdotal character . . .'

42. *China*: The CHINESE Literati have no priests or ecclesiastical establishment. [Literati, in Dr Johnson's definition, are 'the learned'.]

OF THE DIGNITY OR MEANNESS OF HUMAN NATURE

44. *odious in itself*: earlier editions (1741–68) add: 'Women are generally much more flattered in their youth than men; which may proceed from this reason, among others, that their chief point of honour is considered as much more difficult than ours, and requires to be supported by all that decent pride, which can be instilled into them.'

OF CIVIL LIBERTY

50. *made mention of it*: XENOPHON mentions it; but with a doubt if it be of any advantage to a state. Εἰ δὲ καὶ ἐμπορία ὠφελεῖ τι πόλιν, &c. [Xenophon, *Hiero*, 9.9: 'If commerce also brings gain to a city.'] PLATO totally excludes it from his imaginary republic [*Laws* 4].

51. *eminent writers*: Mr ADDISON and LORD SHAFTESBURY. [See Addison, Tatler, no. 161, and Shaftesbury, *Characteristics*, 'Soliloquy', part 2, § 2.]

52. *still alive*: Dr Swift.

54. *Clodius*: Cicero, *Speech on Behalf of Milo*.

55. *Xenophon*: Κτῆσιν δὲ ἀπ' οὐδενὸς ἂν οὕτω καλὴν κτήσαιντο, ὥσπερ ἀφ' οὗ ἂν προτελέσωσιν εἰς τὴν ἀφορμήν—οἱ δέ γε πλεῖστοι Ἀθηναίων πλείονα λήψονται κατ' ἐνιαυτόν ἢ ὅσα ἂν εἰσενέγκωσιν. οἱ γὰρ μνᾶν προτελέσαντες, ἐγγὺς δυοῖν πρόσοδον ἕξουσι—ὃ δοκεῖ τῶν ἀνθρωπίνων ἀσφαλέστατόν τε καὶ πόλυχρονιώτατον εἶναι. ΞΕΝ. ΠΟΡΟΙ. [Xenophon, *Ways and Means*, 3.9–10: 'No investment can yield them so good a return as the money advanced by them for the capital fund . . . most of the Athenians will get over 100 per cent in a year, and those who advance one *mira* will draw an income of nearly two *mirae*, guaranteed by the state, which is all appearances the safest and most durable of human institutions.']

OF THE RISE AND PROGRESS OF
THE ARTS AND SCIENCES

59. *There is . . . animated*: Est Deus in nobis; agitante calescimus illo: / Imperatus hic, sacrae semina mentis habet. Ovid, *Fasti*, 6. 5–6.

61. *Habet . . . alienos*: Tacitus, *Histories*, 1. 37: 'now he keeps us under his heel as if we were his slaves, and regards us as cheap because we belong to another.'

65. *mighty empire*: If it be asked how we can reconcile to the foregoing principles the happiness, riches, and good police of the CHINESE, who have always been governed by a sole monarch, and can scarcely form an idea of a free government; I would answer that though the CHINESE government be a pure monarchy, it is not, properly speaking, absolute. This proceeds from a peculiarity of the situation of that country: they have no neighbours except the TARTARS, from whom they were secured, at least seemed to be secured, by their famous wall, and by the great superiority of their numbers. By this means, military discipline has always been much neglected amongst them; and their standing forces are mere militia, of the worst kind; and unfit to suppress any general insurrection in countries so extremely populous. The sword, therefore, may properly be said to be always in the hands of the people, which is a sufficient restraint upon the monarch, and obliges him to lay his *mandarins* or governors of provinces under the

restraint of general laws, in order to prevent those rebellions, which we learn from history to have been so frequent and dangerous in that government. Perhaps, a pure monarchy of this kind, were it fitted for a defence against foreign enemies, would be the best of all governments, as having both the tranquillity attending kingly power, and the moderation and liberty of popular assemblies.

70. *Holland*: C'est la politesse d'un Suisse / En HOLLANDE civilisé. Rousseau. [Rousseau, 'Sonnet'.]

authors of those ages: It is needless to cite CICERO or PLINY on this head: they are too much noted. But one is a little surprised to find ARRIAN, a very grave, judicious writer, interrupt the thread of his narration all of a sudden, to tell his readers that he himself is as eminent among the Greeks for eloquence, as ALEXANDER was for arms. [*Expedition of Alexander*, 1. 12.]

Lucretius: This poet (see [*De Rerum Natura*, 4. 1175]) recommends a very extraordinary cure for love, and what one expects not to meet with in so elegant and philosophical a poem. It seems to have been the original of some of Dr SWIFT's images. The elegant CATULLUS and PHAEDRUS fall under the same censure.

71. *master*: ATT. Non mihi videtur ad beate vivendum satis esse virtutem. MAR. At hercule BRUTO meo videtur; cujus ego judicium, pace tua dixerim, longe antepono tuo. [Cicero, *Tusculan Disputations*, 5. 5. 12: 'Atticus: It does not appear to me that virtue can be sufficient for leading a happy life. Marcus: I can assure you, my friend Brutus thinks it sufficient, and with your permission I put his judgment far above yours.' Philalethes' dialogues with Philotionus occur in Jeremy Collier's *Essays* (1697).]

Polybius: 18. 4–7.

Plutarch: *Lives*, Life of Titus Flamininus, 2.

Plutarch: ibid. 17. [In earlier earlier editions (1742–68) Hume adds several extra classical examples.]

72. *Macedonians*: ibid. 9.

inscription: Tacitus, *Annals*, 3. 64.

modern: In the *Self-Tormentor* of TERENCE, CLINIAS, whenever he comes to town, instead of waiting on his mistress, sends for her to come to him.

72. *present age*: Lord SHAFTESBURY, see his *Moralists* [in *Characteristics*].

73. *constraint on his guests*: The frequent mention in ancient authors of that ill-bred custom of the master of the family's eating better bread or drinking better wine at table, than he afforded his guests, is but an indifferent mark of the civility of those ages. See JUVENAL, Satire 5. Pliny [*Natural History*, 14. 14. 91]. Also Pliny [the Younger], *Letters*. [Lucian, *De Mercede Conductis*], *Saturnalia*, etc. There is scarcely any part of EUROPE at present so uncivilized as to admit of such a custom.

74. *even*: See *Relation of three Embassies*, by the Earl of CARLISLE [Charles Howard, first Earl of Carlisle (1629–85)].

decency: earlier editions (1742–62) add: 'I must confess, that my own choice rather leads me to prefer the company of a few select companions, with whom I can, calmly and peaceably, enjoy the feast of reason, and try the justness of every reflection, whether gay or serious, that may occur to me. But as such a delightful society is not every day to be met with, I must think, that mixt companies, without the fair-sex, are the most insipid entertainment in the world, and destitute of gaiety and politeness, as much as of sense and reason. Nothing can keep them from excessive dulness but hard drinking; a remedy worse than the disease.'

75. *first arose*: earlier editions (1742–68) add a discussion of the 'pernicious' modern notions of 'honour' and 'gallantry' detached from virtue, using the example of duelling.

THE EPICUREAN

77. Or, *The man of elegance and pleasure*. The intention of this and the three following essays, is not so much to explain accurately the sentiments of the ancient sects of philosophy, as to deliver the sentiments of sects that naturally form themselves in the world, and entertain different ideas of human life and happiness. I have given each of them the name of the philosophical sect to which it bears the greatest affinity. [See Introduction for a discussion of the relationship of 'The Epicurean', 'The Stoic', 'The Platonist', and 'The Sceptic' to the ancient philosophies.]

79. *Pleasure*: Dia Voluptas. 'Divine pleasure': Lucretius, *De Rerum Natura*, 2.172.

81. *Ye favoured of Heaven*: An imitation of the Syrens song in Tasso, 'O Giovinetti, mentre Aprile & Maggio / V'ammantan di fiorité & verde spoglie,' etc. Torquato Tasso, *Jerusalem Delivered*, 14.62. ['You happy youths whom fresh April and May dress in flowering green of lusty age.']

THE STOIC

83. Or, The man of action and virtue.

THE PLATONIST

91. Or, The man of contemplation and *philosophical* devotion.

THE SCEPTIC

101. *understanding of an angel*: Were I not afraid of appearing too philosophical, I should remind my reader of that famous doctrine, supposed to be fully proved in modern times, 'That tastes and colours, and all other sensible qualities, lie not in the bodies, but merely in the senses.' The case is the same with beauty and deformity, virtue and vice. This doctrine, however, takes off no more from the reality of the latter qualities, than from that of the former; nor need it give any umbrage either to critics or moralists. Though colours were allowed to lie only in the eye, would dyers or painters ever be less regarded or esteemed? There is a sufficient uniformity in the senses and feelings of mankind, to make all these qualities the object of art and reasoning, and to have the greatest influence on life and manners. And as it is certain, that the discovery above mentioned in natural philosophy, makes no alteration on action and conduct, why should a like discovery in moral philosophy make any alteration?

107. *say the philosophers*: 'On the Control of Anger', in Plutarch, *Moralia*.

108. *If plagues ... Catiline*: *An Essay on Man*, 1.155–6.

   knaves and robbers: 'Sayings of Spartans', section 217, in Plutarch, *Moralia*.

   one lauguage more: Cicero, *Tusculan Disputations*, 5.40.

109. *Exile . . . to him*: Plutarch, 'On Exile', in *Moralia*.

111. *consolation*: The Sceptic, perhaps, carries the matter too far, when he limits all philosophical topics and reflections to these two. There seem to be others, whose truth is undeniable, and whose natural tendency is to tranquillize and soften all the passions. Philosophy greedily seizes these; studies them, weighs them, commits them to the memory, and familiarizes them to the mind: and their influence on tempers which are thoughtful, gentle, and moderate, may be considerable. But what is their influence, you will say, if the temper be antecedently disposed after the same manner as that to which they pretend to form it? They may, at least, fortify that temper, and furnish it with views, by which it may entertain and nourish itself. Here are a few examples of such philosophical reflections.

  1. Is it not certain, that every condition has concealed ills? Then why envy anybody?
  2. Every one has known ills; and there is a compensation throughout. Why not be contented with the present?
  3. Custom deadens the sense of both the good and the ill, and levels every thing.
  4. Health and humour all. The rest of little consequence, except these be affected.
  5. How many other good things have I? Then why be vexed for one ill?
  6. How many are happy in the condition of which I complain? How many envy me?
  7. Every good must be paid for: fortune by labour, favour by flattery. Would I keep the price, yet have the commodity?
  8. Expect not too great happiness in life. Human nature admits it not.
  9. Propose not a happiness too complicated. But does that depend on me? Yes: the first choice does. Life is like a game: one may choose the game: and passion, by degrees, seizes the proper object.
  10. Anticipate by your hopes and fancy future consolation, which time infallibly brings to every affliction.
  11. I desire to be rich. Why? That I may possess many fine objects; houses, gardens, equipage, etc. How many fine objects does nature offer to every one without expense? If enjoyed, sufficient. If not: see the effect of custom or

of temper, which would soon take off the relish of the riches.

12. I desire fame. Let this occur: if I act well, I shall have the esteem of all my aquaintance. And what is all the rest to me?

These reflections are so obvious, that it is a wonder they occur not to every man. So convincing, that it is a wonder they persuade not every man. But, perhaps, they do occur to, and persuade most men, when they consider human life by a general and calm survey: but where any real, affecting incident happens; when passion is awakened, fancy agitated, example draws, and counsel urges; the philosopher is lost in the man, and he seeks in vain for that persuasion which before seemed so firm and unshaken. What remedy for this inconvenience? Assist yourself by a frequent perusal of the entertaining moralists: have recourse to the learning of PLUTARCH, the imagination of LUCIAN, the eloquence of CICERO, the wit of SENECA, the gaiety of MONTAIGNE, the sublimity of SHAFTESBURY. Moral precepts, so couched, strike deep, and fortify the mind against the illusions of passion. But trust not altogether to external aid: by habit and study acquire that philosophical temper which both gives force to reflection, and by rendering a great part of your happiness independent, takes off the edge from all disorderly passions, and tranquillizes the mind. Despise not these helps; but confide not too much in them neither; unless nature has been favourable in the temper with which she had endowed you.

27

OF NATIONAL CHARACTERS

114. *thoughtless and ignorant*: It is a saying of MENANDER, *Κομψὸς στρατιώτης, οὐδ' ἂν εἰ πλάττει θεὸς Οὐθεὶς γένοιτ' ἄν.* Menander apud Stobaeum. [In the eighteenth century the work of Menander was known only through collections such as those of the fifth-century AD Greek anthologist Stobaeus.] *It is not in the power even of God to make a polite soldier.* The contrary observation with regard to the manners of soldiers takes place in our days. This seems to me a presumption, that the ancients owed all their refinement and civility to books and study; for which, indeed, a soldier's life is not so well calculated. Company and the world is their sphere. And if

there be any politeness to be learned from company, they will certainly have a considerable share of it.

115. *from which it is derived*: Though all mankind have a strong propensity to religion at certain times and in certain dispositions, yet are there few or none who have it to that degree, and with that constancy, which is requisite to support the character of this profession. It must therefore happen, that clergymen, being drawn from the common mass of mankind, as people are to other employments, by the views of profit, the greater part, though no atheists or free-thinkers, will find it necessary, on particular occasions, to feign more devotion than they are at that time possessed of, and to maintain the appearance of fervour and seriousness, even when jaded with the exercises of their religion, or when they have their minds engaged in the common occupations of life. They must not, like the rest of the world, give scope to their natural movements and sentiment: they must set a guard over their looks, and words, and actions: and in order to support the veneration paid them by the multitude, they must not only keep a remarkable reserve, but must promote the spirit of superstition, by a continued grimace and hypocrisy. This dissimulation often destroys the candour and ingenuity of their temper, and makes an irreparable breach in their character.

If by chance any of them be possessed of a temper more susceptible of devotion than usual, so that he has but little occasion for hypocrisy to support the character of his profession, it is so natural for him to overrate this advantage, and to think that it atones for every violation of morality, that frequently he is not more virtuous than the hypocrite. And though few dare openly avow those exploded opinions, *that every thing is lawful of the saints*, and *that they alone have property in their goods*; yet may we observe, that these principles lurk in every bosom, and represent a zeal for religious observances as so great a merit, that it may compensate for many vices and enormities. This observation is so common, that all prudent men are on their guard when they meet with any extraordinary appearance of religion; though at the same time they confess, that there are many exceptions to this general rule, and that probity and superstition, or even probity and fanaticism, are not altogether and in every instance incompatible.

Most men are ambitious; but the ambition of other men

may commonly be satisfied by excelling in their particular profession, and thereby promoting the interests of society. The ambition of the clergy can often be satisfied only by promoting ignorance and superstition, and implicit faith, and pious frauds. And having got what ARCHIMEDES only wanted, (namely, another world, on which he could fix his engines,) no wonder they move this world at their pleasure.

Most men have an overweening conceit of themselves; but *these* have a peculiar temptation to that vice, who are regarded with such veneration, and are even deemed sacred, by the ignorant multitude.

Most men are apt to bear a particular regard for members of their own profession; but as a lawyer, or physician, or merchant, does each of them follow out his business apart, the interests of men of these professions are not so closely united as the interests of clergymen of the same religion; where the whole body gains by the veneration paid to their common tenets, and by the suppression of antagonists.

Few men can bear contradiction with patience; but the clergy too often proceed even to a degree of fury on this head: because all their credit and livelihood depend upon the belief which their opinions meet with; and they alone pretend to a divine and supernatural authority, or have any colour for representing their antagonists as impious and profane. The *Odium Theologicum*, or Theological Hatred, is noted even to a proverb, and means that degree of rancour which is the most furious and implacable.

Revenge is a natural passion to mankind; but seems to reign with the greatest force in priests and women: because, being deprived of the immediate exertion of anger, in violence and combat, they are apt to fancy themselves despised on that account; and their pride supports their vindictive disposition.

Thus many of the vices of human nature are, by fixed moral causes, inflamed in that profession; and though several individuals escape the contagion, yet all wise governments will be on their guard against the attempts of a society, who will for ever be combined into one faction; and while it acts as a society, will for ever be actuated by ambition, pride, revenge, and a persecuting spirit.

The temper of religion is grave and serious; and this is the character required of priests, which confines them to strict rules of decency, and commonly prevents irregularity and intemperance amongst them. The gaiety, much less the excesses of pleasure, is not permitted in that body; and this virtue is, perhaps, the only one which they owe to their profession. In religion, indeed, founded on speculative principles, and where public discourses make a part of religious service, it may also be supposed that the clergy will have a considerable share in the learning of the times; though it is certain that their taste in eloquence will always be greater than their proficiency in reasoning and philosophy. But whoever possesses the other noble virtues of humanity, meekness, and moderation, as very many of them no doubt do, is beholden for them to nature or reflection, not to the genius of his calling.

It was no bad expedient in the old ROMANS, for preventing the strong effect of the priestly character, to make it a law, that no one should be received into the sacerdotal office till he was past fifty years of age. [Dionysius of Halicarnassus, *Roman Antiquities*, 2. 21.] The living a layman till that age, it is presumed, would be able to fix the character.

115. *why not the same with men*: CAESAR [*Gallic War*, 4. 2] says, that the GALLIC horses were very good, the GERMAN very bad. We find in 7. 65 that he was obliged to remount some GERMAN cavalry with GALLIC horses. At present no part of EUROPE has so bad horses of all kinds as FRANCE: but GERMANY abounds with excellent war-horses. This may beget a little suspicion, that even animals depend not on the climate, but on the different breeds, and on the skill and care in rearing them. The north of England abounds in the best horses of all kinds which are perhaps in the world. In the neighbouring counties, north side of the Tweed, no good horses of any kind are to be met with. STRABO, [*Geography*, 2. 3. 7] rejects, in great measure, the influence of climates upon man. All is custom and education, says he. It is not from nature that the ATHENIANS are learned, the LACEDEMONIANS ignorant, and the THEBANS too, who are still nearer neighbours to the former. Even the difference of animals, he adds, depends not on climate.

117. *probity*: A small sect or society amidst a greater, are commonly most regular in their morals; because they are more remarked, and the faults of individuals draw dishonour on the whole. The only exception to this rule is, when the superstition and prejudices of the large society are so strong as to throw an infamy on the smaller society, independent of their morals.

For in that case, having no character either to save or gain, they become careless of their behaviour, except among themselves.

118. *Romans*: Livy, *History of Rome*, 34. 17.

120. *uncertain and fallacious*: I am apt to suspect the negroes to be naturally inferior to the whites. There scarcely ever was a civilized nation of that complexion, nor even any individual, eminent either in action or speculation. No ingenious manufactures amongst them, no arts, no sciences. On the other hand, the most rude and barbarous of the whites, such as the ancient GERMANS, the present TARTARS, have still something eminent about them, in their valour, form of government, or some other particular. Such a uniform and constant difference could not happen, in so many countries and ages, if nature had not made an original distinction between these breeds of men. Not to mention our colonies, there are NEGROE slaves dispersed all over EUROPE, of whom none ever discovered any symptoms of ingenuity; though low people, without education, will start up amongst us, and distinguish themselves in every profession. In JAMAICA, indeed, they talk of one negroe as a man of parts and learning; but it is likely he is admired for slender accomplishments, like a parrot who speaks a few words plainly.

121. *late*: Berkeley, *Alciphron, or the Minute Philosopher*, 5. 26.

122. *for its instruction*: 'Sed Cantaber unde / Stoicus? antiqui prasertim aetate Metelli. / Nunc totus GRAIAS nostrasque habet orbis ATHENAS. / GALLIA causidicos docuit facunda BRITANNOS: / De conducendo loquitur jam rhetore THULE.' Juvenal, *Satires*, 15. 108–10. ['But how could a Cantabrian be a Stoic, and that too in the days of old Metellus? Today the whole world has its Greek and Roman Athens; eloquent Gaul has trained the pleaders of Britain, and distant Thule talks of hiring a rhetorician.']

An eminent writer: William Temple, *Observations upon the United Provinces of the Netherlands* (1673).

124. *Diodorus Siculus*: 5. 26.

Persian manners: BABYLONI *maxime in vinum, & quae ebrietatem, effusi sunt*. Quintus Curtius Rufus, *History of Alexander the Great*, 5. 1. 37–8. ['The Babylonians in particular are devoted to wine and the consequences of drunkenness.']

124. *a better drinker*: Plutarch, *Symposiaca Problemata*, book 1, question 4.

OF TRAGEDY

126. *passion and occupation*: Dubos, *Réflexions critiques sur la poésie et la peinture* (1719–33), part 1, ch. 1.

127. *theory above mentioned*: Fontanelle, 'Réflexions sur la poétique', § 36. *Œuvres*, 3. 34.

129. *calm and indifferent*: Painters make no scruple of representing distress and sorrow, as well as any other passion; but they seem not to dwell so much on these melancholy affections as the poets, who, though they copy every motion of the human breast, yet pass quickly over the agreeable sentiments. A painter represents only one instant; and if that be passionate enough, it is sure to affect and delight the spectator; but nothing can furnish to the poet a variety of scenes, and incidents, and sentiments, except distress, terror, or anxiety. Complete joy and satisfaction is attended with security, and leaves no further room for action.

131. *the elder Pliny*: Pliny, *Natural History*, book 35, ch. 40: Illud vero perquam rarum ac memoria dignum, etiam suprema opera artificum, imperfectasque tabulas, sicut, IRIN ARISTIDIS, TYNDARIDAS NICOMACHI, MEDEAM TIMOMACHI, et quam diximus VENEREM APELLIS, in majori admiratione esse quam perfecta. Quippe in iis lineamenta reliqua, ipsaeque cogitationes artificum spectantur, atque in lenocinio commendationis dolor est manus, cum id ageret, extinctae.

OF COMMERCE

155. *causes*: editions of the *Essays* from 1752 to 1768 read 'cases'.

156. *society*: Mons. MELON, in his political essay on commerce, asserts, that even at present, if you divide FRANCE into 20 parts, 16 are labourers or peasants; two only artizans; one belonging to the law, church, and military; and one merchants, financiers, and bourgeois. This calculation is certainly very erroneous. In FRANCE, ENGLAND, and indeed most parts of EUROPE, half of the inhabitants live in cities; and even of those who live in the country, a great number are artizans, perhaps above a third. [See Melon, *Essai politique sur le commerce* (1734).]

158. *near forty thousand men*: Thucydides, 7.75.

   four hundred sail: Diodorus Siculus [2.5.]. This account, I own, is somewhat suspicious, not to say worse; chiefly because this army was not composed of citizens, but of mercenary forces.

   Gauls and Latins: Livy [*History of Rome*, 7.25.]: 'Adeo in quae laboramus,' says he 'sola crevimus divitias luxuriemque.' ['So strictly has our growth been limited to the only things for which we strive—wealth and luxury.']

159. *as well as pleasure*: The more ancient ROMANS lived in perpetual war with all their neighbours: and in old LATIN, the term, *hostis*, expressed both a stranger and an enemy. This is remarked by CICERO; but by him it is ascribed to the humanity of his ancestors, who softened, as much as possible, the denomination of an enemy, by calling him by the same appellation which signified a stranger [*On Duties*, 1.12.]. It is however much more probable, from the manners of the times, that the ferocity of those people was so great as to make them regard all strangers as enemies, and call them by the same name. It is not, besides, consistent with the most common maxims of policy or of nature, that any state should regard its public enemies with a friendly eye, or preserve any such sentiments for them as the ROMAN orator would ascribe to his ancestors. Not to mention, that the early ROMANS really exercised piracy, as we learn from their first treaties with CARTHAGE, preserved by POLYBIUS [3], and consequently like the SALEE and ALGERINE rovers, were actually at war with most nations, and a stranger and an enemy were with them almost synonymous. [The 'Salee and Algerine rovers' were pirates operating from the Barbary coast.]

OF REFINEMENT IN THE ARTS

171. *400,000*: The inscription on the PLACE-DE-VENDOME says 440,000.

177. *vice is advantageous to the public?*: Mandeville, *The Fable of the Bees: or, Private Vices, Publick Benefits* (1714–29). [Mandeville's paradoxical and deliberately shocking argument offered a very influential model of the economic working of society for writers in the first half of the eighteenth century.]

OF INTEREST

186. *Dion*: Dio Cassius, *Roman History*, 51. 21. 5.

187. *Rome . . . 6 per cent*: COLUMELLA, [On Agriculture, 3. 3. 9.]
   Italy . . . 6 per cent: Pliny the Younger, *Letters*, 7. 18.
   in Bithynia 12: ibid. 10. 54.

OF THE BALANCE OF TRADE

189. *figs and discoverer*: Plutarch, *Moralia*, 'On Curiosity', 16.

191. *external operation*: There is another cause, though more limited in its operation, which checks the wrong balance of trade, to every particular nation to which the kingdom trades. When we import more goods than we export, the exchange turns against us, and this becomes a new encouragement to export; as much as the charge of carriage and insurance of the money which becomes due would amount to. For the exchange can never rise but a little higher than that sum.

193. *L'Abbé du Bos*: see Dubos, *Les intérests de l'Angleterre malentendus dans la présente guerre* (1703).

   level is preserved: It must carefully be remarked, that throughout this discourse, wherever I speak of the level of money, I mean always its proportional level to the commodities, labour, industry, and skill, which is in the several states. And I assert, that where these advantages are double, triple, quadruple, to what they are in the neighbouring states, the money infallibly will also be double, triple, quadruple. The only circumstance that can obstruct the exactness of these proportions, is the expense of transporting the commodities from one place to another; and this expense is sometimes unequal. Thus the corn, cattle, cheese, butter, of DERBYSHIRE, cannot draw the money of LONDON, so much as the manufactures of LONDON draw the money of DERBYSHIRE. But this objection is only a seeming one; for so far as the transport of commodities is expensive, so far is the communication between the places obstructed and imperfect.

195. *advantages*: We observed in Essay III ['Of Money', not included in this selection] that money, when encreasing, gives encouragement to industry, during the interval between the encrease of money and rise of the prices. A good effect of this nature may follow too from paper-credit; but it is dangerous

to precipitate matters, at the risk of losing all by the failing of that credit, as must happen upon any violent shock in public affairs.

199. *all . . . agree*: Thucydides, 2. 13, and Diodorus Siculus, 12. 40; Aeschines, *The Speech on the Embassy*, 17, and Demosthenes, *Third Olympiac Oration*, 24.

Demosthenes and Polybius: Demosthenes, *On the Navy-Boards*, 19; Polybius, 2. 62.

200. *thirty years*: Livy, 14. 40. [Here, Philip is Philip V. The 'thirty years' are from the peace settlement with Rome in 197 BC to the defeat of Perseus by Paullus in 168.]

2,400,000: Lucius Aemilius Paullus brought this treasure back from his victory over Perseus. For the first estimated figure see Velleius Paterculus, [*Historiae Romanae*, 1. 9. 6.] For the second, see Pliny, [*Natural History*, 33. 50.]

Switzerland: The poverty which STANIAN speaks of is only to be seen in the most mountainous cantons, where there is no commodity to bring money. And even there the people are not poorer than in the diocese of SALTSBURGH on the one hand, or SAVOY on the other. [See Stanyan, *An Account of Switzerland Written in the Year 1714* (1714).]

Appian: Roman History, Preface 10.

OF PUBLIC CREDIT

203. *above mentioned*: 'Of the Balance of Trade.'

Plato: Alcibiades, 1. 122d–123b.

Arrian: Expedition of Alexander, 3. 16 and 3. 19.

Plutarch: [*Lives*, Life of Alexander, 36 and 37.] He makes these treasures amount to 80,000 talents, or about 15 millions sterl. QUINTUS CURTIUS [5. 2] says, that ALEXANDER found in SUSA above 50,000 talents.

in reserve: Strabo, 1. 13.

205. *negotiations*: earlier editions (1742–68) continue with comments on 'CIRCULATION', a term which Hume claims not to understand. He admits the benefits of rapid circulation of commodities, but not of stocks, and then comments: 'what production we owe to CHANGE-ALLEY, or even what consumption, except that of coffee, and pen, ink, and paper, I

have not yet learned; nor can one forsee the loss or decay of any one beneficial commerce or commodity, though that place and all its inhabitants were for ever buried in the ocean.'

215. *sed vulgus . . . poterant*: *History*, 3. 55. ['But the mob attended in delight on the great indulgences he bestowed; the most foolish citizens bought them, while the wise regarded as worthless privileges which could neither be granted nor accepted if the state was to stand.' Tacitus is referring to the attempts of the emperor Vitellius to secure popular support against Vespasian in a power struggle in AD 69.]

safety of thousands: I have heard it has been computed, that all the creditors of the public, natives and foreigners, amount only to 17,000. These make a figure at present on their income; but, in case of a public bankruptcy, would, in an instant, become the lowest, as well as the most wretched of the people. The dignity and authority of the landed gentry and nobility is much better rooted; and would render the contention very unequal, if ever we come to that extremity. One would incline to assign to this event a very near period, such as half a century, had not our fathers' prophecies of this kind been already found fallacious, by the duration of our public credit, so much beyond all reasonable expectation. When the astrologers in FRANCE were every year fortelling the death of HENRY IV. *These fellows*, says he, *must be right at last*. We shall, therefore, be more cautious than to assign any precise date; and shall content ourselves with pointing out the event in general.

OF SOME REMARKABLE CUSTOMS

217. *he proved its advantages*: His harangue for it is still extant; περὶ Συμμορίας. [*On the Navy-Boards*, §§ 17–22.]

finances: In Defence of Ctesiphon, §§ 102–9.

enrolling them in the troops: Plutarch, [*Moralia*, 'Lives of the Ten Orators': 'Hypereides'.] DEMOSTHENES gives a different account of this law. [*Against Aristogiton*, Oration 2.] He says that its purpose was, to render the ἄτιμοι ἐπίτιμοι ['the disenfranchised enfranchised'], or to restore the privilege of bearing offices to those who had been declared incapable. Perhaps these were clauses of the same law. [Philip of Macedon defeated the Thebans and Athenians at Chaeronea in 338 BC.]

218. *senate*: The senate of the Bean was only a less numerous mob, chosen by lot from among the people; and their authority was not great.

Democracy to subsist: Aeschines [*Against Ctesiphon*, 5–8]. It is remarkable, that the first step after the dissolution of Democracy to CRITIAS and the Thirty, was to annul the γραζή παρανόμων, as we learn frov Δενοτυθεξετ κατά Τιμοκ. [*Against Timocrates*] The orator in this oration gives us the words of the law, establishing the γραφή παρανόμων. [sec. 33] And he accounts for it, from the same principles we here reason upon.

Thebes: Plutarch, *Lives*, Life of Pelopidas, 25.

repeal of this law: Demosthenes, *Olynthiac Orations*, 1. 2. [The 'demagogue' in question was Eubulus, a fourth-century politician who instigated legislation requiring that the city's surplus revenue be put into the Theoric Fund, for the support of public festivals, and making the repeal of the measure illegal.]

219. *Leptines . . . more*: Demosthenes, *Against Leptines*, §§ 1–4.

bills of attainder: Demosthenes, *Against Aristocrates*, § 86.

Lord Shaftesbury: see Shaftesbury, 'An Essay on the Freedom of Wit and Humour', part 3, § 2, in *Characteristics*.

OF THE POPULOUSNESS OF ANCIENT NATIONS

224. *decay in human nature*: COLUMELLA says [*On Agriculture*, 3. 8] that in AEGYPT and AFRICA the bearing of twins was frequent, and even customary; *gemini partus familiares, ac poene solennes sunt*. If this was true, there is a physical difference both in countries and ages. For travellers make no such remarks on these countries at present. On the contrary, we are apt to suppose the northern nations more prolific. As those two countries were provinces of the ROMAN empire, it is difficult, though not altogether absurd, to suppose that such a man as COLUMELLA might be mistaken with regard to them.

225. *discernment*: Montesquieu, *Lettres Persanes* (1721), letters 112–22, and *L'Esprit des Loix* (1748), book 23.

226. *had perished*: This too is a good reason why the small-pox does not depopulate countries so much as may at first sight be imagined. Where there is room for more people, they will

always arise, even without the assistance of naturalization bills. It is remarked by DON GERONIMO DE USTARIZ, that the provinces of SPAIN, which send most people to the INDIES, are most populous; which proceeds from their superior riches. [See Ustariz, *Theorica y practica de comercio, y de marina* (1724).]

228. *old age or sickness*: Suetonius, *Lives of the Caesars*, Life of Claudius, 23.

useless burden: Plutarch, *Lives*, Life of Marcus Cato, 4.

recommends: *On Agriculture*, 1.6 and 11.1.

Ovid: *Amores*, 1.6.

other authors: Suetonius, [*Of Illustrious Rhetoricians*, 3]. So also the ancient poet, *Janitoris tintinnire impedimenta audio*. ['I hear the door-keeper's impediments rattling.' 'The ancient poet' is Africanus Vopisco.]

Demosthenes: *Against Onetor*, 1.37.

more certain evidence: The same practice was very common in ROME; but CICERO seems not to think this evidence so certain as the testimony of free-citizens. [*A Speech in Defence of Marcus Caelius*, 28.]

229. *custom had assigned for them*: [Seneca, *Epistle* 122] The inhuman sports exhibited at ROME, may justly be considered too as an effect of the people's contempt for slaves, and was also a great cause of the general inhumanity of their princes and rulers. Who can read the accounts of the amphitheatrical entertainments without horror? Or who is surprized, that the emperors should treat that people in the same way the people treated their inferiors? One's humanity, on that occasion, is apt to renew the barbarous wish of CALIGULA, that the people had but one neck. A man could almost be pleased, by a single blow, to put an end to such a race of monsters. You may thank GOD, says the author above cited [*Epistle* 7], addressing himself to the ROMAN people, that you have a master (*viz.* the mild and merciful NERO) who is incapable of learning cruelty from your example. This was spoke in the beginning of his reign, but he fitted them very well afterwards, and no doubt was considerably improved by the sight of the barbarous objects, to which he had, from his infancy, been accustomed.

subjects: We may here observe, that if domestic slavery really encreased populousness, it would be an exception to the general rule, that the happiness of any society and its populousness are necessary attendants. A master, from humour or interest, may make his slaves very unhappy, yet be careful, from interest, to increase their number. Their marriage is not a matter of choice with them, more than any other action of their life.

230. *Cilicia*: Ten thousand slaves in a day have often been sold for the use of the ROMANS at DELUS in CICILIA [Strabo, *Geography*, 14.5.2].

231. *did not increase*: Minore indies plebe ingenua ['The free-born population dwindled day by day'], says Tacitus [*Annals*, 4.27].

verna: As *servus* was the name of the genus, and *verna* of the species, without any correlative, this forms a strong presumption, that the latter were by far the least numerous. It is an universal observation which we may form upon language, that where two related parts of a whole bear any relation to each other, in numbers, rank, or consideration, there are always correlative terms invented, which answer to both the parts, and express their mutual relation. If they bear no proportion to each other, the term is only invented for the less, and marks its distinction from the whole. Thus *man* and *woman*, *master* and *servant*, *father* and *son*, *prince* and *subject*, *stranger* and *citizen*, are correlative terms. But the words, *seaman*, *carpenter*, *smith*, *tailor*, etc. have no correspondent terms, which express those who are no seamen, or carpenters, etc. Languages differ very much with regard to the particular words where this distinction obtains; and may thence afford very strong inferences, concerning the manners and customs of different nations. The military government of the ROMAN emperors had exalted the soldiery so high, that they balanced all the other orders of the state. Hence *miles* and *paganus* became relative terms; a thing, till then, unknown to ancient, and still so to modern languages. Modern superstition exalted the clergy so high, that they overbalanced the whole state: hence *clergy* and *laity* are terms opposed in all modern languages, and in these alone. And from the same principles I infer, that if the number of slaves bought by the ROMANS from foreign countries, had not extremely exceeded those which were bred at home, *verna* would have had a correlative, which would have expressed the former species of slaves. But these, it would seem, composed the main body of the ancient slaves, and the latter were but a few exceptions.

231. *of that kind*: *Verna* is used by Roman writers as a word equivalent to *scurra* ['fashionable idler'], on account of the petulance and impudence of those slaves [Martial, *Epigrams*, 1. 41]. Horace also mentions the *vernae procaces* ['saucy slaves', *Satires*, 2. 6. 66]; and Petronius [*Satyricon*, ch. 24], *vernula urbanitas* ['of the sophistication of the home bred slave']. Seneca [*On Providence*, 1. 6.], *vernularum licentiae* ['slave boys by their forwardness'].

justness of this observation: It is computed in the West Indies, that a stock of slaves grow worse five *per cent* every year, unless new slaves be bought to recruit them. They are not able to keep up their number, even in those warm countries, where clothes and provisions are so easily got. How much more must this happen in European countries, and in or near great cities? I shall add, that, from the experience of our planters, slavery is as little advantageous to the master as to the slave, wherever hired servants can be procured. A man is obliged to clothe and feed his slave; and he does no more for his servant. The price of the first purchase is, therefore, so much loss to him; not to mention, that the fear of punishment will never draw so much labour from a slave, as the dread of being turned off and not getting another service, will from a freeman.

slaves born in it: [Cornelius Nepos, *Lives of Illustrious Men*, Life of Atticus, 13]. We may remark, that Atticus's estate lay chiefly in Epirus, which, being a remote, desolate place, would render it profitable for him to rear slaves there.

Strabo: 7. 3. 12.

Demosthenes: *Against Meidias*, 45–50.

Isocrates: *Panegyricus*.

Politics: 7. 10.

barbarous language: Aristophanes [*The Knights*, 1. 17]. The ancient scholiast remarks on this passage βαρβαρίζει ὡς δοῦλος ['he speaks barbarically like a slave'].

his father: Demosthenes, *Against Aphobus*, 1. 9–11.

232. *cabinet-makers*: κλινοποιοί, makers of those beds which the ancients lay upon at meals.

Plutarch: *Lives*, Life of Cato, 21.

breeding from them: Non temere ancillae eius rei causa comparantur ut pariant. [Justinian, *Digest* 5. 3. 27; 'it is not

ususal for female slaves to be acquired for breeding purposes.']
The following texts are to the same purpose. 'Spadonem
morbosum non esse, neque vitiosum, verius mihi videtur; sed
sanum esse, sicuti illum qui unum testiculum, habet, qui etiam
generare potest.' [*Digest* 21. 1, Law 6: 'A slave who has been
castrated is not, I think, diseased or defective, but sound; just
as one who has only one testicle, and is still capable of
reproduction.'] 'Sin autem quis ita spado sit, ut tam necessaria
pars corporis penitus absit, morbosus est.' [Law 7: 'Where,
however, a slave has been castrated in such a way that any
part of his body required for the purpose of generation is
absolutely absent, he is considered diseased.'] His impotence,
it seems was only regarded so far as his health or life might be
affected by it. In other respects, he was full as valuable. The
same reasoning is employed with regard to female slaves.
'Quaeritur de ea muliere quae semper mortuos parit, an
morbosa sit? et ait Sabinus, si vulvae vitio hoc contingit,
morbosam esse.' [Law 14: 'The question was asked whether a
female slave was diseased who always produced dead children. Sabinus says that if this was caused by an uterine affection, she must be so considered.'] It had even been doubted,
whether a woman pregnant was morbid or vitiated; and it is
determined, that she is sound, not on account of the value of
her offspring, but because it is the natural part or office
of women to bear children. 'Si mulier praegnans venerit,
inter omnes convenit sanam eam esse. Maximum enim ac
praecipuum munus foeminarum accipere ac tueri conceptum.
Puerperam quoque sanam esse; si modo nihil extrinsecus
accedit, quod corpus ejus in aliquam valetudinem immitteret.
De sterili Coelius distinguere Trebatium dicit, ut si natura,
sterilis sit, sana sit; si vitio corporis, contra.' [Ibid.: 'Where a
pregnant female slave is sold, it is held by all the authorities
that she is sound, for it is the greatest and most important
function of a woman to conceive and preserve a child. A
woman in child birth is also sound provided nothing else
happens to cause her bodily illness. Caelius says Trebatius
makes a distinction, in the case of sterility, for if a woman is
sterile by nature she is healthy, but if this occurs through
some bodily defect she is not.']

233. *put to death*: Tacitus, *Annals*, 14. 43.

females to be breeders: The slaves in the great houses had
little rooms assigned to them called *cellae*. Whence the name
of cell was transferred to the monk's room in a convent. See

further on this head, Justus Lipsius, [*Saturnalium Sermonum Libri Duo*, ch. 14 (1585)]. These form strong presumptions against the marriage and propagation of the family slaves.

233. *Hesiod*: *Works and Days*, 1. 405, 1. 602.

individuals: Strabo, 8. 5. 4.

the same author: Xenophon, *Ways and Means*, 4. 14.

to each slave: Cato, *De Re Rustica*, 56; Commentary of Aelius Donatus on Terence's *Phormio*, 1. 1. 9; Seneca, *Letters*, 80. 7–8.

Cato: *De Re Rustica*, 10. 11.

234. *Varro*: *On Agriculture*, 1. 18.

same author: Ibid. 1. 17.

Columella: *On Agriculture*, 1. 8. 5.

Hoc profecere . . . adhibendus: Pliny, *Natural History*, 33. 6. 26: ['This is the progress achieved by our legions of slaves—a foreign rabble in our homes so that we now have to employ an attendant to tell people's names even in the case of slaves.'] See also Tacitus, *Annals*, 14. 44.

Varro: *On Agriculture*, 2. 10.

suspicions: Pastoris duri est hic filius, ille bubulci. [Juvenal, Satire 11, 151: 'One is the son of a hardy shepherd; another of the cattle-man.']

Columella: *On Agriculture*, 1. 8.

235. *Appian*: *The Civil Wars*, 1. 7.

Plutarch: *Lives*, Life of Tiberius Gracchus, 8. 3.

βαρβαρικα δεσμωτηρια: To the same purpose is that passage of the elder SENECA [*The Controversies*, 5. 5]. 'Arata quondam populis rura, singulorum ergastulorum sunt; latiusque nunc villici, quam olim reges, imperant.' ['It is for this that land once ploughed by whole peoples belongs to single slave farms, and bailiffs have wider sway than kings.'] 'At nunc eadem,' says PLINY, 'vincti pedes, damnatae manus, inscripti vultus exercent.' ['But nowadays those agricultural operations are performed by slaves with fettered ankles and by the hands of malefactors with branded faces.' *Natural History*, 18. 4]. So also MARTIAL. 'Et sonet innumera compede Thuscus ager.' ['and Tuscan fields clank with countless fettered slaves.' *Epigrams*, 9. 22]. And LUCAN. 'Tum longos jungere fines / Agrorum, et quondam duro sulcata Camilli / Vomere, et antiquas Curiorum passa ligones / Longa sub ignotis extendere rura colonis.' ['Next they extended the boundaries of their lands until those acres which were once furrowed by the iron plough of Camillus and felt the spade of Curius long ago grew into vast estates tilled by foreign cultivators.' *The Civil War*, 1. 167–70]. 'Vincto fossore coluntur / Hesperiare segetes.' ['The corn fields of Italy are tilled by chained labourers.' *The Civil War*, 7. 402].

235. *Florus*: *Epitome of Roman History*, 2. 7.

same expedient: ibid. 2. 18.

236. *scarcely*: TACITUS blames it [*Germany*, 19].

Plutarch: [*Moralia*, 'On Brotherly Love', 18]. SENECA also approves of the exposing of sickly infirm children ['On Anger', 1. 15].

kill their children: Sextus Empiricus, *Outlines of Pyrrhonism*, 3. 24.

237. *between them*: The practice of leaving great sums of money to friends, though one had near relations, was common in GREECE as well as ROME; as we may gather from LUCIAN. This practice prevails much less in modern times; and BEN JOHNSON'S VOLPONE is therefore almost entirely extracted from ancient authors, and suits better the manners of those times.

It may justly be thought, that the liberty of divorces in Rome was another discouragement to marriage. Such a practice prevents not quarrels from *humour*, but rather increases them; and occasions also those from *interest*, which are much more dangerous and destructive. See further on this head, Essays moral, political, and literary, Part 1. essay XIX. ['Of Polygamy and Divorces', not included in his selection.] Perhaps too the unnatural lusts of the ancients ought to be taken into consideration as of some moment. [The plot of *Volpone* involves Volpone feigning sickness in order to extract gifts from suitors who expect to inherit his wealth in return.]

238. *Xenophon*: *The Expedition of Cyrus*, 7. 6.

ambassadors: Demosthenes ['On the Embassy', 158]. He calls it a considerable sum.

sometimes two: Thucydides, 3. 17.

238. *Polybius's time*: Polybius, 6. 39.

   proportion: Livy, *History of Rome*, 41. 7, 13, and elsewhere.

239. *among the citizens*: CAESAR gave the centurions ten times the gratuity of the common soldiers: [*Gallic War*, 8. 4]. In the RHODIAN cartel, mentioned afterwards, no distinction in the ransom was made on account of ranks in the army.

   proprietors had perished: Diodorus Siculus, 12. 59; Thucydides, 3. 92.

   repeople them: Diodorus Siculus, 12. 82.

   Plutarch: *Lives*, Life of Timoleon, 23.

240. *seven acres*: Pliny [*Natural History*, 18. 4]. The same author, in [18. 7], says, *Verumque fatentibus latifundia perdidere ITALIAM: iam vero et provincias. Sex domi semissem AFRICAE possidebant, cum interfecit eos NERO princeps.* ['And if the truth be confessed, large estates have been the ruin of Italy, and are now proving the ruin of the provinces too—half of Africa was owned by six landlords, when the emperor Nero put them to death.'] In this view, the barbarous butchery committed by the first ROMAN emperors was not, perhaps, so destructive to the public as we may imagine. These never ceased till they had extinguished all the illustrious families, which had enjoyed the plunder of the world, during the latter ages of the republic. The new nobles who rose in their place, were less splendid, as we learn from Tacitus [*Annals*, 3. 55].

   political reasonings: The ancient soldiers, being free citizens, above the lowest rank, were all married. Our modern soldiers are either forced to live unmarried, or their marriages turn to small account towards the increase of mankind. A circumstance which ought, perhaps, to be taken into consideration, as of some consequence in favour of the ancients.

241. *Greeks*: As ABYDUS, mentioned by LIVY [13. 17, 18] and POLYBIUS [16. 34]. As also the XANTHIANS [Appian, *Civil War*, 4. 80].

   Plutarch: *Lives*, Life of Aratus, 6.

242. *slave . . . for 500*: Diodorus Siculus, 20. 84.

   in this respect: LYSIAS, who was himself of the popular faction, and very narrowly escaped from the thirty tyrants, says, that the Democracy was as violent a government as the Oligarchy. [Oration 25, *Defence against a Charge of Subverting the Democracy*, 27].

243. *Greece*: Cicero, *Philippics*, 1.1.

> *Lysias*: As Oration 12, *Against Eratosthenes*; Oration 13, *Against Agoratus*; Oration 16, *In Defence of Mantitheus*.

> *Utica*: Appian, *Civil Wars*, 2.100.

> *Sallust*: See CAESAR's speech, *The War with Catiline*, 51.

> *Lysias*: Oration 25. And in Oration 30 he mentions the factious spirit of the popular assemblies as the only cause why these illegal punishments should displease.

> *In these contests . . . destruction*: Thucydides, 3.83.

> *Dionysius*: Plutarch, *Moralia*, 'On the Fortune or Virtue of Alexander'.

244. *Agathocles*: Diodorus Siculus, 18, 19.

> *Nabis*: Livy, 31, 33, 34.

> *citizens that remained*: see Diodorus Siculus 14.5. ISOCRATES says there were only 5,000 banished. He makes the number of those killed amount to 1,500 [*Areopagiticus*, 67]. AESCHINES [*Against Ctesiphon*, 235] assigns precisely the same number. SENECA [*On Tranquillity*, 5] says 1,300.

> *carry . . . farther*: Diodorus Siculus, 15.58.

> *banished a thousand*: ibid. 13.48.

> *instances*: We shall mention from DIODORUS SICULUS alone a few massacres, which passed in the course of sixty years, during the most shining age of GREECE. There were banished from SYBARIS 500 of the nobles and their partizans [12]. Of CHIANS, 600 citizens banished [13]. At EPHESUS, 340 killed, 1,000 banished [13]. Of CYRENIANS, 500 nobles killed, all the rest banished [14]. The CORINTHIANS killed 120, banished 500 [14]. PHAEBIDAS the SPARTAN banished 300 BAOETIANS [15]. Upon the fall of the LACEDAEMONIANS, Democracies were restored in many cities, and severe vengeance taken of the nobles, after the GREEK manner. But matters did not end there. For the banished nobles, returning in many places, butchered their adversaries at PHIALAE, in CORINTH, in MEGARA, in PHILIASA. In this last place they killed 300 of the people; but these again revolting, killed above 600 of the nobles, and banished the rest [15]. In ARCADIA 1,400 banished, besides many killed. The banished retired to SPARTA and to PALLANTIUM. The latter were delivered up to their countrymen and all killed [15]. Of the banished from ARGOS

and THEBES, there were 509 in the SPARTAN army. Here is a detail of the most remarkable of AGATHOCLES's cruelties from the same author. The people before his usurpation had banished 600 nobles [19]. Afterwards that tyrant, in concurrence with the people, killed 4,000 nobles and banished 6,000. He killed 4,000 people at GELA. By AGATHOCLES's brother 8,000 banished from SYRACUSE [20]. The inhabitants of AEGESTA, to the number of 40,000, were killed, man, woman, and child; and with tortures, for the sake of their money. All the relations, to wit, father, brother, children, grandfather, of his LIBYAN army, killed. He killed 7,000 exiles after capitulation. It is to be remarked, that AGATHOCLES was a man of great sense and courage, and is not to be suspected of wanton cruelty, contrary to the maxims of his age.

244. *20,000 men*: Diodorus Siculus, 18. 8.

in the city: Xenophon, *Banquet*, 4. 29–32.

245. *Lysias*: Oration 29, *Against Nicomachus*.

public service: In order to recommend his client to the favour of the people, he enumerates all the sums he has expended. When χορηγὸς, 30 minas. Upon a chorus of men 20 minas; εἰς πυρριχιστὰς, 8 minas; ἀνδράσι χορηγῶν, 50 minas; κυκλικῷ χορῷ, 3 minas; seven times trierarch, where he spent 6 talent; taxes, once 30 minas, another time 40; γυμνασιαρχῶν, 12 minas; χορηγὸς παιδικῷ χορῷ, 15 minas; κωμῳδοῖς χορηγῶν, 18 minas; πυρριχισταῖς ἀγενείοις, 7 minas; τριήρει ἁμιλλώμενος, 15 minas; ἀρχιθέωρος, 30 minas. In the whole ten talents 38 minas. [The Greek terms above refer to theatre officers.] An immense sum for an ATHENIAN fortune, and what alone would be esteemed great riches. [Oration 21] It is true, he says, the law did not oblige him absolutely to be at so much expence, not above a fourth. But without the favour of the people, no body was so much as safe; and this was the only way to gain it. See further [Oration 24]. In another place, he introduces a speaker, who says that he had spent his whole fortune, and an immense one, eighty talents, for the people. [Oration 26] The μέτοικοι, or strangers, find, says he, if they do not contribute largely enough to the people's fancy, that they have reason to repent it. [Oration 31] You may see with what care DEMOSTHENES displays his expences of this nature, when he pleads for himself *de corona*; and how he exaggerates MIDIAS's stinginess in this particular, in his accusation of that criminal. All this, by the by, is a mark of a very iniquitous judicature. And yet the ATHENIANS valued themslves on having the most legal and regular administration of any people in GREECE.

245. *five generations*: Isocrates, *Panathenaicus*, § 126.

246. *Greek historians*: The authorities cited above, are all historians, orators, and philosophers, whose testimony is unquestioned. It is dangerous to rely upon writers who deal in ridicule and satyr. What will posterity, for instance, infer from this passage of Dr SWIFT? 'I told him, that in the kingdom of TRIBNIA (BRITAIN) by the natives called LANGDON (LONDON) where I had sojourned some time in my travels, the bulk of the people consist, in a manner, wholly of discoverers, witnesses, informers, accusers, prosecutors, evidences, swearers, together with their several subservient and subaltern instruments, all under the colours, the conduct, and pay of ministers of state and their deputies. The plots in that kingdom are usually the workmanship of those persons' etc. [*Gullivers Travels*]. Such a representation might suit the government of ATHENS; but not that of ENGLAND, which is a prodigy, even in modern times, for humanity, justice, and liberty. Yet the Doctor's satire, though carried to extremes, as is usual with him, even beyond other satirical writers, did not altogether want an object. The Bishop of ROCHESTER, who was his friend, and of the same party, had been banished a little before by a bill of attainder, with great justice, but without such proof as was legal, or according to the strict forms of common law.

247. *Solon's*: Plutarch, *Lives*, Life of Solon, 18.

Antipater: Diodorus Siculus, 18. 18.

Servius Tullius's: Livy, 1. 43.

248. *Arrian's account of its inhabitants*: [*Anabasis of Alexander*, 2. 24] There were 8,000 killed during the siege; and the captives amounted to 30,000. DIODORUS SICULUS [17. 46.] says only 13,000, but he accounts for this small number, by saying that the TYRIANS had sent away before-hand part of their wives and children to CARTHAGE.

Herodotus: [*History*, 5. 97.] He makes the number of the citizens amount to 30,000.

same historian observes: History, 8. 132.

Lysias: Oration 32, *Against Diogeiton*.

Demosthenes: *Against Aphobus*, 1. 58.

249. *profit . . . at 12*: ibid. 1. 9.

    12 per cent: ibid., and Aeschines, *Against Ctesiphon*, 104.

    raised money: Cicero, *Letters to Atticus*, 4. 15.

    on such occasions: Cicero, *Against Verres*, 2. 3. 71.

    modern times: See Essay IV ['Of Interest'].

    Thucydides: 7. 28.

    Diodorus Siculus: 13. 81. [Agrigentum was in Sicily.]

    the same author: 12. 9. [Sybaris was in southern Italy.]

250. *Xenophon*: *On Estate Management*, 15. 10–11.

251. *in this particular*: See Part I Essay XI. [Probably 'Of Civil Liberty'.]

252. *in that city*: Aelius Lampridius, *Historia Augusta*, Life of Heliogabalus, 26.

    poets and orators: In general, there is more candour and sincerity in ancient historians, but less exactness and care, than in the moderns. Our speculative factions, especially those of religion, throw such an illusion over our minds, that men seem to regard impartiality to their adversaries and to heretics, as a vice or weakness. But the commonness of books, by means of printing, has obliged modern historians to be more careful in avoiding contradictions and incongruities. DIODORUS SICULUS is a good writer, but it is with pain I see his narration contradict, in so many particulars, the two most authentic pieces of all GREEK history, to wit, XENOPHON'S expedition, and DEMOSTHENES'S orations. PLUTARCH and APPIAN seem scarce ever to have read CICERO'S epistles.

    Diodorus Siculus: 12. 9. and 6. 26.

    Diodorus Siculus: [13. 84.] [This event happened in 406 BC.]

253. *two millions of inhabitants*: DIOGENES LAERTIUS [*Lives of Eminent Philosophers*, 3. 2] says, that AGRIGENTUM contained only 800,000 inhabitants.

    Theocritus: *Idylls*, 17.

    Diodorus Siculus: 1. 31.

    Lysias's: *Funeral Oration*, 27–8.

    Polybius: 2. 24.

    affords at present: The country that supplied this number, was not above a third of ITALY, *viz.* the Pope's dominions,

TUSCANY, and a part of the kingdom of NAPLES. But perhaps in those early times there were very few slaves, except in ROME, or the great cities.

254. *Diodorus Siculus*: 2. 5.

Appian: *Gallic History*, 2.

killed . . . prisoners: PLUTARCH [*Lives*, Life of Caesar, 15] makes the number that CAESAR fought with amount to three millions; JULIAN [*The Caesars*, 321a] to two.

Paterculus: *Roman History*, 2. 47.

Commentaries: PLINY [7. 25] says, that CAESAR used to boast, that there had fallen in battle against him one million one hundred and ninety two thousand men, besides those who perished in the civil wars. It is not probable, that the conqueror could ever pretend to be so exact in his computation. But allowing the fact, it is likely, that the HELVETII, GERMANS, and BRITONS, whom he slaughtered, would amount to near a half of the number.

400 galleys: Diodorus Siculus, 2. 5.

255. *joined him*: Plutarch, *Lives*, Life of Dion, 23–9.

Italy: Strabo, 6. 2. 7.

Plato: *Apology of Socrates*, 29d.

Greek: ARGOS seems also to have been a great city; for LYCIAS contents himself with saying that it did not exceed ATHENS [Oration 34].

Thucydides's time: [6. 3]. See also PLUTARCH [*Lives*, Life of Nicias, 17].

Cicero: [*Against Verrem*, 4. 52]. STRABO [6. 2. 4] says, it was twenty-two miles in compass. But then we are to consider, that it contained two harbours within it, one of which was a very large one, and might be regarded as a kind of bay.

Athenaeus: *Deipnosophistai*, 6. 20.

256. *Athenaeus*: DEMOSTHENES assigns 20,000 [*Against Aristogeiton*, 1. 50–1].

Herodotus says: 5. 97.

Thucydides: 8. 72.

the same historian: [2. 13]. DIODORUS SICULUS's account perfectly agrees [12. 40].

Athens: Xenophon, *Memorabilia*, 2. 6, 14.

256. *Thucydides*: 2. 13.

    Xenophon: *Ways and Means*, 2. 6.

    separate cities: We are to observe, that when DIONYSIUS of HALICARNASSUS says, that if we regard the ancient walls of ROME, the extent of the city will not appear greater than that of ATHENS; he must mean the ACROPOLIS and high town only. No ancient author ever speaks of the PYRAEUM, PHALERUS, and MUNYCHIA, as the same with ATHENS. Much less can it be supposed, that DIONYSIUS would consider the matter in that light, after the walls of CIMON and PERICLES were destroyed, and ATHENS was entirely separated from these other towns. This observation destroys all VOSSIUS'S reasonings, and introduces common sense into these calculations.

    miners: Athenaeus, 6. 272.

257. *Xenophon*: *The Constitution of the Athenians*, 10–12.

    Demosthenes: *Third Philippic*, 3.

    Plautus: *Stichus*, 3. 1. 39.

    Aeschines: *Against Timarchus*, 42.

    Demosthenes: Oration 12, *Against Eratosthenes*, 19.

    fifty-two slaves: *Against Aphobum*, 1. 9.

    Thucydides: 7. 27. [The revolt of the slaves at Decelea occurred in 413 BC.]

    Xenophon: *Ways and Means*, 4. 13–32.

    Demosthenes: *On the Navy Boards*, 19.

    Polybius: 2. 62.

    Xenophon: *Ways and Means*, 4. 14.

258. *Demosthenes*: *Against Aphobum*, 1. 9.

    Thucydides: 8. 40.

    in the country: Plutarch, *Lives*, Life of Lycurgus, 8.

    Thucydides: 4. 80.

    Athenaeus: The same author affirms, that CORINTH has once 460,000 slaves, AEGINA 470,000. But the foregoing arguments hold stronger against these facts, which are indeed entirely absurd and impossible. It is however remarkable, that ATHENAEUS cites so great an authority, as ARISTOTLE for this last fact: and the scholiast on PINDAR mentions the same number of slaves in AEGINA.

258. *Thucydides*: 2. 14–16.

    lodging: Thucydides, 2. 17.

259. *neighbouring territory*: Demosthenes, [*Against Leptines*, 31–3.] The ATHENIANS brought yearly from PONTUS 400,000 medimni or bushels of corn, as appeared from the custom-house books. And this was the greater part of their importation of corn. This, by the by, is a strong proof that there is some great mistake in the foregoing passage of ATHENAEUS. For ATTICA itself was so barren of corn, that it produced not enough even to maintain the peasants. [Livy, 43. 6.] And 400,000 medimni would scarcely feed 100,000 men during a twelvemonth. LUCIAN, in his *The Ship or the Wishes* [4–6] says, that a ship, which, by the dimensions he gives, seems to have been about the size of our third rates, carried as much corn as would maintain ATTICA for a twelvemonth. But perhaps ATHENS was decayed at that time; and, besides, it is not safe to trust to such loose rhetorical calculations.

    Demetrius: Diodorus Siculus, 20. 84.

    Greece: Isocrates, *Panegyricus*, 64.

    Rhodes: [Diodorus Siculus, 17. 14] When ALEXANDER attacked THEBES, we may safely conclude that almost all the inhabitants were present. Whoever is acquainted with the spirits of the GREEKS, especially of the THEBANS, will never suspect that any of them would desert their country when it was reduced to such extreme peril and distress. As ALEXANDER took the town by storm, all those who bore arms were put to the sword without mercy, and they amount only to 6,000 men. Among these were some strangers and manumitted slaves. The captives, consisting of old men, women, children, and slaves, were sold, and they amounted to 30,000. We may therefore conclude, that the free citizens in THEBES, of both sexes and all ages, were near 24,000, the strangers and slaves about 12,000. These last, we may observe, were somewhat fewer in proportion than at ATHENS, as is reasonable to imagine from this circumstance, that ATHENS was a town of more trade to support slaves, and of more entertainment to allure strangers. It is also to be remarked, that 36,000 was the whole number of people, both in the city of THEBES and the neighbouring territory. A very moderate number, it must be confessed; and his computation, being founded on facts which appear indisputable, must have great weight in the present controversy. The above-mentioned numbers of Rhodians, too, were all the inhabitants of the island who were free, and able to bear arms.

259. *Xenophon*: *Hellenica*, 7. 2. 1.

citizens: ibid. 5. 3. 1.

Arcadia: Polybius, 2. 56.

circumference: ibid. 9. 26.

3,000 citizens: Lysias, Oration 34, 7–8.

circumference: Vopiscus, Life of Aurelian, in *Historia Augusta*.

260. *Xenophon*: [*Constitution of the Lacedaemonians*, 1. 1.] This passage is not easily reconciled with that of PLUTARCH above, who says, that SPARTA had 9,000 citizens.

Polybius: 9. 26.

10,000 men: Diodorus Siculus, 28. 24.

Polybius: 29. 24. 8.

Pausanias: *Description of Greece*, Achaia, 15. 7.

Thessalians . . . disorderly: Livy, 34. 51. Plato, *Crito*, 53d.

Thucydides: 4. 3.

Herodotus says: 7. 126.

150,000: Livy, 14. 34.

Justin: Epitome of *Historiae Philippicae*, 9. 5.

261. *Dionysius of Halicarnassus*: 4. 13.

the same author: 10. 32.

Juvenal: Satire 3, 269–70.

other ancient writers: STRABO [5. 3. 7] says, that the emperor AUGUSTUS prohibited the raising houses higher than seventy feet. In another passage [16] he speaks of the houses of ROME as remarkably high. See also to the same purpose VITRUVIUS [*On Architecture*, 2. 8. 17] ARISTIDES the sophist, in his orations εἰς ʽΡώμην [*To Rome*], says, that ROME consisted of cities on the top of cities; and that if one were to spread it out, and unfold it, it would cover the whole surface of ITALY. Where an author indulges himself in such extravagant declamations, and gives so much into the hyperbolical style, one knows not how far he must be reduced. But this reasoning seems natural: If ROME was built in so scattered a manner as DIONYSIUS says,

and ran so much into the country, there must have been very
few streets where the houses were raised so high. It is only
for want of room, that any body builds in that inconvenient
manner.

261. *Pliny's*: [*Letters*, 2. 17, 5. 6] It is true, PLINY there describes a
country house: but since that was the idea which the ancients
formed of a magnificent and convenient building, the great
men would certainly build the same way in town. 'In laxitatem
ruris excurrunt' ['as if they were country houses'] says SENECA
of the rich and voluptuous [Letter 114]. VALERIUS MAXIMUS
[4. 4], speaking of CINCINNATUS'S field of four acres, says,
'Auguste se habitare nunc putat, cujus domus tantum patet
quantum CINCINNATI rura patuerant.' ['He counts himself to
live splendidly now, whose house stands upon as much ground
as all Cincinnatus's farms contained.'] To the same purpose
see [36. 15], also [18. 2].

woods: Vitruvius, 5. 11, Tacitus, *Annals*, 11. 3, Suetonius,
Lives of the Caesars, Life of Octavius, 72, etc.

Pliny: 'MOENIA ejus (ROMAE) collegere ambitu imperatoribus,
censoribusque VESPASIANIS, A. U. C. 828. pass. xiii. MCC.
complexa montes septum, ipsa dividitur in regiones
quatuordecim, compita earum 265. Ejusdem spatii mensura,
currente a milliario in capite ROM. Fori statuto, ad singulas
portas, quae sunt hodie numero 37, ita ut duodecim portae
semel numerentur, praetereanturque ex veteribus septem,
quae esse desierunt, efficit passuum per directum 30,775.
Ad extrema vero tectorum cum castris praetoriis ab eodem
Milliario, per vicos omnium viarum, mensura collegit paulo
amplius septuaginta millia passuum. Quo si quis altitudinem
tectorum addat, dignam profecto, aestimationem concipiat,
fateaturque nullius urbis magnitudinem in toto orbe potuisse
ei comparari.' [Pliny, *Natural History*, 3. 5. 66–7: 'The area
surrounded by its walls at the time of the principate and
censorship of the Vespasians, in the 826th year of its foundation, measured 13,200 paces in circumference, embracing
seven hills. It is itself divided into fourteen regions, with 265
crossways with their guardian Lares. If a straight line is drawn
from the milestone standing at the head of the Roman Forum
to each of the gates, which today number 37 (provided that
the Twelve Gates be counted as one each and the seven of the
old gates that no longer exist be omitted), the result is a total
of 30,775 paces in a straight line. But the total length of all

the ways through the districts from the same milestone to the extreme edge of the buildings, taking into account the Praetorians' Camp, amounts to just over 60 miles. Taking into account the height of the buildings, a very fair estimate would be formed that that would lead us to admit that there has been no city in the whole world that could be compared to Rome in magnitude.']

All the best manuscripts of PLINY read the passage as here cited, and fix the compass of the walls of ROME to be thirteen miles. The question is, What PLINY means by 30,775 paces, and how that number was formed? The manner in which I conceive it, is this. ROME was a semicircular area of thirteen miles circumference. The Forum, and consequently the Milliarium, we know, was situated on the banks of the TYBER, and near the centre of the circle, or upon the diameter of the semicircular area. Though there were thirty-seven gates to ROME, yet only twelve of them had straight streets, leading from them to the Milliarium. PLINY, therefore, having assigned the circumference of ROME, and knowing that that alone was not sufficient to give us a just notion of its surface, uses this farther method. He supposes all the streets, leading from the Milliarium to the twelve gates, to be laid together into one straight line, and supposes we run along that line, so as to count each gate once: in which case, he says, that the whole line is 30,775 paces: or, in other words, that each street or radius of the semicircular area is upon an average two miles and a half; and the whole length of ROME is five miles, and its breadth about half as much, besides the scattered suburbs.

PERE HARDOUIN understands this passage in the same manner; with regard to the laying together the several streets of ROME into one line, in order to compose 30,775 paces: but then he supposes, that streets led from the Milliarium to every gate, and that no street exceeded 800 paces in length. But (1) a semicircular area, whose radius was only 800 paces, could never have a circumference near thirteen miles, the compass of ROME as assigned by PLINY. A radius of two miles and a half forms very nearly that circumference. (2) There is an absurdity in suposing a city so built as to have streets running to its centre from every gate in its circumference. These streets must interfere as they approach. (3) This diminishes too much from the greatness of ancient ROME, and reduces that city below even BRISTOL or ROTTERDAM.

The sense which Vossius in his *Observationes variae* puts on this passage of Pliny, errs widely in the other extreme. One manuscript of no authority, instead of thirteen miles, has assigned thirty miles for the compass of the walls of Rome. And Vossius understands this only of the curvilinear part of the circumference; supposing, that as the Tyber formed the diameter, there were no walls built on that side. But (1) this reading is allowed to be contrary to almost all the manuscripts. (2) Why should Pliny, a concise writer, repeat the compass of the walls of Rome in two successive sentences? (3) Why repeat it with so sensible a variation? (4) What is the meaning of Pliny's mentioning twice the Milliarium, if a line was measured that had no dependence on the Milliarium? (5) Aurelian's wall is said by Vopiscus to have been drawn *laxiore ambitu* [in a wider circuit], and to have comprehended all the buildings and suburbs on the north side of the Tyber; yet its compass was only fifty miles; and even here critics suspect some mistake or corruption in the text; since the walls, which remain, and which are supposed to be the same with Aurelian's, exceed not twelve miles. It is not probable, that Rome would diminish from Augustus to Aurelian. It remained still the capital of the same empire; and none of the civil wars in that long period, except the tumults on the death of Maximus and Balbinus even affected the city. Caracalla is said by Aurelius Victor to have encreased Rome. (6) There are no remains of ancient buildings, which marks any such greatness of Rome. Vossius's reply to this objection seems absurd. That the rubbish would sink sixty or seventy feet under ground. It appears from Spartian [*Life of Severus*] that the five-mile stone *in via Lavicana* was out of the city. (7) Olympiodorus and Publius Victor fix the number of houses in Rome to be betwixt forty and fifty thousand. (8) The very extravagance of the consequences drawn by this critic, as well as Lipsius, if they be necessary, destroys the foundation on which they are grounded: that Rome contained fourteen millions of inhabitants; while the whole kingdom of France contains only five, according to his computation, etc. The only objection to the sense which we have affixed above to the passage of Pliny, seems to lie in this, that Pliny, after mentioning the thirty-seven gates of Rome, assigns only a reason for suppressing the seven old ones, and says nothing of the eighteen gates, the streets leading from which terminated, according to my opinion, before they reached the Forum. But as PLINY was writing to the ROMANS, who perfectly knew the disposition of the streets, it is not strange he should take a circumstance for granted, which was so familiar to every body. Perhaps too, many of these gates led to wharfs upon the river.

261. *two hundred thousand*: Res Gestae Divi Augustii, 15.

262. *Cicero*: Tusculan Disputations, 3. 48.

five modii to each: Sallust, *Histories*, 3. 48. 19.

antiquary: Nicolaus Hortensius, 'On the Provision of Corn at Rome'.

more probable: Not to take the people too much from their business, AUGUSTUS ordained the distribution of corn to be made only thrice a-year: but the people finding the monthly distributions more convenient, (as preserving, I suppose, a more regular economy in their family) desired to have them restored [Suetonius, *Augustus*, 40]. Had not some of the people come from some distance for their corn, AUGUSTUS's precaution seems superfluous.

We are told: Suetonius, *The Deified Julius*, 41.

Suetonius: Life of Nero, 39.

Italy: Suetonius, *Augustus*, 42.

263. *Herodian*: History of the Empire, 4. 3. 7.

Diodorus Siculus: 17. 52.

Paris: QUINTUS CURTIUS says, its walls were ten miles in circumference, when founded by ALEXANDER [*History of Alexander*, 4. 8]. STRABO, who had travelled to ALEXANDRIA as well as DIODORUS SICULUS, says it was scarce four miles long, and in most places about a mile broad [1. 8]. PLINY says it resembled a MACEDONIAN cassock, stretching out in the corners [5. 11]. Notwithstanding this bulk of ALEXANDRIA, which seems but moderate, DIODORUS SICULUS, speaking of its circuit as drawn by ALEXANDER (which it never exceeded, as we learn from AMMIANUS MARCELLINUS [*History of Rome*, 22. 16]), says it was μεγέθει διαφέροντα, *extremely great*. The reason which he assigns for its surpassing all cities in the world (for he excepts not ROME) is, that it contained 300,000 free inhabitants. He also mentions the revenues of the kings, to wit, 6,000 talents, as another circumstance to the same purpose; no such mighty sum in our eyes, even though we make allowance for the different value of money. What

STRABO says of the neighbouring country, means only that it was peopled, οἰκούμενα καλῶς. Might not one affirm, without any great hyperbole, that the whole banks of the river, from GRAVESEND to WINDSOR, are one city? This is even more than STRABO says of the banks of the lake MAREOTIS, and of the canal to CANAPUS. It is vulgar saying in ITALY, that the king of SARDINIA has but one town in PIEDMONT, for it is all a town. AGRIPPA, in Flavius Josephus [*Jewish War*, 2. 385], to make his audience comprehend the excessive greatness of ALEXANDRIA, which he endeavours to magnify, describes only the compass of the city as drawn by ALEXANDER; a clear proof that the bulk of the inhabitants were lodged there, and that the neighbouring country was no .more than what might be expected about all great towns, very well cultivated, and well peopled.

263.   *in Diodorus Siculus's time*: Diodorus Siculus, 17. 52.

women and children: He says ἐλεύθεροι [free residents], not πολῖται, which last expression must have been understood of citizens alone, and grown men.

all the rest of the city: [4. 1.] πάσης πόλεως. POLITIAN interprets it 'aedibus majoribus etiam reliqua urbe'. ['With a palace even greater than the rest of the city.']

Suetonius: He says (in [*Life of Nero*, 6. 31]) that a portico or piazza of it was 3,000 feet long; 'tanta laxitas ut porticus triplices milliarias haberet' ['so extensive that it had a triple colonnade a mile long']. He cannot mean three miles. For the whole extent of the house from the PALATINE to the ESQUILINE was not near so great. So when [Vopiscus, in *The Deified Aurelian*, 49] mentions a portico in SALLUST's gardens, which he calls *porticus milliarensis*, it must be understood of a thousand feet. So also HORACE: 'Nulla decempedis / Metata privatis opacam / Porticus excipiebat Arcton.' [*Odes*, 2. 15: 'No private citizen had a portico measuring its tens of feet, lying open to the shady north.'] So also in [*Satires*, 1. 8. 12]: 'Mille pedes in fronte, trecentos cippus in agrum / Hic dabat.' ['Here a pillar assigned a thousand feet of frontage and three hundred of depth.']

an enormous extent: [Pliny, *Natural History*, 36. 24]: 'Bis vidimus urbem totam cingi domibus principum, Caii ac Neronis.' ['Twice have we seen the whole city girdled by imperial palaces, those of Gaius and Nero.']

263. *the same historian*: Herodian, *History of the Empire*, 2. 4. 6.

   Vopiscus: *Life of Aurelian*, 48.

264. *Polybius*: *Histories*, 12. 4. 5–14.

   Aristotle's: [9. 10.] His expression is ἄνθρωπος, not πολίτης; inhabitant, not citizen.

265. *Pliny*: *Natural History*, 6. 30.

   Strabo: *Geography*, 17. 3. 15.

   many capitals . . . amusement: Such were ALEXANDRIA, ANTIOCH, CARTHAGE, EPHESUS, LYONS, etc. in the ROMAN empire. Such are even BOURDEAUX, THOULOUSE, DIJON, RENNES, ROUREN, AIX, etc. in FRANCE; DUBLIN, EDINBURGH, YORK, in the BRITISH dominions.

266. *L'Abbé du Bos*: *Réflexions Critiques sur la Poesie et sur la Peinture*, 2. 16. 298–9.

   Hibernum . . . mergetur: [*Satires*, 6. 522–3: 'In winter she will go down to the river in the morning, break the ice, and plunge three times into the Tiber.']

   Diodorus Siculus's: 5. 25.

267. *could not live in it*: *Generation of Animals*, 2. 8.

   Strabo: 4. 1. 2.

   Ovid: *Tristia*, 3. 10; *Letters From Pontus*, book 4. Elegies 7, 9, 10.

   Polybius: 4. 21.

   Varro: *On Agriculture*, 1. 2. 4.

   felled: The warm southern colonies also become more healthful: and it is remarkable, that in the SPANISH histories of the first discovery and conquest of these countries, they appear to have been very healthful; being then well peopled and cultivated. No account of the sickness or decay of CORTES's or PIZARRO's small armies.

   Columella: *On Agriculture*, 1. 1. 5.

268. *Saserna*: He seems to have lived about the time of the younger AFRICANUS [1. 1].

   pasturage and plunder: Xenophon, *Expedition of Cyrus*, 7; Polybius, *Histories*, 4. 45.

   uncivilized: in Ovid; Strabo, 7.

   Illyrians no better: Polybius, 2. 12.

269. *Caesar*: *Gallic War*, 6. 23.

   Tacitus: *Germania*.

   Strabo: 7.

   Herodian: *History*, 3. 14. 6.

   Druids: [Caesar, *Gallic War*, 6. 13–14]; Strabo [*Geography*, 7. 2. 1] says, the Gauls were not much improved than the Germans.

   former historian: [Appian] *Roman History*, 6: The Gallic History, 1. 2.

   the latter: [Diodorus Siculus] 5. 25.

270. *little more than twenty*: Ancient Gaul was more extensive than modern France.

   Gauls: Caesar, *Gallic War*, 6. 13, 15.

   Strabo: 4. 1. 2.

   Caesar: *Gallic War*, 2. 4.

   present inhabitants: It appears from Caesar's account, that the Gauls had no domestic slaves (who formed a different order from the *Plebes*). The whole common people were indeed a kind of slaves to the nobility, as the people of Poland are at this day: and a nobleman of Gaul had sometimes ten thousand dependants of this kind. Nor can we doubt, that the armies were composed of the people as well as of the nobility: an army of 100,000 noblemen from a very small state is incredible. The fighting men amongst the Helvetii were the fourth part of the whole inhabitants; a clear proof that all the males of military age bore arms. See Caesar [*Gallic War*, 1.]

   We may remark, that the numbers in Caesar's commentaries can be more depended on than those of any other ancient author, because of the Greek translation, which still remains, and which checks the Latin original.

   same author: Caesar, *Gallic War*, 1. 2.

271. *the Romans*: Livy, 34. 17.

   Plutarch: *Lives*, Life of Caius Martius, 6.

   Hirtius: *The Spanish War*, 8.

   disorders were repressed: Velleius Paterculus, *Roman History*, 2. 90.

   Strabo: 3.

271. *Justin*: *Philippic History*, 44.

formidable: 'Nec numero Hispanos, nec robore Gallos, nec calliditate Poenos, nec artibus Graecos, nec denique hoc ipso hujus gentis, ac terrae domestico nativoque sensu, Italos ipsos ac Latinos—superavimus.' [Cicero, *De Haruspicum Responsis*, 9.19: 'We have excelled neither Spain in population, nor Gaul in vigour, nor Carthage in versatility, nor Greece in art, nor indeed Italy and Latium itself in the sensibility characteristic of this land and its people.'] The disorder of SPAIN seems to have been almost proverbial: 'Nec impacatos a tergo horrebis Iberos.' [Virgil, *Georgics*, 3.408: 'never . . . need you fear . . . restless Spaniards at your back.'] The IBERI are here plainly taken, by a poetical figure, for robbers in general.

neglect of tillage and agriculture: Varro, *On Agriculture*, Preface to book 2; Columella, preface. Suetonius, *Augustus*, 42.

any country: Though the observations of L'Abbé du Bos should be admitted, that ITALY is now warmer than in former times, the consequence may not be necessary, that it is more populous or better cultivated. If the other countries of EUROPE were more savage and woody, the cold winds that blew from them, might affect the climate of ITALY.

272. *government*: The inhabitants of MARSEILLES lost not their superiority over the GAULS in commerce and the mechanic arts, till the ROMAN dominion turned the latter from arms to agriculture and civil life. See STRABO [*Geography*, 1.5]. That author, in several places, repeats the observation concerning the improvement arising from the ROMAN arts and civility: and he lived at the time when change was new, and would be more sensible. So also PLINY: 'Quis enim non, communicato orbe terrarum, majestate ROMANI imperii, profecisse vitam putet, commercio rerum ac societate festae pacis, omniaque etiam, quae occulta antea fuerant, in promiscuo usu facta.' [*Natural History*, 14.1.2: 'For who would not admit that now that intercommunication has been established throughout the world by the majesty of the Roman Empire, life has been advanced by the interchange of commodities and by partnership in the blessings of peace, and that even things that had previously lain concealed have all now been established in general use?'] 'Numine deum electa (speaking of ITALY) quae coelum ipsum clarius faceret, sparsa congregaret imperia,

ritusque molliret, et tot populorum discordes, ferasque linguas
sermonis commercio contraheret ad colloquia, et humanitatem
homini daret; breviterque, una cunctarum gentium in toto
orbe patria fieret. [*Natural History*, 3.5.39: 'Chosen by the
providence of the gods to make heaven itself more glorious,
to unite scattered empires, to make manners gentle, to draw
together in converse by community of language the jarring
and uncouth tongues of so many nations, to give mankind
civilization, and in a word to become throughout the world
the single fatherland of all the races.'] Nothing can be stronger
to this purpose than the following passage from TERTULLIAN,
who lived about the age of SEVERUS. 'Certe quidem ipse orbis
in promptu est, cultior de die et instructior pristino. Omnia
jam pervia, omnia nota, omnia negotiosa. Solitudines famosas
retro fundi amoenissimi obliteraverunt, silvas arva domuerunt,
feras pecora fugaverunt; arenae seruntur, saxa panguntur,
paludes eliquantur, tantae urbes, quantae non casae quondam.
Jam nec insulae horrent, nec scepuli terrent; ubique domus,
ubique populus, ubique respublica, ubique vita. Summum
testimonium frequentiae humanae, onerosi sumus mundo, vix
nobis elementa sufficiunt; et necessitates arctiores, et querelae
apud omnes, dum jam nos natura non sustinet.' [*De Anima*,
30.3–4: 'A glance at the face of the earth shows us that it
is becoming daily better cultivated and more fully peopled
than in olden times. There are few places now that are
not accessible; few, unknown; few, unopened to commerce.
Beautiful farms now cover what once were trackless wastes,
the forests have given way before the plough, cattle have
driven off the beasts of the jungle, the sands of the desert
bear fruit and crops, the rocks have been ploughed under, the
marshes have been drained of their water, and, where once
there was but a settler's cabin, great cities are now to be seen.
No longer do lonely islands frighten away the sailor nor does
he fear their rocky coasts. Everywhere we see houses, people,
stable governments, and the orderly conduct of life. The
strongest witness is the vast population of the earth to which
we are a burden and she scarcely can provide for our needs;
as our demands grow greater, our complaints against nature's
inadequacy are heard by all.'] The air of rhetoric and declamation which appears in this passage, diminshes somewhat
from its authority, but does not entirely destroy it. The
same remark may be extended to the following passage of
ARISTIDES the sophist, who lived in the age of ADRIAN. 'The

whole world,' says he, adressing himself to the ROMANS, 'seems to keep one holiday; and mankind, laying aside the sword which they formerly wore, now betake themselves to feasting and to joy. The cities, forgetting their ancient animosities, preserve only one emulation, which shall embellish itself most by every art and ornament; theatres every where arise, amphitheatres, porticoes, aqueducts, temples, schools, academies; and one may safely pronounce, that the sinking world has been again raised by your auspicious empire. Nor have cities alone received an encrease of ornament and beauty; but the whole earth, like a garden or paradise, is cultivated and adorned; insomuch, that such of mankind as are placed out of the limits of your empire (who are but few) seem to merit our sympathy and compassion' [*To Rome*].

It is remarkable, that though DIODORUS SICULUS makes the inhabitants of AEGYPT, when conquered by the ROMANS, amount only to three millions [*Library of History*, 1.31.6]; yet JOSEPHUS [*Jewish War*, 2.385] says, that its inhabitants, excluding those of ALEXANDRIA, were seven millions and a half, in the reign of NERO: and he expressly says, that he drew this account from the books of the Roman publicans, who levied the poll-tax. STRABO [1.12] praises the superior police of the ROMANS with regard to the finances of Egypt, above that of its former monarchs; and no part of administration is more essential to the happiness of a people. Yet we read in ATHENAEUS [*The Banquet of the Learned*, 1.33d] who flourished during the reign of the ANTONINES, that the town MAREIA, near ALEXANDRIA, which was formerly a large city, had dwindled into a village. This is not, properly speaking, a contradiction. SUIDAS [*Augustus*] says, that the Emperor AUGUSTUS, having numbered the whole ROMAN empire, found it contained only 4,101,017 men (ἄνδρες). There is here surely some great mistake, either in the author or transcriber. But this authority, feeble as it is, may be sufficient to counterbalance the exaggerated accounts of HERODOTUS and DIODORUS SICULUS with regard to more early times.

272. *promising appearances*: Montesquieu, *L'Esprit des Loix*, book 23, ch. 19.

Plutarch: *The Obsolescence of Oracles*, 8.

Roman yoke: [Polybius, 2.62] It may perhaps be imagined, that POLYBIUS, being dependent on ROME, would naturally extol the ROMAN dominion. But, in the *first* place, POLYBIUS, though one sees sometimes instances of his caution, discovers no symptoms of flattery. *Secondly*, this opinion is only delivered in a single stroke, by the by, while he is intent upon another subject; and it is allowed, if there be any suspicion of an author's insincerity, that these oblique propositions discover his real opinion better than his more formal and direct assertions.

272. *Tacitus*: *Annals*, 1. 2.

Strabo: 8 and 9.

273. *increased them*: Plutarch, *On the Delays of the Divine Vengeance*, 32.

Lucian: *De mercede conductis*.

274. *mistake of this nature*: I must confess that that discourse of PLUTARCH, concerning the silence of the oracles, is in general of so odd a texture, and so unlike his other productions, that one is at a loss what judgment to form of it. It is wrote in dialogue, which is a method of composition that PLUTARCH commonly little affects. The personages he introduces advance very wild, absurd, and contradictory opinions, more like the visionary systems or ravings of PLATO than the solid sense of PLUTARCH. There runs also through the whole an air of superstition and credulity, which resembles very little the spirit that appears in other philosophical compositions of that author. For it is remarkable, that though PLUTARCH be an historian as superstitious as HERODOTUS or LIVY, yet there is scarcely, in all antiquity, a philosopher less superstitious, excepting CICERO and LUCIAN. I must therefore confess, that a passage of PLUTARCH, cited from this discourse, has much less authority with me, than if it had been found in most of his other compositions.

There is only one other discourse of PLUTARCH liable to like objections, to wit that *concerning those whose punishment is delayed by the Deity*. It is also wrote in dialogue, contains like superstitious, wild visions, and seems to have been chiefly composed in rivalship to PLATO, particularly his last book, *The Republic*.

And here I cannot but observe, that M. FONTENELLE, a writer eminent for candor, seems to have departed a little from his usual character, when he endeavours to throw a ridicule upon PLUTARCH on account of passages to be met with in this dialogue concerning oracles. The absurdities here put into the mouths of the several personages are not to be ascribed to PLUTARCH. He makes them refute each other; and, in general, he seems to intend the ridiculing of those very opinions, which FONTENELLE would ridicule him for maintaining [*Histoire des Oracles* (1686)].

274. *the world*: [Diodorus Siculus] 2. 5. 4.

most populous: He was contemporary with CAESAR and AUGUSTUS.

OF THE ORIGINAL CONTRACT

281. *Polybius*: 2. 38.

283. *tyranny of that emperor*: Tacitus, *Annals*, 6. 14.

290. *Niger and Albinus*: Herodian, 2. [After the death of the Emperor Commodus in AD 192 Pertinax ruled for three months in 193, after which Didianus Julianus (Julian) bought the title; the ensuing power struggle between him and Lucius Septimus Severus, Pescennius Niger, and Clodius Albinus lasted until 197.]

291. *authority*: It is remarkable, that, in the remonstrance of the duke of BOURBON and the legitimate princes, against this destination of LOUIS the XIVth, the doctrine of *original contract* is insisted on, even in that absolute government. The FRENCH nation, say they, choosing HUGH CAPET and his posterity to rule over them and their posterity, where the former line fails, there is a tacit right reserved to choose a new royal family; and this right is invaded by calling the bastard princes to the throne, without the consent of the nation. But the Comte de BOULAINVILLIERS, who wrote in defence of the bastard princes, ridicules this notion of an original contract, especially when applied to HUGH CAPET; who mounted the throne, says he, by the same arts, which have ever been employed by all conquerors and usurpers. He got his title, indeed, recognized by the states after he had put himself in possession: but is this a choice or a contract? The Comte de BOULAINVILLIERS, we may observe, was a noted republican; but being a man of learning, and very conversant in history, he knew that the people were never almost consulted in these revolutions and new establishments, and that time alone bestowed right and authority on what was

commonly at first founded on force and violence. See [Boulainvilliers, *État de la France*, vol. 3 (1727).]

292. *no form . . . at all*: see Locke, *On Government*, ch. 7, § 90.

   his representatives: see Locke, *ibid*., ch. 9, §§ 138–40.

IDEA OF A PERFECT COMMONWEALTH

301. *It is not*: earlier editions (1752–68) of this essay began with an extra sentence: 'Of all mankind there are none so pernicious as political projectors, if they have power; nor so ridiculous, if they want it. As on the other hand, a wise politician is the most beneficial character in nature, if accompanied with authority; and the most innocent, and not altogether useless, even if deprived of it.'

ON SUICIDE

316. *Tully*: Cicero, *On Divination*, 2. 72 (150).

320. *ills that threaten me*: Agamus Deo gratias, quod nemo in vita teneri potest. [Seneca, *Epistles*, 12, 'On Old Age', § 10: 'And let us thank God that no man can be kept in life.']

324. *danger or misery*: It would be easy to prove that Suicide is as lawful under the *Christian* dispensation as it was to the *heathens*. There is not a single text of scripture which prohibits it. That great and infallible rule of faith and practice, which must control all philosophy and human reasoning, has left us in this particular to our natural liberty. Resignation to providence is indeed recommended in scripture; but that implies only submission to ills that are unavoidable, not to such as may be remedied by prudence or courage. *Thou shalt not kill* is evidently meant to exclude only the killing of others over whose life we have no authority. That this precept, like most of the scripture precepts, must be modified by reason and common sense, is plain from the practice of magistrates, who punish criminals capitally, notwithstanding the letter of the law. But were this commandment ever so express against Suicide, it would now have no authority. For all the law of *Moses* is abolished, except so far as it is established by the law of Nature; and we have already endeavoured to prove, that Suicide is not prohibited by that law. In all cases *Christians* and *Heathens* are precisely upon the same footing; *Cato* and *Brutus*, *Arria* and *Portia* acted heroically; those who now

imitate their example ought to receive the same praises from posterity. The power of committing Suicide is regarded by *Pliny* as an advantage which men possess even above the deity himself. *Deus non sibi potest mortem consciscere, si velit, quod homini dedit optimum in tantis vitae poenis.* ['God cannot, even if he wishes, commit suicide, the supreme boon that he has bestowed on man among all the penalties of life.' Pliny, *Natural History*, 2. 5. 27.]

ON THE IMMORTALITY OF THE SOUL

328. *your father*: Suetonius, *Lives of the Caesars*, Life of Augustus, ch. 3.

LIST OF NAMES

Achilles: Greek hero of the *Iliad*.

Addison, Joseph (1672–1719): essayist, co-author of the *Tatler*, the *Spectator*, the *Guardian*, and other periodicals.

Adrian / Hadrian: Publius Aelius Hadrianus: Roman emperor AD 117–38.

Aemilius, Paulus: Lucius Aemilius Paullus (d. 160 BC): Roman consul who won the Macedonian War.

Aeschines (*c*.397–*c*.322 BC): Athenian orator; opponent of Demosthenes on the issue of whether to make peace with Philip of Macedon.

Agamemnon: legendary leader of the Greeks in the Trojan War.

Agathocles (361–289 BC): demagogue and ruler of Syracuse from 317 BC.

Agesilaus (*c*.444–361 BC): king of Sparta and leader of campaigns against the Persians and Thebans.

Agrippa, Marcus Vipsanius (*c*.63–12 BC): leading supporter of Octavian (later emperor Augustus) in the campaign against Mark Antony; later responsible for extensive public works and rebuilding in Rome.

Agur: described in Proverbs 30: 1 as 'the son of Jakeh'.

Albinus (2nd century AD): author of introductions to the philosophy of Plato.

Albinus, Clodius: contender for the position of Roman emperor after the murder of Pertinax and sale of the succession to Didius Julianus in AD 193.

Alexander the Great (356–323 BC): king of Macedon, son of Philip II; expelled the Persians from Greece and conquered much of Asia Minor.

Ammianus Marcellinus (born *c*. AD 330): historian from Antioch; wrote a continuation of the history of Tacitus in *c*. AD 390.

Angria, Tulagee: 18th-century leader of Indian pirates, eventually defeated in 1756.

Antiochus: name of several Seleucid kings.

Antiochus of Ascalon (1st century BC): Greek philosopher who attempted to reconcile Stoic and Platonic thought and revive the spirit of Plato's Academy.

Antipater: general, and regent of Macedonia under Alexander the Great.

Antonines: Roman emperors—Titus Antoninus Pius, AD 138–61; Marcus Aurelius Antoninus, 161–80.

Antony, Mark: Marcus Antonius (*c*.82–30 BC): supporter of Julius Caesar and victor, with Octavian and Lepidus, in the war against his assassins; later consort of Cleopatra; defeated by Octavian at Actium and committed suicide.

Apelles: Greek painter of the 4th century BC whose work was very highly regarded by many clasical writers.

Appian (2nd century AD): Greek lawyer living in Rome, who compiled narratives of the Roman wars.

Arbuthnot, Dr John (1667–1735): physician, scholar, and satirist; member of the Scriblerian circle.

Ariosto, Lodovico (1474–1533): Italian epic poet, author of *Orlando Furioso*.

Aristagoras: tyrant of Miletus and instigator of a revolt against the Persians in 499 BC.

Aristides (d. *c*.468 BC): democratic leader at Athens; known as 'the Just'.

Aristides, Publius Aelius (AD 117–*c*.180): Greek rhetorician, author of speeches, letters, and prose poems.

Aristophanes (*c*.445–380 BC): Greek comic dramatist.

Aristotle (384–322 BC): Greek philosopher, pupil of Plato, founder of Peripatetic school of philosophical thought; author of numerous highly influential works on philosophy, natural science, and aesthetics.

Arrian (*c*. AD 95–175): Greek officer in the Roman army, consul, legate, and author of works of philosophy, and an account of the campaigns of Alexander the Great.

Artaxerxes I, II, and III: kings of Persia, 464–338 BC.

Athenaeus (3rd century AD): Greek author of the *Deipnosophistai*.

Attalus: name of kings of Pergamum from the 3rd to 1st centuries BC.

Atticus, Titus Pomponius (109–32 BC): Roman businessman; friend of Cicero and recipient of letters from him.

Augustus: Gaius Julius Caesar Octavianus (27 BC–AD 14): victor in the Civil War and the war against Mark Antony, and first emperor of Rome.

Aurelian: Lucius Domitus Aurelianus: Roman emperor AD 270–5.

Aurelius Victor: Sextus Aurelius Victor: author of a history of the Caesars, published *c*. AD 360.

Bacon, Francis (1561–1626): English philosopher and essayist; author of *Essays*, *Novum Organum*, and *Advancement of Learning*.

Bacchus: Greek god of wine.

Balbinus: joint Roman emperor with Maximus in AD 237–8, until both were murdered.

Bartoli, Pietro Santi (*c*.1635–1700): engraver of illustrations of the surviving art of ancient Rome.

Bentivoglio, Cardinal Guido (1579–1644): author of extensive writings on government and diplomacy in Flanders and France, based on his experience as Papal nuncio in both places.

Berkeley, George (1685–1753): philosopher and Bishop of Cloyne; author of works on the principles of knowledge and theory of vision, politics, and economics.

Boccace: Giovanni Boccaccio (1313–75): author of the *Decameron*.

Boileau-Despréaux, Nicholas (1636–1711): poet and literary critic, author of *L'Art Poétique*.

Bolingbroke: Henry St. John, Viscount Bolingbroke (1678–1751): Tory Secretary of State (1710–14) under Queen Anne before going into exile (1715–25) and then returning to cultivate a circle of literary and political opponents to Walpole's administration.

Borgia, Cesare: ruler of Romagna, 1501–3: noted for his ruthlessness.

Boulainvilliers, Henri de (1658–1722): author of *État de la France* (1727).

Bourbon, Duke of: regent of France 1723–6, after the death of Orléans, and before being effectively dismissed by Louis XV.

Brahe, Tycho (1546–1601): Danish astronomer famed for his meticulous observations.

Brutus, Decimus: Roman governor of Cisalpine Gaul who refused to relinquish control to Mark Antony after the assassination of Julius Caesar.

Brutus, Lucius Junius: according to legend, expelled Tarquinius Superbus from Rome and founded the republic in 509 BC.

Brutus, Marcus Junius (85–42 BC): conspirator with Cassius in the plot to murder Julius Caesar. By later reputation an idealist and defender of republican ideals against tyranny.

Bunyan, John (1628–88): author of *The Pilgrim's Progress*, *Grace Abounding*, and other devotional literature.

Busiris: in Greek myth, a son of Poseidon and king of Egypt who sacrificed strangers to Zeus to avert drought, and was killed by Heracles.

Caligula: popular name of Roman emperor Gaius (ruled AD 37–41): normally regarded as having been mentally unbalanced.

Camillus, Marcus Furius: dictator and saviour of Rome after its capture by the Gauls in 387 BC. Later regarded as a model exponent of Roman justice.

Capet, Hugh: king of France *c*.938–96.

Capitolinus, Julius: supposedly author of the lives of Maximus and Balbinus in the *Historia Augusta* (3rd or 4th century AD).

Caracalla: popular name of Marcus Aurelius Severus Antoninus: Roman emperor AD 211–17; remembered for his cruelty and extravagance.

Cassander: one contender for power in Macedonia in the unsettled period after the death of Alexander the Great in 323 BC.

Catiline: Lucius Sergius Catilina (*c*.110–62 BC): Roman politician; conspiritor against Cicero.

Cato the Elder: Marcus Porcius Cato (234–149 BC): active in the war against Hannibal; famous for his attacks on luxury and corruption, and demands for a return to the primitive austerity of Rome.

Cato the Younger: Marcus Porcius Cato (95–46 BC): supporter of Pompey in the Civil War; later reputation as a defender of republican liberty; subject of Addison's tragedy *Cato*.

Catullus, Gaius Valerius (*c*.84–*c*.54 BC): Roman poet of the late republican period.

Charles II (1665–1700): king of Spain.

Charles VII: king of France 1422–61.

Charles VIII: king of France 1488–98.

Cicero, Marcus Tullius (106–43 BC): Roman orator and politician. Overcame Catiline's conspiracy; supported Pompey in the Civil War and was pardoned by Julius Caesar; executed by Octavian and Antony for attacks on the latter. Enormously influential on later orators, writers, and political philosophers.

Clarendon: Edward Hyde, First Earl of Clarendon (1609–74): author of *The True Historical Narrative of the Rebellion and Civil Wars in England* (pub. 1702–4).

Claudius: Tiberius Claudius Nero Germanicus: Roman emperor, ruled AD 41–54, after the murder of Caligula.

Clodius, Publius: associate of Catiline and exemplar of lawlessness in late republican Rome.

Collier, Jeremy (1650–1726): author of *A Short View the Immorality and Profaneness of the English Stage* (1698), a controversial and influential attack on the Restoration theatre.

Columbus, Christopher (1451–1506): Italian explorer travelling from Spain who discovered the New World for Europe.

Columella, Lucius Junius Moderatus (1st century AD): author of *De Re Rustica*, describing the farmer's life and work.

Commodus: Roman emperor AD 180–93.

Condé, Prince of (1621–86): French nobleman and general.

Confucius (551–479 BC): philosopher whose teachings exerted a profound influence on the later development of Chinese culture.

Copernicus, Nicholas (1473–1543): Polish astronomer.

Corneille, Pierre (1606–84): French dramatist.

Cortes, Hernando (1485–1547): Spanish conqueror of Mexico in 1523.

Cromwell, Oliver (1599–1658): leader of the Parliamentary party in the English Civil War and Lord Protector 1653–8.

Curius Dentatus, Manius (3rd century BC): Roman consul, successful in several wars; regarded as a model of probity.

Curius, Marcus: legendary self-sacrificing Roman hero.

Curtius Rufus, Quintus (1st century AD): author of a history of Alexander the Great.

Cyrus: (1) (d. 529 BC): founder of the Persian empire. (2) (d. 401 BC): younger son of Darius II of Persia; helped the Peloponnesians against Athens; killed while attempting to oust his brother Artaxerxes from the Persian throne.

Darius I: king of Persia 521–486 BC; launched military campaigns against Greece.

Datames: Persian army commander who led a rebellion against Artaxerxes II in *c*.362 BC.

De la Vega, Garcilasco (1539–1616): author of a history of Peru.

Demosthenes (384–322 BC): Athenian statesman and celebrated orator.

Descartes, René (1596–1650): French philosopher and mathematician; author of *Discourse on Method*, *Meditations*, and *Principles of Philosophy*.

Diodorus Siculus (1st century BC): author of the *Library of History*, a history of the world in Greek compiled from a wide range of sources, with the history of Rome at its centre.

Dion: Dio Cassius (AD 155–235): author of a history of Rome.

Dionysius the Elder: Dionysius I, tyrant of Syracuse, 405–367 BC.

Dionysius: Dionysius II, tyrant of Syracuse, 367–343 BC.

Dionysius of Halicarnassus (1st century BC): historian and orator.

Domitian: Titus Flavius Domitianus: Roman emperor AD 81–96. Later reputation as a tyrannical ruler.

Drake, Sir Francis (*c*.1545–96): English navigator; commander of the English fleet against the Spanish Armada.

Drusus (*c*.13 BC–AD 23): son of Roman emperor Tiberius.

Dryden, John (1631–1700): English poet, satirist, critic, and dramatist.

Dubos, Jean-Baptiste (1670–1742): author of *Réflexions critiques sur la poésie et la peinture* (1719–33).

Empiricus, Sextus (2nd century AD): author of *Outlines of Pyrrhonism*.

Epictetus (*c*. AD 55–135): Stoic philosopher whose doctrines are known through Arrian's accounts of them.

Epicurus (341–270 BC): founder of the Epicurean school of philosophy.

Euclid (4th to 3rd century BC): Greek mathematician, author of a textbook on geometry, *The Elements*, which remained influential until the late 19th century.

Eumenes: ruler of Pergamum, 263–241 BC, at the start of its rise as a major power.

Fabius: Fabius Cunctator (*c*.275–203 BC): Roman general famous for his tactic of strategic delay in the war with Hannibal.

Fénelon, Francois de Salignac de la Mothe- (1651–1715): author of *Les Aventures de Télémaque, fils d'Ulysse* (1699).

Flamininus, Titus (*c*.225–174 BC): Roman general and statesman, who eventually defeated Philip V of Macedonia.

Fleury, Cardinal André Hercule de (1653–1743): chief minister to Louis XV of France 1726–43.

Florus, Lucius Annaeus (2nd century AD): reputed author of an *Epitome* of Roman history.

Fontenelle: Bernard le Bouvier de Fontenelle (1657–1757): French poet and popularizer of contemporary science.

Francis I: king of France 1515–47.

Francis II: king of France 1559–60.

Galileo Galilei (1564–1642): Italian mathematician and astronomer.

Gee, Joshua: author of *The Trade and Navigation of Great Britain Considered* (1729).

Germanicus: Germanicus Julius Caesar (15 BC–AD 19): adopted son of Roman emperor Tiberius. Successful and popular, his early death was often put down to poisoning.

Geta: son of Septimus Severus; murdered with his supporters by Caracalla in 211 AD, when the latter succeeded as Roman emperor.

Gordian: Roman emperor 238–44 AD, in a period of extreme instability.

Gracchi: the brothers Gracchi, Tiberius Sempronius Gracchus (d. 133 BC) and Gaius Sempronius Gracchus (d. 121 BC) both attempted to reform Roman land law and civil administration during their periods of office as tribunes: both faced considerable opposition and were killed.

Guicciardin: Francesco Guicciardini (1483–1540): Italian historian.

Gustavus Adolphus: king of Sweden 1611–32.

Gustavus Ericson Vasa: Gustav Eriksson Vasa: king of Sweden 1523–60.

Hampden, John (1594–1643): leading English Member of Parliament.

Hannibal (274–183 BC): Carthaginian commander in the Second Punic War, whose feats of military strategy and tactics are still regarded as outstanding.

Hardouin, Jean (1646–1729): publisher of an edition of Pliny's *Natural History* in 1685.

Harrington, James (1611–77): political philosopher and author of *Oceana* (1656).

Heliogabalus: Roman emperor AD 218–22.

Henry III: king of France 1574–89.

Henry IV: king of France 1589–1610.

Heripidas: Spartan general.

Herodian (*c.* AD 165–250): author of a Greek history of the Roman empire from AD 180 to 238.

Herodotus (*c.*484–*c.*420 BC): Greek historian often regarded as the 'father of history' for his history of the wars between Greece and Persia.

Hesiod (*fl. c.*700 BC): earliest known Greek poet after Homer.

Hirtius, Aulus: lieutenant of Julius Caesar and author of the continuation of his *De Bello Gallico*.

Homer: real or fictitious Greek poet (*fl. c.*700 BC): creator of the *Iliad* and *Odyssey*.

Horace: Quintus Horatius Flaccus (65–8 BC): Roman poet whose *Satires* and *Epistles* were particularly influential as models in the 18th century.

Hutchinson: Archibald Hutcheson: 18th-century economic commentator.

Huygens, Christiaan (1629–95): Dutch mathematician and scientist engaged by Louis XIV's minister Colbert to work on problems of shipbuilding and navigation for the French navy.

Isocrates (436–338 BC): Athenian orator; author of political discourses including *Panegyricus*, urging the unity of Greece.

Jonson, Ben (1572–1637): English dramatist and poet.

Josephus, Flavius (AD 37–*c.*100): Jewish soldier and statesman; author of histories of the early Jews, and *The Jewish Wars*, covering the period from 170 BC to AD 70.

Julian: Flavius Claudius Julianus (AD 331–63): Roman emperor 361–3; known to Christian writers as 'The Apostate' for his renunciation of Christianity; author of satires and other writings.

Julianus, Didius: purchaser of the title of Roman emperor after the murder of Pertinax in AD 193.

Julius Caesar: Gaius Julius Caesar (c.100–44 BC): highly successful general and statesman, who extended Roman dominion to Gaul, and whose assassination provoked the second civil war and the end of the republic.

Justin: Marcus Junianus Justinus (2nd or 3rd century AD): author of an epitome of the universal history of Trogus Pompeius.

Justinian: emperor of the eastern Roman empire, AD 527–65.

Juvenal: Decimus Junius Juvenalis (AD c.60–c.130): Roman satirist, a major influence on later Western satiric writing.

Laertius, Diogenes (3rd century AD): biographer of eighty-two of the principal Greek philosophers.

Lampridius, Aelius: supposedly author of the life of Heliogabalus in the *Historia Augusta* (3rd or 4th century AD).

Lipsius, Justus (1547–1606): author of *Saturnalium Sermonum Libri Duo* (1585).

Livy: Titus Livius (59 BC–AD 17): author of a monumental *History of Rome*.

Locke, John (1632–1704): highly influential English philosopher.

Longinus: supposed author of an influential treatise, *On the Sublime*, dating from the 1st or 2nd century AD, the actual authorship of which is unknown.

Longinus, Cassius (c. AD 220–73): author of a treatise on the art of rhetoric.

Louis XI: king of France 1461–83.

Louis XII: king of France 1498–1515.

Louis XIV: king of France 1661–1715.

Lucan: Marcus Annaeus Lucanus (AD 39–65): author of a poetic account of the Roman civil wars.

Lucian (c. AD 120–after 180): Greek author, best remembered for his satiric dialogues.

Lucretius: Titus Lucretius Carus (c.99–55 BC): author of the long philosophical poem *De Rerum Natura* (*On the Nature of Things*).

Lycurgus: (1) legendary legislator of Sparta. (2) administrator of the finances of Athens 338–326 BC; responsible for important public works.

Lysias (5th century BC): orator resident in Athens, many of whose speeches survive.

Machiavel: Niccolo Machiavelli (1469–1527): author of the *Discourses* and *The Prince*; celebrated by later writers as a humanist political theorist, and attacked and demonized for his scandalous analysis of the operation of power.

Maillet, Benoit de (1656–1738): French author of books on the history and political administration of Egypt.

Mandeville, Bernard de (1670–1733): author of *The Fable of the Bees: or, Private Vices, Publick Benefits* (1714–29).

Marcellinus, Ammianus (4th century AD): author of a history of Rome.

Marlborough: John Churchill, Duke of Marlborough (1650–1722): commander of British and Dutch forces during the War of Spanish Sucession.

Martial: Marcus Valerius Martialis (*c.* AD 40–104): Roman poet, author of *Epigrams*.

Maximus: joint Roman emperor with Balbinus 237–8 AD.

Maximus, Valerius (1st century AD): author of a collection of *Memorable Deeds and Sayings*.

Mazarin, Cardinal Jules (1602–61): chief minister of France under Louis XIII and the young Louis XIV, 1642–61.

Melon: Jean-François Melon (*c.*1675–1738): influential French writer on economics.

Menander (342–292 BC): Greek comic poet.

Michael Angelo: Michelangelo Buonaroti (1475–1564): artist.

Milo: Titus Annius Milo Papinianus: participant in fighting in Rome, 57–52 BC; defended by Cicero for murder in 52.

Milton, John (1608–74): English poet, author of *Paradise Lost*, *Paradise Regained*, and prose works in support of press freedom, divorce, and the Parliamentary cause in the English Civil War.

Mithridates: Eupator Mithridates IV: king of Pontus *c.*115–63 BC; leader of a series of successful expeditions against Rome and its colonies in Asia Minor.

Moliere: pseudonym of Jean Baptiste Poquelin (1622–73): French comic dramatist.

Montaigne, Michel de (1533–92): French essayist.

Montesquieu, Baron Charles de Secondat de (1689–1755): author of *De l'esprit des lois*.

More, Thomas (1478–1535): Lord Chancellor of England under Henry VIII until his refusal to recognize the legitimacy of the king's divorce or his right to be head of the Church of England led to his execution; author of *Utopia*.

Nabis: ruler of Sparta during the Macedonian wars.

Nepos, Cornelius (*c.*100–25 BC): Latin author of biographies and (now lost) works on history and geography.

Nero: Roman emperor AD 54–68; later taken as a model of cruelty and bad government.

Newton, Isaac (1642–1727): English mathematician, physicist, and astronomer; author of *Principia Mathematica*.

Nicomachus: son of Aristotle.

Niger, Pescennius: contender for the position of Roman emperor after the murder of Pertinax and sale of the succession to Didius Julianus in AD 193.

Ogilby, John (1600–76): publisher of verse translations of Homer and Virgil.

Olympiodorus (*c.* AD 380–425): author of a now lost history.

Otway, Thomas (1652–85): one of the leading tragic dramatists of the English Restoration stage.

Ovid: Publius Ovidius Naso (43 BC–*c.* AD 18): Roman poet living first in Rome and then in exile in Tomi; author of lyric and erotic poems.

Paterculus, Velleius Gaius (*c.*19 BC–*c.* AD 30): author of a history of Rome.

Pausanias (2nd century AD): author of a descriptive guidebook to Greece.

Perseus: in Greek mythology, the son of Zeus and Danae, who cut off the Gorgon's head, and rescued and married Andromeda.

Pertinax: Roman emperor for three months in AD 193, after the murder of Commodus, and before his own murder, which in turn provoked civil war. Celebrated by later writers as an innocent victim of others' political ambitions.

Peter the Great: Czar of Russia 1689–1725.

Petrarch: Francesco Petrarca (1304–74): Italian Renaissance lyric poet.

Petronius (d. AD 65): Emperor Nero's official 'arbiter of taste', and the author of the *Satyricon*.

Phaedrus (*c.*15 BC–AD 50): Roman writer of fables.

Phalereus, Demetrius (*c.*354–283 BC): writer of politics and oratorical works; governor of Athens 317–307; later influential in developing Alexandria as a centre of Greek culture.

Philip II, III, IV: kings of Spain 1556–98, 1598–1621, 1621–65.

Philip of Macedon: Philip II, ruler of Macedon 359–336 BC; father of Alexander the Great.

Philip V: king of Macedon 221–179 BC.

Philistus: historian at the time of Dionysius the elder.

Pindar (518–438 BC): Greek lyric poet, best known for his influential *Odes*.

Pizarro, Francisco (*c.*1475–1541): Spanish conqueror of Peru.

Plato (*c.*429–347 BC): Athenian philosopher; pupil of Socrates and teacher of Aristotle. His political ideas were influential in Greece and Rome, and continued to have an enormous influence on later Western thought.

Plautus, Titus Maccius (*c.*254–184 BC): Roman comic dramatist; imitator of the Greek New Comedy.

Pliny the Elder: Gaius Plinius Secundus (AD 23–79): Roman administrator and author of an encyclopaedic *Natural History*.

Pliny the Younger: Gaius Plinius Caecilius Secundus (*c.* AD 61–113): adopted son of above; known particularly for his ten published books of letters.

Plutarch (*c.* AD 46–126): Greek biographer and essayist; author of *Parallel Lives* of Greek and Roman public figures.

Poliorcetes, Demetrius: conqueror of Athens in 307 BC.

Politian, Angelus (1454–94): translator of Herodian into Latin.

Polybius (*c.*202–120 BC): Greek historian; author of the *Universal History*, an account of Roman history from 220 to 145 BC.

Pompey: Gnaeus Pompeius (106–48 BC): Roman general; opponent of Julius Caesar in the civil war, in which he was finally defeated at Pharsalus.

Pope, Alexander (1688–1744): English satirical poet.

Ptolemy: Claudius Ptolemaeus (2nd century AD): Greek geographer and astronomer.

Ptolemies: name of the dynasty that ruled Egypt from the death of Alexander the Great to the Roman invasion.

Publius Victor: the author's name under which *De Regionibus Urbis Romae*, a catalogue of the buildings of ancient Rome, was published.

Pyrrhus (319–272 BC): king of Epirus and military campaigner against Rome on behalf of the Greek cities of southern Italy. His defeat of the Romans at Asculum involved crippling losses for his own army: hence 'pyrrhic victory'.

Racine, Jean Baptiste (1639–99): French neoclassical dramatist.

Raleigh, Sir Walter (1552–1618): English courtier, explorer, and writer; eventually executed for conspiracy.

Raphael: Raffaello Santi (1483–1520): Italian painter.

Rapin: Paul de Rapin-Thoyras (1661–1725): author of a popular *History of England*, published in French in 1723–7 and rapidly translated into English.

Retz, Cardinal de (1614–79), author of *Mémoirs* (1717).

Richelieu, Caudinal: chief minister to Louis XIII and effective ruler of France 1624–42.

Rochester: John Wilmott, earl of Rochester (1648–80): English poet and libertine.

Rousseau, Jean-Baptiste (1671–1741), French poet and writer.

Rowe, Nicholas (1674–1718): English dramatist.

Rubens, Peter Paul (1577–1640): Flemish painter.

Sallust: Gaius Sallustius Crispus (86–34 BC): Roman politician and historian, author of the *War with Catiline* and the *War with Jugurtha*.

Sasern: Saserna: name of two Latin writers on agriculture.

Scipio Africanus, Publius Cornelius (*c*.235–183 BC): Roman general who defeated Hannibal at Zama in 202 BC.

Sejanus: Lucius Aelius Sejanus (d. AD 31): prefect of the Praetorian Guard; gained considerable power while the emperor Tiberius was in retirement on Capri, but was eventually denounced and executed.

Seneca the Elder: Lucius Annaeus Seneca (*c*.55 BC–AD 40): Roman author of the *Controversiae*.

Seneca, Lucius Annaeus (*c*.4 BC–AD 65): Roman philosopher and tragedian; tutor to Nero in the first years of his reign.

Severus, Lucius Septimus: one of three contenders for the position of Roman emperor after the murder of Pertinax and sale of the succession to Didius Julianus in AD 193; Roman emperor 193–211.

Shaftesbury: Anthony Ashley Cooper, Third Earl of Shaftesbury (1671–1713): author of *Characteristics*; an influential and controversial aesthetician and moralist for 18th-century commentators.

Socrates (469–399 BC): Greek philosopher whose method of challenging received ideas through pointed questioning is recounted in Plato's early dialogues.

Solon (*c*.640–560 BC): Athenian statesman who brought an end to civil strife in 594; in later life revered as a sage.

Spartian: Aelius Spartianus: supposedly author of the life of Severus in the (3rd or 4th century AD) *Historia Augusta*.

Spencer: Edmund Spenser (*c*.1552–99): English poet, author of *The Fairy Queen*.

Sprat, Thomas (1635–1713): first historian of the Royal Society.

Stanian: Abraham Stanyan: author of *An Account of Switzerland Written in the Year 1714* (1714).

Strabo (*c*.64 BC–AD 19): Greek historian and author of *Geographica*, a geography of the Roman empire.

Suetonius (*c*. AD 70–141): author of *Lives of the Caesars*.

Suidas: name of a 10th-century Greek encyclopaedia, containing articles on history and literature.

Swift, Jonathan (1667–1745): Dean of Dublin, satirist and political polemicist.

Tacitus, Cornelius (*c.* AD 55–120): historian of imperial Rome whose work exerted considerable influence on writers after its redicovery during the Renaissance.

Tasso, Torquato (1544–95): Italian epic and pastoral poet.

Temple, Sir William (1628–99): essayist and historian.

Terence: Publius Terentius Afer (*c.*195–159 BC): Roman comic dramatist; imitator of Greek New Comedy.

Theocritus (*c.*300–250 BC): Greek pastoral poet. An enormously important influence on Virgil and the later pastoral tradition.

Thrasybulus: Athenian who overthrew the Thirty Tyrants and restored democracy to Athens in 404–403 BC.

Thucydides (*c.*460–*c.*400 BC): Greek historian of the Peloponnesian War.

Tiberius: Tiberius Claudius Nero Caesar: Roman emperor AD 14–37; hostile accounts of Tiberius's reign by Tacitus and Suetonius dwell on his habit of ruling through favourites while remaining in retirement, and his sexual excesses.

Timoleon: Corinthian who in 365 BC helped in the killing of his brother to prevent him becoming tyrant; the subject of one of Plutarch's *Lives*.

Titus: Titus Flavius Sabinus Vespasianus: Roman emperor, AD 79–81; earlier, commanded the Roman armies in the capture of Jerusalem in AD 70. Regarded sympathetically by later commentators.

Titus Flamininus: Roman consul in 198 BC; victor over Philip of Macedon in 197 BC.

Tournefort, Joseph: 18th-century author of an account of travels in the Levant.

Trajan: Marcus Ulpius Trajanus: Roman emperor AD 98–117; famed as a soldier and for public buildings and welfare reforms within the empire.

Tullius, Servius: sixth king of Rome, ruled 578–525 BC.

Tully: the name by which Marcus Tullius Cicero was often referred to by English writers until the 19th century.

Ulysses: Latin name for Homer's Odysseus.

Ustariz, Don Geronimo De: author of Spanish commentaries on commerce.

Varro, Marcus Terentius (116–27 BC): Roman author of many works, of which *De Re Rustica* and parts of a Latin Grammar are the most substantial to have survived.

Vauban: Sébastien Le Prestre, Seigneur de Vauban (1633–1707): French military engineer and later royal administrator.

Verres, Gaius: notoriously corrupt Roman governor of Sicily, prosecuted by Cicero in 70 BC.

Vespasian: Titus Flavius Vespasianus (Roman emperor AD 69–79): succeeded Nero as emperor after a civil war during which three other contenders were briefly declared emperor. Regarded as an efficient administrator who left Rome well regulated and solvent.

Virgil: Publius Vergilius Maronis (70–19 BC): Roman poet, author of *Eclogues*, *Georgics*, and the *Aeneid*.

Vitruvius Pollio (c.50–26 BC): Roman architect and engineer, serving under Julius Caesar and Augustus; author of *De Architectura*, a treatise on architecture which had a wide influence in the Renaissance.

Voltaire: pseudonym of François Marie Arouet (1694–1778): one of the leading authors of the French Enlightenment.

Vopiscus, Flavius: supposedly author of biographies of Roman emperors in the *Historia Augusta*.

Vossius, Isaak (1618–89): author of *Variarum Observationum Liber*.

Waller, Edmund (1606–87): English lyric poet.

Walpole, Robert (1676–1745): English politician and statesman; effectively first Prime Minister 1721–42.

Wolsey, Cardinal Thomas (1471–1530): administrator vested with enormous power under Henry VIII, before eventually falling from favour.

Xenophon (c.428–c.354 BC): Greek historian, author of the *Persian Expedition*, and *Hellenica*, a history of Greece from 411 to 362, as well as numerous general works.

Xerxes: king of Persia 485–465 BC; invaded Greece and occupied Athens, but forced to retreat after defeat in the naval battle of Salamis.

	Classical Literary Criticism
	Greek Lyric Poetry
	Myths from Mesopotamia
APOLLODORUS	The Library of Greek Mythology
APOLLONIUS OF RHODES	Jason and the Golden Fleece
APULEIUS	The Golden Ass
ARISTOTLE	The Nicomachean Ethics
	Physics
	Politics
CAESAR	The Civil War
	The Gallic War
CATULLUS	The Poems of Catullus
CICERO	The Nature of the Gods
EURIPIDES	Medea, Hippolytus, Electra, and Helen
GALEN	Selected Works
HERODOTUS	The Histories
HESIOD	Theogony and Works and Days
HOMER	The Iliad
	The Odyssey
HORACE	The Complete Odes and Epodes
JUVENAL	The Satires
LIVY	The Rise of Rome
LUCAN	The Civil War
MARCUS AURELIUS	The Meditations
OVID	The Love Poems
	Metamorphoses
	Sorrows of an Exile

GEORGE ELIOT	Adam Bede
	Daniel Deronda
	Middlemarch
	The Mill on the Floss
	Silas Marner
ELIZABETH GASKELL	Cranford
	The Life of Charlotte Brontë
	Mary Barton
	North and South
	Wives and Daughters
THOMAS HARDY	Far from the Madding Crowd
	Jude the Obscure
	The Mayor of Casterbridge
	A Pair of Blue Eyes
	The Return of the Native
	Tess of the d'Urbervilles
	The Woodlanders
WALTER SCOTT	Ivanhoe
	Rob Roy
	Waverley
MARY SHELLEY	Frankenstein
	The Last Man
ROBERT LOUIS STEVENSON	Kidnapped and Catriona
	The Strange Case of Dr Jekyll and Mr Hyde and Weir of Hermiston
	Treasure Island
BRAM STOKER	Dracula
WILLIAM MAKEPEACE THACKERAY	Barry Lyndon
	Vanity Fair
OSCAR WILDE	Complete Shorter Fiction
	The Picture of Dorian Gray

	Oriental Tales
WILLIAM BECKFORD	Vathek
JAMES BOSWELL	Boswell's Life of Johnson
FRANCES BURNEY	Camilla
	Cecilia
	Evelina
	The Wanderer
LORD CHESTERFIELD	Lord Chesterfield's Letters
JOHN CLELAND	Memoirs of a Woman of Pleasure
DANIEL DEFOE	Captain Singleton
	A Journal of the Plague Year
	Memoirs of a Cavalier
	Moll Flanders
	Robinson Crusoe
	Roxana
HENRY FIELDING	Joseph Andrews and Shamela
	A Journey from This World to the Next and
	The Journal of a Voyage to Lisbon
	Tom Jones
	The Adventures of David Simple
WILLIAM GODWIN	Caleb Williams
	St Leon
OLIVER GOLDSMITH	The Vicar of Wakefield
MARY HAYS	Memoirs of Emma Courtney
ELIZABETH HAYWOOD	The History of Miss Betsy Thoughtless
ELIZABETH INCHBALD	A Simple Story
SAMUEL JOHNSON	The History of Rasselas
CHARLOTTE LENNOX	The Female Quixote
MATTHEW LEWIS	The Monk

A SELECTION OF OXFORD WORLD'S CLASSICS

American Literature

British and Irish Literature

Children's Literature

Classics and Ancient Literature

Colonial Literature

Eastern Literature

European Literature

History

Medieval Literature

Oxford English Drama

Poetry

Philosophy

Politics

Religion

The Oxford Shakespeare

A complete list of Oxford Paperbacks, including Oxford World's Classics, OPUS, Past Masters, Oxford Authors, Oxford Shakespeare, Oxford Drama, and Oxford Paperback Reference, is available in the UK from the Academic Division Publicity Department, Oxford University Press, Great Clarendon Street, Oxford OX2 6DP.

In the USA, complete lists are available from the Paperbacks Marketing Manager, Oxford University Press, 198 Madison Avenue, New York, NY 10016.

Oxford Paperbacks are available from all good bookshops. In case of difficulty, customers in the UK can order direct from Oxford University Press Bookshop, Freepost, 116 High Street, Oxford OX1 4BR, enclosing full payment. Please add 10 per cent of published price for postage and packing.